11th European Workshop on Natural Language Generation 2007

(ENLG 07)

Schloss Dagstuhl, Germany
17-20 June 2007

Editor:

Stephan Busemann

ISBN: 978-1-61738-516-2

Printed from e-media with permission by:

Curran Associates, Inc.
57 Morehouse Lane
Red Hook, NY 12571

Some format issues inherent in the e-media version may also appear in this print version.

Printed by Curran Associates, Inc. (2010)

For permission requests, please contact the Association for Computational Linguistics at the address below.

Association for Computational Linguistics
209 N. Eighth Street
Stroudsburg, Pennsylvania 18360

Phone: 1-570-476-8006
Fax: 1-570-476-0860

acl@aclweb.org

Additional copies of this publication are available from:

Curran Associates, Inc.
57 Morehouse Lane
Red Hook, NY 12571 USA
Phone: 845-758-0400
Fax: 845-758-2634
Email: curran@proceedings.com
Web: www.proceedings.com

Preface

This volume contains the proceedings of the 11th European Workshop on Natural Language Generation (ENLG07).

The workshop takes place at Schloss Dagstuhl in Germany. It continues a biennial series of workshops on natural language generation that has been running since 1987. Previous European workshops have been held at Toulouse, Budapest and Aberdeen. The series provides a regular forum for presentation and discussion of research in this area, both for NLG specialists and for researchers from other areas.

The 2007 workshop spans the interest areas of Natural Language Generation to Artificial Intelligence, Computational Linguistics and Semantic Web techniques. One of the key themes is evaluation of NLG systems, including two sessions on recent activities in this area.

The invited talk is given by Dr Kristiina Jokinen. Kristiina's work focusses on adaptive interactive systems, including dialogue and, of course, NLG. We are grateful for being able to include into this volume her paper on "Quality of service and communicative competence in NLG evaluation".

There were 41 submissions, of which 30 were accepted by the program committee (19 paper and 11 poster presentations). Two papers were retracted as they also had been accepted at other events, and the authors decided to publish there. One poster was retracted as the authors could unfortunately not find sponsorship to attend the workshop. This volume thus contains the invited paper, 17 paper and 10 poster presentations.

My sincere thanks go to the program committee who has accomplished a strenuous task in providing three reviews for each paper in due time.

I also wish to thank Andrei Voronkov for his marvelous EasyChair system that made everything from submission to proceedings generation so much easier (http://www.easychair.org). At DFKI, Danish Nadeem designed and helped maintaining the workshop webpage at http://enlg07.dfki.de. Nadiya Yampolska provided valuable support in the organization of the workshop. Thank you, Danish and Nadiya!

Last not least, the excellent cooperation of the Schloss Dagstuhl team is highly appreciated, who patiently answered my many questions and showed a great deal of flexibility in accommodating the event to our liking.

Stephan Busemann
Program Chair and Organizer

Program Committee

John Bateman, University of Bremen, Germany
Anja Belz, Brighton University, England
Kalina Bontcheva, University of Sheffield, England
Stephan Busemann (Chair), DFKI GmbH, Germany
Charles Callaway, University of Edinburgh, Scotland
Robert Dale, Macquarie University, Australia
Michael Elhadad, Ben Gurion University, Beer Sheva, Israel
Helmut Horacek, University of the Saarland, Germany
Emiel Krahmer, Tilburg University, Netherlands
Geert-Jan Kruijff, DFKI GmbH, Germany
Elena Not, IRST, Italy
Ehud Reiter, University of Aberdeen, Scotland
Manfred Stede, University of Potsdam, Germany

Additional Reviewer

Meni Adler, Ben Gurion University, Israel

Local Organization

Stephan Busemann, DFKI GmbH, Germany
Danish Nadeem, DFKI GmbH, Germany
Nadiya Yampolska, DFKI GmbH, Germany

Table of Contents

Invited Paper

Quality of service and communicative competence in NLG evaluation

Kristiina JOKINEN
University of Helsinki and University of Tampere
Finland
Kristiina.Jokinen@helsinki.fi

Abstract

The paper discusses quality of service evaluation which emphasises the user's experience in the evaluation of system functionality and efficiency. For NLG systems, an important quality feature is communicatively adequate language generation, which affects the users' perception of the system and consequently, evaluation results. The paper drafts an evaluation task that aims at measuring quality of service, taking the system's communicative competence into account.

1 Introduction

The state of the art Natural Language Generation systems can generate summaries and short texts which exhibit variation in sentence structure, anaphoric references, and amount of information included in the text, as well as some adaptation to different users. The starting point can be a structured database or a specifically designed representation, while the output can be text and also spoken language given a suitable text-to-speech component. The standard architecture (Reiter and Dale 2000) provides basis for generation technology which ranges from rule-based systems via XML transformations to statistical generators.

As the academic research extends out to industrial markets, high priority should be given to evaluation techniques. The goal is not only to provide diagnostic feedback about the system performance, but to enable researchers and developers to test and compare different techniques and approaches with respect to generation tasks. Moreover, evaluation allows self-assessment to guide and focus future research. To potential users, customers, and manufacturers evaluation offers slightly different benefits: with an increased number of applications which can integrate an NLG component, evaluation provides surveys of the available generation components and their suitability to particular practical tasks. Vivid interest has thus been shown in finding suitable evaluation tasks and methods, e.g. in the recent workshop (Dale and White 2007), resulting in the Shared Task Evaluation Campaign.

Setting up a framework that addresses (some of) the motivations and requirements for evaluation is a complex task, and to structure the goals, three fundamental questions need to be asked:

1. Definition: what is it that we are interested in and require from an NLG?
2. Measures: which specific property of the system and its performance can we identify with the goal and use in evaluation?
3. Method: how to determine the appropriate value for a given measure and a given NLG system? Can the results predict properties of future systems?

The paper seeks to answer these questions from the perspective of communicative systems. The starting point is that generation products are not generated or read in void: they are produced as communicative acts in various communicative situations. NLG evaluation thus resembles that of dialogue systems: besides task completeness, one need to measure intangible factors such as impact of the text on the user and the user's expectations and satisfaction concerning the output. Moreover, it is important to measure the quality of service, or the system's effectiveness as perceived by the users through their experience with the system.

The paper starts with the definition (Section 2), continues with a discussion about metrics (Section 3) and methods (Section 4), and concludes with a concrete evaluation proposal (Section 5).

2 Definition of evaluation

We distinguish between assessment and evaluation (Möller 2007), or performance and adequacy evaluation (Hirschman and Thompson 1997). Assessment refers to the measurement of system performance in specific areas with respect to certain criteria, whereas evaluation refers to the determination of the fitness of a system for a specific purpose. Assessment also requires well-defined baseline performance for the comparison of alternative technologies, but adequacy evaluation is mainly determined by the user needs.

Performance of a system should be distinguished from its quality. According to Möller (2007), performance is "an ability of the module to provide the function it has been designed for". Quality, on the other hand, is determined by the perceptions of the system users. It "results from a perception and a judgment process, in which the perceiving subject (e.g. a test user of the system) establishes a relationship between the perceptive event and what he/she expects or desires from the service". Quality is thus everything that is perceived by the user with respect to what she expects from the system. User factors like attitude, emotions, experience, task/domain knowledge, etc., will influence the perception of quality.

It is also common to talk about usability of a system, referring to issues that deal with effectiveness and user satisfaction. The ISO definition of usability goes as follows:

> *The extent to which a product can be used by specified users to achieve specified goals with effectiveness, efficiency and satisfaction in a specified context of use.*

In usability testing, a test supervisor observes real users as they use the product in real tasks, and analyses the results for the purpose of learning how to improve the product's usability. Usability and quality evaluations seem similar and in practice, both use similar techniques (user questionnaires, interviews). An important difference is that in the latter, user expectations are explicitly taken into consideration by relating the perceived system properties to the expectations that the user had about the system. A system can be useful and usable, but in order to become utilised it must also provide a special value for the users. Considering NLG systems, it may be difficult to obtain usability or quality information as such: usually generators are not stand-alone systems but components of bigger systems. However, if a NL generator is a component e.g. in a dialogue system, its quality affects the quality of the whole system. Thus evaluating generators in the context of the same dialogue system, it is possible to obtain explicit quality judgements of the NLG component, too.

3 Evaluation metrics

Different measures can be used depending on the goals and the system itself. For individual components, quantifiable measures and glass-box evaluation provide useful information about how to optimize a component further, or which component to choose over another. Performance can be quantified by providing suitable metrics for:

- effectiveness for the task (the system provides the desired information),
- efficiency (time needed to complete the task, or the effort required from the user).

In NLG, such metrics deal with the time it takes to generate a text, or the length and complexity of sentences and syntactic constructions. The BLEU type metrics can be used to automatically compare generated texts with the target as in translation studies, while comprehensibility judgement tests can be used to determine if the texts effectively communicate the intended message.

However, the system is always situated in a context. Glass-box evaluation does not tell us how the system functions as a whole when used in its context, and black-box evaluation, focusing on the system's functioning and impact on users in real situations, should thus complement performance evaluation. This includes measures for:

- satisfaction of the user (experienced comfort, pleasantness, or joy-of-use),
- utility (involves cost measures),
- acceptability (whether a potential user is willing to use the system).

Accordingly, NLG systems should be evaluated with respect to the context where the generated text is meant to appear, and by the users who are likely to use the system. This brings us back to the evaluation of the quality of the system: we need to determine quality features which capture differences in the users' perception of the system and consequently, contribute to the system quality. Since language is used to communicate ideas and meanings, communicative competence is one of the most visible aspects of language- based applications. The quality of the system can thus be measured by its communicative capability: how accurately and reliably the intended message is conveyed to the user in a given context.

4 Evaluation methods

Good evaluation methods are generic in that they allow comparison of different systems and also predictions to be made about their future versions. One of the frameworks used in dialogue system evaluation is the PARADISE framework (Walker et al. 2000) which learns the evaluation parameters from the data and produces a performance function which specifies relative contributions of the various cost factors to the overall performance. The goal of the evaluation is to maximize user satisfaction by maximizing task success and minimizing task cost measured using various task and dialogue metrics. PARADISE is a rigorous framework, but the data collection and annotation cost for deriving the performance function is high. When considering development of complex systems, or the need for evaluation of prototypes with a large number of users, semi-automatic evaluation with less manual annotation would be preferable. Möller (2007) also points out that it may be too simplistic to relate interaction parameters in a linear fashion, since quality is a multi-dimensional property of the system.

As the correlation between the designers' and the users' views of the system can be weak, a comprehensive glass-box evaluation cannot be based solely on the interaction parameters, i.e. assessing how the designed system functionalities work with respect to various users, but also the way how the users experience the system should be explored. Extending the PARADISE type evaluation, Möller (2007) presents a taxonomy of quality aspects (for speech-based interactive systems but it can be applied to NLG systems, too) which includes quality evaluation of the system from the user's perspective. It aims at generic prediction power concerning quality aspects (categories of quality) and quality features (perceptual dimensions). The extra value of the system can be approximated by comparing the users' actual experience of the system with the expectations they had of the system before its evaluation (cf. case studies reported in Möller 2007; Jokinen and Hurtig 2006). The differences are indicative of the users' disappointments and satisfactions in regard to the quality aspects, and by applying more complex algorithms to calculate parameter dependencies, the model's prediction power can also be improved.

5 NLG evaluation

For a given generation task, there is usually not only one correct solution but several: the text may be constructed in more than one way. This kind of variation is typical for language-based applications in general: there is no "golden standard" to compare the results with, but the ratings about the success of a contribution depend on the situation and the evaluator's attitudes and likings. In interactive system development, the success of responses is usually related to the "contextual appropriateness", based on Grice's Cooperation Principle, and made explicit in the recommendations and best practice guidelines (see e.g. Gibbon et al., 1997). Analogously, the task in the NLG evaluation is not to measure various outputs in regard to one standard solution but rather, to provide a means to abstract away from the details of the individual outputs into the space of quality features that characterise the contextual appropriateness of the texts, i.e. the system's communicative competence with respect to the user's expectations and experience.

As mentioned, one way to organise this kind of quality evaluation is to integrate the NLG system in an interactive prototype and evaluate the output which is produced as a response to a particular communicative goal.[1] The goals can be rather straightforward information providing goals with the topic dealing with weather forecasts or traffic information (what is the weather like in X, tell about the weather in Y in general, the wind speed later in the afternoon, etc.), or more complex ones that require summaries of news texts or comparisons of database items (e.g. how the weather is expected to change tomorrow, compare air quality in X and Y, how has precipitation changed in recent years; how do I get to X). They simulate plausible "real" situations in which to evaluate one's experience of the system, and also provide discourse contexts in which to judge the appropriateness of the generated text.

The goals can be directly mapped to an interface language that enables the NLG system to be called with the selected parameter settings. A structured database can be provided as the shared

[1] The task resembles the one proposed by Walker (2007), but has been independently sketched at the ENLGW 2005 in Aberdeen with Stephan Busemann.

input, and output is a short text, possibly spoken, which can be varied by allowing the users to choose between a short or a full text, or if they wish the text to appear in a mobile phone screen (concise) or on a webpage (verbose).

The user is also instructed to evaluate each generated text(s) by answering questions that ask the user's opinion e.g. of the comprehensibility of the text, its syntactic correctness, acceptability, appropriateness, reliability, style, and the user's overall impression. The questions may also ask if the text is informative or ambiguous, if it gives too much information (what could be left out) or too little information (what is missing), and if it conforms to the user's expectations.

In the beginning of the evaluation session, before their actual experience with the system, the users are asked to estimate their familiarity with generation systems and, by going through the evaluation questions, to describe how quick, informative, fluent, and useful they expect the system to be. All the answers are given in a 5-point Likert scale, and in the analysis, evaluation answers are related to those of expectations.

Evaluation can be performed via web-based interaction (cf. the Blizzard Challenge for evaluating corpus-based speech synthesis: http://festvox.org/blizzard/). Using the web, it is possible to recruit participants from different countries, and they can also rank the texts anywhere any time. Given that several generators will take part in the evaluation, software share and installation can also be simplified. A drawback is that there is no control over the users or their environment: the users may not complete the evaluation or they may fill in random values. Web connection may also break, and degrade the system performance and speed.

6 Conclusion

The paper has discussed the quality of service evaluation which emphasises the user's perception of the system in the evaluation setup. The system's communicative competence, i.e. ability to provide reliable and useful information, is regarded as an important quality feature, and a web-based evaluation set-up is drafted in order to evaluate the quality of NLG systems with respect to their communicative capability. We finish the paper with some general questions concerning the evaluation setup.

- How realistic interactions are necessary in order to get reliable evaluation data? E.g. should the system provide meta-communication besides the factual text?
- The users should not be burdened with too many similar parameter settings. How many different features can be varied to maintain user interest and yet to guarantee systematic variation and collection of enough data?
- Even though it is not necessary to define an "ideal" text for each communicative goal, some guidelines may be useful to describe e.g. necessary/optional features of the generated texts for the participating systems.

References

Dale, R. and M. White (Eds) 2007. Proceedings of the Workshop on Shared Tasks and Comparative Evaluation in Natural Language Generation, http://www.ling.ohio-state.edu/~mwhite/nlgeval07/

Gibbon, D., R. Moore and R. Winski (Eds.) 1997. *Handbook of Standards and Resources for Spoken Language Systems*. Mouton de Gruyter, New York.

Hirschman, L. and H. Thompson 1997. Overview of evaluation in speech and natural language processing. In: Cole, R., Mariani, J., Uszkoreit, H., Zaenen A., and Zue, V. (Eds.) 1997. *Survey of the State of the Art in Human Language Technology,* Cambridge University Press and Giardini Editori, Pisa.

Jokinen, K. 1996. Adequacy and Evaluation. *Procs of the ECAI-96 workshop "Gaps and Bridges: New Directions in Planning and Natural Language Generation"*. Budapest, Hungary. pp. 105-107.

Jokinen, K. and T. Hurtig 2006. User Expectations and Real Experience on a Multimodal Interactive System. *Procs of Interspeech-2006*.

Möller, S. 2007. Evaluating Speech-based Interactive Systems. In: Fang, C. and K. Jokinen (Eds.) *New Trends in Speech-based Interactive Systems*. Springer Publishers.

Reiter, E and R.Dale 2000 *Building Natural Language Generation Systems*. Cambridge University Press.

Walker, M, Kamm, C, and Litman, D. 2000. Towards developing general models of usability with PARADISE. *Natural Language Engineering*, 6:363–377.

Walker, M. 2007. *Share and Share Alike: Resources for Language Generation*. In R. Dale and M. White (Eds.) pp. 28-30.

Long and Short Papers

Generation of Repeated References to Discourse Entities

Anja Belz
Natural Language Technology Group
University of Brighton
A.S.Belz@brighton.ac.uk

Sebastian Varges
Information and Communication Technology
University of Trento
varges@dit.unitn.it

Abstract

Generation of Referring Expressions is a thriving subfield of Natural Language Generation which has traditionally focused on the task of selecting a set of attributes that unambiguously identify a given referent. In this paper, we address the complementary problem of generating repeated, potentially different referential expressions that refer to the same entity in the context of a piece of discourse longer than a sentence. We describe a corpus of short encyclopaedic texts we have compiled and annotated for reference to the main subject of the text, and report results for our experiments in which we set human subjects and automatic methods the task of selecting a referential expression from a wide range of choices in a full-text context. We find that our human subjects agree on choice of expression to a considerable degree, with three identical expressions selected in 50% of cases. We tested automatic selection strategies based on most frequent choice heuristics, involving different combinations of information about syntactic MSR type and domain type. We find that more information generally produces better results, achieving a best overall test set accuracy of 53.9% when both syntactic MSR type and domain type are known.

1 Introduction

Generation of Referring Expressions (GRE) is one of the most lively and thriving subfields of Natural Language Generation (NLG). GRE has traditionally addressed the following question:

> [G]iven a symbol corresponding to an intended referent, how do we work out the semantic content of a referring expression that uniquely identifies the entity in question? (Bohnet and Dale, 2005, p. 1004)

This view of GRE is mainly concerned with ruling out 'distractors' to achieve unique identification of the target referent. Our research is concerned with a complementary question: given an intended referent and a discourse context, how do we generate appropriate referential expressions (REs) to refer to the referent at different points in the discourse? While existing GRE research has taken discourse context into account to some extent (see Section 2), the question why people choose different REs in different contexts has not really been addressed:

> Not only do different people use different referring expressions for the same object, but the same person may use different expressions for the same object on different occasions. Although this may seem like a rather unsurprising observation, it has never, as far as we are aware, been taken into account in the development of any algorithm for generation of referring expressions. (Viethen and Dale, 2006, p. 119)

Selection of a particular RE in a particular context is likely to be affected by a range of factors in addition to discourse-familiarity and unique identification. In our research we ultimately aim to (i) investigate the factors that influence choice of RE in context, (ii) determine what information is needed for a GRE module to be able to generate appropriate REs in context, and (iii) develop reliable methods for automatically generating REs in context.

Our basic approach is to annotate occurrences of MSR in naturally occurring texts, analyse the texts in various ways, and obtain multiple, human-produced alternatives to the REs in the texts. The results are used to inform the design of automatic methods for RE selection. The success of such methods can in turn be evaluated in terms of similarity of output REs with the human-produced REs.

In our current work we are focusing on a text type that has a single, easily identifiable main subject for which we can therefore expect to find a range of different REs: encyclopaedic entries. In this paper, we describe a corpus of such texts we have compiled and annotated (Section 3), and report first insights from our analysis of the corpus data (Section 4). We further report the results of an experiment where subjects selected REs in context (Section 5), and establish baseline results for automatic methods of selection (Section 6).

2 Related Research

The most classical form of GRE algorithm takes into account two main factors in selecting expressions: unique identification (of the intended referent from a set including possible distractors), and brevity (Dale, 1989; Reiter and Dale, 1992). Most GRE research focuses on definite, non-first mentions of the target referent. The most influential of these algorithms, the 'incremental algorithm' (IA) (Dale and Reiter, 1995), originally just selected attributive properties, but a range of extensions have been reported. Siddharthan and Copestake's algorithm (2004) is able to identify attributes that are particularly discriminating given the entities in the contrast set, and van Deemter's SET algorithm can generate REs to sets of entities (van Deemter, 2002).

Krahmer and Theune (2002) moved away from unique identification, also taking discourse context into account: they replaced the requirement that the intended referent be the *only* entity that matches the RE, to the requirement that it be the *most salient* in a given context. Several versions of centering theory have been used as a basis for pronominalisation algorithms (Dale, 1992; McCoy and Strube, 1999; Henschel et al., 2000). Jordan (2002) highlighted a factor other than salience that influences choice of RE: she found a large proportion of overspecified redescriptions in the Coconut corpus of dialogues and showed that some dialogue states and communicative goals make overspecific REs more likely.

Among the few corpora of texts within which REs have been annotated in some way (as opposed to corpora of annotated REs such as those created by van Deemter et al. (2006)) are the GNOME, Coconut and Maptask corpora. In the GNOME Corpus (Poesio, 2000; Poesio, 2004) different types of discourse and semantic information are annotated, including reference and semantic attributes. The corpus annotation was e.g. used to train a decision tree learner for NP modifier generation (Cheng et al., 2001).

The RE annotations in the Coconut corpus represent information at the discourse level (reference and attributes used) and at the utterance level (information about dialogue state). The 400 REs and annotations in the corpus were used to train an RE generation module (Jordan and Walker, 2000). Gupta and Stent (2005) annotated both the Maptask and Coconut corpora for POS-tags, NPs, referent of NPs, and knowledge representations for each speaker which included values for different attributes for potential referents.

While context has been taken into account to some extent in existing research on generation of REs, our goal is to model a range of contextual factors and the interactions between them. Our corpus creation work provides — for the first time, as far as we are aware — a resource that includes multiple human-selected REs for the same referent in the same place in a discourse. In contrast to the resources cited above, our corpus is a collection of naturally occurring texts. It is also somewhat larger, containing approximately 8,000 REs in total.

3 The Corpus

We created a corpus of short encyclopaedic texts by collecting just over 1,000 introductory sections from Wikipedia entries for cities, countries, rivers and people. An introductory section was defined as the part of the entry preceding the table of contents (we only used entries with tables of contents). We removed Wikipedia mark-up, images, HTML tags etc. from the entries to yield text-only versions. These were then annotated for references to the subject of the entry by five annotators, and the annotations double-checked by the first author. Annotators managed to do between 5 and 10 texts per hour. The inter-annotator agreement was 86%, as checked on a randomly selected 20-text subset of the corpus for which we had annotations by all five annotators (these annotations were not double-checked). The final corpus consists of 1,078 texts in four subdomains: rivers (83 texts), cities (248 texts), countries (255 texts) and people (492 texts).

3.1 Types of referential expression annotated

We annotated three broad categories of main subject referential expressions (MSREs) in our corpus[1] — subjects, objects and possessives. These are rel-

[1] In our terminology and view of grammar in this section we rely heavily on Huddleston and Pullum (2002).

atively straightforward to identify, and account for virtually all cases of main subject reference (MSR) in our texts. Annotators were asked to identify subject, object and possessive NPs and decide whether or not they refer to the main subject of the text. The three MSR types were defined as follows (NPs that we annotated are underlined):

I Subject MSREs: referring subject NPs, including pronouns and special cases of VP coordination where the same MSRE is the subject of the coordinated VPs, e.g:

1. *He was proclaimed dictator for life.*
2. *Alexander Graham Bell (March 3, 1847 - August 2, 1922) was a Scottish scientist and inventor who emigrated to Canada.*
3. *Most Indian and Bangladeshi rivers bear female names, but this one has a rare male name.*
4. *"The Eagle" was born in Carman, Manitoba and _ grew up playing hockey.*

II Object MSREs: referring direct or indirect objects of VPs and prepositional phrases; e.g.:

1. *People from the city of São Paulo are called paulistanos.*
2. *His biological finds led him to study the transmutation of species.*

III Possessive MSREs: genitive NPs including genitive forms of pronouns, but excluding genitives that are the subject of a gerund-participial[2]:

1. *Its estimated length is 4,909 km.*
2. *The country's culture, heavily influenced by neighbours, is based on a unique form of Buddhism intertwined with local elements.*
3. *Vatican City is a landlocked sovereign city-state whose territory consists of a walled enclave within the city of Rome.*

3.2 Comments on annotation scheme

We interpret relative pronouns in a particular type of relative clause as anaphorically referential (I(2) and III(3) above): the type that Huddleston and Pullum call *supplementary relative clauses* (as opposed to integrated relative clauses). The main difference in meaning between the two types of relative clause is that in supplementary ones, the relative clause can be dropped without affecting the meaning of the clause containing it. From the point of view of generation, the meaning could be equally expressed in two independent sentences or in two clauses one of which is a relative clause. The single-sentence construction is very common in the People subdomain of our corpus. One example is shown in (1) below, with the semantically equivalent two-sentence alternative shown in (2):

(1) *Hristo Stoichkov is a football manager and former striker who was a member of the Bulgaria national team that finished fourth at the 1994 FIFA World Cup.*

(2) *Hristo Stoichkov is a football manager and former striker. He was a member of the Bulgaria national team that finished fourth at the 1994 FIFA World Cup.*

We also annotated 'non-realised' MSREs in a restricted set of cases of VP coordination where an MSRE is the subject of the coordinated VPs. Consider the following example, where the subclausal coordination in (3) is semantically equivalent to the clausal coordination in (4):

(3) *He stated the first version of the Law of conservation of mass, _ introduced the Metric system, and _ helped to reform chemical nomenclature.*

(4) *He stated the first version of the Law of conservation of mass, he introduced the Metric system, and he helped to reform chemical nomenclature.*

According to Huddleston and Pullum (p. 1280), utterances as in (3) can be thought of as a reduction of longer forms as in (4), even though the former are not syntactically derived by ellipsis from the latter. Our reason for annotating the approximate place where the subject NP would be if it were realised (the gap-like underscores above) is that from a generation perspective there is a choice to be made about whether to realise the subject NP or not. Note that because we only included cases where subclausal coordination is at the level of VPs, these are all cases where only the subject NP is 'missing'[3].

Apart from titles and anything in quotations we included all NPs in our analysis. There are other forms of MSR that we could have included in our analysis, but decided against, because annotation simply proved too difficult: MSRs that are true gaps

[2] E.g. *His early career was marred by *his being involved in a variety of social and revolutionary causes.*

[3] E.g. we would not annotate a non-realised MSRE e.g. in *She wrote books for children and books for adults.*

and ellipses, adjective and noun modifiers, and implicit or anaphorically derivable references (other than those mentioned above).

4 Examining the Evidence

During the annotation process, the annotators found that the question 'does this expression refer to the main subject of this entry' was not always straightforward to answer. Consider the following passage:

(5) *A troop of Siberian Cossacks from Omsk founded the fort Zailiysky in 1854 at the foot of the Tian Shan mountain range, and renamed it one year later to Vernyj, a name that remained until 1921. In 1921, the name Alma-Ata ("father-apple") was created by the Bolsheviks. In a devastating earthquake in 1911, almost the only large building that remained standing was the Russian Orthodox cathedral. In the 1920s, after the completion of the Turkestan-Siberia Railway, Alma-Ata, as it was then known, became a major stopping point along the track. In 1929, Almaty became the capital of the Kazakh SSR.*

The actual MSREs (*Fort Zailiysky*, *Alma-Ata*, *it*, *Almaty*) are underlined, but there are a range of other terms that could be used to refer to the main subject (*father-apple*, *Vernyi*, *the capital of the Kazakh SSR*). There are three main issues. The first is metalinguistic use[4] of potential REs (as in *the name Alma-Ata* above) which did not cause major difficulties. Another issue is lexical ambiguity, e.g. an occurrence of *Australia* could refer to the continent or the country, and *Dubai* could refer to the city or the emirate. However, by far the more difficult issue arises where, if there are two referents, they cannot be said to be entirely distinct. Consider the following examples:

(6) *The Indus system is largely fed by the snows and glaciers of the Karakoram, Hindu Kush and Himalayan ranges. The Shyok, Shigar and Gilgit streams carry glacieral waters into the main river.*

(7) *Aruba's climate has helped tourism as visitors to the island can reliably expect warm, sunny weather.*

In (6) if one were to say that *the main river* and *the Indus system* had two distinguishable referents, the relation between them would clearly be one of part and whole. In (7), it could be argued that there are two referents (the country Aruba and the geological formation that it occupies), but this is not entirely satisfactory. One of the aspects of a country is its geographical dimension, so *the island* could be said to refer to that aspect of Aruba.

These issues are simpler in the People subdomain (and this is the reason why we decided to include more people entries in the corpus): at least it is fairly clear when and where people begin and end, but there are still many 'partial' references, e.g. *the young man* in the following sentence:

(8) *His aptitude was recognized by his college headmaster, who recommended that the young man apply for the École Normale Supérieure.*

It is clearly not entirely a matter of deciding whether two REs refer to two distinct referents or to the same referent, but there appear to be a whole range of intermediate cases where referents are neither identical nor entirely distinct. Most REs refer to one or more aspects of a referent more strongly than the others. E.g. *the island* refers most strongly to the geographical aspect of Aruba, *the democracy* to its political aspect, and so on. However, there also appear to be default REs that are neutral with regard to these different aspects, e.g. *Aruba* in the current example.

From the point of view of the generation process, the fact that some potential REs refer to one or more aspects of the intended referent more strongly than others is important, because it is one of the reasons why different REs are chosen in different contexts, and this is an issue largely orthogonal to discourse-familiarity, addressee-familiarity and whether the intended referent as a whole is in focus or not.

Such matters of aspectual focus are likely to interact with other discourse-level and contextual factors that may influence choice of RE in a repeated reference, such as salience, discourse focus and structure, distance from last mention, presence of potential distractors, and text genre.

5 Human Choice of MSR

We had two reasons for conducting an experiment with human subjects as described below. For one, we wanted to get an idea of the degree to which RE choice followed patterns that we could hope to replicate with automatic methods. If our subjects agreed substantially, then this would seem likely. The other reason was that we needed a reference test set with multiple REs (in addition to the corpus

[4]"[T]he case where we cite a linguistic expression in order to say something about it qua linguistic expression." (Huddleston and Pullum, 2002, p. 401).

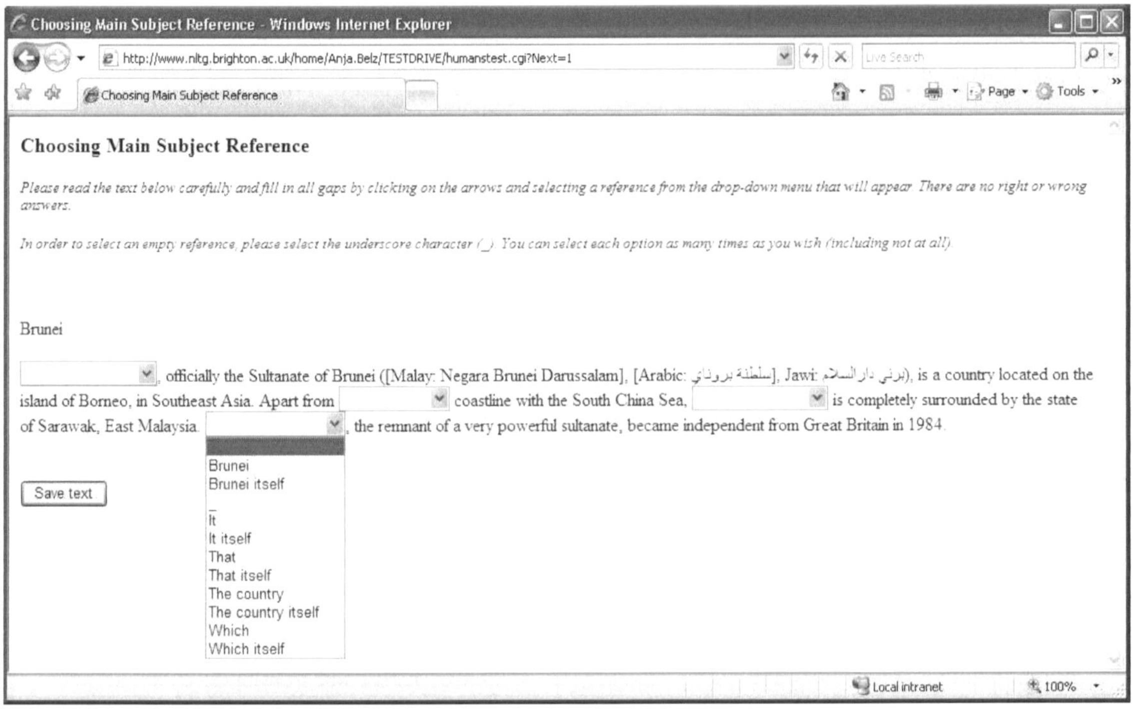

Figure 1: Screen shot of Choosing MSR Experiment.

texts) for each MSR to evaluate our automatic methods against, as is standard e.g. in MT and document summarisation.

We randomly selected a 10% subset of our corpus as our test set, ensuring that there were an equal number of texts from each subdomain and annotator. We then conducted an experiment in which we deleted all annotated MSREs and asked subjects to select an RE from a list of possible REs. Subjects were asked to do at least three texts each, over the web in a set-up as shown in Figure 1. The list of possible REs was automatically generated from the REs that actually occurred in each text, also using some additional generic rules (e.g. adding REs based on category nouns such as *the country* in the screen shot). We did not monitor who did the experiment, but asked members of the Corpora mailing list, colleagues and friends to participate anonymously. Approximately 80 different subjects did the experiment. Texts were randomly selected for presentation to subjects. Each text was removed from the pool of texts after three subjects had done it. As a result of the experiment we had three human-selected REs for each of the MSR slots. There were a total of 764 MSR slots in this set of texts (an average of 8.4 per text).

There was a considerable amount of agreement among the subjects, despite the fact that there were on average 9.5 different REs to choose from for each MSR slot[5]. Table 1 shows an overview of the agreement figures. In just 8.9% of MSRs, all three subjects chose a different RE, whereas in 50.1% of MSRs, all subjects chose exactly the same RE. In 64.9% of cases the subjects all made the same decision about whether to pronominalise or not, and in 95.3% of cases they all agreed about whether to realise the MSR or not (this does, however, include a large number of cases where the non-realised reference is not grammatical, as e.g. in the example in Figure 1).

To assess agreement between the subjects and the corpus texts we computed the average of the three pairwise agreement figures, shown in Table 2. The average agreement figures here are somewhat higher than those in Table 1.

6 Automatically Chosing MSREs

We conducted experiments to obtain baseline results for automatically choosing among a given set of REs. The task definition was the same as in the

[5]Not all available choices are guaranteed to be grammatical, since they are not generated by a grammar-based component.

Total MSRs	764
Average MSRs per file	8.4
All three different	8.9%
All three exactly same	50.1%
All three same pronominalisation decision	64.9%
All three same non-realisation decision	95.3%

Table 1: (Dis)agreement among subjects in Choosing MSR Experiment.

Total MSRs	764
Average MSRs per file	8.4
Average pairwise agreement	65.0%
Same pronominalisation decision (avg)	76.7%
Same non-realisation decision (avg)	97.2%

Table 2: (Dis)agreement between subjects in Choosing MSR Experiment and corpus texts.

human experiments, i.e. we deleted all MSRs and replaced them with lists of possible REs.

Our goal was to determine the accuracy that can be obtained by making the most frequent choice in a given context. This kind of baseline has been shown to be very powerful for example in word sense disambiguation and POS-tagging. In POS-tagging, each word is tagged with its (generally) most frequent POS-tag; in WSD, each ambiguous word is tagged with its most frequent sense.

6.1 Automatic classification of REs

Methods for automatically choosing from a previously unseen set of REs need to map the REs to a generalized representation/classification that allows one to apply statistics obtained from the training corpus to new sets of REs. We devised a general classification scheme for REs which is based on the notion of default RE (see Section 4), RE length relative to length of default RE, and generally identifiable linguistic features (such as presence of a determiner and pronouns). The scheme distinguishes the following types and subtypes of REs:

1. Default name of the main subject of the article which we set to the title for each entry (e.g. *United Kingdom* for the entry on the United Kingdom of Britain and Northern Ireland).
2. Pronoun: (a) personal, (b) relative, (c) possessive.
3. REs with determiner: subcategorised according to length relative to default RE, length of the default +/- X, $1 \leq X \leq 6$.
4. Any other REs, subcategorised according to length relative to default RE: length of the default +/- X, $0 \leq X \leq 6$.

The idea in taking length into account is that this may enable us to capture length-related phenomena such as the fact that references to the same object in a discourse tend to become shorter over the course of a text (known as *attenuation* in the psycholinguistic literature).

6.2 Frequencies of MSR types in training set

We determined the frequencies of the above RE types in the training set as a whole, and individually for each subdomain (Rivers, Cities, Countries, People) and for each syntactic MSR type (Subjects, Objects, Possessives), as shown in Table 3. There are interesting differences in frequencies between different subdomains. Pronouns are overall the most frequent type of RE in our corpus, accounting for nearly half of all REs, but are more dominant in some subdomains than others: percentages range from 28% (Cities) to 63% (People). The default name (which we set to the entry title) is the second most frequent type overall, accounting for between 2% (Rivers[6]) and 37% (Cities).

REs that contain determiners are very rare in the People subdomain. REs shorter than the default are far more frequent in People (where reference by surname alone is common) than the other subdomains.

6.3 Most frequent choice selection

We tested most frequent choice selection on the test set (the same set of texts as was used in the human experiment) using four different ways of subdividing the corpus and calculating frequencies (S1–S4 below). For each corpus subdivision we ranked the RE types given above (Section 6.1) according to their frequency of occurrence in the corpus subdivision (these rank lists are referred to as *frequency lists* below). The four ways of subdivding the corpus were as follows:

S1. All texts, resulting in a single, global frequency list;

S2. Texts divided according to subdomain, resulting in four frequency lists (cities, countries, rivers, people);

S3. Texts divided according to MSR type, resulting in three frequency lists (subjects, objects, possessives);

S4. Texts divided according to both subdomain and MSR type, resulting in 12 frequency lists (one for each combination of subdomain and MSR type).

[6]The title in River entries often includes the word 'river', e.g. *Amazon River* whereas in REs in the texts it is rare.

length	Default	Pronoun (all)	RE +det $> d$	RE +det $< d$	RE +/-det $= d$	Other RE $> d$	Other RE $< d$
All texts (7277)	1491	3372	601	91	492	184	1046
All city texts (1735)	666	483	273	15	183	26	89
All country texts (1469)	521	506	227	57	112	6	40
All river texts (572)	13	245	98	10	143	3	50
All people texts (3501)	291	2138	3	9	54	149	867
All subject MSREs (4940)	1241	1863	398	50	364	171	853
All object MSREs (681)	184	148	129	31	102	13	74
All possessive MSREs (1656)	66	1361	74	10	26	0	119

Table 3: Training set frequencies of different RE types, computed for entire training set, subdomains and syntactic MSR types; d = length of default name.

	All	Cities	Countries	Rivers	People
All	29.6% (757)	49.7% (141)	36.7% (191)	4.2% (24)	57.1% (182)
Subject MSREs	34.8% (523)	49.1% (110)	43.0% (142)	29.4% (17)	42.1% (254)
Object MSREs	42.3% (52)	61.9% (16)	43.8% (16)	0% (2)	46.2% (13)
Possessive MSREs	85.2% (182)	50.0% (33)	90.9% (33)	80.0% (5)	86.6% (134)

Table 4: Test set results (in percent) obtained with several most frequent choice strategies 'trained' on different subsets of the training set.

This gave us 20 frequency lists in total which we applied to RE selection as follows. First, the alternative REs given in the test set inputs were classified with the scheme described in Section 6.1. Then the RE classified as belonging to the RE type at the top of the frequency list was selected. If no alternative was in the top RE category, we backed off to the second most frequent category, and so on.

Table 4 shows the percentages of correct decisions over the test set. The results clearly show that overall performance improves as more knowledge about the tasks is included. Subset sizes are shown in brackets in each cell, as they are informative: e.g. of the two objects MSRs in Rivers in the test set, neither was in the most frequent Object/River type according to the training set.

The 'global' accuracy figure (All/All) achieved with the frequency list computed from the entire training set is 29.6%; for the other sets, accuracy ranges from the very low 4.2% (All/River) to the very high 90.9% (Possessive/Country).

The more we know about what kind of MSR we are looking for, the better we can do. As computed on the entire test set, if we know nothing in addition to it being an RE, then we get 29.6%; if we (only) know whether the referent is a river, city, country or person, this figure rises to 48.9%; if we (only) know whether we are looking for a subject, object or possessive RE, then we get 47.4%. If we know both subdomain and MSR type, then we get as much as 53.9%. This is still considerably less than the 65% achieved on average by the human subjects (Table 2), but it is a very strong baseline.

7 Further research

The distinct task we are planning to address in the immediate future is how well we can predict choice of REs using only input that is derivable from the full-text context, as would be required e.g. for text summarisation. The most frequent choice results presented in this paper represent baselines in this respect. In future work, we intend to look at more sophisticated approaches, including linguistic features (POS-tags, grammatical relations, etc.); optimal sequences of REs (e.g. modelled by n-gram models); and determining the current topic to decide which aspects of a referent are in focus (as described in Section 4).

We will also extend our annotation of the corpus texts in various ways, initially focussing on syntactic annotations such as POS-tags and dependencies. We also plan to look at annotating (or automatically identifying) potential distractors.

8 Conclusion

In this paper we presented and described our corpus of introductory encyclopaedic texts in which we have annotated three types of reference to the main subject. We described an experiment with human subjects in which we found that the subjects agreed in their choice to a considerable degree. In our experiments with automatic RE selection we found that the simple strategy of selecting the most frequent type of RE provides a strong baseline, particularly if information regarding subdomain type and syntactic type of RE is included.

Acknowledgments

The annotation effort was supported under EPSRC (UK) Grant GR/S24480/01. We are very grateful to the members of the Corpora mailing list, our colleagues and friends who helped us complete the online experiment. We thank the anonymous reviewers who provided very helpful feedback. Particular thanks are due to Helen Johnson, University of Colorado, who spotted and reported a bug early enough for us to fix it.

Sebastian Varges was partially supported by the European Commission ADAMACH project contract N 022593, and by DARPA under Contract No. NBCHD030010. Any opinions, findings, and conclusions or recommendations expressed in this material are those of the authors and do not necessarily reflect the views of DARPA or the Department of Interior–National Business Center.

References

Bernd Bohnet and Robert Dale. 2005. Viewing referring expression generation as search. In *Proceedings of IJCAI'05*, pages 1004–1009.

Hua Cheng, Massimo Poesio, Renate Henschel, and Chris Mellish. 2001. Corpus-based np modifier generation. In *Proceedings of NAACL 2001*.

Robert Dale and Ehud Reiter. 1995. Computational interpretations of the Gricean maxims in the generation of referring expressions. *Cognitive Science*, 19(2):233–263.

Robert Dale. 1989. Cooking up referring expressions. In *Proceedings of the 27th Annual Meeting of the Association for Computational Linguistics*.

Robert Dale. 1992. *Generating Referring Expressions: Constructing Descriptions in a Domain of Objects and Processes*. Bradford Books, MIT Press, Cambridge, MA.

Surabhi Gupta and Amanda Stent. 2005. Automatic evaluation of referring expression generation using corpora. In *Proceedings of the 1st Workshop on Using Copora in Natural Language Generation*, pages 1–6, Brighton, UK.

Renate Henschel, Hua Cheng, and Massimo Poesio. 2000. Pronominalization revisited. In *Proceedings of COLING'00*, pages 306–312.

Rodney Huddleston and Geoffrey Pullum. 2002. *The Cambridge Grammar of the English Language*. Cambridge University Press.

Pamela W. Jordan and M. Walker. 2000. Learning attribute selections for non-pronominal expressions. In *Proceedings of ACL'00*.

Pamela W. Jordan. 2002. Contextual influences on attribute selection for repeated descriptions. In Kees van Deemter and Rodger Kibble, editors, *Information Sharing: Reference and Presupposition in Language Generation and Interpretation*. CSLI, Stanford, CA.

Emiel Krahmer and Mariet Theune. 2002. Efficient context-sensitive generation of referring expressions. In K. van Deemter and R. Kibble, editors, *Information Sharing: Reference and Presupposition in Language Generation and Interpretation*, pages 223–264. CSLI, Stanford, CA.

Kathy McCoy and Michael Strube. 1999. Generating anaphoric expressions: Pronoun or definite description. In *Proceedings of the ACL'99 Workshop on Reference and Discourse Structure*, pages 63–71.

Massimo Poesio. 2000. Annotating a corpus to develop and evaluate discourse entity realization algorithms: issues and preliminary results. In *Proceedings of LREC 2000*.

Massimo Poesio. 2004. Discourse annotation and semantic annotation in the GNOME corpus. In *Proc.* ACL*'04 Discourse Annotation Workshop*.

Ehud Reiter and Robert Dale. 1992. A fast algorithm for the generation of referring expressions. In *Proceedings of the 14th International Conference on Computational Linguistics*, pages 232–238, Nantes, France, 23-28 August.

Advaith Siddharthan and Ann Copestake. 2004. Generating referring expressions in open domains. In *Proc. of ACL-04*.

Kees van Deemter, Ielka van der Sluis, and Albert Gatt. 2006. Building a semantically transparent corpus for the generation of referring expressions. In *Proceedings of the 4th International Conference on Natural Language Generation*, pages 130–132, Sydney, Australia, July.

Kees van Deemter. 2002. Generating referring expressions: Boolean extensions of the Incremental Algorithm. *Computational Linguistics*, 28(1):37–52.

Jette Viethen and Robert Dale. 2006. Towards the evaluation of referring expression generation. In *Proc. of the 4th Australasian Language Technology Workshop (ALTW'06)*, pages 115–122.

Stochastic Realisation Ranking for a Free Word Order Language

Aoife Cahill, Martin Forst and Christian Rohrer
Institute of Natural Language Processing
University of Stuttgart, Germany
{cahillae|forst|rohrer}@ims.uni-stuttgart.de

Abstract

We present a log-linear model that is used for ranking the string realisations produced for given corpus f-structures by a reversible broad-coverage LFG for German and compare its results with the ones achieved by the application of a language model (LM). Like other authors that have developed log-linear models for realisation ranking, we use a hybrid model that uses linguistically motivated learning features *and* a LM (whose score is simply integrated into the log-linear model as an additional feature) for the task of realisation ranking. We carry out a large evaluation of the model, training on over 8,600 structures and testing on 323. We observe that the contribution that the structural features make to the quality of the output is slightly greater in the case of a free word order language like German than it is in the case of English. The exact match metric improves from 27% to 37% when going from the LM-based realisation ranking to the hybrid model, BLEU score improves from 0.7306 to 0.7939.

1 Introduction

Most traditional approaches to stochastic realisation ranking involve applying language model n-gram statistics to rank alternatives (Langkilde, 2000; Bangalore and Rambow, 2000; Langkilde-Geary, 2002). Much work has been carried out into statistical realisation ranking for English. However, n-grams alone (even if they are efficiently implemented) may not be a good enough measure for ranking candidate strings, particularly in free-word order languages.

Belz (2005) moves away from n-gram models of generation and trains a generator on a generation treebank, achieving similar results to a bigram model but at much lower computational cost. Cahill and van Genabith (2006) do not use a language model, but rather rely on treebank-based automatically derived LFG generation grammars to determine the most likely surface order.

Ohkuma (2004) writes an LFG generation grammar for Japanese separate from the Japanese LFG parsing grammar in order to enforce canonical word order by symbolic means. In another purely symbolic approach, Callaway (2003; 2004) describes a wide-coverage system and the author argues that there are several advantages to a symbolic system over a statistical one. We argue that a reversible symbolic system, which is desirable for maintainability and modularity reasons, augmented with a statistical ranking component can produce systematically ranked, high quality surface realisations while maintaining the flexibility associated with hand-crafted systems.

Velldal et al. (2004) and Velldal and Oepen (2005) present discriminative disambiguation models using a hand-crafted HPSG grammar for generation from MRS (Minimal Recursion Semantics) structures. They describe three statistical models for realization ranking: The first is a simple n-gram language model, the second uses structural features in a maximum entropy model for disambiguation and a third uses a combination of the two models. Their results show that the third model where the n-gram language model is combined with the structural features in the maximum entropy disambiguation model performs best. Nakanishi et al. (2005) present similar probabilistic models for a chart generator using a HPSG grammar acquired from the Penn-II Treebank (the Enju HPSG), with the difference that, in their experiments, the model that only uses structural features outperformed the hybrid model. We present a model for realisation ranking similar to the models just mentioned. The main differences between our work and theirs is that we are working within the LFG framework and concentrating on a less configurational language: German.

2 Background

2.1 Lexical Functional Grammar

The work presented in this paper is couched in the framework of Lexical Functional Grammar (LFG). LFG is a grammar formalism which makes use of two representation levels to encode syntactic properties of sentences: constituent structure (c-structure) and functional structure (f-structure). C-structures are context-free trees that encode constituency and linear order. F-structures are attribute-value matrices that encode grammatical relations and morphosyntactic features. While translational equivalents of sentences may vary considerably across languages at the c-structure level, it is assumed that, at the f-structure level, where linear order is abstracted away from, languages behave much more alike. Also, f-structures are taken as the interface from syntax to semantics. From a language-technological perspective, f-structures are the level of representation various (prototypes of) question-answering systems, a sentence condensation system and machine translation systems operate on and generate from.

Figures 1 and 2 illustrate the c-structure and the f-structure that the German broad-coverage LFG presented in the next paragraph produces for (1).

(1) Verheugen habe die Worte des
Verheugen had the words the-GEN
Generalinspekteurs falsch interpretiert.
inspector-general wrongly interpreted.
'Verheugen had mis-interpreted the words of the inspector-general.'

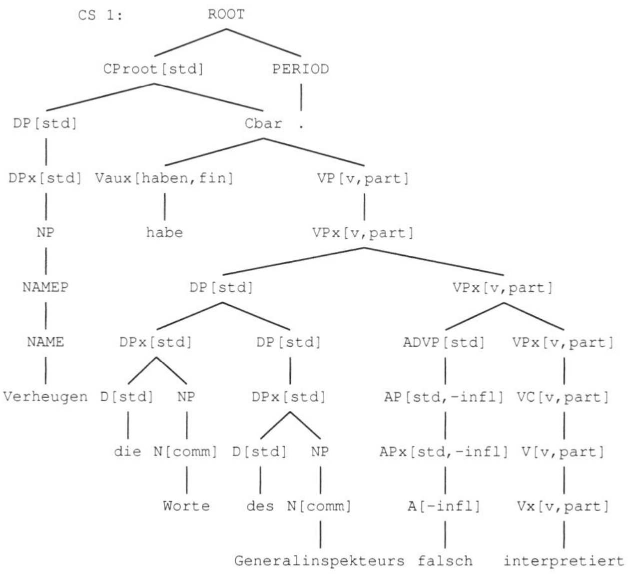

Figure 1: C-structure for (1)

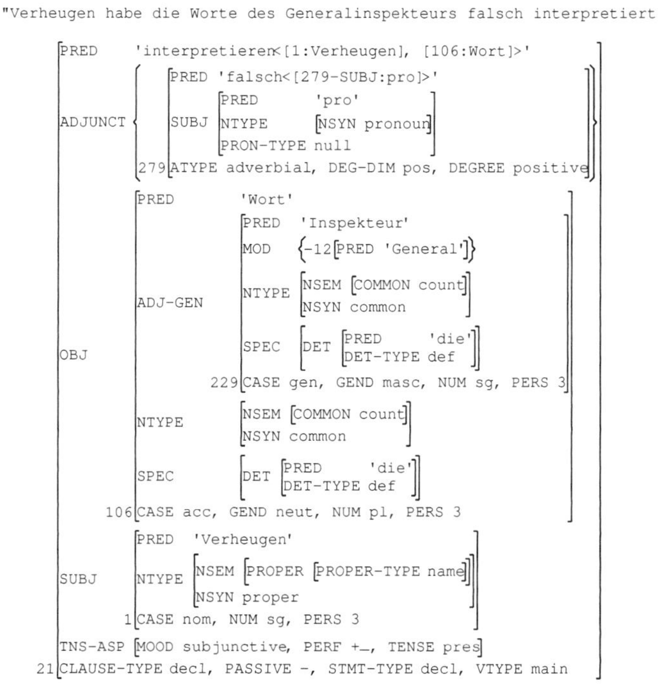

Figure 2: F-structure for (1)

2.2 A broad-coverage LFG for German

For the construction of our data, we use the German broad-coverage LFG documented in Dipper (2003) and Rohrer and Forst (2006). It is a hand-crafted grammar developed in and for the LFG grammar development and processing platform XLE (Crouch et al., 2006). It achieves parsing coverage of about 80% in terms of full parses on newspaper text, and for sentences out of coverage, the robustness techniques described in Riezler et al. (2002) (fragment grammar, 'skimming') are employed for the construction of partial analyses. The grammar is reversible, which means that the XLE generator can produce surface realisations for well-formed input f-structures.

Recently, the grammar has been complemented with a stochastic disambiguation module along the lines of Riezler et al. (2002), consisting of a log-linear model based on structural features (Forst, 2007). This module makes it possible to determine one c-/f-structure pair as the most probable analysis of any given sentence.

2.3 Surface realisation

As XLE comes with a fully-fledged generator, the grammar can be used both for parsing and for surface realisation. Figure 3 shows an excerpt of the set of strings (and their LM ranking) that are generated from the f-structure in Figure 2. Note that all of these (as well as the the remaining 139 strings in the set) are grammatical; however, some of them are clearly more likely or unmarked than others.

1. `Falsch interpretiert habe die Worte`
   `Wrongly interpreted had the words`
   `des Generalinspekteurs Verheugen.`
   `the-GEN inspector-general Verheugen.`
2. `Falsch interpretiert habe die Worte des Generalinspekteures Verheugen.`
3. `Die Worte des Generalinspekteurs falsch interpretiert habe Verheugen.`
5. `Die Worte des Generalinspekteurs habe Verheugen falsch interpretiert.`
7. `Verheugen habe die Worte des Generalinspekteurs falsch interpretiert.`

Figure 3: Excerpt of the set of 144 strings generated from the f-structure in Figure 2, ordered according to their LM score

Just as hand-crafted grammars, when used for parsing, are only useful for most applications when they have been complemented with a disambiguation module, their usefulness as a means of surface realisation depends on a reliable module for realisation ranking. A long list of arbitrarily ordered output strings is useless for practical applications such as summarisation, QA, MT etc.

Very regular preferences for certain realisation alternatives over others can be implemented by means of so-called optimality marks (Frank et al., 2001), which are implemented in XLE both for the parsing and the generation direction. For ranking string realisations on the basis of 'soft' and potentially contradictory constraints, however, the stochastic approach based on a log-linear model, as it has previously been implemented for English HPSGs (Nakanishi et al., 2005; Velldal and Oepen, 2005), seems more adequate.

3 Experimental setup

3.1 Data

We use the TIGER Treebank (Brants et al., 2002) to train and test our model. It consists of just over 50,000 annotated sentences of German newspaper text. The sentences have been annotated with morphological and syntactic information in the form of functionally labelled graphs that may contain crossing and secondary edges.

We split the data into training and test data using the same data split as in Forst (2007), i.e. sentences 8,001–10,000 of the TIGER Treebank are reserved for evaluation. Within this section, we have 422 TIGER annotation-compatible f-structures, which are further divided into 86 development and 336 test structures. We use the development set to tune the parameters of the log-linear model. Of the 86 heldout sentences and the 336 test sentences, 78 and 323 respectively are of length >3 and are actually used for our final evaluation.

For training, we build a symmetric treebank of 8,609 packed c/f-structure representations in a similar manner to Velldal et al. (2004). We do not include structures for which only one string is generated, since the log-linear model for realisation ranking cannot learn anything from them. The symmetric treebank was established using the following strategy:

1. Parse input sentence from TIGER Treebank.
2. Select all of the analyses that are compatible with the TIGER Treebank annotation.
3. Of all the TIGER-compatible analyses, choose the most likely c/f-structure pair according to log-linear model for parse disambiguation.
4. Generate from the f-structure part of this analysis.

String Realisations	#str.	Avg # words
> 100	1206	18.3
≥ 50, < 100	709	14.3
≥ 10, < 50	3029	11.8
> 1, < 10	3665	7.6
Total	8609	11.3

Table 1: Number of structures and average sentence length according to ambiguity classes in the training set

String Realisations	#str.	Avg # words
> 100	61	23.7
≥ 50, < 100	26	13.5
≥10, < 50	120	11.6
> 1, < 10	129	7.8
Total	336	12.8

Table 2: Number of structures and average sentence length according to ambiguity classes in the test set

5. If the input string is contained in the set of output strings, add this sentence and all of its corresponding c/f-structure pairs to training set. The pair(s) that correspond(s) to the original corpus sentence is/are marked as the intended structure(s), while all others are marked as unintended.

Theoretically all strings that can be parsed should be generated by the system, but for reasons of efficiency, punctuation is often not generated in all possible positions, therefore resulting in an input string not being contained in the set of output strings. Whenever this is the case for a given sentence, the c/f-structure pairs associated with it cannot be used for training. Evaluation can be carried out regardless of this problem, but it has to be kept in mind that the original corpus string cannot be generated for all input f-structures. In our test set, it is generated only for 62% of them.

Tables 1 and 2 give information about the ambiguity of the training and test data. For example, in the training data there are 1,206 structures with more than 100 string realisations. Most of the training and test structures have between 2 and 50 possible (and grammatical) string realisations. The average sentence length of the training data is 11.3 and it is 12.8 for the test data.[1] The tables also show that the structures with more potential string realisations correspond to longer sentences than the structures that are less ambiguous when generating.

[1] This is lower than the overall average sentence length of roughly 16 in TIGER because of the restriction that the structure produced by the reversible grammar for any TIGER sentence be compatible with the original TIGER graph. As the grammar develops further, we hope that longer sentences can be included in both training and test data.

3.2 Features for realisation ranking

Using the feature templates presented in Riezler et al. (2002), Riezler and Vasserman (2004) and Forst (2007), we construct a list of 186,731 features that can be used for training our log-linear model. Out of these, only 1,471 actually occur in our training data. In the feature selection process of our training regime (see Subsection 3.3), 360 features are chosen as the most discriminating; these are used to rank alternative solutions when the model is applied. The features include c-structure features, features that take both c- and f-structure information into account, sentence length and language model scores. Examples of c-structure features are the number of times a particular category label occurs in a given c-structure, the number of children the nodes of a particular category have or the number of times one particular category label dominates another. Examples of features that take both c- and f-structure information into account are the relative order of functions (e.g. 'SUBJ precedes OBJ'). As in Velldal and Oepen (2005), we incorporate the language model score associated with the string realisation for a particular structure as a feature in our model.

3.3 Training

We train a log-linear model that maximises the conditional probability of the observed corpus sentence given the corresponding f-structure. The model is trained in a (semi-)supervised fashion on the 8,609 (partially) labelled structures of our training set using the `cometc` software provided with the XLE platform. `cometc` performs maximum likelihood estimation on standardised feature values and offers several regularisation and/or feature selection techniques. We apply the combined method of incremental feature selection and l_1 regularisation

Exact Match Upper Bound	62%
Exact Matches	27%
BLEU score	0.7306

Table 3: Results with the language model

Exact Match Upper Bound	62%
Exact Matches	37%
BLEU score	0.7939

Table 4: Results with the log-linear model

presented in Riezler and Vasserman (2004), the corresponding parameters being adjusted on our heldout set.

For technical reasons, the training was carried out on unpacked structures. However, we hope to be able to train and test on packed structures in the future which will greatly increase efficiency.

4 Evaluation

4.1 Evaluating the system's output

We evaluate the most likely string produced by our system in terms of two metrics: **exact match** and **BLEU score** (Papineni et al., 2002). Exact match measures what percentage of the most probable strings are exactly identical to the string from which the input structure was produced. BLEU score is a more relaxed metric which measures the similarity between the selected string realisation and the observed corpus string.

We first rank the generator output with a language model trained on the Huge German Corpus (a collection of 200 million words of newspaper and other text) using the SRILM toolkit. The results are given in Table 3, achieving exact match of 27% and BLEU score of 0.7306. In comparison to the results reported by Velldal and Oepen (2005) for a similar experiment on English, these results are markedly lower, presumably because of the relatively free word order of German.

We then rank the output of the generator with our log-linear model as described above and give the results in Table 4. There is a noticeable improvement in quality. Exact match increases from 27% to 37%, which corresponds to an error reduction of 29%,[2] and BLEU score increases from 0.7306 to 0.7939.

There is very little comparable work on realization ranking for German. Gamon et al. (2002) present work on learning the contexts for a particular subset of linguistic operations; however, no evaluation of the overall system is given.

4.2 Evaluating the ranker

In addition to the exact match and BLEU score metrics, which give us an indication of the quality of the strings being chosen by the statistical ranking system, the quality of the ranking itself is interesting for internal evaluation during development. While exact match tells us how often the correct string is selected, in all other cases, it gives the developers no indication of whether the correct string is close to being selected or not. We propose to evaluate the ranker by calculating the following **ranking score**:

$$s = \begin{cases} \frac{n-r+1}{n} & \text{if } r \text{ is defined,} \\ 0 & \text{if } r \text{ is not defined,} \end{cases}$$

where n is the total number of potential string realisations and r is the rank of the gold standard string. If the gold standard string is not among the list of potentials, i.e. r is undefined, the ranking score is defined as 0.

The ranking scores for the language model and the hybrid log-linear model are given in Table 5. Since the original string is not necessarily in the set of candidate strings, we also provide the upper bound (i.e. if the ranker had chosen the correct string any time the correct string was available). The table shows that in almost 62% of the cases, the original string was generated by the system. The hybrid model achieves a ranking score of 0.5437 and the language model alone achieves 0.4724. The structural features in the hybrid model result in an error reduction of 49% over the baseline language model ranking score. The hybrid model is thus noticeably better at ranking the original string (when available) higher in the list of candidate strings. This error reduction is considerably higher than the error reduction of the much stricter exact match score.

[2]Remember that the original corpus string is generated only from 62% of the f-structures of our test set, which fixes the upper bound for exact match at 62% rather than 100%.

Language Model	0.4724
Hybrid Model	0.5437
Upper Bound	0.6190

Table 5: Evaluating the ranking

5 Error Analysis

We had initially expected the increase in BLEU score to be greater than 0.0633, since German is far less configurational than English and therefore we thought the syntactic features used in the log-linear model would play an even greater role in realisation ranking. However, in our experiments, the improvement was only slighlty greater than the improvement achieved by Velldal and Oepen (2005). In this section, we present some of the more common errors that our system still produces.

Word Choice Often there is more than one surface realisation for a particular group of morphemes. Sometimes the system chooses an incorrect form for the sentence context, and sometimes it chooses a valid, though marked or dispreferred, form. For example, from the structure in Figure 2, the system chooses the following string as the most probable.

Verheugen habe die **Wörter** des
Verheugen had the **words** of the
Generalinspekteures falsch interpretiert.
inspector-general wrongly interpreted.

There are two mis-matches in this output string with respect to the original corpus string. In the first case the system has chosen *Wörter* as the surface realisation for the morpheme sequence *Wort+NN.Neut.NGA.Pl* rather than the, in this case, correct form *Worte*. In the second (less critical) case, the system has chosen to mark the genitive case of *Generalinspekteur* with *es* rather than the *s* that is in the original corpus. This is a relatively frequent alternation that is difficult to predict, and there are other similar alternations in the dative case, for example. In the development set, this type of error occurs in 6 of the 78 sentences. In order to correct these errors, the morphological component of the system needs to be improved.

Placement of adjuncts Currently, there is no feature that captures the (relative) location of particular types of adjuncts. In German, there is a strong tendency for temporal adjuncts to appear early in the sentence, for example. Since the system was not provided with data from which it could learn this generalisation, it generated output like the following:

Frauenärzte haben die Einschränkung
Gynaecologists have the restriction
umstrittener Antibabypillen wegen
controversial birth control pills because of
erhöhter Thrombosegefahr **am Dienstag**
increased risk of thrombosis **on Tuesday**
kritisiert.
critisised.
'Gynaecologists criticised the restriction on controversial birth control pills due to increased risk of thrombosis on Tuesday.'

where the temporal adjunct *on Tuesday* was generated very late in the sentence, resulting in an awkward utterance. The most obvious solution is to add more features to the model to capture generalisations about adjunct positions.

Discourse Information In many cases, the particular subtleties of an utterance can only be generated using knowledge of the context in which it occurs. For example, the following sentence appears in our development corpus:

Israel stellt den Friedensprozess nach Rabins
Israel puts the peace process after Rabin's
Tod nicht in Frage
death not in question
'Israel does not challenge the peace process after Rabin's death'

Our system generates the string:

Nach Rabins Tod stellt Israel den
After Rabin's death puts Israel the
Friedensprozess nicht in Frage.
peace process not in question.

which, taken on its own, gets a BLEU score of 0. The sentence produced by our system is a perfectly valid sentence and captures essentially the same information as the original corpus sentence. However, without knowing anything about the information structure within which this sentence is uttered, we have no way of telling where the emphasis of the sentence is. The work described in this paper is part of a much larger project, and future research is already planned to integrate information structure into the surface realisation process.

6 Discussion and future work

In the work of Callaway (2003; 2004), a purely symbolic system is presented. Our system makes use of a symbolic grammar, but we apply a statistical ranking model to the output. We believe that this gives us the power to restrict the output of the generator without under-generating. The symbolic grammar enforces hard constraints and the statistical ranking models (possibly conflicting) soft constraints to weight the alternatives.

Satisfactory methods for the automatic evaluation of surface realisation (as well as machine translation) have not yet been developed (Belz and Reiter, 2006). The shortcomings of current methods, particularly BLEU score, seem to be even more pronounced for German and other relatively free word-order languages. Given that all of the sentences generated by our system are syntactically valid, one would expect much higher results. A human inspection of the results and investigation of other evaluation metrics such as NIST will be carried out to get a clearer idea of the quality of the ranking.

There is a potential bias in the learning algorithm, in that the average length of the training data sentences is lower than the average length of the test data. In particular, the length of the sentences with more than 100 potential string realisations seems to be considerably longer (cf. Tables 1 and 2). Therefore, it is possible that the system has not learnt enough features from longer sentences to be able to correctly rank the intended string. We plan to increase the size of the training set to also include longer sentences that would hopefully avoid this bias. Moreover, more data will allow us to investigate in detail the effect of more or less training data on the results of a stastical realisation ranking system trained on them.

Finally, more feature design is clearly necessary for the improvement of the system. We already have several features in mind, which have not been implemented for technical reasons. Examples are the distance between a relative clause and its antecedent as well as its weight, which will hopefully allow us to learn which types of relative clauses tend to appear in extraposed position. Another thing that features for realization ranking should capture is the information-structural status of constituents. Information structure is an important factor when generating the correct surface realisation (Kruijff et al., 2001). German is a language in which word order is largely driven by information structure rather than grammatical function, which is often marked morphologically. In future work, we plan to integrate information structure features into the log-linear model and hope that results will improve.

7 Conclusions

In this paper, we have presented a log-linear realisation ranking system for a German LFG system. The reversibility of the grammar ensures that all output strings will be grammatical. The task then becomes to choose the most likely one. We train on over 8,600 partially labelled structures and test on 323 sentences of length >3. To our knowledge, this is the largest statistical realisation experiment carried out for German. The number of structures used is also much greater than the data used in Velldal and Oepen (2005), although the improvement over a baseline language model was only slightly better. We achieved an increase in exact match score from 27% to 37% and an increase in BLEU score from 0.7306 to 0.7939. The fact that our scores are lower than that of Velldal and Oepen (2005) suggests that it may be more difficult to achieve high scores for German data, although this is not necessarily a reflection of the quality of the strings chosen. We also show, using a ranking score, that the log-linear ranking system generally ranks the correct solution considerably higher than our baseline system.

Acknowledgements

The work described in this paper has been carried out as part of the COINS project of the linguistic Collaborative Research Centre (SFB 732) at the University of Stuttgart, which is funded by the German Research Foundation (DFG). Furthermore, we would like to thank John Maxwell of the Palo Alto Research Center for being so responsive to our requests for extensions of the XLE generator functionalities, some of which were crucial for our work.

References

Srinivas Bangalore and Owen Rambow. 2000. Exploiting a probabilistic hierarchical model for generation. In *Proceedings of COLING 2000*, pages 42–48, Saarbrücken, Germany.

Anja Belz and Ehud Reiter. 2006. Comparing automatic and human evaluation of NLG systems. In *Proceedings of EACL 2006*, pages 313–320, Trento, Italy.

Anja Belz. 2005. Statistical generation: Three methods compared and evaluated. In *Proceedings of ENLG 2005*, pages 15–23, Aberdeen, Scotland.

Sabine Brants, Stefanie Dipper, Silvia Hansen, Wolfgang Lezius, and George Smith. 2002. The TIGER Treebank. In *Proceedings of the Workshop on Treebanks and Linguistic Theories*, Sozopol, Bulgaria.

Aoife Cahill and Josef van Genabith. 2006. Robust PCFG-Based Generation using Automatically Acquired LFG Approximations. In *Proceedings of COLING/ACL 2006*, pages 1033–1040, Sydney, Australia.

Charles B. Callaway. 2003. Evaluating coverage for large symbolic NLG grammars. In *Proceedings of IJCAI 2003*, pages 811–817, Acapulco, Mexico.

Charles B. Callaway. 2004. Wide coverage symbolic surface realization. In *Proceedings of ACL 2004*, pages 125–128, Barcelona, Spain.

Dick Crouch, Mary Dalrymple, Ron Kaplan, Tracy King, John Maxwell, and Paula Newman. 2006. XLE documentation. Technical report, Palo Alto Research Center, CA.

Stefanie Dipper. 2003. *Implementing and Documenting Large-scale Grammars – German LFG*. Ph.D. thesis, IMS, University of Stuttgart.

Martin Forst. 2007. *Disambiguation for a Linguistically Precise German Parser*. Ph.D. thesis, University of Stuttgart.

Anette Frank, Tracy Holloway King, Jonas Kuhn, and John T. Maxwell. 2001. Optimality Theory Style Constraint Ranking in Large-Scale LFG Grammars. In Peter Sells, editor, *Formal and Empirical Issues in Optimality Theoretic Syntax*, pages 367–397. CSLI Publications, Stanford, CA.

Michael Gamon, Eric Ringger, Simon Corston-Oliver, and Robert Moore. 2002. Machine-learned contexts for linguistic operations in German sentence realization. In *Proceedings of ACL 2002*, pages 25–32, Philadelphia, PA.

Geert-Jan M. Kruijff, Ivana Kruijff-Korbayova, John Bateman, and Elke Teich. 2001. Linear Order as Higher-Level Decision: Information Structure in Strategic and Tactical Generation. In *Proceedings of ENLG 2001*, pages 74–83, Toulouse, France.

Irene Langkilde-Geary. 2002. An Empirical Verification of Coverage and Correctness for a General-Purpose Sentence Generator. In *Proceedings of INLG 2002*, NY.

Irene Langkilde. 2000. Forest-based statistical sentence generation. In *Proceedings of NAACL 2000*, pages 170–177, Seattle, WA.

Hiroko Nakanishi, Yusuke Miyao, and Jun'ichi Tsujii. 2005. Probabilistic models for disambiguation of an HPSG-based chart generator. In *Proceedings of IWPT 2005*.

Tomoko Ohkuma. 2004. Japanese generation grammar. Presentation at the ParGram fall meeting, Dublin, Ireland.

Kishore Papineni, Salim Roukos, Todd Ward, and WeiJing Zhu. 2002. BLEU: a Method for Automatic Evaluation of Machine Translation. In *Proceedings of ACL 2002*, pages 311–318, Philadelphia, PA.

Stefan Riezler and Alexander Vasserman. 2004. Gradient feature testing and l_1 regularization for maximum entropy parsing. In *Proceedings of EMNLP'04*, Barcelona, Spain.

Stefan Riezler, Tracy Holloway King, Ronald M. Kaplan, Richard Crouch, John T. Maxwell, and Mark Johnson. 2002. Parsing the Wall Street Journal using a Lexical-Functional Grammar and Discriminative Estimation Techniques. In *Proceedings of ACL 2002*, Philadelphia, PA.

Christian Rohrer and Martin Forst. 2006. Improving coverage and parsing quality of a large-scale LFG for German. In *Proceedings of LREC-2006*, Genoa, Italy.

Erik Velldal and Stephan Oepen. 2005. Maximum entropy models for realization ranking. In *Proceedings of the 10th MT Summit*, pages 109–116, Thailand.

Erik Velldal, Stephan Oepen, and Dan Flickinger. 2004. Paraphrasing treebanks for stochastic realization ranking. In *Proceedings of TLT Workshop*, pages 149–160, Tübingen, Germany.

Modelling control in generation*

Roger Evans[†], David Weir[‡], John Carroll[‡], Daniel Paiva[‡], Anja Belz[†]

[†]**University of Brighton**
Brighton, UK

[‡]**University of Sussex**
Brighton, UK

Abstract

In this paper we present a view of natural language generation in which the control structure of the generator is clearly separated from the content decisions made during generation, allowing us to explore and compare different control strategies in a systematic way. Our approach factors control into two components, a 'generation tree' which maps out the relationships between different decisions, and an algorithm for traversing such a tree which determines which choices are actually made. We illustrate the approach with examples of stylistic control and automatic text revision using both generative and empirical techniques. We argue that this approach provides a useful basis for the theoretical study of control in generation, and a framework for implementing generators with a range of control strategies. We also suggest that this approach can be developed into tool for analysing and adapting control aspects of other advanced wide-coverage generation systems.

1 Introduction

Natural Language Generation (NLG) has traditionally been most successful when applied to restricted domains using hand-crafted, carefully tuned systems[1] In such scenarios, the range of outputs to be generated is generally quite small, and controlling the generator is often trivial (for example, if the process is deterministic) or unimportant (if all solutions are equally good). Moving beyond such systems, however, requires control issues to be taken more seriously, in order to efficiently generate suitable output from among a range of options, some of which may not be appropriate. Delivering re-usable generation components, or components with sufficient breadth to be empirically tuned, requires a better understanding of control in generation.

The problem is exacerbated by the complexity of the generation process, and correspondingly of generation systems. The simple pipeline model of Reiter and Dale (2000) actually conceals a wide range of underlying approaches to generation (cf. (Mellish et al., 2006, section 2.1)), and a recent initiative to provide a 'reference architecture' for such systems (involving some of the present authors) abandoned any attempt to harmonise control aspects of the systems it studied (Mellish et al., 2006). In such a situation, it is difficult to see how any general statements, results or techniques relating to controlling generation can be developed, although Paiva and Evans (2005) report an approach that has the potential for wider applicability.

In the present paper, we introduce a view of the generation process which abstracts away from specific generation systems or architectures, to a point at which it is possible to separate control from content decisions in the generation process. This allows us to explore systematically different control strategies for constructing the same content (mapping from an input to the same output), and examine different approaches (e.g. generative, empirical) to the problem of controlling generation. The approach we develop is quite abstract, but we see potential for using it in at least three ways: as a theoretical framework for studying and understanding control; as a directly implementable generation framework in its own right, at least for small scale systems, and with suitable care over data representations, larger scenarios too; and as a tool for modelling the control behaviour of other generation systems, perhaps with a view to tuning them to a particular domain.

The paper is organised as follows. Section 2 introduces the model and discusses in general terms

* This research was part of COGENT (Controlled Generation of Text) project, supported by the EPSRC under grants GR/S24480/01 (Brighton) and GR/S24497/01 (Sussex).

[1]See, for example, Paiva (1998) for a survey of such systems.

the ways it can be used for studying control. Section 3 describes two examples of the model being used for practical generation research: using the pCRU system for exploring stylistic variation in weather forecasts, and developing an automatic text revision system for medical leaflets. Section 4 explores some wider issues and summarises the contribution of this work and possible future directions.

2 The control model

We start with a very general view of the generation process[2]. Generation takes an input and produces an output, which is a 'more linguistically instantiated' representation of the input (but we will not say precisely what that means — cf. (Evans et al., 2002; McDonald, 1993). In the process of doing this, the generator makes various decisions about the content of its output — it reaches a choice-point at which several options are possible and selects one to follow, and then reaches another choice point, and so on. In fact, this is all any generation algorithm does: visit choice points one after another and make a decision relating to the content of output at each one. Each decision may be constrained by the input, constrained by other decisions already made, or determined by the generation algorithm itself. These constraints may not reduce the number of choices at a choice point to exactly one, in which case the algorithm may be capable of returning several solutions, all deemed to be equally good, or no solutions at all. A simple way to think of this behaviour is as a tree structure, where each node corresponds to a choice-point, and each branch corresponds to a choice (leading to the next choice-point etc.).

But now let us abstract this process a little more. Consider first the input. It is common in generation to distinguish between different kinds of information that an algorithm may appeal to. Reiter and Dale (2000, p.43) specify four kinds of information in their generic generator definition: knowledge source, communicative goal, user model and discourse history. But we shall take a 'black box' view of the generator's input – the input is simply a collection of constraints on the process of producing the output. On this view, the generator does not 'transform' an input into an output, but creates an output 'from nowhere', guided in some way by the input information.

Turning now to the output, we assume this takes the form of some kind of data structure, for example a string of characters, a list of words, a parse tree or even a forest representing multiple realisations. We further assume that such a structure is in general constructed incrementally through applying a sequence of operations, which we shall call *content operations*, and that there may be some flexibility in how these operations are applied to produce 'the same' output (thinking algebraically, content operations may be commutative, or may combine together in various ways). The potential for applying these operations in different orders to produce the same output gives rise to one source of variation of control. We are not interested in what outputs are, but only how they are constructed, and so we think of them purely in terms of the content operations that give rise to them.

Adopting this very abstract view, we can conceptualise a generator as having the following principal components:

1. a set of *content operations* – these are possible operations that can be taken with respect to an output (for example, in a feature-based approach, a content operation might be to set a feature in the data-structure under construction to a particular value);

2. a way of organising content operations into a *generation tree* – each node in the tree corresponds to a choice-point for the generator, each branch is labelled with a set of content operations, and selecting that branch corresponds to choosing those operations on the output, and then traversing the branch to a new choice-point node;

3. an *input constraint algorithm* – at each choice point, the tree provides a set of possible options, and this algorithm applies constraints imposed by the input to reduce these options (possibly removing some or even all of them);

4. a *traversal algorithm* for the generation tree – at each choice point, this algorithm selects which branches to follow from among those still available after the intervention of the input constraint algorithm.

This view of generation may seem a little unusual, but it is, we believe, uncontroversial, in the sense that most implemented generators could in principle be 'unwrapped' into such a structure,

[2] In principle, this view applies far more generally than language generation, but we only consider NLG here.

though it may be very large, or even in principle unbounded. Its value from the present perspective is that it allows us to separate out control aspects from content in a uniform way. Specifically, we maintain that control resides in (a) the structure of the generation tree (that is, the grouping of content operations into choice point options, and the ordering of choice points in the tree) and (b) the traversal algorithm. In contrast, the content aspects of the algorithm arise from its input/output specification: the form of the input gives rise to the input constraint algorithm (independently of the control context, that is, the position in a generation tree at which the algorithm is applied), and the set of outputs, viewed as content operation combinations, gives rise to the set of content operations.

Our interest in these control components arises because they represent the *process* of generation, rather than, for example, the linguistic structure of the sentence generated. Understanding and controlling generation can thus be expressed and studied in terms of generation tree structures and traversal algorithms independently from actual systems and their linguistic representations. In the following subsections, we discuss these control components in more detail.

2.1 Generation trees

A **generation tree** is an unordered tree whose branches are labelled with sets of content operations, and whose leaves are labelled with output structures. Although we do not stipluate what content operations or output structures are, we do intend that the output structure is in some sense the result of applying content operations, and also allow that not all content operations are compatible with each other (for example, some may be mutually exclusive). This allows us to place a general consistency requirement on generation trees: a generation tree is **consistent** if each output structure labelling a leaf is compatible with the sequence of content operation sets labelling the path from the leaf to the root.

To make this definition more concrete, here are two possible interpretations:

- Consider a simple generator which uses a context-free grammar to specify its output language. Generation consists of starting at the initial category (S) and using grammar rules to expand non-terminals, until no non-terminals are left. One possible generation tree representation would have each node corresponding to a sentential form of the grammar (a string of terminals and nonterminals which could expand to a sentence in the grammar), with the root node corresponding to S, and each branch corresponding to the expansion of one or more non-terminals in the sentential form to produce a new sentential form. Here, the content operations are the individual rule expansions, and there is some flexibility in how they are applied to produce a particular output. Different generation trees correspond to different control strategies for grammar expansion – for example, always expanding just the left-most non-terminal would correspond to a left-to-right depth-first strategy, expanding all non-terminals simultaneously would result in a breadth-first strategy.

- Consider a generator that produces a complex feature structure (such as an HPSG sign (Pollard and Sag, 1994), or an MRS representation (Copestake et al., 2005)), by taking an underspecified input and further instantiating it. Here, content operations are feature specifications (of the form 'the value of feature f is v'), the output structures are feature structures and an output structure is compatible with a feature specification if it instantiates the feature with the specified value. Then a generation tree is consistent if each feature structure labelling a leaf node instantiates all the features specified on the path from the root to that leaf. Thinking more algorithmically, as we move down from the root towards a leaf, each decision instantiates some additional features in the output structure, until the structure is completed at the leaf.

Generation trees describe the process of generating outputs. Each path from root to leaf corresponds to a different 'run' of the generator leading to an output. Thus the structure of the generation tree bears no necessary relationship to the structure of the representations returned, or to any underlying linguistic formalism used to specify them. In the context-free generator described above, it is possible to read off parse trees associated with each leaf, but the generation tree itself is not directly related to the generator's grammar – in general there is no requirement that a generation tree is itself a derivation tree according to some grammar, or has any other formal property.

This notion of a generation tree has its roots in two earlier ideas. Paiva (2004) introduces 'tracing trees' to analyse the behaviour of a generation algorithm and discusses two variants, a tree representation of the generation of an individual sentence, and a single tree representation of all the sentences that can be generated. In that work and subsequent publications (Paiva and Evans, 2004; Paiva and Evans, 2005), the first variant is used, but the second variant is very similar in structure to generation trees as defined here. Belz (2004) introduces generation trees which are a direct precursor to the present definition, representing a generation algorithm directly as traversal of a tree mapping from partially specified to more specified content (this system is the basis of example 3.1, discussed below).

2.2 The structure of generation trees

Generation trees provide a framework for organising the decisions made by the generator. The structure of the generation tree is a key component in the control structure of the algorithm, because it captures two important factors:

- how content operations group together into choice-points – each node in the tree has a number of branches leading from it, and each branch is labelled with a set of content operations; selecting a branch commits to the content operations which label it as a group, and in preference to the content operations of other branches (although nothing prevents those operations occurring again further down the selected branch);
- the order in which choice-points are visited – each branch leads to another node and hence another choice;

The primary content of a generation tree is the set of output structures labelling leaves, and these are 'constructed' from the content operations on the path from the tree root. But where there is scope for varying how content operations are applied to produce the same output, it is possible to alter the structure of the tree without changing the output structures, in other words, changing the control structure without changing the content. As we saw in the context-free generator, above, depth-first and breadth-first strategies may have radically different trees, but result in the same output sentences.

A range of control considerations may come into play when we think about what the structure of the tree should be. Examples that can be directly measured in the tree structure include how balanced the tree should be, how many daughters a node may have, or how many content operations may label a single branch. These will each correspond to aspects of the processing, for example, how much variation in processing time there is for different outputs or how much the system commits in one step. Other aspects of structure may only be observable when the tree is combined with actual inputs, for example, how often this branch results in dead ends (choice-points with no admissible choices remaining). There may also be interactions with the traversal algorithm, since the tree shape provides the domain for making choices and the branch labels provide the way of discriminating choices. In the examples below, we shall consider traversal algorithms trained on corpus data – this will only work well if the choices available at a choice point correspond to 'events' in a corpus which can be effectively measured.

2.3 The traversal algorithm

The second control component in our model is the tree traversal algorithm. This gets applied once all other constraints (those imposed by the tree structure and the input) have been applied. So in effect, if there are still choices remaining at this point, they are 'free choices' as far as the generator tree and input structure are concerned. The simplest traversal algorithm is to accept all the remaining choices as valid, and pursue them all to return potentially multiple solutions. Serialised variants on this theme include pursuing any one choice, chosen at random (on the basis that they are all equally suitable), or imposing an order on the tree and then pursing a left-to-right depth-first traversal. In either of these cases, the possibility of dead-ends (no solutions at a descendant node) needs to be accommodated, perhaps by backtracking.

A more interesting scenario is where the traversal algorithm does not treat all options as the same, but imposes a preferential order on them. A familiar example of this would be where choices have probabilities associated with them, learned from some corpus, with the intention that the generator is attempting to generate sentences most like those that occur in the corpus. We will see several examples of this approach in section 3. We note here that this probability information is not part of the input, nor is it part of the generation tree as we have defined it above. However the traversal algorithm associates these probabilities with individual choices-points in the tree, so that in effect it views the tree as being annotated with these probabilities. We refer to such a tree as a **trained** generation tree, while remembering that strictly speaking, according to our model the training parameters are part of the traversal algorithm, not the tree.

3 Examples of this control model

3.1 Example 1 – pCRU

pCRU (Belz, 2006; Belz, 2007) is a probabilistic language generation framework for creating NLG systems that contain a probabilistic model of the entire generation space, represented by a context-free underspecification grammar. The basic idea is to view all generation rules as context-free rules and to estimate a single probabilistic model from a corpus of texts to guide the generation process. In non-probabilistic mode, the generator operates by taking any sentential form of the grammar as an input and expanding it using the grammar to all possible fully specified forms, which are the outputs. Thus a pCRU grammar looks rather like a conventional grammar for syntax, except that it is used to model deep generation as well as surface realisation.

The probabilistic version of pCRU introduces a probability distribution over the generator decisions. This is achieved by using **treebank training**, that is, estimating a distribution over the expansion rules that encode the generation space from a corpus using two steps[3]:

1. *Convert corpus into multi-treebank:* use the underlying grammar to parse the corpus and annotate strings with the derivation trees obtained
2. *Train the generator:* Obtain frequency counts for each individual generation rule from the multi-treebank; convert into probability distributions over alternative rules

The resulting probability distribution is used in one of three ways to control generation.

1. *Viterbi generation:* undertake a Viterbi search of the generation forest for a given input, which maximises the joint likelihood of all decisions taken in the generation process. This selects the most likely generation process, but is considerably more expensive than the greedy modes.
2. *Greedy generation:* make the single most likely decision at each choice point (rule expansion) in a generation process. This is not guaranteed to result in the most likely generation process, but the computational cost is very low.
3. *Greedy roulette-wheel generation:* use a non-uniform random distribution proportional to the likelihoods of alternatives.

Belz (2006) describes an application of the system to weather forecast generation, and compares the different control techniques with human generation and a more traditional generate-and-test probabilistic architecture (Langkilde-Geary, 2002).

pCRU can be interpreted using the model introduce here in the following way (cf. the first example given in section 2.1). The **generation tree** is defined by all the possible derivations according to the grammar. Each node corresponds to a sentential form and each child node is the result of rewriting a single non-terminal using a grammar rule. Thus the **content operations** are grammar rules. The **content structures** are sentences in the grammar. The input is itself a sentential form which identifies where in the complete tree to start generating from, and the **input constraint algorithm** does nothing (alternatively, the input constraint algorithm only admits paths that pass through nodes associated with the input sentential form). Treebank training associates probabilities with all the possible expansion rules at a given choice-point, and three **traversal algorithms** Viterbi, greedy, and greedy roulette-wheel are defined.

3.2 Example 2 – Automatic Text Revision

Our second example of the generation model is in a system currently under development for Automatic Text Revision (ATR). The core idea here is that all the leaves in a generation tree are in a sense equivalent to each other (modulo any leaves rules out by particular input constraints). Hence they are, in a sense, paraphrases of each other. If they are text strings, the paraphrasing relationship may be obvious, but even generation trees over more abstract representations have this paraphrasing quality. Hence they support a notion of **generalised paraphrasing**: substituting one data structure used during generation for another one, whose equivalence

[3]See Belz (2006) for a more complete description.

is licensed by a generation tree.

We are using this type of generation tree to experiment with a model of ATR, intended for applications such as automatic improvement of drafts, or texts written by non-native writers, editorial adjustment to a house style, stylistic modification of a finished document for a different audience, or smoothing out stylistic differences in a multi-authored document.

Our ATR system uses generation trees whose output structures are Minimal Recursion Semantics (MRS) representations (Copestake et al., 2005), and whose content operations are instantiations of particular features in MRS structures (cf. example 2 in section 2.1). Thus a conventional use of such a generation tree might be to walk down the tree, instantiating MRS features at each choice-point guided by some input information, until a completely specified MRS realisation is reached at one of the leaves. However, for ATR we use the trees somewhat differently: the input to the process is one of the content structures labelling a leaf of the tree. The objective is to locate another output structure (a 'paraphrase') by walking up the tree from the input leaf (*de-generating*), and then taking alternative decisions to come back down to a different leaf (*re-generating*). In the absence of an 'input', the generation tree cannot distinguish between its output structures, and so the result might be a random alternative leaf. To overcome this, we need to add control in the sense introduced above.

The control questions we are exploring in this scenario are:

- How can we train a generation tree so that it is possible to locate 'better' paraphrases than the input?
- Can we structure a tree so that 'better' paraphrases are close to the input (that is, limited de-generation will always result in significant improvement)?

We address the first question using probabilistic training against a corpus of texts like the ones we want to paraphrase into (the 'target' corpus). In a simlar way to the pCRU example, we train the tree by estimating frequency distributions for different branches at each choice-point in the tree. In this case the branches are labelled with sets of feature instantiations. We train by parsing a corpus of target texts to MRS structures and then counting instances of the sets of feature instantiations on each branch, smoothing and normalising. In effect, we are using MRS features to characterise the 'style' of the corpus. Once we have done this, each leaf MRS can be assigned an overall probability score, and each interior node can compare the incoming score (from the branch leading to the input MRS) with scores for MRS's on the other branches, deciding whether to de-generate higher (in the hope of more improvement, but at greater cost) or start re-generating from this point.

The second question is interesting both from a computational complexity point of view (can we structure the tree to make the ATR more efficient?) and also because our goal is *minimal* paraphrasing: in many ATR contexts, it is bad to change the text unnecessarily, and so we are looking for minimal changes that improve the style. Our approach to this problem is to induce the generation trees themselves from a pool of MRS structures. We automatically construct different decision trees which gather together choices about groups of feature assignments in MRS's in different ways and different orders. This results in a set of generation trees with different structures, but all covering the same set of MRS leaves (and all with the same very abstract specification at their root – the fragment of MRS structure shared by *all* the MRS's). We then experiment with these trees to find which trees are more efficient for ATR from one text domain to another. Our long-term aim is to use the difference between our two corpora (for example pharmaceutical leaflet written for doctor and or for patients) to allow us to construct or select efficient generation trees automatically.

The description of this system makes reference to concepts in the generation model introduced here, but it may be useful to be more explicit, as we did with the pCRU example. The **output structures** are MRS's (more accurately, de-lexicalised MRS's) and the **generation trees** are labelled with abstractions over MRS's. The **content operations** are instantiations of MRS features, and typically there is more than one content operation on each branch in a generation tree (where features tend to co-occur with each other). The input is one of the leaf MRS's, **the input constraint algorithm** does nothing (as the influence of the input is entirely captured by its position in the tree) and the **traversal algorithm** uses the probability distributions to locate the best (or a better) paraphrase, relative to the training corpus.

4 Discussion

The examples just discussed illustrate how the model introduced in this paper offers a uniform perspective which is still flexible. The model separates out control and content aspects of the generation process and makes it possible to reason about and compare different control strategies in different generation scenarios. In the examples described here, we have illustrated generation trees over two different kinds of structure (strings in a language and MRS's), created in two different ways (generatively from the sentential forms of a grammar, and induced from data), with two kinds of content operation (grammar expansion and feature instantiation), two notions of training and four different traversal algorithms, and two very different notions of input. And of course this does not exhaust the range. Additional sources for generation trees, for example, may include manually crafted trees (somewhat akin to systemic grammars, although concerned more with control than linguistics) or trees induced from implemented generation systems (in the manner used by Paiva (2004) for his tracing trees).

This last option highlights one of several potential uses for the model proposed here. On the one hand our aim is to promote a clearer theoretical perspective on control issues in generation, by introducing a model in which they can be represented and explored in a common framework. The two examples given above constitute direct implementations of the model. Although they are both quite small scale systems, they indicate the prospects for direct implementation in larger systems (and help identify where scaling up may be problematic). But we also envisage using this approach as an analytic tool for studying and tuning other generation systems – by mapping a system into this generation model it may become possible to understand how it might most effectively be empirically controlled, for example, to identify deficiencies in the design, or to reason about computational complexity and efficiency.

Although we have discussed generation trees as if they cover the entire generation process (from non-linguistic input, whatever that may be, to textual realisation), nothing in the definitions above forces this. In practice a generation tree might be used to model just some part of the generation process (such as content selection or realisation), and multiple generation trees might be used collectively in a more complex algorithm. We also believe that this approach suggests a way forward for hybrid symbolic/probabilistic systems. By making the control structures of the generator more explicit it becomes easier to see how (and in how many ways) one can introduce empirically informed processing into even quite complex symbolic systems.

Finally, the model presented here is not 'just' a classical search algorithm, because the process is in a sense constructive – content actions are intended to further specify the solution, rather than distinguish between fully-formed solutions, and the internal nodes of the tree are intended not to be solutions in themselves. A search perspective is also possible, by associating internal nodes with the set of realisations they dominate and construing the algorithm as a search for the right set of realisations generation trees can be embedded in. But such a view presupposes the enumeration of the set of realisations which we are keen to avoid. This may seem like a procedural nicety, and of course in a sense it is, but in addressing control issues at all we are committed to looking at procedural aspects of a system. In fact, ultimately what we are trying to achieve here is to provide a theoretical and formal foundation for exactly those aspects of a system generally regarded as procedural details.

References

A. Belz. 2004. Context-free representational underspecification for NLG. Technical Report ITRI-04-08, Information Technology Research Institute, University of Brighton.

A. Belz. 2006. Probabilistic generation using representational underspecification. Technical Report NLTG-06-01, Natural Language Technology Group, CMIS, University of Brighton.

A. Belz. 2007. Probabilistic generation of weather forecast texts. In *Proceedings of the Conference of the North American Chapter of the Association for Computational Linguistics (NAACL-HLT 2007)*.

A. Copestake, D. Flickinger, I. Sag, and C. Pollard. 2005. Minimal recursion semantics: An introduction. *Research on Language and Computation*, 3(2/3):281–332.

R Evans, P. Piwek, and L. Cahill. 2002. What is NLG? In *Proceedings of International Conference on Natural Language Generation*.

I. Langkilde-Geary. 2002. An empirical verification of coverage and correctness for a general-purpose sentence generator. In *Proceedings of the 12th International Conference on Natural Language Generation*, pages 17–24.

D. McDonald. 1993. Issues in the choice of a source for natural language generation. *Computational Linguistics*, 19(1):191–197.

C. Mellish, D. Scott, L. Cahill, R. Evans, D. Paiva, and M. Reape. 2006. A reference architecture for natural language generation systems. *Journal of Natural Language Engineering*, 12(1):1–34.

D. Paiva and R. Evans. 2004. A framework for stylistically controlled generation. In *Proceedings of the International Conference on Natural Language Generation*, pages 120–129.

D. Paiva and R. Evans. 2005. Empirically-based control of natural language generation. In *Proceedings of the 43th Annual Meeting of the Association for Computational Linguistics*, pages 58–65.

D. Paiva. 1998. A survey of applied natural language generation systems. Technical Report ITRI-98-03, ITRI, University of Brighton.

D. Paiva. 2004. *Using Stylistic Parameters to Control a Natural Language Generation System*. Ph.D. thesis, University of Brighton.

Carl J. Pollard and Ivan A. Sag. 1994. *Head-Driven Phrase Structure Grammar*. University of Chicago Press, Chicago.

E. Reiter and R. Dale. 2000. *Building Natural-Language Generation Systems*. Cambridge University Press.

Avoiding Repetition in Generated Text

Mary Ellen Foster
Informatik VI: Robotics and Embedded Systems
Technische Universität München
Boltzmannstr. 3, 85748 Garching, Germany
foster@in.tum.de

Michael White
Department of Linguistics
The Ohio State University
Columbus, OH 43210 USA
mwhite@ling.osu.edu

Abstract

We investigate two methods for enhancing variation in the output of a stochastic surface realiser: choosing from among the highest-scoring realisation candidates instead of taking the single highest-scoring result (*ε-best sampling*), and penalising the words from earlier sentences in a discourse when generating later ones (*anti-repetition scoring*). In a human evaluation study, subjects were asked to compare texts generated with and without the variation enhancements. Strikingly, subjects judged the texts generated using these two methods to be better written and less repetitive than the texts generated with optimal n-gram scoring; at the same time, no significant difference in understandability was found between the two versions. In analysing the two methods, we show that the simpler ε-best sampling method is considerably more prone to introducing dispreferred variants into the output, indicating that best results can be obtained using anti-repetition scoring with strict or no ε-best sampling.

1 Introduction

A classic rule of writing, found in many style guides, is to avoid repetition in order to keep text interesting and make it more lively. When designing systems to automatically generate text, it is often taken for granted that this stylistic goal should be met as well: for example, van Deemter et al. (2005) incorporated random choice into a language generation system "to maximise the *variety* of sentences produced" (emphasis original).

Repetitiveness may take several forms: using the same words or syntactic structures, repeatedly giving the same facts, or even repeating entire turns (for example, error-handling turns in dialogue systems). At the level of word choice and phrasing, recent advances in stochastic text generation have made it possible to implement corpus-based approaches to varying output. However, as Stone et al. (2004) note, there is an inherent conflict between producing output that is optimally similar to the corpus and incorporating variability: varying output requires choosing less frequent options, which inevitably reduces scores on corpus similarity measures. To the extent that corpus-based measures (such as n-gram scores) are used to avoid overgeneration and select preferred paraphrases, it is not obvious how to enhance variation without reducing output quality.

With this question in mind, we investigate in this paper the impact of two different methods for enhancing variation in the output generated by the COMIC multimodal dialogue system.[1] Both methods take advantage of the periphrastic ability of the OpenCCG surface realiser (White, 2006a). In the usual OpenCCG realisation process, when a logical form is transformed into output text, n-gram models are used to steer the realiser towards the single highest-scoring option for the sentence. This process tends to select the same syntactic structure for every sentence describing the same feature: for example, in the COMIC domain (describing and comparing bathroom tiles), the structure *The colours are [colours]* would be used every time the colours of a tile design are to be presented, even though alternative paraphrases are available.

The first (and simplest) means of avoiding such repetition using OpenCCG, *ε-best sampling*, is to perform n-best realisation and then to select randomly from among those options whose score is within a threshold ε of the top score. The second

[1] http://www.hcrc.ed.ac.uk/comic/

means of adding variation, *anti-repetition scoring*, is to store the words from recently generated sentences and to penalise a proposed realisation based on the number of words that it shares with these sentences. OpenCCG provides a built-in facility for implementing such anti-repetition scorers and integrating them with the normal n-gram–based scoring algorithm (White, 2005).

To verify that it can be beneficial for a natural language generation system to strive to avoid repetition, we first conducted a human evaluation study in which subjects were asked to compare texts generated with and without the two variation-enhancing methods. Strikingly, subjects judged the versions generated using ε-best sampling and anti-repetition scoring to be both better written and less repetitive than the versions generated with optimal n-gram scoring. To our knowledge, this study is the first to show a clear benefit for enhancing variation; while other recent studies (e.g., Stent et al., 2005; Belz and Reiter, 2006) have shown that automatic evaluation metrics do not always correlate well with human judgments of high quality generated texts with periphrastic variations, these studies examined sentences out of context, and thus could not take into account the benefit of avoiding repetition as a discourse progresses.

Following the human evaluation study, we varied the main parameters used in ε-best sampling and anti-repetition scoring and analysed the resulting impact on the amount of periphrastic variation and the number of dispreferred paraphrases in the generated outputs. The analysis revealed that the simpler ε-best sampling method is considerably more prone to introducing dispreferred variants into the output. It also showed that essentially the same amount of variation can be achieved using anti-repetition scoring on its own, or just with strict ε-best sampling, as using both methods together. This suggests a way of resolving the conflict between enhancing variation and maximising corpus similarity.

The rest of this paper is structured as follows. In Section 2, we describe previous work on generating paraphrases. In Section 3, we next summarise the realisation process of the OpenCCG surface realiser, concentrating on its use of n-gram models in the generation process and its support for disjunctive logical forms. In Section 4, we then give details of how the two anti-repetition methods were integrated into this realisation algorithm. Section 5 next presents the result of the human evaluation study. In Section 6, we then explore the impact of the two anti-repetition methods on the variability and quality of the generated text, using a range of parameter settings. In Section 7, we discuss the results of both studies and compare them with related work. Finally, in Section 8, we give some conclusions and outline possible extensions to this work.

2 Previous Work

The acquisition and generation of paraphrases has been studied for some time (cf. Iordanskaja et al., 1991; Langkilde and Knight, 1998; Barzilay and McKeown, 2001; Barzilay and Lee, 2003; Pang et al., 2003). Much recent work in this area has focussed on the automated acquisition of paraphrases from corpora, along with the use of the resulting paraphrases in language-processing areas such as information extraction and retrieval, question-answering, and machine translation.

The main technique that has been used for adding variation to stochastically-generated output is to modify the system so that it does not always choose the same option in a given situation, normally by modifying either the weights or the selection strategy. When selecting a combination of speech and body-language output for an animated character based on a corpus of recorded behaviour, for example, Stone et al. (2004) introduced variation by perturbing the scores slightly to choose from among low-cost utterances. The outputs from the system with perturbed weights scored nearly as high on an automated evaluation as those from the optimised system, and also made use of a wider range of corpus data. Belz and Reiter's (2006) "greedy roulette" *p*CRU text-generation system selected among generation rules weighted by their corpus probabilities, while Foster and Oberlander (2006) used a similar technique to select facial displays for an animated talking head. Both of these systems scored higher on a human evaluation than at least one competing system that always chose the single highest-scoring option; see Section 7 for further discussion.

The CRAG-2 system (Isard et al., 2006) generates dialogues between pairs of agents who are linguistically distinguishable but able to align with each other. It uses the OpenCCG surface realiser to select appropriate paraphrases for the desired personality of the simulated character and the stage of the dialogue, integrating cache models built from the preceding discourse with the primary n-gram models to attain lexico-syntactic alignment. The method of anti-repetition scoring described in this paper is similar, but the goal is opposite: instead of increasing alignment with an interlocutor, here we modify the *n*-gram scores to avoid alignment with the system's own previous utterances.

3 Surface Realisation with OpenCCG

The studies described in this paper use the OpenCCG open source surface realiser (White, 2006a,b), which is based on Steedman's (2000) Combinatory Categorial Grammar (CCG). A distinguishing feature of OpenCCG is that it uses a hybrid symbolic-statistical chart realisation algorithm combining (1) a theoretically grounded approach to syntax and semantic composition with (2) integrated language models for making choices among the options left open by the grammar. In so doing, it brings together the traditions of symbolic chart realisation (Kay, 1996; Carroll et al., 1999) and statistical realisation (Langkilde and Knight, 1998; Langkilde, 2000; Bangalore and Rambow, 2000; Langkilde-Geary, 2002). Another recent approach to combining these traditions appears in (Carroll and Oepen, 2005), where parse selection techniques are incorporated into an HPSG realiser.

In OpenCCG, the search for complete realisations makes use of *n*-gram language models and proceeds in one of two modes, *anytime* or *two-stage* (packing/unpacking). In the anytime mode, a best-first search is performed with a configurable time limit: the scores assigned by the *n*-gram model determine the order of the edges on the agenda, and thus have an impact on realisation speed. In the two-stage mode, a packed forest of all possible realisations is created in the first stage; in the second stage, the packed representation is unpacked in bottom-up fashion, with scores assigned to the edge for each sign as it is unpacked, much as in (Langkilde, 2000).

To realise a broad range of paraphrases, OpenCCG implements an algorithm for efficiently generating from disjunctive logical forms (LFs) (White, 2006a). A disjunctive LF represents the full set of possible syntactic paraphrases of a sentence: the differences may be subtle (e.g., choosing between *the design* or *it* as the subject), or may involve entirely different structures (e.g., *here we have a design in the classic style* vs. *this design is classic*). The algorithm uses packed representations similar to those initially proposed by Shemtov (1997), enabling it to run many times faster than sequential realisation of an equivalent set of non-disjunctive LFs.

The implementation described here makes use of the OpenCCG grammar developed as part of the COMIC multimodal dialogue system. This grammar was manually written with the aim of achieving very high quality. However, to streamline grammar development, the grammar was allowed to overgenerate in areas where rules are difficult to write and where *n*-gram models can be reliable; in particular, the grammar does not sufficiently constrain modifier order, which in the case of adverb placement especially can lead to a large number of possible orderings. To select preferred word orders among those allowed by the grammar for the input LF, we used a backoff 4-gram model trained on approximately 750 example target sentences, where certain words were replaced with their semantic classes (e.g. MANUFACTURER, COLOUR) for better generalisation, much as in (Oh and Rudnicky, 2002).

4 Anti-Repetition Methods

For both studies in this paper, we used OpenCCG to realise a range of texts describing and comparing bathroom-tile designs. The starting point for this implementation was the XSLT-based text planner from the COMIC system (Foster and White, 2004), which transforms sets of facts about tile designs into OpenCCG logical forms. We enhanced this text planner to produce disjunctive logical forms covering the full range of paraphrases permitted by the most recent version of the COMIC grammar, and then used OpenCCG realise those forms as text.

In the normal OpenCCG realisation process outlined above, corpus-based *n*-grams are used to select the single highest-scoring realisation for a given logical form. To allow the realiser to choose paraphrases other than the top-scoring one, we modified the realisation process in two ways: *ε-best sampling* and *anti-repetition scoring*.

ε-best sampling was implemented by creating the full set of possible surface realisations for a given disjunctive LF, and then randomly selecting one from the set whose *n*-gram score is within a given threshold of the top score. As the scores for sentences can vary by several orders of magnitude, the threshold was specified as a distance in log-10 space. Depending on the threshold value, this method can add more or less variation to the generated text. There is a danger that, if the threshold is too large and the grammar overgenerates, the output may include paraphrases that are dispreferred, or even ungrammatical.

Default (no anti-repetition methods)		With anti-repetition methods
This design is country. It is based on the Sandstein collection by Porcelaingres. The colours are brown, grey and black. There are geometric shapes on the decorative tiles.		Here is a design in the country style. It uses tiles from the Sandstein collection by Porcelaingres. It has brown, grey and black in the colour scheme. The decorative tiles have geometric shapes.
This design is also country. It is based on the Cardiff collection by Aparici. The colours are cream and dark red. It also has geometric shapes on the decorative tiles.		This one is also country. It draws from Cardiff, by Aparici. The colour scheme features cream and dark red. The decorative tiles also have geometric shapes.

Figure 1: Sample description sequence realised in both modes

Anti-repetition scoring was implemented as follows. First, for a proposed realisation, the number c of open-class words repeated from the preceding discourse was counted. This count was weighted: a word that appeared in the immediately preceding context received a full count of 1, one that appeared only in the context before that was weighted at 0.5, one from further back at 0.25, and so on. The repetition score r for a proposed realisation was then 10^{-p*c}, where p is the specific penalty value. This formula returns 1 if there are no repeated items, and returns a score that is linear in log space with the number of repeated items otherwise. The overall score for a proposed realisation was computed by multiplying r by the normal corpus-based n-gram score. In this way, preferences regarding word order and function words are still determined by the n-gram model, since the anti-repetition scorer only considers single open-class words.

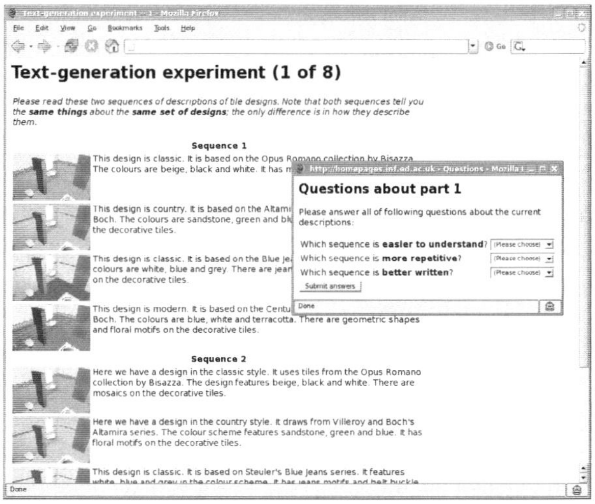

Figure 2: Evaluation interface

5 Human Judgement Study

As a first test of the effectiveness of the two anti-repetition methods, we measured human judges' subjective responses to texts generated with and without these methods.

5.1 Materials and presentation

For this study, we used the text planner to create disjunctive logical forms for a set of eight description sequences. Each sequence consisted of four consecutive descriptions of tile patterns, using a fixed structure for all descriptions. We then used OpenCCG to generate text from these logical forms in two ways: in the default mode with no anti-repetition methods enabled, and with both ε-best sampling and anti-repetition scoring enabled, using a value of 20 for the parameter in each. For the anti-repetition scorer, each description as a whole provided the context for the sentences in the next: that is, an entire set of sentences describing one design was realised, and then the words from all of those sentences were added to the context before the next description was processed. Figure 1 shows the first two descriptions of one of the generated sequences realised in both modes.

The experiment was run over the world-wide web and proceeded as follows. A participant was presented with both versions of each generated sequence in turn, in an individual randomly-chosen order. The order of presentation was counterbalanced so that each participant saw the default version first for four of the sequences, and the anti-repetition version first for the other four. A small thumbnail image of the tile design being described was shown beside each description. For each sequence, participants answered three forced-choice questions: which of the versions was (1) easier to understand, (2) more repetitive, and (3) better written. Figure 2 shows the user interface for this evaluation running in a web browser.

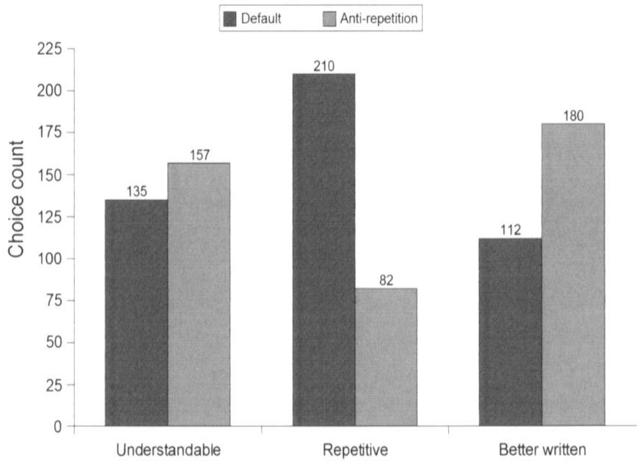

Figure 3: Results of the human evaluation

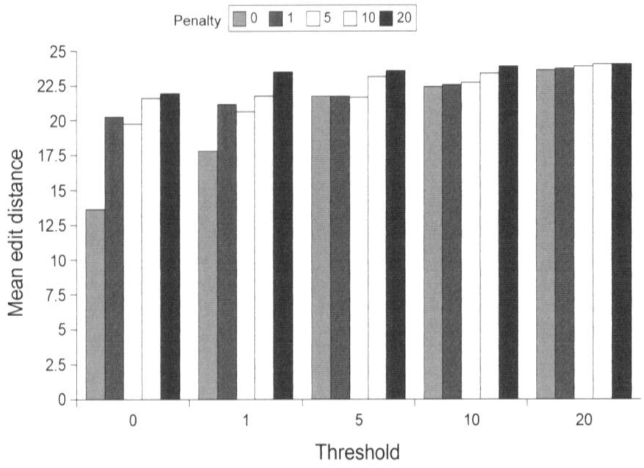

Figure 4: Mean edit distances

5.2 Participants and results

A total of 37 subjects took part in the evaluation study. All were native speakers of English; 20 were female, and 17 male. Since one subject answered half of the questions, this resulted in a total of 292 responses for each question.

The overall results are presented in Figure 3. For the understandability question, subjects chose the anti-repetition version in 157 cases (54%); this preference was not significant on a binomial test ($p \approx 0.2$). However, the responses to the other two questions did show significant preferences: subjects chose the default version as more repetitive 210 times (72%) and the anti-repetition version as better written 180 times (62%). Both of these preferences are significant at the $p < 0.0001$ level.

6 Exploring the Parameter Settings

The results of the user evaluation show that subjects found text generated with anti-repetition methods both less repetitive and better written. However, both methods depend on the value of a parameter: the threshold for ε-best sampling, and the repetition penalty for anti-repetition scoring. In the human evaluation, both parameters were set to the rather large value of 20. In this section, we explore the relative impact of the two methods by varying the configuration of the realiser and examining the generated texts for two factors: the variability across descriptions and the rate of dispreferred paraphrases.

For this experiment, we created the logical forms for a new set of 20 sequences of four descriptions, similar to those created for the human evaluation. For each sequence, we ran the realiser on all of the logical forms in turn, using all combinations of the following values for each parameter: 0, 1, 5, 10, and 20. A threshold of 0 means that the realiser choose the highest-scoring result, while a repetition penalty of 0 amounts to no repetition penalty at all. When both parameters are set to 0, this corresponds to the default sequences from the human evaluation; when both parameters are 20, this corresponds to the anti-repetition sequences from that study.

As in the previous study, we realised all of the sentences for a given description and then added the results to the context for the anti-repetition scorer for the next descriptions. To compensate for any variability introduced into the process by the random choice in ε-best sampling, we realised the whole set of 20 sequences a total of six times.

6.1 Variability

To assess the variability in a generated description sequence, we computed the edit distance between all pairs of descriptions in the sequence; that is, the number of insertions, deletions, and replacements required to transform one description into another. Guégan and Hernandez (2006) used a similar edit-distance-based metric to detect parallelism in texts. The score for a sequence was the mean edit distance between all pairs of descriptions in the sequence, where a higher score indicates greater variability. As a concrete example, the edit distance between the two default descriptions in Figure 1 is 10, while the distance between the anti-repetition descriptions is 24; the mean edit distance for the sequences from the human evaluation was 13.4 for the default versions and 23.1 for the anti-repetition versions.

Figure 4 shows the mean edit distance for all settings of the parameters. Each set of five bars corresponds to a different setting of the threshold pa-

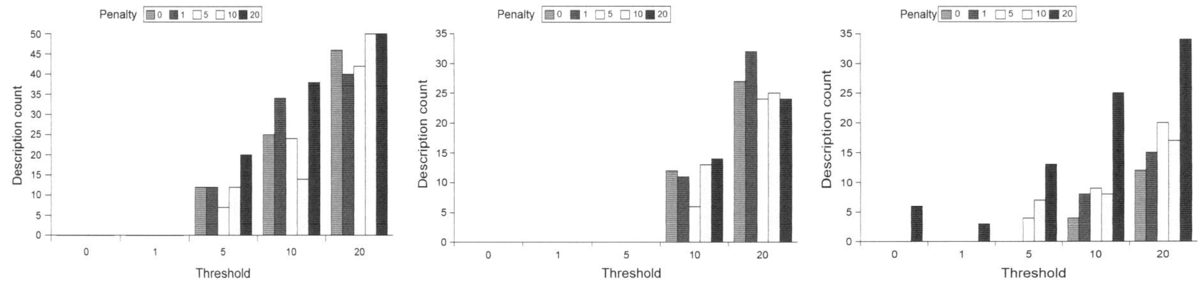

(a) Sentence-initial and sentence-final *also* (b) *we have ... here* and *we here have* (c) *is family*

Figure 5: Counts for dispreferred paraphrases

rameter; within a set of bars, each shows the result with a different value for the penalty. To assess the significance of these results, we performed a linear regression, treating the values of each parameter as levels of an ordered factor. The resulting model explained approximately 70% of the total variance ($R^2 = 0.71$). The regression coefficients for each of the individual factors (threshold and penalty) were both significantly greater than 0 ($p < 0.0001$), showing that an increase in either tended to result in a corresponding increase in the edit distance. However, the regression coefficient for the interaction of the factors is negative (also $p < 0.0001$), indicating that the effect of the two methods is not simply additive.

6.2 Dispreferred paraphrases

To measure the rate of dispreferred paraphrases, we searched for specific word sequences that are permitted by the COMIC grammar, but that were deliberately not included in the OpenCCG *n*-gram models. Normally, the corpus-based *n*-grams ensure that such realisations are never included in the output; however, when the selection strategy is modified as described here, such word sequences can end up being selected. The occurrences of the following substrings were counted: sentence-initial and sentence-final *also*; *we here have ...* and *we have ... here* (instead of *here we have*); *is family* (instead of *is in the family style*).[2] In the anti-repetition descriptions used in the human evaluation, there was one instance each of *is family* and sentence-initial *also*.

Figure 5 shows the counts of dispreferred paraphrases under all of the parameter settings; again, each group of bars corresponds to a different setting of the ε-best threshold, while each bar within the group represents a different value for the anti-repetition penalty. A total of 480 descriptions were generated under each combination of parameter settings: 20 sequences, each consisting of 4 descriptions, each generated 6 times. The count for each setting indicates the number of those descriptions that contained the specific substring. For example, 35 (7%) of the descriptions generated with both parameters set to 20 contained *is family* (Figure 5(c)). By inspection, it is clear that all dispreferred paraphrases tend to occur very infrequently at low parameter settings and to increase as the threshold increases; increasing the anti-repetition appears to have an effect only on *is family*.

To assess the significant factors for each of the dispreferred paraphrases, we analysed the influence of both parameters on the rate of that paraphrase by fitting a log-linear model to the contingency table of frequency counts for each of the paraphrase types; this type of model is suitable for use on count data and allows us to assess the influence of each of the factors on the counts in the table. The results confirm what is evident from the graph: increasing the threshold has a significant influence on the rate of all three of the paraphrases ($p < 0.0001$, ANOVA), while increasing the repetition penalty affects only the occurrence of *is family* (also $p < 0.0001$).

7 Discussion

The results of the user evaluation show that human judges strongly preferred the texts generated with the anti-repetition methods, even though the corpus-based *n*-gram score of such texts is lower than the score of the texts generated without such methods. This result agrees with the results of other recent studies that compared human preferences on gener-

[2]Unlike *classic style*, *family style* is actually a noun-noun compound, but is not modelled that way in the grammar for uniformity. This means that the grammar also generates *is family*, which is odd, so *n*-grams were used to avoid this wording.

ated output with the prediction of corpus-based similarity measures (e.g., Stent et al., 2005; Belz and Reiter, 2006; Foster and Oberlander, 2006). In all of these studies, human judges generally preferred outputs that incorporated more variation, even if the results were less similar to the corpus examples; on the other hand, corpus-based measures tended to favour output that did not diverge far, on average, from the corpus data.

By specifically concentrating on the effect of repetition in a discourse context, the results of the user study extend those of previous evaluations of the impact of variation in automatically-generated output, which generally presented the materials as a series of isolated examples. For example, Belz and Reiter (2006) evaluated a range of knowledge-based stochastic surface realisers. Their "greedy roulette" implementation, which selected generation rules based on corpus probabilities, had a similar effect on the generated texts as our variation methods: their implementation "will tend to use different words and phrases in different texts, whereas the other statistical generators will stick to those with the highest frequency." This generator was penalised by automated evaluation measures because it tended to diverge from the corpus more than the others; however, the expert human judges ranked the output of this generator better than their bigram generator, though not as highly at their greedy one.

We considered two methods for avoiding repetition while generating text: ε-best sampling and anti-repetition scoring. These two methods were both straightforward to add to OpenCCG's stochastic realisation process. Both had a significant effect on the variability across a sequence of descriptions, as measured by the mean edit distance between the elements of the sequence, although the effect of the two techniques was not additive. ε-best sampling also tended to increase the incidence of all dispreferred *n*-grams as the threshold value is increased, while anti-repetition scoring increased the rate only of the dispreferred *n*-grams that involved lexical choice.

If we compare the preferences in the user evaluation with the results of the automated studies, we see that the users tended to prefer the outputs that had higher variability. The materials generated for the user study happened to have very few dispreferred paraphrases—one instance each of *is family* and sentence-initial *also*—so it is difficult to draw definitive conclusions. The responses for the *also* description are similar to those on the entire set; however, for the description with *is family*, the responses were significantly different. On this single item, 70% of the subjects chose the description generated without the anti-repetition methods (and therefore without the dispreferred paraphrase) as being better written; the responses on this question are significantly different than those on the rest of the items ($\chi^2 = 12.5$, $df = 1$, $p < 0.0001$). This suggests that, while the variability introduced by the anti-repetition methods is indeed appreciated by the human judges, there is nevertheless a real danger that departing too far from the corpus examples can lead to undesirable outputs.

8 Conclusions and future work

We have described two methods for enhancing the variation in the output of the OpenCCG surface realiser: *ε-best sampling* and *anti-repetition scoring*. In a human evaluation comparing text generated with and without these enhancements, subjects judged the versions generated with these methods to be better written and less repetitive significantly more often than the reverse, and did not report any difference in understandability between the versions. To our knowledge, this is the first study that specifically demonstrates the benefits of avoiding syntactic repetition as a discourse progresses.

When the impact of each of the two implemented methods on the generated text is examined, both have a similar effect on the variation across a sequence of descriptions. However the simpler ε-based technique is more prone to introducing dispreferred variants into the output, indicating that better results can be obtained using anti-repetition scoring with strict or no ε-based sampling. Using anti-repetition scoring also allows the anytime mode of the OpenCCG realiser to be employed.

In the human evaluation, participats were asked to give direct judgements on the quality of generated output presented as text: their responses indicated that they both were aware of and appreciated the variation in the output. In future evaluations, we would like to measure the impact of this type of variation on actual user interactions using tools such as subjective user satisfaction, objective dialogue quality, and performance on a recall task.

An important consideration when automatically generating paraphrases is that any changes to the words or syntax should not alter the meaning; that is, in machine-translation terms, a paraphrase must be *adequate*. In our implementation, we ensured adequacy through domain-specific text-planning rules that add options to a disjunctive logical form only if they are considered equivalent in the domain. It remains for future work to examine whether the engineering of such rules can be streamlined through automatic acquisition. Another question for future work is to investigate whether cases where repetition is useful can be identified, e.g. to achieve desired parallelism, and whether such insights can be incorporated into rules which restrict the paraphrase space accordingly.

Acknowledgements

This work was partly supported by the COMIC project (IST-2001-32311). Thanks to Jon Oberlander and the ENLG reviewers for useful comments.

References

S. Bangalore and O. Rambow. 2000. Exploiting a probabilistic hierarchical model for generation. In *Proceedings, COLING-00*. ACL C00-1007.

R. Barzilay and L. Lee. 2003. Learning to paraphrase: An unsupervised approach using multiple-sequence alignment. In *Proceedings, HLT-NAACL 2003*. ACL N03-1003.

R. Barzilay and K. McKeown. 2001. Extracting paraphrases from a parallel corpus. In *Proceedings, ACL/EACL 2001*. ACL P01-1008.

A. Belz and E. Reiter. 2006. Comparing automatic and human evaluation of NLG systems. In *Proceedings, EACL 2006*. ACL E06-1040.

J. Carroll, A. Copestake, D. Flickinger, and V. Poznański. 1999. An efficient chart generator for (semi-) lexicalist grammars. In *Proceedings, EWNLG-99*.

J. Carroll and S. Oepen. 2005. High efficiency realization for a wide-coverage unification grammar. In *Proceedings, IJCNLP-05*.

K. van Deemter, E. Krahmer, and M. Theune. 2005. Real versus template-based natural language generation: A false opposition? *Computational Linguistics*, 31(1):15–24.

M. E. Foster and J. Oberlander. 2006. Data-driven generation of emphatic facial displays. In *Proceedings, EACL 2006*. ACL E06-1045.

M. E. Foster and M. White. 2004. Techniques for text planning with XSLT. In *Proceedings, NLPXML 2004*. ACL W04-0601.

M. Guégan and N. Hernandez. 2006. Recognizing textual parallelisms with edit distance and similarity degree. In *Proceedings, EACL 2006*. ACL E06-1036.

L. Iordanskaja, R. Kittredge, and A. Polguère. 1991. Lexical selection and paraphrase in a meaning-text generation model. In C. L. Paris, W. R. Swartout, and W. C. Mann, editors, *Natural Language Generation in Artificial Intelligence and Computational Linguistics*, pages 293–312. Kluwer.

A. Isard, C. Brockmann, and J. Oberlander. 2006. Individuality and alignment in generated dialogues. In *Proceedings, INLG 2006*. ACL W06-1405.

M. Kay. 1996. Chart generation. In *Proceedings, ACL-96*. ACL P96-1027.

I. Langkilde. 2000. Forest-based statistical sentence generation. In *Proceedings, NAACL-00*. ACL A00-2023.

I. Langkilde and K. Knight. 1998. Generation that exploits corpus-based statistical knowledge. In *Proceedings, COLING-ACL 1998*. ACL P98-1116.

I. Langkilde-Geary. 2002. An empirical verification of coverage and correctness for a general-purpose sentence generator. In *Proceedings, INLG-02*.

A. H. Oh and A. I. Rudnicky. 2002. Stochastic natural language generation for spoken dialog systems. *Computer, Speech & Language*, 16(3/4):387–407. doi:10.1016/S0885-2308(02)00012-8.

B. Pang, K. Knight, and D. Marcu. 2003. Syntax-based alignment of multiple translations: Extracting paraphrases and generating new sentences. In *Proceedings, HLT-NAACL 2003*. ACL N03-1024.

H. Shemtov. 1997. *Ambiguity Management in Natural Language Generation*. Ph.D. thesis, Stanford University.

M. Steedman. 2000. *The Syntactic Process*. MIT Press.

A. Stent, M. Marge, and M. Singhai. 2005. Evaluating evaluation methods for generation in the presence of variation. In *Computational Linguistics and Intelligent Text Processing*, volume 3406/2005 of *Lecture Notes in Computer Science*, pages 341–351. Springer. doi:10.1007/b105772.

M. Stone, D. DeCarlo, I. Oh, C. Rodriguez, A. Stere, A. Lees, and C. Bregler. 2004. Speaking with hands: Creating animated conversational characters from recordings of human performance. *ACM Transactions on Graphics (SIGGRAPH)*, 23(3). doi:10.1145/1186562.1015753.

M. White. 2005. Designing an extensible API for integrating language modeling and realization. In *Proceedings, ACL-05 Workshop on Software*.

M. White. 2006a. CCG chart realization from disjunctive inputs. In *Proceedings, INLG 2006*. ACL W06-1403.

M. White. 2006b. Efficient realization of coordinate structures in Combinatory Categorial Grammar. *Research on Language and Computation*, 4(1):39–75. doi:10.1007/s11168-006-9010-2.

Spotting Overgeneration Suspects

Claire Gardent
CNRS/LORIA
Nancy, France
claire.gardent@loria.fr

Eric Kow
INRIA/LORIA/UHP
Nancy, France
eric.kow@loria.fr

Abstract

We present a method for quickly spotting overgeneration suspects (i.e., likely cause of overgeneration) in hand-coded grammars. The method is applied to a medium size Tree Adjoining Grammar (TAG) for French and is shown to help reduce the number of outputs by 70% almost all of it being overgeneration.

1 Introduction

A generative grammar should describe all and only the sentences of the language it describes. In practice however, most grammars both under- and overgenerate. They under-generate in that they fail to describe all the language sentences and they overgenerate in that they licence as grammatical, strings that are not.

In a computational setting, this theoretical shortcoming means that processing will yield either too many or too few sentence analyses. Undergeneration results in insufficient coverage (some sentences cannot be parsed). Conversely, overgeneration leads to an explosion of generated strings.

Here we focus on overgeneration. There are several reasons why grammars overgenerate.

First, as is now well-known, grammar engineering is a highly complex task. It is in particular, easy to omit or mistype a constraint thereby allowing for an illicit combination and indirectly, an illicit string.

Second, a computational grammar is a large object and predicting all the interactions described by even a medium size grammar is difficult, if not impossible. Indeed this is why a surface realiser that produces all the strings associated with a given semantics is a valuable tool: it permits checking these predictions on concrete cases.

Third, grammars are often compiled from more abstract specifications and this additional layer of abstraction introduces the risk of licensing an illicit elementary structure. This is the case in particular in our approach where the TAG used by the realiser is compiled from a so-called "metagrammar" (cf. section 2). As we shall see in section 4, this added level of abstraction means that elementary trees are present in the grammar that shouldn't. These trees may also induce overgeneration.

In this paper, we propose a method for reducing overgeneration in a computational grammar. We apply the proposed approach to a Tree Adjoining Grammar for French (SEMFRAG) and show that it results in a 70% decrease of the generation output on a graduated test suite of 140 input semantics.

The paper is structured as follows. We start (section 2) by presenting the computational framework in which our experiment is based namely SEMFRAG, a tree adjoining grammar for French and GENI, a surface realiser. In section 3, we then go on to describe the methodology we propose to identify and eradicate sources of overgeneration. Section 4 presents the results of the evaluation. Section 5 concludes with pointers for further research.

2 The computational framework

We now briefly describes the GENI surface realiser and the SEMFRAG TAG on which we tested our debugging method.

2.1 SemFraG, a TAG for French integrating semantic information

SEMFRAG is a Feature-based lexicalised TAG (FTAG, (VSJ88)) for French extended with semantic information as described in (GK03).

A Feature-based TAG (FTAG, (VSJ88)) consists of a set of (auxiliary or initial) elementary trees and of two tree composition operations: substitution and adjunction. Initial trees are trees whose leaves are labelled with substitution nodes (marked with a downarrow) or terminal categories. Auxiliary trees are distinguished by a foot node (marked with a star) whose category must be the same as that of the root node. Substitution inserts a tree onto a substitution node of some other tree while adjunction inserts an auxiliary tree into a tree. In an FTAG, the tree nodes are furthermore decorated with two feature structures (called **top** and **bottom**) which are unified during derivation as follows. On substitution, the top of the substitution node is unified with the top of the root node of the tree being substituted in. On adjunction, the top of the root of the auxiliary tree is unified with the top of the node where adjunction takes place; and the bottom features of the foot node are unified with the bottom features of this node. At the end of a derivation, the top and bottom of all nodes in the derived tree are unified.

To associate semantic representations with natural language expressions, the FTAG is modified as proposed in (GK03).

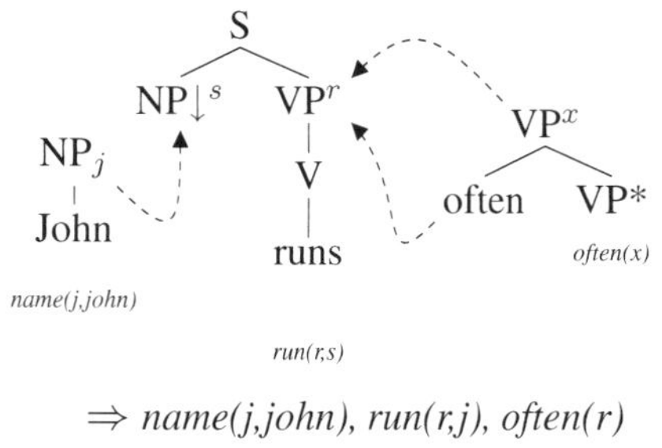

Figure 1: Flat semantics for "John often runs"

Each elementary tree is associated with a flat semantic representation[1]. For instance, in Figure 1, the trees[2] for *John, runs* and *often* are associated with the semantics *name(j,john)*, *run(r,s)* and *often(x)* respectively.

The arguments of a semantic functor are represented by unification variables which occur both in the semantic representation of this functor and on some nodes of the associated syntactic tree. In the same example, the semantic index s occurring in the semantic representation of *runs* also occurs on the subject substitution node of the associated elementary tree.

The value of semantic arguments is determined by the unifications resulting from adjunction and substitution. For instance, the semantic index s in the tree for *runs* is unified during substitution with the semantic indices labelling the root nodes of the tree for *John*. As a result, the semantics of *John often runs* is

(1) `{name(j,john),run(r,j),often(r)}`

The grammar used describes a core fragment for French and contains around 6 000 elementary trees. It covers some 35 basic subcategorisation frames and for each of these frames, the set of argument redistributions (active, passive, middle, neuter, reflexivisation, impersonal, passive impersonal) and of argument realisations (cliticisation, extraction, omission, permutations, etc.) possible for this frame. As a result, it captures most grammatical paraphrases that is, paraphrases due to diverging argument realisations or to different meaning preserving alternation (e.g., active/passive or clefted/non clefted sentence).

2.2 SemFraG and XMG

SemFraG is compiled from a higher-level XMG (eXtensible MetaGrammar) specification (CD04). Briefly, the XMG formalism permits specifying basic classes and then combining them (by inheritance, conjunction and disjunction) to produce SemFraG elementary trees and their associated semantics (cf. (CD04; Gar06)). For instance, the tree for an active intransitive verb taking a nominal canonical subject will result from specifying and then conjoining classes for the canonical nominal subject, the active verb form and the unary relation.

Importantly, the compilation process keeps track of which classes are used to produce each elementary tree. As a result, each SemFraG elementary tree is associated with the set of classes used to produce that tree. For instance, in SemFraG, the tree for the active form of intransitive verbs taking a nominal canonical subject will be associated by the XMG compiler with the following set of properties:

> CanonicalSubject, n0Vn1, ActiveForm, UnaryRel, NonInvertedNominalSubject

More generally, the set of classes associated by the XMG compilation process with each elementary

[1] The examples given actually show a simplified version of the flat semantics used y GenI where in particular, so-called labels are omitted. A full specification is given in (?).

[2] C^x/C_x abbreviate a node with category C and a top/bottom feature structure including the feature-value pair { **index** : x}.

tree (we will call this the *tree properties*) provides clear linguistic information about these trees. As we shall see in section 3, this information is extremely useful when seeking to identify *overgeneration suspects* i.e., elementary trees which are likely to cause overgeneration.

2.3 The GenI surface realiser

The basic surface realisation algorithm[3] used is a bottom up, tabular realisation algorithm (Kay96) optimised for TAGs. It follows a three step strategy which can be summarised as follows. Given an empty agenda, an empty chart and an input semantics ϕ:

Lexical selection. Select all elementary trees whose semantics subsumes (part of) ϕ. Store these trees in the agenda. Auxiliary trees devoid of substitution nodes are stored in a separate agenda called the auxiliary agenda.

Substitution phase. Retrieve a tree from the agenda, add it to the chart and try to combine it by substitution with trees present in the chart. Add any resulting derived tree to the agenda. Stop when the agenda is empty.

Adjunction phase. Move the chart trees to the agenda and the auxiliary agenda trees to the chart. Retrieve a tree from the agenda, add it to the chart and try to combine it by adjunction with trees present in the chart. Add any resulting derived tree to the agenda. Stop when the agenda is empty.

When processing stops, the yield of any syntactically complete tree whose semantics is ϕ yields an output i.e., a sentence.

The workings of this algorithm can be illustrated by the following example. Suppose that the input semantics is (1). In a first step (**lexical selection**), the elementary trees selected are the ones for *John, runs, often*. Their semantics subsumes part of the input semantics. The trees for *John* and *runs* are placed on the agenda, the one for *often* is placed on the auxiliary agenda.

The second step (the **substitution phase**) consists in systematically exploring the possibility of combining two trees by substitution. Here, the tree for *John* is substituted into the one for *runs*, and the resulting derived tree for *John runs* is placed on the agenda. Trees on the agenda are processed one by one in this fashion. When the agenda is empty, indicating that all combinations have been tried, we prepare for the next phase.

All items containing an empty substitution node are erased from the chart (here, the tree anchored by *runs*). The agenda is then reinitialised to the content of the chart and the chart to the content of the auxiliary agenda (here *often*). The **adjunction phase** proceeds much like the previous phase, except that now all possible adjunctions are performed. When the agenda is empty once more, the items in the chart whose semantics matches the input semantics are selected, and their strings printed out, yielding in this case the sentence *John often runs*.

3 Reducing overgeneration

We now present the methodology we developed for identifying and eradicating sources of overgeneration. In essence, the idea is to first, manually annotate the realiser output as either PASS or OVERGENERATION and to then use the annotated data to:

> *automatically spot the items ((sets of) TAG elementary trees, pairs of combined trees) which systematically occur only in overgeneration cases.*

More specifically, the procedure we defined to reduce overgeneration can be sketched as follows (cf. also Figure 2).

1. Surface realisation is applied to a graduated test suite of input semantics thus producing a (detailed) derivation log of all the derivations associated with each input in the testsuite
2. The outputs given by the derivation log are (manually) classified into PASS or OVERGENERATION sentences, the overgeneration mark indicating strings that either do not actually belong in the target language, or should not be associated to the input semantics.
3. The annotated output is used to automatically produced a *suspects report* which identifies a list of suspects i.e., a list of TAG trees or derivation steps which are likely to cause the overgeneration because they only occur in overgeneration cases.
4. The grammar is debugged and re-executed on the data

[3] See (GK05) for more details.

5. The derivations results are compared with the previous ones and any discrepancy (less or more sentences generated) signalled.

In a sense, this is an approach that might already be widespread in generation: produce some output, and correct the grammar possibly with the aid of a derivation log. Our contributions are a systematic, incremental approach; a high level of automation, which increases our throughput by focusing human attention on correcting the grammar rather than the unrelated details; and research into summarisation of the operations log so that we can more easily identify the source of error.

3.1 An incremental approach

First experiments with SEMFRAG showed that the grammar strongly overgenerates both because it was initially developed for parsing and because it is automatically compiled from an abstract specification (cf. section 1). Indeed for some inputs, the realiser produced over 4000 paraphrases, a large portion of them being overgeneration. More generally, Figure 3 shows that the number of outputs for a given input varies between 0 and 4908 with an average of 201 outputs per input (the median being 25).

To avoid having to manually annotate large amounts of data, we relied on a graduated test suite and proceeded through the data from simplest to more complex. Concretely, this means that we first eliminated overgeneration in input corresponding to sentences with one finite verb (INPUT1) before moving on to inputs corresponding to sentences with two (INPUT2) and three (INPUT3) finite verbs. This means that as we moved from the simplest to the more complex data, overgeneration was incrementally reduced thereby diminishing the number of output to be annotated.

Indeed this worked very well as by simply looking at INPUT1 we achieved a 70% decrease in the number of outputs for the total testsuite (cf. section 4).

3.2 Semi-automated grammar debugging

The debugging procedure described above was implemented through a test harness interleaving manual annotations with machine-generated output. Three points are worth stressing. First, the suspects report is produced automatically from the annotated derivation log. That is, except for the derivation log manual annotation, the identification of the suspects information is fully automated. Second, regression

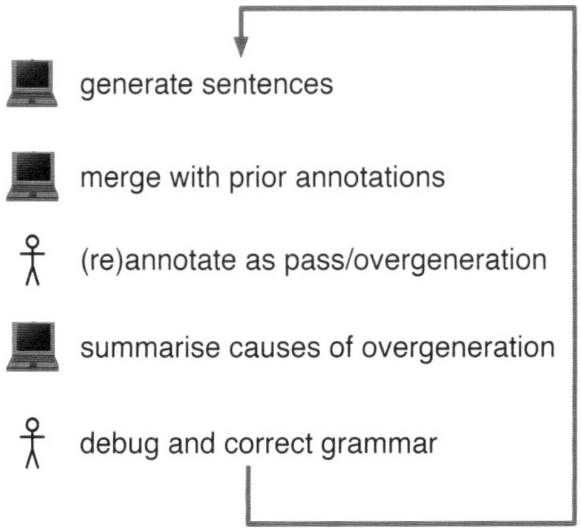

Figure 2: Test harness

testing is used to verify that corrections made to the grammar do not affect its coverage (all PASS remains PASS). Third, the harness provides a linguist friendly environment for visualising, modifying and running the grammar on the inputs being examined.

3.3 Listing the suspects

The derivation log produced by GENI contains detailed information about each of the derivations associated with a given input. More specifically, for each generated string, the derivation log will show the associated derivation tree together with the tree family, tree identifier and tree properties associated with each elementary tree composing that derivation tree.

```
Output: jean se demande si c'est
        paul qui vient
demander:n8 <-(s)- venir
demander:n1 <-(s)- jean
venir:n4 <-(s)- paul

demander Tn0ClVs1int-630
  CanonicalSubject
  NonInvertedNominalSubject
  SententialInterrogative
venir Tn0V-615
  CleftSubject
  NonInvertedNominalSubject
paul TproperName-45
jean TproperName-45
```

However, the derivation log can be both very long and very redundant. To extract from it information that points more directly to the likely causes of overgeneration, we first manually annotate each string as *pass* or *overgeneration*. We then automatically extract from the annotated derivation log, a much shorter "suspects report" which identifies suspects i.e., likely causes for overgeneration.

In essence, this suspects report lists trees, sets of trees or derivation items that *only occur in overgeneration cases* (i.e., strings that have manually been annotated as OVERGENERATION). Moreover, information about the suspects is displayed in a compact and informative way. Specifically, for a given generation input, the suspects report will consist of a (possibly empty) list of items of the following form[4]:

1. Lemma
2. TreeFamily ?(all) – ?($\wedge$ tree-property)
3. ?(TreeId* ? ($\wedge$ tree-property))
4. ?($\text{TreeId}_i\text{:nodeId}_j \xleftarrow{Op} \text{TreeId}_k$)

That is, a suspect report item (SR-ITEM) indicates, for a given lemma (line 1), the tree family (line 2), the specific trees (line 3), the specific tree properties (lines 2 and 3) and/or the specific derivation items[5] (line 4) that consistently occur only in overgeneration cases.

The suspects report is compact in that it only outputs information about likely suspects i.e., trees, tree family, tree properties and/or derivation items which consistently occur only in overgeneration cases. Furthermore, it groups together overgeneration sources which share a common feature (same tree family, same tree family and same tree properties, same derivation items). As we shall see, displaying the commonalities between suspects makes it easier for the linguist to understand the likely cause of overgeneration (for instance, if all the trees of a given family lead to overgeneration, then it is likely that the grammar is not sufficiently constrained to block the use of this family in the particular context considered).

It is informative in that it gives detailed information about the likely cause of overgeneration. In particular, tree properties can be extremely useful in understanding the commonalities between the trees involved and thereby the likely cause of overgeneration.

[4]The $*$ is the Kleene star, ? indicates optionality.

[5]A derivation item of the form $\text{TreeId}_i\text{:nodeId}_j \xleftarrow{Op} \text{TreeId}_k\text{:nodeId}_l$ indicates that TreeId_k has been added to the node nodeId_j of TreeId_i using the operation Op where Op is either adjunction or substitution.

To better illustrate the type of information contained in a suspects report, we now go through a few examples.

Example 1: "il faut partir/? devoir partir" Given the input semantics for e.g., *il faut partir* (we must go), the suspects report tells us that the presence in a derivation of any trees of the family `SemiAux` leads to overgeneration.

```
consistent overgeneration for devoir
TSemiAux (all) - SemiAux
  [506]
```

Indeed, in this context (i.e., given the input semantics considered), the use of a `SemiAux` tree results in the production of such strings as *devoir partir* which are grammatical but do not yield a finite sentence as output. If desired, this particular overgeneration bug can be fixed by constraining the generator output to be a finite sentence.

Example 2: "Jean dit accepter/*C'est par Jean qui accepte qu'être dit". In the previous example, the SR-ITEM indicates that all trees of a given family lead to overgeneration but there is only one tree in that family. A more interesting case is when there are several such trees. For instance, the SR-ITEM below indicates that all derivations involving an n0Vn1 tree anchored with *dire* lead to overgeneration and that there are 6 such trees (trees 699 ...750). Moreover the tree properties information indicates that all these trees share the `InfinitiveSubject Passive` tree properties. Inspection of the data shows that these trees combine with a finite form of *accepter* to yield highly agrammatical strings such as *c'est par Jean qui accepte qu'être dire* (instead of e.g., *Jean dit accepter*. In short, the SR-ITEM indicates that the grammar is not sufficiently constrained to block the combination of the infinitive passive form of the n0Vn1 trees anchored with *dire* with some of the trees associated by the grammar with *accepter*.

```
input t90
Lemma: dire
Tn0Vn1 (all) - InfinitiveSubject
        Passive
  [699] CanonicalCAgent Passive
  [746] CanonicalGenitive dePassive
  [702] CleftCAgentOne Passive
  [752] CleftDont dePassive
  [751] CleftGenitiveOne dePassive
  [750] RelativeGenitive dePassive
```

Example 3: "Jean doit partir/*C'est Jean il faut que qui part" Sometimes overgeneration will only occur with some of a family trees and in this case the third line of the SR-ITEM indicates which are those trees and which are their distinguishing properties (i.e. the properties that always result in overgeneration). For instance, the suspects report for the input semantics of *Jean doit partir* (Jean must leave), contains the following single SR-ITEM:

```
Input t30
consistent overgeneration for partir
Tn0V - CleftSubject
  [604]
```

This indicates that all derivations including tree 604 of the n0V family anchored with *partir* lead to overgeneration. Indeed such derivations license highly ungrammatical sentences such as *C'est Jean il faut que qui part* where a cleft subject tree for *partir* combines with the canonical tree for *il faut*. This overgeneration bug can be fixed by constraining n0V cleft subject trees to block such illicit combinations.

Example 4: "L'homme riche part/* riche l'homme part" Finally, overgeneration may sometimes be traced back to a specific derivation item i.e., to a specific tree combination. This will then be indicated in the last line of the trace item. For instance, the following SR-ITEM indicates that adjoining the adjective auxiliary tree `Tn0vA-90` to the root of a determiner tree always lead to overgeneration. Indeed such an adjunction results in sentences where the adjective precedes the determiner which in French is agrammatical.

```
Input t70
consistently overgenerating derivation
item
le:Tdet-17:n0 <-(a)- riche:Tn0vA-90
```

4 Results and Evaluation

4.1 Before and after figures

We have used the test harness over a period of one week, roughly 12 consecutive man hours. Over that period we have run over ten iterations of the test harness, making 13 modifications to the grammar as a result. In the process of revising this grammar, we have studied 40 cases (under one third of the whole suite) and manually annotated 1389 outputs with pass/overgeneration judgements. On the whole 140 cases of the test suite, the original grammar produced 28 167 outputs (4908 for the worst case, 201 mean, 25 median). The revised grammar produces 70% fewer likely agramatical outputs, leaving behind 8434 sentences (201 worst case, 60 mean, 12 median). We believe that this reduction is especially noteworthy given the little time we have spent in this process.

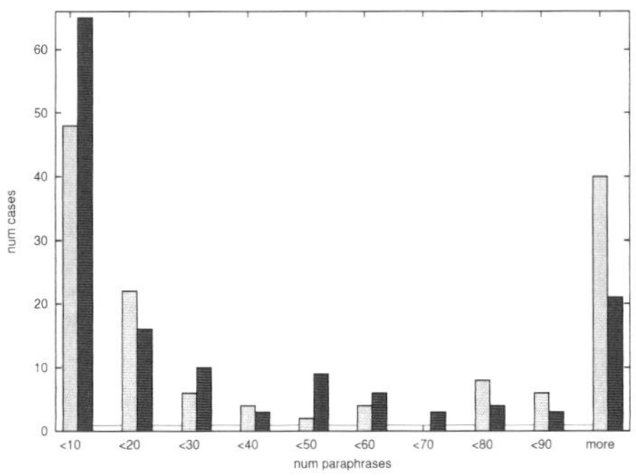

Figure 3: Distribution of generation outputs before and after debugging

It is very well to be cutting out overgeneration, but only so long as we are not cutting out linguistically valid sentences along the way. The test suite had been built semi-automatically, by parsing some sentences and hand-picking the valid semantic representations among the proposed outputs. As a basic sanity check, we reparsed the original sentences with the new grammar and found that 136 out of 140 sentences were parsed successfully, 4 less than with the original grammar. The difference was due to an over-restrictive constraint and was easily corrected.

4.2 Typing the suspects

As mentioned above, the overall 70% overgeneration reduction was achieved by a total of 13 modifications to the (meta)-grammar. Two points are worth stressing here.

First, the small number of modification is due to the fact that the metagrammar is a very compact description of the grammar where in particular, shared tree fragments are factored out and used in the production of several trees. As a result, one change to the metagrammar usually induces a change in not one but several (sometime hundred of) TAG trees. For instance, a modification stated in the fragment describing the verb spine of the active verb form will affect all trees in the grammar that realise an active verb form i.e., several hundreds of trees.

Second, the drastic reduction in overgeneration is made possible by a combination of 3 factors. First, the suspects report allows for a quick identification of the overgeneration sources. Second, the metagrammar architecture makes it possible to generalise. Suppose for instance, that a given SR-ITEM indicates that the grammar incorrectly allows the adjunction of a given type of auxiliary tree β to a subject cleft tree. It might be the case that in fact, the grammar should be modified to block the combination of β with *all* cleft trees (not just the subject ones). Then the metagrammar architecture makes it possible to state the required modification at the level of the cleft description so that in effect, all cleft trees will be modified. In this way, the identification of an overgeneration cause linked to a specific example can be generalised to a larger class of examples. Third, the input data was organised in a graduated testsuite where first simple (basic) sentences where considered then sentences of complexity 2 (cases whose canonical verbalisation involve two finite verbs), then sentences of complexity 3 (three finite verbs). By proceeding incrementally through the testsuite, we ensured that early modifications propagate to more complex cases.

Let us now look at the types of errors which, we found, induce overgeneration.

Missing constraints Unsurprisingly, the main source of overgeneration was the lack of sufficient constraints to block illicit tree combinations. For instance, the grammar overgenerated the string *devoir c'est Jean qui part* (instead of *c'est Jean qui doit partir*) because the tree for *devoir* was not sufficiently constrained to block adjunction on the VP node of cleft trees. In such cases, adding the relevant constraints (e.g., CEST = - on the foot node of the *devoir*-tree and CEST = + on the VP node of the cleft-tree for *partir*) eliminates the overgeneration.

Incomplete constraints and incorrect feature percolation In some cases, we found that the constraint was only partially encoded by the grammar in that it was correctly stated in one of the combining trees but incorrectly or not at all in the other. Thus for instance, the adjective tree was correctly constrained to adjoin to DET = - N-trees but the corresponding DET = + constraint on the root node of determiner trees was missing. In other cases, the feature was present but incorrectly percolated. In both cases, the partial implementation of the constraint lead to a lack of unification clash and thereby to an overgenerating combination of trees.

Illicit elementary trees A third type of errors was linked to the fact that the grammar was produced semi-automatically from an abstract grammar description. In some cases, the linguist had failed to correctly foresee the implications of her description so that an elementary tree was produced by the compiler that was in fact incorrect. For instance, we had to introduce an additional constraint in the metagrammar to rule out the formation of trees describing a transitive verb with impersonal subject (in French, transitive verb cannot take an impersonal subject).

Incorrect semantics A more complex type of error to deal with concern cases where the semantics is insufficiently constrained thereby allowing for illicit combinations. For instance, in the imperative form, the grammar failed to constrain the first semantic argument to be YOU i.e., the hearer denotation. As a result, the input for sentences such as *Jean demande si Paul part* incorrectly generated strings such as *demande à Jean si Paul part*. In such cases thus, it is the semantics associated by the metagrammar with the elementary tree that needs to be modified.

Lexical exceptions As is well known, grammatical generalisation often are subject to lexical exceptions. For instance, transitive verbs are generally assumed to passivise but verbs of measure such as *to weigh* are transitive and do not. As is usual in TAG, in GENI, such exceptions are stated in the lexicon thereby blocking the selection of certain trees (in this case, all the passive trees) for the lexical items creating the exception (here the measure type verbs). Relatedly, some of the overgeneration cases stem from insufficient lexical information.

5 Conclusion

Debugging grammars for overgeneration need not be slow and tedious. We have found that with a certain dose of automation – a test harness to mechanise the regression-testing parts of the process, and computer-generated summaries to identify trouble spots – we can obtain major reductions in overgeneration with little effort.

Whilst these initial results are encouraging, a more sophisticated approach should help to detect more errors more efficiently. One shortcoming of our current approach is that we focus mostly on unitary sources of overgeneration: a single lexical item, tree property or derivation operation that consistently occurs in overgenerated strings. However, grammar flaws essentially consist of unexpected interactions between (at least) two items, so it would seem that the most sensible place to look for mistakes would be where they interact. For example, instead of identifying single items that fail, we could look for *pairs* of items that consistently overgenerate when they co-occur. Note that this is not necessarily a subset of single-source failures. A given item X may consistently overgenerate in the presence of another item Y, but not with Z. If we were only looking for consistent single-source failures, we would ignore X altogether, whereas if we were looking for pairs, we would indeed detect (X,Y).

Another shortcoming of our approach is that it requires us to be disciplined in our pass/overgeneration annotations. If we mismark a sentence as pass, the derivation summariser will neglect every tree property or derivation item that occurs in that sentence, as it is only looking for items that consistently overgenerate. Perhaps a more robust approach would be to instead return items that *tend* to occur with overgeneration. This would make it more tolerant to imperfect annotations.

Producing these annotations is time-consuming. It would be worthwhile to explore some automatic means of making pass/overgeneration judgements on a large number of sentences, for example, using an n-gram based language model, like one that would be employed by a speech recogniser. We could then take the best N% of the sentences as passes or establish a threshold of improbability, below which sentences will be considered as overgeneration. We could also use more sophisticated tools, a statistical parser or a symbolic one with a wide coverage grammar in an alternate formalism. Even a relatively liberal parser which itself overgenerates might be useful in that (i) it may overgenerate in different areas than our grammar (ii) anything that *it* marks as a failure would be highly suspicious indeed.

The annotations do not need to be produced by a full-fledged parser either. Indeed, for each sentence that it produces, the surface realiser outputs its parse tree. So another way to classify the generated strings might be through assessing not the quality of the strings themselves but of their parses. For example, we could determine if the elementary trees that were used to build a sentence are likely to occur together in the same sentence. This kind of information can be extracted from a systemic functional grammar for instance. SFGs are largely generation-oriented grammars which encode as a network, the motivations behind each linguistic choice and the linguistic choices they allow for. If we associated each choice in the SFG network with a set of tree properties from our TAG grammar, we would essentially have an encoding of what tree properties go together. If the sentence contains a set of tree properties for which there is no equivalent system network traversal, it should be flagged as suspicious.

Our use of this test harness has so far been limited to the syntactic aspects of surface realisation. It could also be applied to other realiser tasks such as, for instance, morphological generation. It would also be interesting to see to what extent the method used here to spot overgeneration suspects could be adapted to other linguistic formalisms such as HPSG, LFG or CCG.

Finally, it would be interesting to investigate in how much overgeneration reduction helps reduce parsing ambiguity. Given a large scale symbolic grammar, parsing will often yield several hundreds of parses many of them are probably incorrect. We believe that reducing overgeneration should help reduce the number of output parses and thereby improve both parsing efficiency and the quality of the output parses.

GENI is free (GPL) software and can be downloaded at `http://trac.loria.fr/~geni`.

References

B. Crabbé and D. Duchier. Metagrammar redux. In *International Workshop on Constraint Solving and Language Processing - CSLP 2004, Copenhagen*, 2004.

C. Gardent. Integration d'une dimension semantique dans les grammaires d'arbres adjoints. *TALN*, 2006.

C. Gardent and L. Kallmeyer. Semantic construction in FTAG. In *10th EACL*, Budapest, Hungary, 2003.

C. Gardent and E. Kow. Generating and selecting grammatical paraphrases. In *Proceedings of the 10th European Workshop on Natural Language Generation*, Aberdeen, Scotland, 2005.

M. Kay. Chart Generation. In *34th ACL*, pages 200–204, Santa Cruz, California, 1996.

K. Vijay-Shanker and AK Joshi. Feature Structures Based Tree Adjoining Grammars. *Proceedings of the 12th conference on Computational linguistics*, 55:v2, 1988.

Evaluating algorithms for the Generation of Referring Expressions using a balanced corpus

Albert Gatt and **Ielka van der Sluis** and **Kees van Deemter**
Department of Computing Science
University of Aberdeen
{agatt,ivdsluis,kvdeemte}@csd.abdn.ac.uk

Abstract

Despite being the focus of intensive research, *evaluation* of algorithms that generate referring expressions is still in its infancy. We describe a corpus-based evaluation methodology, applied to a number of classic algorithms in this area. The methodology focuses on *balance* and *semantic transparency* to enable comparison of human and algorithmic output. Although the Incremental Algorithm emerges as the best match, we found that its dependency on manually-set parameters makes its performance difficult to predict.

1 Introduction

The current state of the art in the Generation of Referring Expressions (GRE) is dominated by versions of the Incremental Algorithm (IA) of Dale and Reiter (1995). Focusing on the generation of "first-mention" definite descriptions, Dale and Reiter compared the IA to a number of its predecessors, including a Full Brevity (FB) algorithm, which generates descriptions of minimal length, and a Greedy algorithm (GR), which approximates Full Brevity (Dale, 1989). In doing so, the authors focused on Content Determination (CD, which is the purely semantic part of GRE), and on a description's ability to *identify* a referent for a hearer. Under this problem definition, GRE algorithms take as input a Knowledge Base (KB), which lists domain entities and their properties (often represented as attribute-value pairs), together with a set of intended referents, R. The output of CD is a distinguishing description of R, that is, a logical form which distinguishes this set from its distractors.

Dale and Reiter argued that the IA was a superior model, and predicted that it would be the better match to human referential behaviour.[1] This was due in part to the way the IA searches for a distinguishing description by performing gradient descent along a predetermined list of domain attributes, called the *preference order*, whose ranking reflects general or domain-specific preferences (see §4.1).

The Incremental Algorithm has served as a starting point for later models (Horacek, 1997; Kelleher and Kruijff, 2006), and has also served as a yardstick against which to compare other approaches (Gardent, 2002; Jordan and Walker, 2005). Despite its influence, few empirical evaluations have focused on the IA. Evaluation is even more desirable given the dependency of the algorithm on a preference order, which can radically change its behaviour, so that in a domain with n attributes, there are in principle $n!$ different algorithms.

This paper is concerned with applying a corpus-based methodology to evaluate content determination for GRE, comparing the three classic algorithms that formed the basis for Dale and Reiter's (1995) contribution, adapted to also deal with pluralities and gradable properties.

1.1 Requirements for GRE evaluation

One of the problems with evaluating GRE is that it interfaces with several other sub-tasks of NLG including, among others, realisation and discourse coherence (especially where anaphoric reference is concerned). On the other hand, a large amount of work in the area has focused on the semantic heart of the problem. Given *identification* as the over-

[1] Dale and Reiter also observed that IA is computationally more efficient than its competitors, although GR has only polynomial complexity. Consistent with subsequent research, we shall be de-emphasising complexity issues here.

arching goal of such algorithms, a crucial question concerns the extent to which their choice of content from the available attributes for a referent matches that produced by a speaker in a comparable situation. This is the main focus of this paper, whose evaluation methodology therefore targets content determination, abstracting away from issues of lexical choice and realisation. A corpus-based evaluation of a content determination GRE algorithm requires a resource that satisfies the following desiderata.

Semantic transparency: The human 'gold standard' descriptions in the corpus need to be paired with a domain representation so that, as far as possible, an algorithm is exposed to the same domain as an author. To evaluate content determination, descriptions need to be semantically annotated, abstacting away from variations in syntax and lexicalisation. For example, *the right-facing sofa* and *the settee which is oriented towards the right* are, from the point of view of a content determination procedure, semantically equivalent.

Pragmatic transparency: Ideally, the communicative intention underlying corpus descriptions should match those for which an algorithm was designed. If an algorithm is primarily aimed at identification, then human gold-standards should, as far as possible, be restricted to this intention.

Balance: To assess the extent to which an algorithm matches human performance, the corpus should contain an equal number of instances where each attribute is required. Only in this way would the claim that *algorithm* X *matches humans on content y% of the time* be reliable[2].

These desiderata suggest that the way forward in evaluation in this area is to design controlled studies for corpus construction. The rest of this paper describes the construction of such a corpus, and the results of an evaluation that addressed the differences between IA and its predecessors against human descriptions in domains of varying complexity, containing both singular and plural descriptions. The study also aimed to contribute to a growing debate in the NLG community, on the evaluation of NLG systems, arguing in favour of the careful construction of *balanced* and *transparent* corpora to serve as resources for NLG.

2 Related work

We are aware of three studies on GRE evaluation, all of which compare the IA to some alternative models. Two of these (Jordan and Walker, 2005; Gupta and Stent, 2005) used the COCONUT dialogue corpus. The third (Viethen and Dale, 2006) used a small corpus collected in a monologue setting. These studies meet the transparency requirements to different degrees. Though COCONUT dialogues were elicited against a well-defined domain, Jordan (2000) has emphasised that reference, in COCONUT, was often intended to satisfy intentions over and above identification. Gupta and Stent used an evaluation metric that included aspects of the syntactic structure of descriptions (specifically, modifier placement), thus arguably obscuring the role of content determination (CD).

Our approach is closest in spirit to that of Viethen and Dale, who elicited descriptions from people in a setting where identification was the sole communicative aim. However, in the case of the IA, the authors averaged over 24 different preference orders, potentially averaging over 24 very different incarnations of the algorithm and masking the impact of any one order. Similarly, neither Jordan/Walker nor Gupta/Stent are explicit about the determination of the preference order for the IA in their studies. No obvious attempts were made to make sure that the corpora in question were semantically balanced.

One question that these studies raise relates to how human-authored and automatically generated descriptions should be compared. For instance, both Jordan/Walker and Viethen/Dale use a measure of recall. This indicates the coverage of an algorithm in relation to a corpus, but does not measure the *degree* of similarity between a description generated by an algorithm and a description in the corpus, punishing all mismatches with equal severity.

3 The TUNA corpus

We built a corpus consisting of ca. 1800 descriptions, collected through a controlled experiment run over the web for three months. Half of this corpus contains descriptions of real photographs of people; the other half contains descriptions of artificially constructed pictures of household items. In this paper, the main focus is on the 'furniture' subcorpus,

[2]For example, the IA overspecifies descriptions by selecting attributes not strictly required for identification, because of its preference order. A claim that this feature improves performance implies that the relative priority of attributes is important. To be reliable, such a claim would have to be made against a corpus in which 'preferred' and 'dispreferred' attributes were required the same number of times.

TYPE	COLOUR	ORIENTATION	SIZE
chair	blue	forward	large
sofa	red	backward	small
desk	green	leftward	
fan	grey	rightward	

Table 1: Non-numeric attributes in the domains

which represents the simpler of the two domains, consisting of digitally constructed pictures of objects with well-defined properties. Therefore, it provides a good test case for the algorithms evaluated, since it allows us to probe into a number of issues that arise even with straightforwardly describable objects. The 'people' sub-corpus is more complex, since the objects are real photographs and afford an author with many descriptive alternatives. We explicitly compare the results of the present evaluation with a similar study on the 'people' sub-corpus, in §5.

3.1 Materials, design and procedure

The furniture sub-corpus consists of 900 descriptions from 45 native or fluent speakers of English. Participants described objects in 20 trials, each corresponding to a domain where there were one or two clearly marked target referents (the *target set*) and six distractor objects, placed in a 3 (row) $\times$ 5 (column) grid. Pictures of the objects represented combinations of values of the four attributes shown in the top panel of Table 1. In a pilot study involving 19 participants, we found that instances in which descriptions used semantic content beyond that indicated in the Table were extremely rare with these simple objects. In each trial, the horizontal and vertical position of the objects is represented using two numeric-valued attributes, X-DIM (row) and Y-DIM (column). Their value was randomly determined with every fresh trial. Approximately half the corpus descriptions include locative expressions[3]. We will refer to this as the +LOC dataset, containing 412 descriptions from 26 authors. The other half, the −LOC dataset (444 descriptions; 27 authors), consists of descriptions using only COLOUR, SIZE and ORIENTATION, apart from TYPE.

Participants were exposed to the 20 trials in randomised order; in each case, they typed a description for the target set. They were told that they would be interacting with a language-understanding program which would remove the referents from the domain, based on their description. Identification was emphasised as the primary goal of descriptions. Each time a participant submitted a description, one or two objects were automatically removed from the domain by a function which had been preset to remove the wrong objects on approximately one-fourth of the trials. This was intended to make the interaction seem more natural. We discuss an evaluation of this methodology in §3.3.

The trials in the experiment were balanced. For each possible combination of the attributes in Table 1, there was an equal number of domains in which an identifying description of the target(s) required the use of those attributes. We refer to this as the *minimal description* (MD) of the target set. For example, there was a domain in which a target could be minimally distinguished by using COLOUR and SIZE. TYPE was never included in the minimal description, leaving 7 possible attribute combinations. The experiment manipulated one within-subjects variable, Cardinality/Similarity (3 levels):

Singular (SG): 7 domains contained a single referent

Plural/Similar (PS): 6 domains had two referents, which had identical values on the MD attributes. For example, both targets might be blue in a domain where the minimally distinguishing description consisted of COLOUR.

Plural/Dissimilar (PD): In the remaining 7 Plural trials, the targets had different values of the minimally distinguishing attributes.

Plural referents were taken into account because plurality is pervasive in NL discourse. The literature (e.g. Gardent (2002)) suggests that they can be treated adequately by minor variations of the classic GRE algorithms (as long as the descriptions in question refer distributively, cf. Stone (2000)), which is something we considered worth testing.

3.2 Corpus annotation

The XML annotation scheme (van der Sluis et al., 2006) pairs each corpus description with a representation of the domain in which it was produced. The domain representation, exemplified in Figure 1(a)), indicates which entities are target referents or distractors, and what combination of the attributes and values in Table 1 they have, as well as their numeric X-DIM and Y-DIM values (row and column numbers).

[3]This was manipulated as a second, between-subjects factor. Participants were randomly placed in groups which varied in whether they could use location or not, and in whether the communicative situation was fault-critical or not. For more details, we refer to van Deemter *et al.* (2006).

```
<ENTITY type=target'>
<ATTRIBUTE name='orientation' value='right' />
<ATTRIBUTE name='type' value='sofa' />
<ATTRIBUTE name='size' value='large' />
...
</ENTITY>
<ENTITY type='target'>
<ATTRIBUTE name='colour' value='red' />
<ATTRIBUTE name='type' value='desk' />
<ATTRIBUTE name='size' value='small' />
...
</ENTITY>
```

(a) Fragment of a domain

```
<DESCRIPTION num='plural'>
<DESCRIPTION num='singular'>
<ATTRIBUTE name='size' value='large'>large</ATTRIBUTE>
<ATTRIBUTE name='type' value='sofa'>settee</ATTRIBUTE>
<ATTRIBUTE name='orientation' value='right'>
at oblique angle</ATTRIBUTE>
</DESCRIPTION>
and
<DESCRIPTION num='singular'>
<ATTRIBUTE name='size' value='small'>small</ATTRIBUTE>
<ATTRIBUTE name='type' value='desk'>desk</ATTRIBUTE>
</DESCRIPTION>
</DESCRIPTION>
```

(b) 'large settee at oblique angle and small desk'

Figure 1: Corpus annotation examples

Figure 1(b) shows the annotation of a plural description. ATTRIBUTE tags enclose segments of a description corresponding to properties, with `name` and `value` attributes which constitute a semantic representation compatible with the domain, abstracting away from lexical variation. For example, in Figure 1(b), the expression *at an oblique angle* is tagged as ORIENTATION, with the value *rightward*. If a part of a description could not be resolved against the domain representation, it was enclosed in an ATTRIBUTE tag with the value `other` for `name`. Consistent with our pilot study, this was only necessary in 39 descriptions (3.2%).

The DESCRIPTION tag in Figure 1(b) indicates the logical form of a description. Thus, Figure 1(b) is a `plural` description enclosing two `singular` ones. Correspondingly, the logical form of each embedded description is a conjunction of attributes, while the two sibling descriptions are disjoined:

$$(large \wedge sofa \wedge right) \vee (small \wedge desk) .$$

3.3 Annotator reliability and experimental validity

The reliability of the annotation scheme was evaluated in a study involving two independent annotators (hereafter A and B), both postgraduate students with an interest in NLG, who used the same annotation manual (van der Sluis et al., 2006). They were given a stratified random sample of 270 descriptions, 2 from each Cardinality/Similarity condition, from each author in the corpus. To estimate inter-annotator agreement, we compared their annotations against the consensus labelling made by the present authors, using a version of the Dice coefficient. Let D_1 and D_2 be two descriptions, and $att(D)$ be the attributes in any description D. The coefficient, which ranges between 0 (no agreement) and 1 (perfect agreement) is calculated as in (1). Because descriptions could contain more than one instance of an attribute (e.g. Figure 1(b) contains two instances of SIZE), the sets of attributes for this comparison were represented as multisets.

$$dice(D_1, D_2) = \frac{2 \times |att(D_1) \cap att(D_2)|}{|att(D_1)| + |att(D_2)|} \quad (1)$$

In the present context, Dice is more appropriate than agreement measures (such as the κ statistic) which rely on predefined categories in which discrete events can be classified. The 'events' in the corpus are NL expressions, each of which is 'classified' in several ways (depending on how many attributes a description expresses), and it was up to an annotator's judgment, given the instructions, to select those segments and mark them up.

Both annotators showed a high mean agreement with the authors, as indicated by their mean and modal (most frequent) scores (A:: mean $= 0.93$, mode $= 1$ (74.4%); B: mean $= 0.92$; mode $= 1$ (73%)). They also evinced substantial agreement among themselves (mean $= 0.89$, mode $= 1$ (71.1%)). These results suggest that the annotation scheme used is replicable to a high degree, and that independent annotators are likely to produce very similar semantic markup.

In the evaluation study reported below, we use the same measure to compare algorithm and human output, because an optimally informative comparison should take into account the number of attributes that an algorithm omits in relation to the human gold standard, and the number of attributes that it includes. We also evaluated the validity of the experimental setup. Since communicating with a machine may have biased participants, they were asked, during a debriefing phase, to assess the performance of their virtual interlocutor, by indicating agreement to the statement *The system performed well on this task*. Of the 5 response categories, ranging from 1 *strongly disagree* to 5 (*strongly agree*), 34 individuals selected *agree* or *strongly agree* while no one selected *strongly disagree*. The mean score was 3.9.

4 Evaluating the algorithms

The three algorithms mentioned in §1 can be characterised as search problems (Bohnet and Dale, 2005) which differ primarily in the way they structure a search space populated by KB properties:

Full Brevity (FB): Finds the smallest distinguishing combination of properties.
Greedy (GR): Adds properties to a description, always selecting the property with the greatest discriminatory power.
Incremental (IA): Performs gradient descent along a predefined list of properties. Like GR, IA incrementally adds properties to a description until it is distinguishing.

The evaluation was carried out separately for the −LOC and +LOC datasets introduced in §3.1. Algorithms were compared to a random baseline (RAND) which selected a property randomly, and added it to a description if it removed distractors and was true of the referents. In the −LOC dataset, only GR and IA were compared, because GR and FB give identical output[4]. By contrast, the +LOC dataset, where there are 5 attributes including X-DIM and Y-DIM, and the values of the locative attributes were randomly determined in all domains, there is much greater scope for variation.

All four algorithms also included TYPE by default. Adding TYPE, despite its lack of contrastive value, was the norm in the corpus descriptions (93.5%). While the IA always adds TYPE, as proposed by Dale and Reiter (1995), we applied the same trick to FB and GR to avoid penalising their performance unnecessarily. In addition, we extended each algorithm in two ways:

Plurality: To cover the plural descriptions in the corpus, we used the algorithm of (van Deemter, 2002), which is an extension to the IA. The algorithm first searches through the KB to find a distinguishing conjunction of properties, failing which, it searches through disjunctions of increasing length until a distinguishing description is found. FB and GR can easily be extended in the same way.
Gradable properties: Locative expressions in the corpus are essentially gradable. For instance, *the table on the left* could be used even if the table was located in the right half of the grid, as long as it was the *leftmost* table. van Deemter (2006) proposed an algorithm to deal with such gradable properties, which can use any of the GRE algorithms (FB, GR, IA). Gradable properties are represented in the form $\langle A = n \rangle$, for example $\langle \text{X-DIM} = 3 \rangle$ (i.e., the property of being located in the middle column of the grid). This equality is converted into a number of inequalities of the forms $\langle \text{X-DIM} > m \rangle$ and $\langle \text{X-DIM} < m' \rangle$. For example, in a domain with 2 objects, in column 2 and 3, this results in the inequalities $\langle \text{X-DIM} > 2 \rangle$ and $\langle \text{X-DIM} < 4 \rangle$. Inequalities are used by a GRE algorithm in the same way as other properties. A postprocessing phase transforms them into superlative form. For example, if a referent is identified by $\langle \text{TYPE} : sofa \rangle \wedge \langle \text{X-DIM} > 2 \rangle$, this yields a combination expressible as "the rightmost sofa", or "the sofa on the right".

4.1 Preference orders for the IA

In assessing the impact of preference orders on the IA, we compare some psycholinguistically-motivated versions to a baseline version which reverses the hypothesised trends. In what follows, we denote a preference order using the first letter of the attributes shown in Table 1.

Psycholinguists have shown that attributes such as COLOUR are included in descriptions of objects even when they are not required (Pechmann, 1989; Eikmeyer and Ahlsèn, 1996). Attributes such as SIZE, which require comparison to other objects, are more likely to be omitted (Belke and Meyer, 2002). Based on this research, we hypothesise a 'best' preference order for the IA (IA-BEST_1) in the −LOC dataset, and a reverse baseline order (IA-BASE_1):

IA-BEST_1: C >> O >> S

[4]This is because objects were distinguishable on the basis of three attributes. When only 1 or 2 attributes suffice to distinguish an object, GR and FB always return identical output. In the case of 3 attributes, GR and FB are identical in the present corpus because the minimal description consists of all the properties that have some discriminatory value.

	−LOC			+LOC					
	IA-BEST$_1$	IA-BASE$_1$	GR/FB	IA-BEST$_2$	IA-BEST$_3$	IA-BEST$_4$	IA-BASE$_2$	FB	GR
Mean	.83	.75	.79	.64	.61	.63	.54	.57	.58
Mode	1	.67	.8	.67	.67	.67	.67	.67	.67
PRP	24.1	7.4	18.7	10	4.6	3.9	1.7	6.6	5.8
$\mathbf{t}_S$	7.002*	−5.850*	3.333*	3.934*	2.313	3.406	.705	.242	.544
$\mathbf{t}_I$	4.632*	−1.797	1.169	4.574*	3.352*	4.313*	1.776	1.286	1.900

Table 2: Comparison to the Random Baseline ($^*p < .05$)

IA-BASE$_1$: S >> O >> C

In the more complex +LOC dataset, the inclusion of the numeric-valued X-DIM and Y-DIM increases the number of attributes to 5. Arts (2004) found that locatives in the vertical dimension were much more frequent than those in the horizontal (see also Kelleher and Kruijff (2006)). Two different descriptive patterns dominate her data: Either Y-DIM and COLOUR are strongly preferred and X-DIM is strongly dispreferred, or Y-DIM and X-DIM are both highly preferred. This leaves us with three groups of preference orders, namely CY >> {O,S} >> X, YXC >> {O,S}, and Y,C >> {O,S} >> X. Assuming that ORIENTATION preceeds SIZE (which involves comparisons), three promising orders emerge, with a baseline, IA-BASE$_2$, which is predicted to perform much worse.

IA-BEST$_2$: C >> Y >> O >> S >> X

IA-BEST$_3$: Y >> X >> C >> O >> S

IA-BEST$_4$: Y >> C >> O >> S >> X

IA-BASE$_2$: X >> O >> S >> Y >> C

4.2 Differences between algorithms

Table 2 displays mean and modal (most frequent) scores of each algorithm, as well as the *perfect recall percentage* (PRP: the proportion of Dice scores of 1). Pairwise t-tests comparing each algorithm to RAND are reported using subjects (t_S) and items (t_I) as sources of variance. These figures average over all three Cardinality/Similarity conditions; we return to the differences between these below.

With the exception of IA-BASE, the different versions of IA performed best on both datasets. In the simpler −LOC dataset, IA-BEST$_1$ achieved a modal score of 1 24% of the time. Both the modal score and the PRP of GR/FB were lower. Only IA-BEST$_1$ was significantly better than RAND both by subjects and items. This suggests that while IA-BEST$_1$ reflects overall preferences, and increases the likelihood with which a preferred attribute is included in a description, a consideration of the relative discriminatory power of a property, or the overall brevity of a description, does not reflect human tendencies.

A comparison of IA-BEST$_1$ to FB/GR on this dataset showed that the IA was significantly better, though this only approached significance by items. ($t_S = 2.972$, $p = .006$; $t_I(19) = 2.117$, $p = .08$). Though this ostensibly supports the claim of Dale and Reiter (Dale and Reiter, 1995), it should be discussed in the light of the performance of IA-BASE$_1$, which performed significantly *worse* than RAND by subjects, as shown in Table 2, indicating a very substantial impact of the attribute order.

In the +LOC dataset, there is an overall decline in performance. The much poorer performance of FB and GR on this dataset (neither is better than RAND) is due to their not selecting preferred attributes with the same frequency as the better-performing orders of the IA, since the chances of selecting them are contingent on their discriminatory power.

A comparison of GR to FB revealed that the small difference in their mean scores was not significant ($t_1(24) = .773$, ns; $t_2(19) = 1.455$, ns). Pairwise contrasts involving IA-BEST$_2$ showed that it performed significantly better than both FB ($t_S = 4.235$, $p < .05$; $t_I = -2.539$, ns) and GR ($t_S = 4.092$, $p < .05$; $t_I = 2.091$, ns), though only by subjects. This was also the case for IA-BEST$_4$ against FB ($t_S = 3.845$, $p = .01$; $t_I = 2.248$, ns), though not against GR ($t_S = 3.072$, ns; $t_I = 1.723$, ns). None of the comparisons involving IA-BEST$_3$ reached significance. Once again, the performance of the IA on the more complex dataset displays a strong dependency on the predetermined attribute order.

4.3 Plurals and similarity

The final part of the analysis considers the relative performance of the algorithms on singular and plural data, focusing on the best IA in each dataset,

	−LOC		+LOC	
	IA-BEST$_1$	GR	IA-BEST$_2$	GR
SG	.92	.8	.71	.59
PS	.80	.74	.59	.56
PD	.79	.79	.59	.59
F_S	50.367*	22.1*	11.098*	1.893
F_I	40.025*	2.171	13.210 ∗ ∗	.611

Table 3: Effect of Cardinality/Similarity $^*p < .001$

IA-BEST$_1$ and IA-BEST$_2$, and on GR (which did not differ from FB in +LOC). As Table 3 shows, the algorithms' performance declined dramatically on the plural data; the difference between the Singular (SG), Plural Similar (PS) and Plural Dissimilar (PD) domains is confirmed by a one-way ANOVA with Cardinality/Similarity as independent variable, though this is not significant for GR in +LOC.

With PS domains (where the minimally required description is always a conjunction), van Deemter's algorithm will succeed at first pass, without needing to search through combinations, except that a disjunction is required for TYPE values (e.g. 2a, below). People tend to be more redundant, because they partition a set if its elements have different values of TYPE, describing each element separately (2b). In the PD condition, the main problem is that the notion of 'preference' becomes problematic once the search space is populated by combinations of attributes, rather than literals.

(2) (a) $(desk \vee fan) \wedge red \wedge large \wedge forward$

(b) the large red desk facing forward and the large red fan facing forward

5 The People Domain

Like most work in GRE, the preceding results focus on very simple objects, with attributes such as *colour*. With complex objects, the relevant properties are not always easy to ascertain. Similarly, we expect less agreement between corpus annotators and we expect GRE algorithms to perform worse on complex domains, compared to those where objects are simple and stylised. A separate study on the 'people' sub-corpus described in §3 was conducted, using the same overall setup as the present study. In this section, we briefly discuss our main findings in this sub-corpus. A more detailed comparison of the evaluation results on the furniture domain with parallel results on the people domain is reported elsewhere.

The targets in the people corpus differ from their distractors only in whether they had a beard (HASBEARD), wore glasses (HASGLASSES) and/or were young or old (AGE). But as expected, speakers used other attributes than the ones that are necessary to identify the photographed people. As a result descriptions include, for instance, whether a referent wears a tie, or has a certain hairstyle. To be able to match the descriptions with the domain representation a total of 9 attributes were defined per photograph. The first indication that complexity results in much higher variation comes from results on annotator agreement on this data, with the same annotators discussed in §3.3. Though again suggesting a high degree of replicability, the figures indicate greater difficulty in annotating complex data (A: mean = .84, mode = 1 (41.1%); B: mean = .78; mode = 1 (36.3%)).

Another problem is that complex objects, with several attributes, give rise to several possible orders, making it difficult to determine preference orders for the IA *a priori*, particularly since, unlike attributes such as COLOUR and SIZE, there is little psycholinguistic data on reference with attributes such as HASHAIR. Although in the 'people' domain there exists a particular IA algorithm that performs better than the GR algorithm, only a few of the possible preference orders yield significantly better results than GR. When comparing the mean scores of the best IAs from both domains, the best IA in the furniture domain performed much better than the best IA in the people domain. Their mean scores differ substantially: while IA-BEST$_1$ obtained a mean of .83 on furniture descriptions, the best-performing order on the 'people' corpus had a mean of .69, with a lower recall percentage score of 21.3%.

6 Conclusions

In recent years, GRE has extended considerably beyond what was seen as its remit a decade ago, for example by taking linguistic context into account (Krahmer and Theune, 2002; Siddharthan and Copestake, 2004). We have been conservative by focusing on three classic algorithms discussed in Dale and Reiter (1995), with straightforward extensions to plurals and gradables.

We tested the Incremental Algorithm's match against speaker behaviour compared to other models using a a balanced, semantically and pragmatically transparent corpus. It turns out that performance depends on the preference order of the attributes that are used by the IA. Preliminary indications from a study on a more complex sub-corpus support this view. This evaluation took a *speaker-oriented* perspective. A *reader-oriented* perspective might yield different results. This is our main target for future follow-ups of this work.

One lesson to be drawn from this study is of a practical nature. Suppose a GRE algorithm were required for an NLG system, to be deployed in a novel domain. If the IA is the prime candidate, which preference order should be chosen? Psycholinguistic principles can be good predictors, but an application may involve attributes whose degree of preference is unknown. Investigating how the subjects/authors of interest behave requires time and resources, in the absence of which, an algorithm like GR (suitably adapted to make sure that the TYPE attribute is represented) may be a better bet.

Finding correct preference orders is comparable to a situation wherein a doctor has a choice of two medicines with which to fight the flu. One of these (nicknamed GR) produces reasonable results against all variants of the flu; the success of the other (called IA) depends crucially on a balancing of ingredients that differs from case to case. Finding the right balance is an art rather than a science. – This, we feel, is the situation in GRE today.

7 Acknowledgements

Thanks to Richard Power, Ehud Reiter, Ross Turner, Imtiaz Khan and Emiel Krahmer for helpful comments. This work forms part of the TUNA project (`www.csd.abdn.ac.uk/research/tuna/`), supported by EPSRC grant GR/S13330/01.

References

A. Arts. 2004. *Overspecification in Instructive Texts*. Ph.D. thesis, University of Tilburg.

E. Belke and A. Meyer. 2002. Tracking the time course of multidimensional stimulus discrimination. *European Journal of Cognitive Psychology*, 14(2):237–266.

B. Bohnet and R. Dale. 2005. Viewing referring expression generation as search. In *Proc. IJCAI-05*.

R. Dale and E. Reiter. 1995. Computational interpretation of the Gricean maxims in the generation of referring expressions. *Cognitive Science*, 19(8):233–263.

Robert Dale. 1989. Cooking up referring expressions. In *Proc. ACL-89*.

H. J. Eikmeyer and E. Ahlsèn. 1996. The cognitive process of referring to an object. In *Proc. 16th Scandinavian Conference on Linguistics*.

C. Gardent. 2002. Generating minimal definite descriptions. In *Proc. ACL-02*.

S. Gupta and A. J. Stent. 2005. Automatic evaluation of referring expression generation using corpora. In *Proc. 1st Workshop on Using Corpora in NLG*.

H. Horacek. 1997. An algorithm for generating referential descriptions with flexible interfaces. In *Proc. ACL-97*.

P. W. Jordan and M. Walker. 2005. Learning content selection rules for generating object descriptions in dialogue. *Journal of Artificial Intelligence Research*, 24:157–194.

P. W. Jordan. 2000. Influences on attribute selection in redescriptions: A corpus study. In *Proc. CogSci-00*.

J. D. Kelleher and G-J Kruijff. 2006. Incremental generation of spatial referring expressions in situated dialog. In *Proc. ACL-COLING-06*.

E. Krahmer and M. Theune. 2002. Efficient context-sensitive generation of referring expressions. In Kees van Deemter and Rodger Kibble, editors, *Information Sharing*. Stanford: CSLI.

T. Pechmann. 1989. Incremental speech production and referential overspecification. *Linguistics*, 27:89–110.

A. Siddharthan and A. Copestake. 2004. Generating referring expressions in open domains. In *Proc. ACL-04*.

M. Stone. 2000. On identifying sets. In *Proc. INLG-00*.

K. van Deemter, I. van der Sluis, and A. Gatt. 2006. Building a semantically transparent corpus for the generation of referring expressions. In *Proc. INLG-06*.

K. van Deemter. 2002. Generating referring expressions: Boolean extensions of the incremental algorithm. *Computational Linguistics*, 28(1):37–52.

K. van Deemter. 2006. Generating referring expressions that contain gradable properties. *Computational Linguistics*. to appear.

I. van der Sluis, A. Gatt, and K. van Deemter. 2006. Manual for the TUNA corpus: Referring expressions in two domains. Technical Report AUCS/TR0705, University of Aberdeen.

J. Viethen and R. Dale. 2006. Algorithms for generating referring expressions: Do they do what people do? In *Proc. INLG-06*.

Generating Politeness in Task Based Interaction: An Evaluation of the Effect of Linguistic Form and Culture

Swati Gupta
Department of Computer Science,
University of Sheffield
Regent Court, 211 Portobello street,
Sheffield, UK, S1 4DP
s.gupta@dcs.shef.ac.uk

Marilyn A. Walker
Department of Computer Science,
University of Sheffield
Regent Court, 211 Portobello street,
Sheffield, UK, S1 4DP
m.walker@dcs.shef.ac.uk

Daniela M. Romano
Department of Computer Science,
University of Sheffield
Regent Court, 211 Portobello street,
Sheffield, UK, S1 4DP
d.romano@dcs.shef.ac.uk

Abstract

Politeness is an integral part of human language variation, e.g. consider the difference in the pragmatic effect of realizing the same communicative goal with either "Get me a glass of water mate!" or "I wonder if I could possibly have some water please?" This paper presents POLLy (Politeness for Language Learning), a system which combines a natural language generator with an AI Planner to model Brown and Levinson's theory of politeness (B&L) in collaborative task-oriented dialogue, with the ultimate goal of providing a fun and stimulating environment for learning English as a second language. An evaluation of politeness perceptions of POLLy's output shows that: (1) perceptions are generally consistent with B&L's predictions for choice of form and for discourse situation, i.e. utterances to strangers need to be much more polite than those to friends; (2) our indirect strategies which should be the politest forms, are seen as the rudest; and (3) English and Indian native speakers of English have different perceptions of the level of politeness needed to mitigate particular face threats.

Introduction

Politeness is an integral part of human language variation in conversation, e.g. consider the difference in the pragmatic effect of realizing the same communicative goal with either "Get me a glass of water mate!" or "I wonder if I could possibly have some water please?", with choices of these different forms driven by sociological norms among human speakers (Brown & Levinson, 1987). Recent work on conversational agents suggests that such norms are an important aspect of language generation for human-computer conversation as well (Walker et al., 1997; André et al., 2000; Reeves & Nass, 1996; Cassell & Bickmore, 2003; Porayska-Pomsta, 2003; Johnson et al., 2004). (Walker et al., 1997) were the first to propose and implement Brown & Levinson's (1987) theory of politeness, henceforth B&L, in conversational agents. Their goal was to provide interesting variations of character and personality in an interactive narrative application. Subsequent work has shown the value of politeness strategies based on B&L in many conversational applications, e.g. tutorial dialogue (Porayska-Pomsta, 2003; Johnson et al., 2004), animated presentation teams (André et al.,2000; Rehm and Andre, 2007), real estate sales (Cassell & Bickmore, 2003), and has also shown that the cross-cultural claims of B&L hold up in these contexts (Johnson et al., 2005).

This paper presents POLLy (Politeness for Language Learning), a system which combines a natural language generator with an AI Planner to model B&L's theory of politeness in task-oriented dialogue. Our hypothesis is that politeness forms are difficult for non-native speakers to learn, and that a virtual environment where learners can interact with virtual agents embodying different politeness strategies in different discourse contexts, will provide a fun and stimulating environment for learning English as a second language (ESL). As a first step, we evaluate the use of different politeness strategies in task-oriented dialogues in a

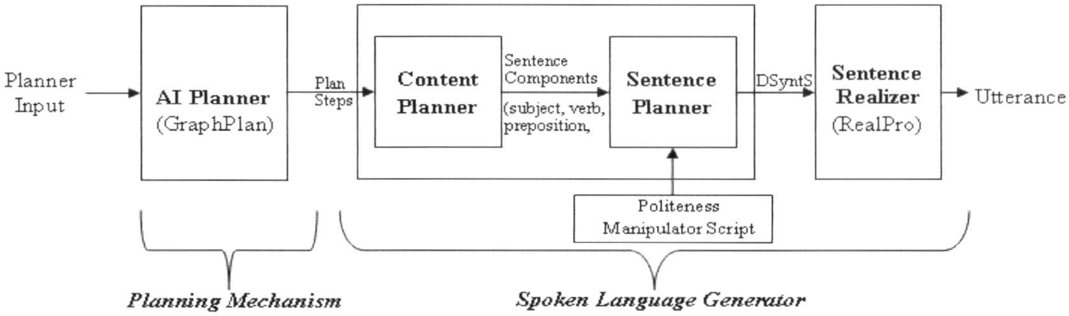

Figure 1: Complete System Architecture

collaborative task domain of cooking, where subjects are asked to collaborate with another person to make a recipe. We show that: (1) politeness perceptions of POLLy's output are generally consistent with B&L's predictions for choice of form and for discourse situation, i.e. utterances to strangers need to be more polite than those to friends; (2) our indirect strategies which should be the politest forms, are seen as the rudest; and (3) English and Indian speakers of English have different perceptions of the level of politeness needed to mitigate particular face threats. Section 1 describes POLLy's architecture and functionality. Section 2 describes an experiment to evaluate user's perceptions of automatically generated task-oriented polite language and Section 3 presents the experimental results. Section 4 sums up and compares our results with previous work.

1 POLLy's architecture and theoretical basis

POLLy consists of two parts: an AI Planner based on GraphPlan (Blum & Furst, 1997) and a spoken language generator (SLG), as illustrated in Figure 1. GraphPlan is a class STRIPS-style planner which, given a goal, e.g. cook pasta, produces a plan of the steps involved in doing so. POLLy then allocates the plan steps to two agents as a shared collaborative plan to achieve the cooking task, with goals to communicate about the plan via speech acts (SAs) needed to accomplish the plan collaboratively, such as Requests, Offers, Informs, Acceptances and Rejections (Grosz & Sidner, 1990; Sidner 1994). The SLG then generates variations of the dialogue based on B&L's theory of politeness that realizes this collaborative plan, as in (Walker et al, 1997; Andre et al, 2000). This is explained in more detail below and an example dialogue is shown in Figure 4. When this dialogue is embedded in our virtual reality environment (Romano, 2005), the human English language learner should be able to play the part of one of the agents in order to practice politeness in a real-time immersive environment.

1.1 Brown and Levinson's theory

B&L's theory states that speakers in conversation attempt to realize their speech acts (SAs) to avoid threats to one another's **face**, which consists of two components. **Positive face** is the desire that at least some of the speaker's and hearer's goals and desires are shared by other speakers. **Negative face** is the want of a person that his action be unimpeded by others. Utterances that threaten the conversants' face are called Face Threatening Acts (FTAs). B&L predict a universal of language usage that the choice of linguistic form can be determined by the predicted Threat Θ as a sum of 3 variables:

1. P: power that the hearer has over the speaker;
2. D: social distance between speaker & hearer;
3. R: a ranking of imposition of the speech act.

Linguistic strategy choice is made according to the value of the Threat Θ. We follow (Walker et al, 1997)'s four part classification of strategy choice. The **Direct strategy** is used when Θ is low and executes the SA in the most direct, clear and unambiguous way. It is usually carried out either in urgent situations like "Please Help!", or where the face threat is small as in informing the hearer "I have chopped the vegetables" or if the speaker has power over the hearer, "Did you finish your homework today?". The **Approval strategy** (Positive Politeness) is used for the next level of threat Θ - this strategy is oriented towards the need for the hearer to maintain a

B&L	Request Forms	Strategy Names	Inform Forms	Strategy Names
Direct	Do X.	RD1Imperative	X	ID1DirectAssert
	Do X please.	RD2ImperativePlz	-	-
	You must do X.	RD3ImperativeInsist	-	-
	You could do X.	RD4AsModAbility	-	-
Approval	Could you please do X mate?	RAp1QModAbility	Do you know that X?	IAp1QKnowledge
	If you don't mind you can do X.	RAp2AsModAbility	Do you know that X mate?	IAp2QueryKNowledgeAddress
	Would it be possible for you to do X?	RAp3AsPossible	-	-
	I'm sure you won't mind doing X.	RAp4AsOptimism	-	-
Autonomy	Could you possibly do X for me?	RAu1QModAbility	It seems that X.	IAu2AsAppear
	I know I'm asking you for a big favour but could you please do X?	RAu2ApologizeQModAbility	I am wondering if you know that X.	IAu1AsConfuse
	I'm wondering whether it would be possible for you to do X.	RAu3AsConfusePossibility	-	-
	Would you not like to do X?	RAu1QOptimism	-	-
Indirect	X is not done yet.	RI1AsNegation	-	-
	X should have been done.	RI2AsModRight	-	-
	Someone should have done X.	RI3AsModRightAbSub	-	-
	Someone has not done X yet.	RI4AsNegationAbsSub	-	-
	Where X is a task request. For example 'You could chop the onions,' or 'Would it be possible for you to clean the spill on the floor?'	*These strategies are applied to the various tasks requests X.*	*Where X is an inform event, like 'Do you know that the milk is spoilt mate?' or 'I'm wondering if you know that you have burnt the pasta.'*	*These strategies are applied to the various inform events X.*

Figure 2: The individual B&L strategies used for Request and Inform speech acts

positive self-image. Positive politeness is primarily based on how the speaker approaches the hearer, by treating him as a friend, a person whose wants and personality traits are liked, and by using friendly markers "Friend, would you please close the door?" or exaggerating "Amazing, you are the best cook in the world!" The **Autonomy Strategy** (Negative Politeness) is used for great face threats, when the speaker may be imposing on the hearer, intruding on their space or violating their freedom of action. These face threats can be mitigated by using hedges, "I wonder if you would mind closing the door for me," or by minimizing imposition, "I just want to ask you if you could close the door." The **Indirect Strategy** (Off Record) is the politest strategy and is therefore used when Θ is greatest. It depends on speaking in an indirect way, with more than one attributable intention so that the speaker removes himself from any imposition. For ex., using metaphor and irony, rhetorical questions, understatement, hints etc. "Its cold in here," which implies a request to close the door, or being vague like "Perhaps someone should clean the table."

1.2 SLG (Spoken Language Generation)

The SLG is based on a standard architecture (Dale & Reiter, 1995) with three components: Content planning, sentence planning and surface realization. See Figure 1. The politeness strategies are implemented through a combination of content selection and sentence planning. The linguistic realizer RealPro is used for realization of the resulting sentence plan (Lavoie & Rambow, 1997), and the content planning and sentence planning components produce outputs that can be transformed into RealPro input, which we discuss first.

The **Surface Realizer** RealPro takes a dependency structure called the Deep-Syntactic Structure (DSyntS) as input and realizes it as a sentence string. DSyntS are unordered *trees* with labelled nodes and arcs where the nodes are lexicalized. Only meaning bearing lexemes are represented and not function words. An example of a DSyntS for the sentence "I have chopped the vegetables." is given below. The attributes to all the nodes are explicitly specified, tense, article, etc. The two nodes are specified with relations I and II, where I is the subject and II is the object.

```
"chop" [ lexeme: "chop" class: "verb" taxis: "perf" tense: "pres" ]
(
  I "<PRONOUN>" [ lexeme:"<PRONOUN>" number: "sg"
    person:"1st" rel: "I" ]
  II "vegetable" [ lexeme: "vegetable" article: "def" class: "com
    mon_noun" number: "pl" rel: "II"]
)
```

The **Content Planner** interfaces to the AI Planner, selecting content from the preconditions, steps and effects of the plan. According to B&L, direct strategies are selected from the steps of the plan, while realizations of preconditions and negating the effects of actions are techniques for implementing indirect strategies. For instance, in case of the first direct request strategy RD1Imperative (stands for Request SA, Imperative direct strategy) shown in Figure 2, which is realised as 'Do X', task X is selected from the steps of the plan and since it is a request SA and imperative strategy, it is realized simply as 'Do X'. Similarly, in case of the first indirect strategy RI1AsNegation (Request SA, Assert Negation Indirect strategy) which is realized as 'X is not done yet', the content is selected by the negation of effects of the action of doing X. The content planner extracts the components of the sentences to be created, from the plan and assigns them their respective categories, for example, lexeme get/add under category verb, knife/oil under direct object etc and sends them as input to the Sentence Planner.

The **Sentence Planner** then converts the sentence components to the lexemes of DSyntS nodes to create basic DsyntS for simple sentences (Berk, 1999), which are then transformed to create variations as per B&L's politeness strategies. The SAs for which the Sentence Planner creates sentences can be divided into two kinds: Initiating SAs like request, inform, suggest, offer etc and Response SAs like inform SA and acceptance and rejection of various SAs. In the conversation, first the initiating SAs are created followed by response SAs. The subject is implicitly assumed to be first person singular (I) in case of offer, inform, accept and reject, second person singular (you) in request_act and request_inform and first person plural (we) in case of suggest and accept_suggest. Each SA has multiple variants for realizing its politeness strategies as shown in Figure 2.

For realizing these B&L strategies, transformations to add lexical items such as 'please', 'if you don't mind', and 'mate' were added to the DSyntS to make a sentence less or more polite. These politeness formulas are divided into four categories: **Address** form which means a friendly manner of addressing someone like 'mate'. **Abstracting the subject** by saying 'someone should have washed the dishes' instead of addressing the hearer directly. **Softeners** like 'if you don't mind,' 'if you know,' 'please' and 'possibly'. **Additives** consisted of *Apologizing* like admitting impingement as in "I know I'm asking you for a big favour", using *must* "You must take out the trash" and explicitly stating that you are asking a favour as in "Could you chop the onions for me?" For example if we want variations for a Request_act SA in which one agent requests the other to cook vegetables, the Content Planner sends the verb (cook) and the direct object (vegetable) to the Sentence Planner which then creates a base DsyntS. Figure 3 shows the RAu9QOptimism transformation for the CookVeg task (which stands for Request act

```
"cook" [lexeme: "cook" class: "verb" tense: "pres" mood:"imp"]
(
  II "vegetable" [lexeme: "vegetable" article: "def" class: "com
    mon_noun" number: "pl" rel: "II" ]
)
```

This would be realized simply as *"Cook the vegetables."* It is transformed to create utterances which vary in politeness according to B&L.

Base DSyntS

```
"cook" [lexeme:"cook" class:"verb" mood:"cond" question:"+" ]
(
  I  "<PRONOUN>" [lexeme:"<PRONOUN>" number:"sg"
     person:"2nd" rel:"I" ]
  II "vegetable" [lexeme:"vegetable" article:"def" class:"com
     mon_noun" number:"pl" rel:"II" ]
  ATTR "like_to" [lexeme:"like_to" class:"adverb" rel:"ATTR"]
  ATTR "mate" [lexeme:"buddy" rel:"ATTR" ]
)
```

Realized as "Would you like to cook the vegetables mate?"

Base DSyntS manipulated to create polite DSyntS

Figure 3: Transformation from base DSyntS to the RAu9QOptimism strategy for CookVeg task

Agent	Utterance	SA and Politeness Strategy
Agent1	*Could you tell me if you have placed the pan on the burner?*	Approval: REQUEST_INFORM
Agent2	*Oh yes, I have placed the pan on the burner.*	Direct: ACCEPT_REQUEST_INFO
Agent1	*Have you turned-on the burner mate?*	Approval: REQUEST_INFORM
Agent2	*I am not sure.*	Direct: REJECT_REQUEST_INFO
Agent2	*Could I boil the pasta in the pan for you?*	Autonomy: OFFER
Agent1	*Alright if it is not a problem.*	Autonomy: ACCEPT_OFFER
Agent2	*Do you know that I have chopped the vegetables with the knife?*	Approval: INFORM
Agent1	*Ok.*	Direct: ACCEPT_INFORM
Agent2	*Do you know that I have added the oil to the pan my friend?*	Approval: INFORM
Agent1	*Yeah.*	Direct: ACCEPT_INFORM
Agent1	*I have added the vegetables to the pan.*	Direct: INFORM
Agent2	*Alright.*	Direct: ACCEPT_INFORM
Agent1	*Could I add the other-ingredients to the vegetables?*	Approval: OFFER
Agent2	*That is nice of you but no please do not bother yourself.*	Approval: REJECT_OFFER
Agent2	*I am wondering whether you would like to cook the vegetables in the pan.*	Autonomy: REQUEST_ACT
Agent1	*Please do not mind but I can not do that.*	Autonomy:REJECT_REQUEST_ACT

Figure 4: An example run of the system for two agents cooking pasta with vegetables

speech act, Query optimism autonomy strategy for the task cook vegetables). In addition, in the second row of Figure 2, the sentence planner transforms the selected content by adding 'please' for the second direct request strategy RD2ImperativePlz, and in the third row, it adds 'must' to the RD3ImperativeInsist. Under indirect strategy in Figure 2, the strategy of abstracting the subject by saying 'someone' instead of addressing the hearer directly is shown as RI4AsNegationAbsSub. An example run of a dialogue generated by the system for two agents cooking pasta is given in Figure 4.

2 Experimental Method

We conducted an experiment to study the perception of politeness by subjects in different discourse contexts, with subjects from two different cultural backgrounds: 11 were British and 15 Indians and their average age was between 20 to 30 years. Subjects were presented with a series of tasks implemented as a web-based questionnaire, and were asked to rate various utterances as though the utterances had been said to them by their partner in the collaborative task. The survey asked the subjects how polite their partner is perceived to be, on a five point Likert-like scale: Excessively Overpolite, Very Polite, Just Right, Mildly Rude or Excessively Rude. All of the tasks were selected to have relatively high R (ranking of imposition) as per B&L's theory. Requests were to 'chop the onions', 'wash the dishes', 'take out the rubbish' and 'clean the spill on the floor.' The events for the propositional content of the Inform SAs were "You have burnt the pasta" and "The milk is spoilt", "You have broken the dish" and "The oven is not working". Subjects rated a total of 84 sentences spread over these 8 different tasks. There was also a text box for subjects to write optional comments.

There were five experimental variables: (1) Speech act type (request vs. inform); (2) B&L politeness strategy (direct, approval, autonomy, indirect); (3) discourse context (friend vs. stranger); (4) linguistic form of the realization of the B&L strategy; (5) cultural background (Indian vs. British). The politeness strategies were selected from strategies given by B&L for each level of politeness, as shown in Figure 2.

For each task, subjects were told that the discourse situation was either they were working on the cooking task with a **Friend**, or with a **Stranger**. This was in order to implement B&L's D variable representing social distance. A friend has a much lower social distance than a stranger, thus Θ should be much greater for strangers than friends. We did not manipulate the power variable of B&L.

We tested two speech acts: **Request** and **Inform**. The ranking of imposition R for speech acts has Requests with higher R than Inform, so Θ should be greater for requests, implying the use of a more polite B&L strategy. For the Request speech act, subjects judged 32 example sentences, 16 for each situation, Friend vs. Stranger. There were 4 examples of each B&L strategy, direct, approval, autonomy, indirect. The B&L strategies for requests are given in Figure 2. For the Inform speech act, subjects judged 10 example utterances for each situation, friend and stranger, with 5 B&L strategies, used to inform the hearer of some potentially face-threatening event. Of the five, there was one direct, two approval and two autonomy utterances. No Indirect strategies were used for Inform SAs because those given by B&L of hints, being vague, jokes, tautologies are not implemented in our system. The B&L strategies for Informs are also in Figure 2.

3 Results and Observations

We calculated ANOVAs with B&L category, situation (friend/stranger), speech act, syntactic form, politeness formula and the nationality of subjects as the independent variables and the ratings of the perception of politeness by the subjects as the dependent variable. Results are in Tables 1, 2, and 3 and are discussed below.

B&L strategies Effect: The four B&L strategies (Direct, Approval, Autonomy and Indirect) had a significant effect on the interpretation of politeness (df=3, F=407.4, p<0.001). See Table 1. The overall politeness ratings from least polite to most were Indirect, Direct, Approval and then Autonomy strategy as shown in the graph in Figure 5.

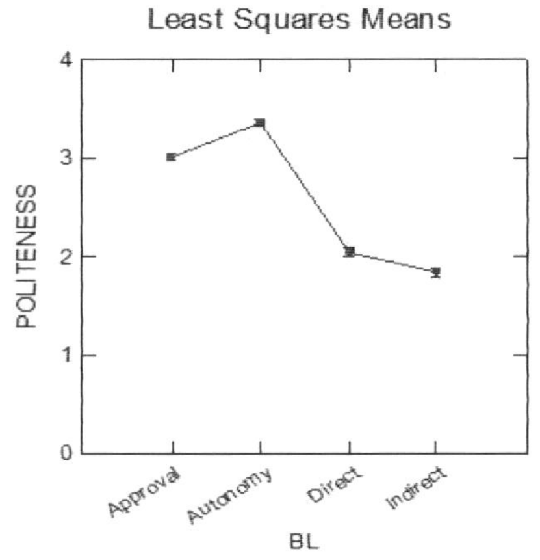

Figure 5: The B&L Strategies effect

It must be noted that as opposed to our findings, B&L regard the indirect strategy as the most polite of all. We hypothesize that this is so because of the limitations of our system for making different kinds of indirect strategies. The indirect realizations that our generator produces from the AI planner are the *effect not achieved* forms like the indirect request strategies (RI1AsNegation, RI2AsModRight, RI3AsModRightAbSub and RI4AsNegationAbsSub) as shown in Figure 2 which sound like a complaint or sarcasm. Other Indirect strategies given by B&L like giving hints, being vague, sarcasm or jokes are situation dependent and require general language knowledge and are not implemented. We plan to address this issue as part of our future work.

Situation Effect (Friend/Stranger): Table 1 also shows that sentences spoken by the Friend were rated to be overall more polite than those spoken by the Stranger (df=1, F=123.6, p<0.001). This shows B&L's social distance variable that when the distance is large, a more polite sentence is appropriate but if we use a sentence with too much politeness in case of lesser social distance, the sentence would be regarded as over polite.

SA Effect (Request/ Inform): The inform SA was rated as more polite than Request SA (df=1, F=61.4, p<0.001). Requests have more face threat than Informs as they impede upon hearer's freedom of action and need to be more polite.

Sentence Form Effect: We divided the sentences into four categories, used for B&L strategy realizations, as per their syntactic forms. *Queries* interrogate the listener, like strategy RAp1QModAbility, "Could you please wash the dishes mate?" *Assertions* in case of request SA refer to sentences that make a request by asserting something like by asserting that the precondition holds or asserting the ability of the hearer like strategy RAp2AsModAbility, "If you don't mind you can chop the onions." In case of inform SA, they refer to polite declaratives that use some politeness formulas or additives with autonomy and approval strategies. *Direct Assertions* refer to sentences that directly assert something without much politeness tactic and are used to realize the direct form of the Inform SA, like ID1DirectAssert strategy, "You have burnt the pasta." Lastly, *Imperatives* are those

		Direct	Approval	Autonomy	Indirect	Overall
Speech Act	Request	2.0	3.0	3.4	1.8	2.6
	Inform	2.4	3.0	3.2	NA	3.0
Situation	Friend	2.3	3.3	3.6	2.0	3.0
	Stranger	1.8	2.8	3.1	1.7	2.4

Table 1: Mean values of the politeness ratings of SAs and situations for B&L's strategies and their overall mean score

		Overall Score
Sentence Form	Imperative	1.8
	Assertion	2.5
	Queries	3.2
	Direct Assertions	2.4
Politeness Formula	AddressForm	3.1
	AbstractSubject	2.0
	Softeners	3.3
	Additives	3.0

Table 2: Overall mean values of the sentence forms and politeness formulas

sentences that directly command the user to perform some action, like the RD3ImperativeInsist strategy, "You must clean the spill on the floor" In case of requests, Imperatives were rated as least polite followed by Assertions and then Queries with (df=2, F=279.4, p<0.001). In case of Inform SA, Assertions are considered to be most polite, followed by Queries and then Direct Assertions with (df=2, F=36.0, p<0.001).

Politeness Formula Effect: We observed that sentences with address form 'mate' were rated more polite than those without it (df=1, F= 49.8, p<0.001). Abstracting the subject (used in indirect strategy) made the sentence less polite (df=1, F=125.0, p<0.001) and adding Softeners notably increased politeness (df=4, F=104.0, p<0.001). In case of additives, apologies were rated to be most polite, followed by those that asked for favour and sentences that used an insisting adverb such as must were least polite of all (df=3, F=185.6, p<0.001).

Nationality Effect: We found that the politeness interpretation of Indian and British subjects was significantly different. Indians rated the sentences as overall more polite than British. This was most evident in case of a Friend saying something, (df=1, F=6.0, p<0.01) and in case of Requests (df=1, F=6.37, p<0.01) whereas in case of a stranger their measures were almost equal. This shows the culture effect that Indians are more informal in their communication, especially when they are talking to a friend. Although the overall degrees of politeness of the four B&L strategies was rated higher by Indians, which opposes the universality assumption of B&L, the order of the ranking of the strategies was the same for both Indians and British (indirect being the least polite, followed by approval, autonomy and direct) which shows that the broad universality is still preserved.

		Request	Inform
Situation	Friend	2.8	3.2
	Stranger	2.3	2.8
Sentence Form	Imperative	1.9	NA
	Assertion	2.4	3.2
	Queries	3.3	3.0
	Direct Assertions	NA	2.4

Table 3: Mean values of situation and sentence forms in relation to the speech acts

Conclusion

We presented an implementation of a system, called POLLy, that combines a general AI planner with a spoken language generator behaviour, for generating polite language as per the theory of Brown and Levinson, and demonstrated how to extract language from a plan to generate conversations that are oriented towards performing an action (Sidner, 1994). (Walker et al., 1997) were the first to propose an application of B&L to conversational agents, but while they used a planner representation, they did not integrate a planner and their approach was not evaluated. Here, we have presented an experiment which shows that the B&L strategies have a significant effect on humans' perception of politeness. The utterances evaluated by our subjects were produced by POLLy and there was no human moderator unlike the evaluation experiment of (Cassell & Bickmore, 2002) which was wizard-of-oz. Where cultural differences are concerned, our experiment showed strong differences in the perception of politeness by Indian and British native speakers of English in case of SAs with B&L's high ranking of imposition like requests and where B&L's social distance variable was less when the discourse situation was specified as that of talking to a friend, whereas in their experiment, (Johnson et al., 2005) showed that the perceptions of politeness of American and German speakers in the domain of tutorial dialogues was identical. (André et al., 2000) proposed the idea of animated presentation teams for presenting information to the user but they investigated only personality and not politeness and their NLG was template based. Our generator is to be applied in the domain of teaching ESL. Previously, (Porayska-Pomsta, 2003) applied B&L's theory in the tutorial domain for modelling teacher's corrective responses, with a generator based on case based reasoning, selecting utterances from human-human dialogues rather than building a generator based on B&L. (Johnson et al., 2004) also had a similar approach for generating socially appropriate tutorial dialogue, with a template based NLG component, for a language training system that provides training in a foreign language and culture through AI enhanced story driven gaming, task-oriented spoken language instruction and intelligent tutoring. Their language courses have a strong task-based focus on skills needed to cope with specific situations; they give people enough knowledge of language and culture to enable them to carry out particular tasks in a foreign country, like introducing yourself, obtaining directions and arranging meetings. Rehm and Andre have shown that the interpretation of politeness strategies is affected by the gestures used in an embodied conversational agent (Rehm and Andre, 1997). In future work, we aim to modify the language generator to make it more robust and integrate POLLy into a virtual reality environment for learning politeness when learning English as a second language.

References

André, E., Rist, T., Mulken, S.v., Klesen, M., & Baldes, S. (2000) *The automated design of believable dialogues for animated presentation teams*. In Embodied Conversational Agents (pp. 220–255). Cambridge, MA, USA: MIT Press.

Berk, Lynn M. (1999) *English syntax: from word to discourse*, Oxford University Press.

Blum, A., Furst, M. (1997) *Fast Planning Through Planning Graph Analysis*. Artificial Intelligence, 90:281-300.

Brown, Penelope & Levinson, S. (1987) *Politeness: Some Universals in Language Usage*. Cambridge u.a.: Cambridge University Press.

Cassell, J. Bickmore, Timothy W. (2003) *Negotiated Collusion: Modeling Social Language and its Relationship Effects in Intelligent Agents*. User Model. User-Adapt.Interact.13(1-2):89-132.

Dale, R. and Reiter, E. (1995). *Building Natural Language Generation Systems*. Studies in Natural Language Processing. Cambridge University Press.

Grosz, B. J. and Sidner, C. L. (1990) *Plans for discourse*. In P. R. Cohen, J. L. Morgan, and M. E. Pollack, editors, Intentions in Communication, pages 417- 444. MIT Press, Cambridge, MA.

Johnson, L.W. and Rizzo, P. and Bosma, W.E. and Ghijsen, M. and van Welbergen, H. (2004) *Generating socially appropriate tutorial dialog*. In: ISCA Workshop on Affective Dialogue Systems, Kloster Irsee, Germany. pp. 254-264.

Johnson, L., Mayer, R., André, E., & Rehm, M. (2005). *Cross-cultural evaluation of politeness in tactics for pedagogical agents*. Proc. of the 12th Int. Conf. on Artificial Intelligence in Education.

Lavoie, B., and Rambow, O. (1997) *RealPro – a fast, portable sentence realizer*. In Proceedings of the Conference on Applied Natural Language Processing (ANLP'97), Washington DC.

Porayska-Pomsta, K. (2003) *Influence of Situational Context on Language Production: Modelling Teachers' Corrective Responses*. School of Informatics, University of Edinburgh.

Reeves, B. and Nass, C. (1996). *The Media Equation*. University of Chicago Press.

Rehm, M. and Andre, E. (2007) *Informing the Design of Agents by Corpus Analysis*. (to appear in) Conversational Informatics, Edited by T. Nishida.

Romano, D.M. (2005). *Virtual Reality Therapy*. Developmental Medicine & Child Neurology Journal. 2005 Sep; 47(9):580

Sidner, C. L. (1994) *An artificial discourse language for collaborative negotiation*. In Proc. 12th National Conf. on AI, pages 814–819, Seattle, WA.

Walker, M., Cahn, J. and Whittaker, S. J. (1997). Improving linguistic style: Social and affective bases for agent personality. In Proc. Autonomous Agents'97, 96–105. ACM Press.

Interactive sentence combining and paraphrasing in support of integrated writing and grammar instruction: A new application area for natural language sentence generators

Karin HARBUSCH, Camiel VAN BREUGEL, Ulrich KOCH & Gerard KEMPEN
University of Koblenz-Landau, Computer Science Dept.
Universitätsstraße 1
56070 Koblenz, GERMANY
{harbusch, camiel, koch}@uni-koblenz.de

Max Planck Institute
PO Box 310
6500 AH Nijmegen, NETHERLANDS
gerard.kempen@mpi.nl

Abstract

The potential of sentence generators as engines in Intelligent Computer-Assisted Language Learning and teaching (ICALL) software has hardly been explored. We sketch the prototype of COMPASS, a system that supports integrated writing and grammar curricula for 10 to 14 year old elementary or secondary schoolers. The system enables first- or second-language teachers to design controlled writing exercises, in particular of the "sentence combining" variety. The system includes facilities for error diagnosis and on-line feedback. Syntactic structures built by students or system can be displayed as easily understood phrase-structure or dependency trees, adapted to the student's level of grammatical knowledge. The heart of the system is a specially designed generator capable of lexically guided sentence generation, of generating syntactic paraphrases, and displaying syntactic structures visually.

1 Introduction: sentence combining

In many countries, a satisfactory level of writing proficiency is increasingly being recognized as an important goal of first- and second-language instruction at all levels of education. In response to this trend, language technology is beginning to contribute computational tools for writing curricula—(semi-)automatic essay grading being a recent example (e.g. Shermis & Burstein, 2003). The software system described in the present paper supports elementary or secondary schoolers in developing the SYNTACTIC aspects of their writing skills, with German as target language.

The following little story was written by a 10 year old German student as part of a writing exercise. It comprises 15 short sentences, each consisting of a single finite clause. The first and last sentences of the text[1] are as follows:

(1) *Die Kinder wollen zum Mond fliegen.*
The children want to-the moon fly
(2) *Sie bauen eine Rakete. [...]*
They build a rocket
(3) *Sie fliegen nach Hause.* (4) *Zu Hause*
They fly to home At home
erzählen sie alles ihren Eltern.
tell they all (to) their parents

An important goal of writing instruction in elementary and secondary schools in Germany and elsewhere is to raise the level of syntactic diversity of the texts produced by the students. Combining simple clauses into complex or compound sentences is one of the means to this goal. For example, the author of the present story could have combined sentences (1) and (2) as in (5), or (3) and (4) as in (6).

(5) *Die Kinder bauen eine Rakete, weil sie zum Mond fliegen wollen.* [*weil* 'because']
(6) *Sie fliegen nach Hause und erzählen alles ihren Eltern.* [*und* 'and']

At the end of the 1960s, "sentence combining" originated in the United States as a form of "controlled writing" exercises, and various em-

[1]From sentence material collected by our partners at the Psychology Department of the University of Koblenz-Landau under research grant "Wissen-schaf(f)t Zukunft" from the Ministry of Education, Science, Youth and Culture of Rheinland-Pfalz, Germany. The work presented here is partially funded by that grant.

pirical evaluation studies have since confirmed its usefulness (Daiker et al., 1985). In a sentence-combining exercise, students are presented with a sequence of short clauses each expressing a simple proposition. Together, the propositions make up a little story or essay. By transforming the short clauses and combining them into longer sentences, the students then produce a coherent and fluent piece of text. Exercises are often accompanied by instructions to combine clauses in a particular syntactic way (e.g. "use a relative clause"). This requires understanding by the student of grammatical terminology. Actually, empirical studies show that writing instruction as well as grammar teaching yield better results when trained in an integrated manner than when trained in isolation (e.g. Mellon 1969; Schuurs, 1990).

Currently, computer support for sentence combining is restricted to multiple-choice questions or quizzes. To our knowledge, no software tool currently exists that deploys generation technology to evaluate student responses to sentence combining exercises. As a matter of fact, virtually the entire literature on the application of NLP to the syntactic aspects of first- and second-language teaching is based on syntactic parsing technology (Heift & Schulze 2003). To our knowledge, Zamorano Mansilla (2004) is the only project that applies a sentence generator (KPML; Bateman 1997) to the recognition and diagnosis of writing errors ("fill-in-the-blank" exercises, not sentence combining).

The system introduced in the present paper is a first attempt to fill this gap. It supports students in producing diverse sentence structures on-line while focusing on grammatical structure, i.e. without the need to pay much attention to semantic content generation, word inflection, spelling, and typing. The system evaluates grammatical correctness of student-generated output and compliance with the task assignment online, and provides accurate feedback.

2 The COMPASS system

The kernel of the COMPASS system (for COMbinatorial and Paraphrastic Assembly of Sentence Structure) is a specially designed sentence generator capable of LEXICALLY GUIDED SENTENCE CONSTRUCTION, and of PARAPHRASING. It takes as input (1) a set of lexically anchored "treelets" that specify the subcategorization frames of the lexical anchors, together with (2) a specification of the grammatical relations between lexical anchors that the to-be-generated sentences should realize. (This in contrast with familiar generators that take a semantic structure as input.) The key structure building operation in the generator is DISJUNCTIVE FEATURE UNIFICATION (for details of the underlying Performance Grammar formalism, see Kempen & Harbusch 2002). Moreover, instead of generating a single sentence as output, it produces the full set of well-formed syntactic paraphrases licensed by the current lexical input in conjunction with the grammar (Harbusch et al., 2006).

The user interface lets the student describe a visually displayed scene by selecting words from a list of inflected word forms. To this purpose, s/he drags the word forms out of the list and drops them into the system's workspace on the screen, where COMPASS displays the treelets associated with them (Figure 1). Then, the student combines them in accordance with the required grammatical relations, and orders the branches of the resulting hierarchical structure from left to right (also by drag & drop), until s/he judges that the word form string dominated by the tree (which may contain crossing branches) expresses the intended meaning in the form of a grammatically correct sentence. The generator produces all possible word-order paraphrases and checks whether the terminal string of at least one paraphrase is identical to the string produced by the student. If not, COMPASS attempts to diagnose the error by checking if the latter string could have resulted from mis- or non-application of a linear order rule, and provides feedback accordingly. The rule base of the system also includes MAL-RULES, which generate structures occurring in frequently observable errors. If the generator has to apply a mal-rule in order to match student output exactly, a feedback message is displayed (e.g. "Don't use main clause word order in a subordinate clause").

Notice that, because the students compose all sentences and phrases under generator control, COMPASS can evaluate their responses WITHOUT THE HELP OF A PARSER: Based on its paraphrastic capabilities and its mal-rules, the system

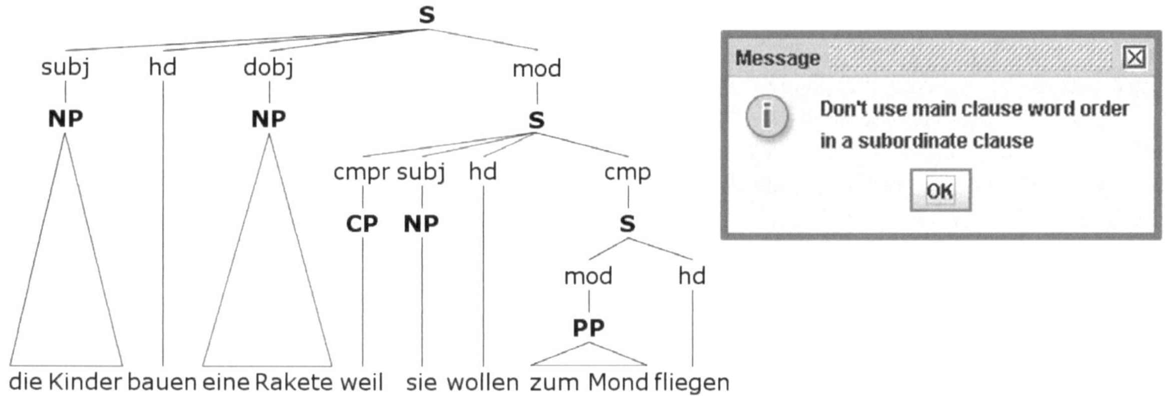

Figure 1. A COMPASS exercise for English speaking students learning German as a second language (Workspace snapshot). The students are instructed first to assemble two main clauses (sentences (1) and (2)), then to combine them with *weil* 'because' and to pronominalize one of the subject NPs. The student failed to place *wollen* 'want' in clause-final position.

can often 're-construct' the well- or ill-formed sentences produced by students.

The design of the generator enables sentence combining in direct-manipulation style. At student request, it can join together two or more independent clauses or sentences into a larger complex or compound sentence—e.g., with one clause becoming a subordinate adverbial or relative clause within the other (as in (5); Figure 1), or by linking them together as coordinate structures (as in (6)). By dragging a function word from the word list—e.g. a relative pronoun, a subordinating or coordinating conjunction—and attaching the current clauses or sentences to it, the student can specify which sentence combination s/he wants. The generator's linguistic rule base ensures that the linguistic constraints entailed by the combination are obeyed (e.g. linear order changes, pronominalization, ellipsis).

This sentence-combining procedure is hard to realize in generators embodying the three-stage pipeline architecture described in Reiter & Dale (2000), which is not intended to deal with structural changes. Actually, COMPASS allows students not only to link trees together, but also to break them apart after making a mistake. By dragging a lexical treelet or a larger subtree away from the current overall tree, they disconnect the former from the latter. The feature composition of the nodes of the separated partial trees is immediately adapted to the constraints prevailing in the new configurations.

The above drag & drop facilities are realized by a user interface with powerful capabilities for drawing and manipulating trees interactively (Kempen 2004). Trees can be displayed with varying levels of morphosyntactic detail (e.g. showing vs. hiding structure within major phrases of a clause) and in different styles (e.g. phrase-structure vs. dependency trees). These facilities support visual grammar instruction tailored student's level of grammatical knowledge (Kempen 1999). The grammatical nomenclature in the tree diagrams and the error messages are close to that used by language teachers in traditional curricula (e.g., emphasizing grammatical FUNCTIONS; cf. Reuer 2003). Also, the 'flat' trees generated by the underlying Performance Grammar are relatively easy to understand for beginning learners of grammatical notions.

3 Current implementation

A prototype version of COMPASS has been implemented in Java, based on the Performance Grammar Workbench (PGW)—the generator described in Harbusch et al. (2006). It is intended as a software tool in support of integrated writing and grammar curricula for 10 to 14 year old elementary and secondary schoolers. The grammar and the lexicon of the system are in German; this also holds for the grammatical nomenclature in tree diagrams displayed on the screen, although users who are studying German as a second language can opt for trees with English or Dutch terminology.

When COMPASS starts, it shows three windows, called TASK, VOCABULARY, and WORKSPACE, respectively. The Task window specifies the problem to be solved in the Workspace, e.g., to construct the tree for a given sentence, to change the number and/or tense of a given sentence, or to build a few sentences describing a comic strip. The Vocabulary window lists a small set of inflected words from which the student has to choose. S/he drags the words s/he thinks are appropriate from the Vocabulary window and drops them in the Workspace. There, COMPASS displays the treelets associated with the selected word forms, enabling the student to combine them and assemble the target sentence. The sentence generator evaluates each attachment attempt and provides feedback in case of student errors (as explained in Section 2).

The exercise in Figure 1 deals with word order differences in main and subordinate clauses (the modal verb *wollen* 'want' in "second" and "final" position, respectively). By applying a mal-rule that allows verb-second in subordinate clauses, COMPASS can match the ill-formed subordinate *weil* clause assembled by the student and issue an accurate error message. The student can correct the errors by dragging the *wollen* branch to the final position.

4 Conclusion and discussion

At the time of writing, COMPASS exists only in the form of a prototype with a limited vocabulary and grammar. Together with the Psychology Department of the university of Koblenz-Landau and with teachers of German, we are designing and implementing grammar and writing exercises that are useful, attractive and motivating for the target group, and that can be tried out in the classroom. This enables us to test whether the on-line diagnostic performance of our generator-based system is at least as good as that attained by modern parser-based systems.

References

Bateman, J. A. (1997). Enabling technology for multilingual natural language generation: The KPML development environment. *Journal of Natural Language Engineering, 3,* 15—55.

Daiker, D. A., Kerek, A. & Morenberg, M. (Eds.). (1985). *Sentence Combining: A rhetorical perspective.* Carbondale: Southern Illinois University Press.

Delmonte, R., Delcloque, Ph. & Tonelli, S. (Eds.) (2004). *Procs. InSTIL/ICALL2004 Symposium on NLP and speech technologies in advanced language learning systems* (Venice, Italy). Padova: Unipress.

Harbusch, K., Kempen, G., van Breugel, C. & Koch, U. (2006). A generation-oriented workbench for Performance Grammar: Capturing linear order variability in German and Dutch. In: *Procs. 4th Internat. NLG Conference* (Sydney, Australia).

Heift, T. & Schulze, M. (Eds.) (2003). Error diagnosis and error correction in CALL. *CALICO Journal, 20(3).* (Special issue).

Kempen, G. (1999). Visual Grammar: Multimedia for grammar and spelling instruction in primary education. In: Cameron, K.C. (Ed.). *CALL: Media, design, and applications.* Lisse: Swets & Zeitlinger.

Kempen, G. (2004). Interactive visualization of syntactic structure assembly for grammar-intensive first- and second-language instruction. In: Delmonte et al. (Eds.).

Kempen, G. & Harbusch, K. (2002). Performance Grammar: A declarative definition. In: Nijholt, A., Theune, M. & Hondorp, H. (Eds.), *Computational linguistics in the Netherlands 2001.* Amsterdam: Rodopi.

Mellon, J. C. 1969. *Transformational sentence-combining: A method for enhancing the development of syntactic fluency in english composition.* Urbana, IL: National Council of Teachers of English.

Reiter. E. & Dale, R. (2000). *Building natural language generation systems.* Cambridge UK: Cambridge University Press.

Reuer, V. (2003). Error recognition and feedback with Lexical Functional Grammar. *CALICO Journal, 20,* 497-512.

Schuurs, U. R. I. (1990). *Leren schrijven voor lezers: Het effect van drie vormen van probleemgericht schrijfonderwijs op de zinsbouwvaardigheid.* PhD Dissertation, Twente University, Enschede.

Shermis, M. D., & Burstein, J. (2003). *Automated essay scoring: A cross-disciplinary perspective.* Hillsdale, NJ: Erlbaum.

Zamorano Mansilla, J. R. (2004). Text generators, error analysis and feedback. In: Delmonte et al. (Eds.).

Using WYSIWYM to Create an Open-ended Interface for the Semantic Grid

F. Hielkema, C. Mellish & P. Edwards
Department of Computing Science
University of Aberdeen
Aberdeen
AB24 3UE
{fhielkem, cmellish, pedwards}@csd.abdn.ac.uk

1 Introduction

Central to the vision of the Semantic Grid is the adoption of metadata and ontologies to describe resources, to promote and enhance collaboration (De Roure et al., 2005). This raises the question of how such metadata comes into existence. Ideally the users should create it themselves, which raises the issue of how a scientist should create RDF. In our work in the area of e-social science[1], we aim to support social scientists in their research, using (Semantic) Grid technologies. For this, a tool is needed that facilitates easy creation of RDF by non-experts, to enable researchers to deposit and describe their own data. We believe that, for social scientists, natural language is the best medium to use, as the way they conduct their research and the structure of their documents and data indicate that they are more oriented towards text than graphics.

We originally envisaged such tools as being driven by an underlying ontology. However, from the start users expressed a fear of 'being trapped in the ontology', due to the contested nature of many social science concepts (Edwards et al., 2006). We therefore aim to maximise the users' freedom, keeping the tools open-ended by supporting dynamic evolution of metadata and integrating ontologies with folksonomies (Guy and Tonkin, 2006). A folksonomy is a social classification process where users can annotate their resources with keywords or tags, which are not restricted in any way. In some folksonomies, e.g. Flickr[2], users can use other users' tags, so that a set of frequent tags emerges. Using a folksonomy, we could suggest feasible tags to influence user-behaviour, without restricting the user to a pre-defined set of concepts.

Natural language applications are often domain specific and not very flexible. This makes the open-endedness we need a great challenge. Existing elicitation approaches, such as using Controlled Languages, restrict in great measure what the user can and cannot say. We believe that to achieve the desired open-endedness and flexibility, the best approach is not based on natural language processing, as it is as yet beyond the state of the art to reliably parse all user utterances, but based on natural language generation. In WYSIWYM (Power et al., 1998), the user can specify information by editing a feedback text that is generated by the system, based on a semantic representation of the information that the user has specified already. This NLG-approach, we believe, can give us both the flexibility we need and fluent language output. The expressivity of the language need not be restricted as it is generated by the system, and does not need to be parsed; and if we enable the user to modify the underlying data structure while using the tool, we have the desired open-endedness.

Figure 1 shows a feedback text (generated by the current system) for a scenario in which a social scientist is depositing data that forms part of a study into rural accessibility. Existing options for depositing such data (e.g. the UK Data Archive[3]) are found to be too restrictive by some social scientists. We therefore think there is scope for a tool that allows scientists to describe their data themselves, in a way they see fit.

In the next sections we will first describe some related work in NLG and the Semantic Grid community, then describe the design and implementation of our metadata-elicitation tool. We will discuss possible methods for keeping the tool open-ended and unrestrictive, and how folksonomies may be a part of the solution, and conclude with a description of remaining issues and plans for the future.

2 Related Work

Existing Semantic Grid tools that avoid the need to write RDF are often graphical (Handschuh et al., 2001). Natural language approaches include GINO (Bernstein and Kaufmann, 2006), an ontology editor with an approach reminiscent of NL-Menus (Tennant et al., 1983), and Controlled languages, e.g. PENG-D (Schwitter and Tilbrook, 2004).

Natural language approaches tend to restrict expressivity to ensure that every entry can be parsed,

[1] http://www.policygrid.org/
[2] http://www.flickr.com/
[3] http://www.data-archive.ac.uk/

Bibliography
Access to *'APAT'* is public. It was deposited on 9 March 2007.
It was deposited by *John Farrington*. John Farrington's email address is j.farrington@abdn.ac.uk. He is an employee of *the University of Aberdeen*. John Farrington is the principal investigator of 'APAT'.

Methodology
'APAT's' observation units were individuals and focus groups.

Domain
'APAT' supports *'Settlements, Services and Access'*. John Farrington, *Jon Shaw*, *Matthew Leedal* and *Margaret Maclean* are the authors of 'Settlements, Services and Access.'

Figure 1: Example of a WYSIWYM description

limiting the language and often making it stilted, so that there is a small learning curve before the user knows which structures are allowed. Tools that generate natural language from ontologies (though not for elicitation purposes) include Wilcock (2003) and ONTOSUM (Bontcheva, 2005). Wilcock uses templates, achieving portability but paying a price in expressivity and accuracy. ONTOSUM assumes the ontologies contain labels with the appropriate lexicalisation of their resources, and that their part-of-speech tags can be easily derived.

In order to maintain full expressivity and to shorten the learning curve, we have elected to use WYSIWYM (What You See Is What You Meant) (Power et al., 1998). This is a natural language generation approach where the system generates a feedback text for the user that is based on a semantic representation. This representation is edited directly by the user by manipulating the feedback text. Figure 1 shows a feedback text generated by our system.

As the text is generated by the system and does not have to be parsed, we do not have to restrict what can be said, so the language retains its expressivity and the user does not need to learn what is acceptable input. The system is guided by an underlying datastructure, in our case a lightweight ontology. While the original WYSIWYM could only be ported to new domains by having an expert create a new lexicon, we wish to allow the user to extend the ontology while using the tool (i.e. while describing a resource). This, provided we have a NLG-component robust enough to deal with this, will ensure the desired open-endedness.

In the next section we describe the ongoing implementation of a WYSIWYM-tool for metadata elicitation from users unfamiliar with RDF. In section 4 we discuss ways to keep the tool open-ended.

3 Design and Implementation

We are building a tool that elicits metadata from the user in the form of RDF triples, i.e. statements of the form: 'subject - predicate - object'. The tool presents the users with a text containing an expansion point (anchor) for each object that is mentioned, which has a menu with possible properties associated with that object. These objects and properties are defined by an underlying OWL-Lite ontology[4]. The ontology we use for development is based on the UK Data Archive. This lightweight ontology is only a seed; users can extend or replace it (see section 4). We intend to ensure that other OWL-Lite ontologies can be substituted. Such ontologies should be well-formed, be clear about which objects are permitted in the domain and range of properties, and for the benefit of the generated text should have clear object and property names (e.g. HasAuthor), as these names are used for generation with only some minor adjustments (such as adding determiners and removing capitals).

The current system consists of five components: the semantic graph, the ontology reader, the RDF-creator, the natural language generator (text planner and surface realiser) and the interface.

The **interface** shows the feedback text with anchors indicating expansion points, which contain menus with types of information that can be added. Google Web Toolkit[5] was used to create the prototype interface.

The **semantic graph** stores the information the user is adding. Initially a generic graph is created, so an initial feedback text can be produced; the graph is updated each time the user adds information.

The **ontology reader** creates a model of a given OWL-Lite ontology, which is consulted throughout the building of the semantic graph and extended with all new properties or objects that the user adds. The ontology specifies the range and domain of the properties; i.e. the properties in each anchor menu, and the (type(s) of) resource that can be selected or added as the range of a selected menu item.

The semantic graph is translated to a list of RDF triples by the **RDF-creator**. These triples are stored, with the relevant resource(s), in a shared repository of social science resources on the Semantic Grid. The RDF-creator will in the future also store any changes the user made to the ontology.

The **natural language generator** maps the semantic graph to (HTML) text that contains anchors. It consists of a text planner and a surface realiser:

- Text Planner
  This component creates paragraph boundaries and headers. Each property in the semantic graph is mapped to a dependency tree (Mel'cuk, 1988). Before this mapping, the properties are grouped firstly for their source node (so all information about an object is grouped), secondly

[4]http://www.csd.abdn.ac.uk/research/policygrid/ontologies/UKDA/UKDA.owl
[5]http://code.google.com/webtoolkit/

for their label and thirdly for their target. Properties with identical source and label are marked for aggregation in the surface realiser.

- Surface Realiser

  The surface realiser maps the dependency trees to text using the SimpleNLG package[6]. To improve the conciseness of the text, it performs (at present) limited aggregation, when a group of properties has the same source and label (e.g. 'x and y are the authors of z'). It also keeps track of which objects are salient, in order to use pronouns. The text in Figure 1 was generated by the system.

The next section outlines our ideas for extending the system to make it open-ended and flexible.

4 Achieving Open-endedness

To avoid trapping the user in an ontology, two strategies present themselves: first, to make the ontology less restrictive by making it open-ended, and second, to do away with ontologies entirely. We are not prepared to do the latter, as ontologies provide a useful framework and are at the core of the Semantic Grid. We will therefore try to make the most of the first strategy in two ways: enabling the user to adapt any ontologies that are used, and where possible using a much less complex structure: the folksonomy.

4.1 Open-endedness in Ontologies

Although our system is driven by an ontology, we have kept this very lightweight (OWL-Lite, using only domain and range of properties and cardinality restrictions), and will give the user the power to adapt this ontology to his/her own needs. Extending an ontology with new classes and properties is no great problem; but those properties then need a suitable natural language representation. In our system this means they need an entry in the lexicon that maps them to a dependency tree (classes merely need a noun phrase).

A straightforward way to obtain such entries is to let a system administrator create them when needed. However, this would cause considerable delays for the user and would look almost as restrictive as not allowing new property creation at all. Instead, we want to enable the system to create these lexicon entries immediately, so the user can use the new property that session. Using the property name that the user provides, the system should generate an appropriate lexicon entry.

Hallett (2006) describes a portable WYSIWYM application that generates its lexicon automatically. It is unclear, however, how such a fully automated approach would work in practice. ONTOSUM (Bontcheva, 2005) depends on the user to provide lexicalisations of ontology resources. Their application generates the lexicon automatically, assigning pos-tag 'noun' to classes and 'verb' to properties; the user can then change the ontology or correct the pos-tags through an iterative process. This approach assumes that the user is willing to, and capable of, editing the ontology and providing pos-tags.

In contrast, we have decided to use a semi-automatic approach, but one that requires little expertise from the user. The system has the linguistic knowledge, and the user knows what the surface realisation should be; together they can generate a new lexicon entry. We are trying to identify common sentence types to mould into templates. The system inserts the root form of the property name into each template, and presents them for the user to choose from. For instance, given the property 'deposit', with domain 'Person' and range 'Document', the system may generate the following:

1. John Farrington deposits APAT
2. The depositor of APAT is John Farrington
3. APAT has the depositor John Farrington
4. APAT's depositor is John Farrington

The user chooses the most suitable representation, e.g. the first option, and then fine-tunes it by manipulating verb tense, actor and root, adding or removing determiners and prepositions, and switching the domain and range. In our example, changing the verb to past tense and passive action results in the surface form: 'APAT was deposited by John Farrington'. Once the user is satisfied with the representation, the corresponding dependency tree is stored in the lexicon and used for realising all future instances of this property.

4.2 The Freedom of Folksonomies

There are two types of property in OWL-Lite: object and datatype properties. The object properties have a class as their range, the datatype properties a data-type, such as 'string' or 'date'. The implementation allows the user complete freedom in specifying the value of a 'string' datatype, using free text to enter them. Unfortunately this means that we have no control over the quality of the entered data; we cannot prevent a user from entering nonsense.

This is unavoidable when the major goal is to afford the user freedom. However, the problem can be alleviated. Spelling mistakes can be prevented by checking all entries against a dictionary - but this can be very frustrating for the user, and a problem when he/she wants to enter new, foreign or subject-specific words. We believe folksonomies are a better solution here. A folksonomy stores which tags have been used with which frequency. In our system, each datatype property has its own folksonomy, as people would specify different values for the property

[6] http://www.csd.abdn.ac.uk/~ereiter/simplenlg/

'country' than for 'sampling method'. Every time the user selects a datatype property and is prompted to enter a value, the corresponding 'tag cloud' is generated and shown to the user. A tag cloud gives an overview of tags used by other users; their frequency is reflected in the relative font size.

We believe that folksonomies will stimulate the emergence of a community set of tags (Guy and Tonkin, 2006), prompting the user to use the same values as other users, or to adopt a similar style. It should in large part protect the system from mistakes such as spelling errors, and, when queried, increase the likelihood of a search term being associated with more than one resource. The user however retains complete freedom, as he/she does not have to use the folksonomy values but can still use free text; and every entry the user makes is immediately added to the folksonomy. The folksonomy, then, allows us to subtly guide user behaviour, while being completely unrestrictive.

5 Conclusion and Future Work

We have outlined our ongoing development of a open-ended metadata elicitation tool, that allows users to create RDF by editing text. By using natural language generation instead of parsing we ensure that all user input is understood by the system. The system is driven by a lightweight ontology; open-endedness is achieved by enabling the user to extend the ontology where necessary. To enable this, a lexical specification for an appropriate surface realisation is generated by the system using feedback from the user, who chooses the most appropriate realisation and fine-tunes it.

To guide user behaviour without being restrictive, we employ folksonomies, collections of tags with information about how, when, where and how often they have been used. For each datatype property, a tag cloud is generated suggesting appropriate tags to use. When the user enters a new value, this is added to that property's folksonomy.

We intend to use our tool to populate a repository of social science resources. This will help us investigate user requirements on querying. Our aim is to use the same approach, using WYSIWYM with open-ended ontologies and folksonomies, for querying and information presentation. This way the user works with the same interface for each repository-related task, which should greatly improve usability. The folksonomy will be very useful in querying, with the tag cloud showing possible search terms and their frequency in the repository. A search term taken from the folksonomy would guarantee a result.

We believe that WYSIWYM will be as suitable for query formulation as for metadata elicitation. Information presentation in WYSIWYM could be an interactive process, allowing the user to request extra information where needed. Eventually, WYSIWYM will furnish us with an interesting and highly useful set of tools for the Semantic Grid.

References

A. Bernstein and E. Kaufmann. 2006. Gino - a guided input natural language ontology editor. In *International Semantic Web Conference 2006*, pages 144–157.

Kalina Bontcheva. 2005. Generating tailored textual summaries from ontologies. In *ESWC*, pages 531–545.

D. De Roure, N.R. Jennings, and N.R. Shadbolt. 2005. The Semantic Grid: Past, Present and Future. In *Proceedings of the IEEE 93(3)*, pages 669–681.

P. Edwards, J. Aldridge, and K. Clarke. 2006. A Tree Full of Leaves: Description Logic and Data Documentation. In *Proceedings of the Second International Conference on e-Social Science*, Manchester, UK.

M. Guy and E. Tonkin. 2006. Folksonomies: Tidying up Tags? *D-Lib Magazine*, 12(1).

C. Hallett. 2006. Generic Querying of Relational Databases using Natural Language Generation Techniques. In *Proceedings of the Fourth International Natural Language Generation Conference*, pages 88–95, Nottingham, UK.

S. Handschuh, S. Staab, and A. Maedche. 2001. Cream: Creating relational metadata with a component-based, ontology-driven annotation framework. In *K-CAP '01: Proceedings of the 1st international conference on Knowledge capture*, pages 76–83, New York, NY, USA. ACM Press.

I.A. Mel'cuk. 1988. *Dependency Syntax: Theory and Practice*. State University of New York.

R. Power, D. Scott, and R. Evans. 1998. What You See Is What You Meant: Direct Knowledge Editing with Natural Language Feedback. In *Proceedings of the Thirteenth European Conference on Artificial Intelligence*, Brighton, UK.

R. Schwitter and M. Tilbrook. 2004. Controlled Natural Language meets the Semantic Web. In *Proceedings of the Australasian Language Technology Workshop 2004*.

H.R. Tennant, K.M. Ross, R.M. Saenz, C.W.Thompson, and J.R. Miller. 1983. Menu-based Natural Language Understanding. In *Proceedings of the Twenty-first Annual Meetings on Association for Computational Linguistics*, pages 151–158, Cambridge, Massachusetts.

G. Wilcock. 2003. Talking OWLs: Towards an Ontology Verbalizer. In *Human Language Technology for the Semantic Web and Web Services (ISWC'03)*, pages 109–112, Sanibel Island, Florida.

Lexical choice of modal expressions

Ralf Klabunde
Department of Linguistics
Ruhr-Universität Bochum
Germany
klabunde@linguistics.rub.de

Abstract

This paper describes a model of the choice of modal verbs and modal particles. The choice mechanism does not require a modality-specific input as, e.g., a modal logical formula. Instead semantic (modal force) and pragmatic constraints (speech act marking) are applied to the available information on the whole and constrain the set of modal candidates to those that are appropriate in the respective contexts. The choice model is realized in the CAN system that generates recommendations about courses of study.

1 Motivation

Modality is a ubiquitous phenomenon. Speakers use modals very frequently to express that a state of affairs is not simply true or false, but that the propositional content of the respective sentence must be evaluated against some background information. For example, a sentence like *she must study computer science* expresses that, given some contextual information, it follows necessarily from this information that she studies computer science. Pragmatically, in the same context, the use of the modal verb *must* is able to signal the existence of a certain speech act, for example an advice.

Such an estimation of the validity of a proposition against contextual restrictions and signalling a speech act at the same time is rather the rule than the exception so that it is not surprising that modality concerns all relevant processing levels in NLG.

If we take the standard division of labour for an NLG system (cf. Reiter and Dale 2000), basically each module affects modality:

- Trivially, content selection is a modality-related task since a decision must be drawn which content shall be modalized.
- Discourse structuring may be modality-sensitive for two reasons: first, some rhetorical relations suggest the use of modals within their arguments,[1] and second, if information is grouped, this chunk might serve as conversational background triggering the use of modals.
- Since sentence connectives can bear modal meanings (Blühdorn 2004), sentence aggregation is modality-sensitive as well.
- Modals are no content words, but they are polysemous lexical items and candidates for lexical choice.
- Even the generation of referring expressions is sensitive to modality because pronouns behave differently in certain modal contexts (a phenomenon labelled in formal semantics as modal subordination, see Roberts 1989).
- Finally, the grammatical realization requires modal-specific grammar rules.

Although modality is anything but a peripheral phenomenon, it did not receive much attention in research on NLG yet. This is even more astonishing if one considers generated texts produced by NLG systems. Many systems generate texts with modals, but the use of these modals is not driven by semantic decisions. For example, the STOP system (Reiter et al. 2003) generates letters which contain modal verbs

[1] The examples given on the RST website (`http://www.sfu.ca/rst/index.hmtl`) show this very clearly.

and/or conditionals (whose meaning is closely linked to modality) as, e.g., *However, you* ***might*** *like to be a non-smoker if it was easy to stop.* The question-answering system described in Moriceau (2006) uses web page extracts in addition to the generated answer. These extracts contain modal expressions (e.g., *it* ***could*** *also be explained by random movements*).

ADVISOR II (Elhadad 1995) is a generation system that covers exactly the same domain as the CAN system described in this paper. Its generated sentences contain modal verbs (e.g., *You have little experience with writing papers. So it* ***could*** *be difficult.*), and it realizes several of the speech acts that play a role in CAN as well. However, since ADVISOR II is based on a theory of argumentation that focuses on scalars and lexical items with a scalar semantics, respectively, the choice of modals is not driven by the underlying theory. Lexical choice concerns primarily scalar adjectives, connectives, and judgement determiners.

In general, the papers on the mentioned systems suggest that the use of these modal expressions is not based on a meaningful representation of modality or processes that systematically result in the use of appropriate modal expressions. Rather these systems seem to realize modals by means of template-based approaches. A semantically or pragmatically motivated choice does not occur.

1.1 Aim of this paper

In this paper, we present such a model of the choice of modals. This model is integrated into the CAN system (*conceptualization for modal expressions*), an NLG system that generates recommendations for courses of study (Klabunde 2007). Currently, the choice of modals is confined to modal verbs like *können* (can) or *müssen* (must) and modal particles (*ja, doch;* these particles have no direct counterparts in English). The model does not require a content representation as formulas of some modal logic. The only concession to modality is the existence of more than one content plan. We operate with ordinary content plans created by a planner, and simulate the semantics of modal operators by means of quantification. Additionally, we formulate pragmatic conditions as speech act markers. The combination of semantic with pragmatically motivated conditions allows the selection of modal verbs and particles, respectively.

In what follows, we will first describe the semantic and pragmatic particularities of modal verbs and particles and some relevant analyses of these modals in formal semantics and pragmatics (section 2). Based on these approaches, we present the CAN system in section 3. The choice of modals in CAN is described in detail in section 4. We conclude this paper with an outline of our future work.

2 Modal verbs and particles

Modality is a blurred concept that centers around the notions of possibility and necessity (cf. Kratzer 1981; Papafragou 2006, Werner 2006, and many others). Independent of what modal expression is used, a modal sentence expresses that the propositional content of the sentence possibly or necessarily holds with respect to some contextual restrictions.

2.1 Modal verbs

Standard approaches to the semantics of modal verbs emphasize the relevance of two parameters for a semantic analysis: the *modal force*, i.e. the expression of possibility or necessity, and contextual restrictions by means of a *conversational background*. Some German examples shall demonstrate the relevance of these parameters:

(1) *Du musst den Semantik-Kurs besuchen*
You must attend the semantics course
Modal force: necessity
No restriction on the conversational background

(2) *Du sollst den Semantik-Kurs besuchen*
You are to attend the semantics course
Modal force: necessity
Preferably a teleological, deontic or epistemic conversational background

(3) *Du darfst den Semantik-Kurs besuchen*
You may attend the semantics course
Modal force: possibility
Preferably a deontic conversational background

Meaning differences between modal verbs are explained by different admissible modal forces and conversational backgrounds. For example, the difference between *müssen* and *sollen* is just the class of admissible backgrounds: both express necessity as modal force, but while *müssen* is not confined to specific conversational backgrounds, *sollen* requires a teleological, a deontic, or an epistemic background.

In Kratzer's (1981) seminal work – inspired by modal logics - propositions and conversational backgrounds are represented as sets of possible worlds, so that the whole approach boils down to set-theoretic operations on possible world sets. For our approach it is especially important that the semantics of the modal operators $\Box$ (necessity) and $\Diamond$ (possibility) is traced back to universal and existential quantification over possible worlds, respectively: if [p] denotes the set of possible worlds, where the proposition p holds, and R(w) is the set of accessible possible worlds for a given world w, then: $[\Box(p)] = \lambda w. (R(w) \subseteq [p])$, and $[\Diamond(p)] = \lambda w. (R(w) \cap [p] \neq \emptyset)$.

For example, the sentence *you must attend the semantics course* is true iff, given an actual world w, all worlds that are accessible from w belong to the set of worlds in which the addressee attends the semantics course.

Although truth-conditions do not play an essential role for the choice of modals, modal forces do. We describe in section 4 how modal forces are modelled by quantification over plan nodes.

In addition to semantic constraints, modal verbs may also serve as speech act markers (cf. Zeevat 2003). Many modal verbs are associated with preferred conversational backgrounds, and this background suggests a certain speech act. For example, *dürfen* (may) expresses possibility as modal force and can be used if a deontic background becomes relevant. With such a background, *dürfen* expresses a permission.

2.2 Modal particles

Contrary to modal verbs, modal particles do not have a semantics at all; their function is to relate the propositional content to the speech situation. For example, *ja* as modal particle indicates the speaker's evidence that the propositional content is true:

(4) *Du besuchst ja den Semantik-Kurs*
You are attending the semantic course – as we both know

Stressed *doch* marks a contradiction with the listener's assumptions or - with normal intonation - that the content is probably present in the common ground:

(5) *Du besuchst DOCH/doch den Semantik-Kurs*
You are attending the semantics course – I am right/ am I right?

The particles always express possibility as modal force, since the speaker signals that according to his belief state it is not definitely the case that the propositional content is true. Furthermore, the particles are typically used with an epistemic conversational background.

Zeevat (2004) points out that particles function as context- and speech act markers. As context markers, they signal the existence of a specific relation between the common ground CG and proposition ϕ. For example, the particle *ja* signals the relation *old*(CG, ϕ).

As for speech act marking, the modal particles behave analogous to modal verbs. The pragmatic function of the particles is to map the default speech act – the assertion - to a non-default one as, e.g., a reminder or a recommendation. If the particles function as speech act markers, their meaning may be represented as planning operators (cf. Appelt 1985 for an axiomatic approach to speech act planning). In this case, context marking belongs to the preconditions, and using the particle has certain effects with respect to the speaker's goal and the listener's information state.

In choosing modal particles we benefit from the vicinity of the formal characteristics of modal particles to planning operators. As described in section 4.2, we formulate speech acts as operator-like rules that manipulate the common ground.

3 The CAN system

The CAN system supports students in choosing courses for their course of study within the B.A. program at the University of Bochum. The users provide the system with the courses they attended so far, the maximal number of semesters they would like to study, and the courses they want to attend. Based on this information, the system generates recommendations/pieces of advice etc. which courses the user should/must/can/may take. The architecture of the system is given in figure 1.

Content determination and linearization is realized by a forward planner. The planner produces a sequence of plans that are all of equal value. More than one plan is needed in order to have alternative scenarios as "possible worlds" at hand, which is a prerequisite for the use of any modal expression.

Since students have to major in two independent areas, plans can contain conflicts. For example, it could be the case that the user selects two courses that take place at the same time. In these cases the existence of the conflict will be linguistically indicated and the conflict must be resolved. Conflicts are resolved either by considering the internal hierarchy of the course types (obligatory courses are ranked higher than optional ones), or – if both courses are of equal value – by the user.

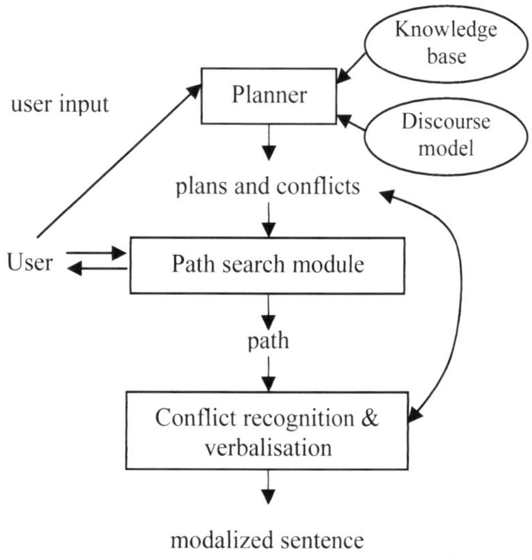

Fig. 1: Architecture of CAN

The modals are chosen by considering semantic and pragmatic constraints as described in section 4.

Currently, the system is able to choose the following modal expressions: *müssen* (must), *können* (can), *wollen* (want), *dürfen* (may), *nicht brauchen* (does not need to), the subjunctive *sollten* (should), and the particles *ja* and *doch.*

The sentences are realized by means of sentential templates with slots for the courses, semesters, and modal expressions.

4 The choice of modals in CAN

The basic idea in the choice of modals is to use semantic and pragmatic constraints as filters for all modal candidates.

The conversational background fixes those modals that can be used at all. Based on this initial set, the computed modal force restricts the initial set to those modals that express that force. Finally, we check whether the speech acts associated with the remaining modals are appropriate in the respective context.

4.1 Semantic constraints

The conversational background is constituted by the application domain. Since the knowledge base contains information about the conditions of study, we are primarily dealing with deontic uses of the modals. The user's input as well as the information provided so far are stored in a discourse model that constitutes an epistemic background.[2]

The modal force is computed by quantification over plan nodes. Basically, the content planner works in a STRIPS-like fashion (Fikes et al. 1972). In order to achieve a definition of modal forces in planning terms, it might be useful to remind some definitions:

A plan $\pi = \langle\alpha_1, \ldots, \alpha_n\rangle$ is a sequence of tasks α_i.

A plan graph G is a set of plans which have the same starting node and the same final node: $G = \{\pi_1, \ldots, \pi_m\}$ such that $\forall\pi_i$: $\alpha_1, \alpha_n \in \pi_i$.

We use a simplified version of operator definitions that does without a delete list of items to be removed from the current state description: an operator is a pair $\langle P,E\rangle$ with P being a formula as precondition and E a set of formulas that describes the effects of the action.

States are modified just by extending the current state by the effects of an instance of an operator: $M_i = M_{i-1} \cup E$. A plan $\pi = \langle\alpha_1, \ldots, \alpha_n\rangle$ will be

[2] We should note that our approach is actually too simple to treat all epistemic uses. Epistemic interpretations express the speaker's estimation of the probability that a state of affairs comes true; we are just able to check whether some information was already given or is assumed to be new for the user.

accepted if all tasks α_i are applicable in the corresponding states: $M_{i-1} \vdash P_{\alpha i}$

Given these standard definitions, the conditions for the modal forces are as follows:

$\Box(\alpha_j)$ iff $\forall \pi_i \in G: M\alpha_{j-1} \vdash P_{\alpha j}$

$\Diamond(\alpha_j)$ iff $\exists \pi_i \in G: M\alpha_{j-1} \vdash P_{\alpha j}$

4.2 Pragmatic constraints

Our formulation of pragmatic constraints is based on Zeevat's (2003, 2004) work on speech act marking. Basically, Zeevat describes speech act markers (focus markers, modal particles, and others) as planning operators with preconditions and effects. Three speech acts and their constraints shall demonstrate how speech act marking works in our approach.

4.2.1 Permissions

Generally, a permission expresses that the addressee's goal is compatible with the goals of the speaker. Preconditions for realizing this speech act are:

- The speaker is socially superordinate to the listener. We believe that this essential condition is satisfied due to the user's acceptance of CAN as a supporting system.
- The propositional content of the sentence is compatible with the plan graph.

Context marking is not necessary. The system checks whether the user's favoured courses $\{c_1, \ldots, c_n\}$ can be mapped onto at least one of the generated plans: $\exists \pi_i: \forall c_j: c_j \in \pi_i$.

If these conditions are satisfied, the modal verb *dürfen* (may) is used since (1) it is an admissible modal verb for the underlying deontic background, (2) it expresses possibility as modal force, i.e. the mentioned compatibility of the conversational background with the propositional content (the user's courses), and – due to the first condition mentioned above - it may be used as illocutionary indicator of permissions.

4.2.2 Reminders

Reminders draw on the discourse record as epistemic conversational background. The preconditions concern context marking: the content must already be suggested in the conversational background.

We are able to adopt Zeevat's (2004:102) characterisation who takes the relation *old* as context marker:

> *old*(CG,ϕ) iff CG $\models$ *suggested*(ϕ), and *suggested* is defined by means of a set of operators $\{O_1, .., O_n\}$ like *x dreams that, x believes that* etc.: *suggested*(ϕ) $\leftrightarrow$ $\phi \vee O_1$ *suggested*(ϕ) $\vee \ldots \vee O_n$ *suggested*(ϕ).

Since we are not dealing with attitude contexts, our approach is a scaled-down version of Zeevat's proposal. The system checks whether the proposition had been inserted into the discourse record some time ago (in this case, CG $\models \phi$ is trivially satisfied). If this is the case, the modal particle *ja* or *doch* is used because these particles expresses possibility as modal force (compatibility of the propositional content with a plan) and signal the reminder.

4.2.3 Recommendations

Recommendations declare a certain state of affairs as advantageous with respect to some goal. Computationally, this is an optimization problem: attending a course in a specific semester is advantageous for the completion of the course of study, if its attendance optimizes the number of semesters for that completion.

If some course c becomes relevant – either it was selected by the user or is given in the knowledge base – the precondition is: $\exists \pi_i, \pi_j$ with $c \in \pi_i, \pi_j$ and $|\pi_i| < |\pi_j|$.

If such an optimal attendance exists, the subjunctive form *sollte* (should) is used. *Sollte* expresses possibility, may be used for deontic backgrounds, and is an illocutionary indicator of recommendations.

4.3 Example outputs

The following three examples show the context-dependent choice of modals, depending on the user's input, the information in the knowledge base, and the previous course of the interaction with the system. Note that the multiple occurrence of modals within one clause is possible:

- The user selects a course of type „synchronic linguistics“:

CAN: *Wenn Sie einen Kurs [Typ Synchronie] im Grundkursmodul „Germanistische Linguistik" besuchen wollen, dann müssen Sie den Grundkurs Germanistische Linguistik, Teil 2 besuchen.*

If you want to attend a synchronic linguistics course in the basic module „Germanic Linguistics", then you must attend part 2 of the basic course on Germanic Linguistics.

The generated conditional sentence contains a modal verb in the if-clause (*wollen*, want) and in the main clause (*müssen*, must). *Wollen* is used because the user declares attending a course of some type as his goal. This goal is compatible with at least one plan, viz. the plan that declares such a course in the current semester. Since this course must necessarily be attended to achieve the user's goal (every plan with the user's goal as final task contains this course), *müssen* is used. Speech act-related conditions are not relevant for this sentence.

- The user selects the semantics course again, after some other course selections:

  CAN: *Sie dürfen doch dieses Semester den Kurs „Semantik" nicht belegen, weil Sie nicht alle Voraussetzungen erfüllen.*

  You must not attend the semantics course, because you do not satisfy all prerequisites – did you forget this?

The generated sentence contains the negated modal verb *dürfen* (may) and the modal particle *doch*. The former (*nicht dürfen*) is used because there is no plan containing the wanted course in the respective semester (incompatibility of the user's input with the generated plans). For the same reason, the preconditions of a permission are not applicable. The particle has been chosen because the user selected the same course some time ago. The incompatibility is derived from the discourse model so that the sentence is a reminder on speech act level. The sentence also explains why the course is incompatible with each plan.

- The user selects two courses with overlapping hours:

  CAN: *Sie wollen „Strukturen einer Einzelsprache" und „Einführung in die Linguistik" besuchen. Allerdings überschneiden sie sich zeitlich. Sie müssen eine andere Auswahl treffen.*

  You want to attend „Structures of a Language" and „Introduction to Linguistics". Both courses temporally overlap, however. You must make a different decision.

This example shows the linguistic output in case of a conflict. The modal verb *wollen* expresses the compatibility of the user's goal with a plan. This plan contains the conflict mentioned in the second sentence. The use of *müssen* in the final sentence is motivated by the necessity to find a conflict-free plan.

5 Summary and future work

The approach to the choice of modals described in this paper does not require modal logic formulas as content representations. However, since the use of modals signals talking about alternative scenarios/ worlds, one needs a way of representing these alternatives. We solved this problem by letting the planner create all possible plans for the same initial and final state. This bundle of equal plans allows us to determine the modal force by means of quantifying plan nodes. This semantic analysis restricts the set of modal candidates to those items that are able to express the determined modal force. A further diminution of this set is achieved by considering speech-act related conditions the modals must satisfy.

Our future work comprises broadening the set of modals (especially modal adverbs and syntactic constructions with modal meanings), a more elaborated treatment of modal forces, and the evaluation of the system's behaviour.

Thus far we treat modal forces from a traditional viewpoint: there are two forces and nothing in between. However, there are several linguistic means to signal different degrees of modal forces (various modal adverbs, the subjunctive, and others). Quantifying over the plan nodes should be a suitable means to model these varying modal forces. Just as generalized quantifiers express different relations between two sets, we should be able to trace back the modal forces to relations between all available nodes and those that express propositional units.

Finally, we are planning to provide CAN with a web interface in order to gain comments on the linguistic adequacy of the generated modals. Comments from students who played around with the system seem to suggest that the modal verbs are appropriate but the use of the modal particles could be bemusing. The use of modal particles seems to be deeply rooted in ordinary, "real" conversation so that some students were confused when CAN generates a sentence with a chummy connotation. The evaluation shall clarify whether the modals support the acceptance of the expressed content.

Acknowledgements

I thank Alexander Linke and Arne Ruhnau for their implementation work in Perl and the reviewers for their helpful comments.

References

Appelt, D.E. (1985) *Planning English sentences.* Cambridge University Press, Cambridge.

Blühdorn, H. (2004) *Temporalkonnektoren: Einleitung.* In H. Blühdorn, E. Breindl and U. Hermann (eds.), Brücken schlagen. Grundlagen der Konnektorensemantik, de Gruyter, Berlin/New York, pp. 125-136.

Elhadad, M. (1995) *Using argumentation in text generation.* Journal of Pragmatics, 24, pp. 189-220.

Fikes, R., P. Hart & N.J. Nilsson (1972) *Learning and executing generalized robot plans.* Artificial Intelligence, 3(4), pp. 251-288.

Klabunde, R. (2007) *Generating modals.* Proceedings of the Seventh International Workshop on Computational Semantics, Tilburg; pp. 342-345.

Kratzer, A. (1981) The notional category of modality. In H.-J. Eikmeyer & H. Rieser (eds.) Words, Worlds, and Contexts. De Gruyter, Berlin, pp. 38-74.

Moriceau, V. (2006) *Generating intelligent numerical answers in a question-answering system.* Proceedings of the Fourth International Natural Language Generation Conference, Sydney, pp. 96-103.

Papafragou, A. (2006) *Epistemic modality and truth conditions.* Lingua, 116, pp. 1688-1702.

Reiter, E. and Dale, R. (2000) *Building Natural Language Generation Systems.* Cambridge. Cambridge University Press.

Reiter, E., R. Robertson & L. Osman (2003) *Lessons from a Failure: Generating Tailored Smoking Cessation Letters.* Artificial Intelligence, 144, pp. 41-58.

Roberts, C. (1989) *Modal subordination and pronominal anaphora in discourse.* Linguistics & Philosophy, 12 (6), pp. 683-721.

Werner, T. (2006) *Future and non-future modal sentences.* Natural Language Semantics, 14, pp. 235-255.

Zeevat, H. (2003) The syntax semantic interface of speech act markers. *Proceedings of Diabruck 03.* 7th Workshop on the Semantics and Pragmatics of Dialogue.

Zeevat, H. (2004) *Particles: Presupposition Triggers, Context Markers or Speech Act Markers.* In R. Blutner & H. Zeevat (eds.) Optimality Theory and Pragmatics. Palgrave Macmillan, London, pp. 91-111.

Measuring Variability in Sentence Ordering for News Summarization

Nitin Madnani[a,b] **Rebecca Passonneau**[c] **Necip Fazil Ayan**[a,b] **John M. Conroy**[d]
Bonnie J. Dorr[a,b] **Judith L. Klavans**[e] **Dianne P. O'Leary**[a,b] **Judith D. Schlesinger**[d]
[a]Department of Computer Science
[b]Institute for Advanced Computer Studies
University of Maryland, College Park
{nmadnani,nfa,bonnie,oleary}@cs.umd.edu
[c]Center for Computational Learning Systems, Columbia University
becky@cs.columbia.edu
[d]IDA/Center for Computing Sciences
{conroy,judith}@super.org
[e]College of Information Studies, University of Maryland, College Park
jklavans@umd.edu

Abstract

The issue of sentence ordering is an important one for natural language tasks such as multi-document summarization, yet there has not been a quantitative exploration of the range of acceptable sentence orderings for short texts. We present results of a sentence reordering experiment with three experimental conditions. Our findings indicate a very high degree of variability in the orderings that the eighteen subjects produce. In addition, the variability of reorderings is significantly greater when the initial ordering seen by subjects is different from the original summary. We conclude that evaluation of sentence ordering should use multiple reference orderings. Our evaluation presents several metrics that might prove useful in assessing against multiple references. We conclude with a deeper set of questions: (a) what sorts of independent assessments of quality of the different reference orderings could be made and (b) whether a large enough test set would obviate the need for such independent means of quality assessment.

1 Introduction

The issue of ordering content in a multi-document extractive summary is an important problem that has received little attention until recently. Sentence ordering, along with other factors that affect coherence and readability, is of particular concern for multi-document summarization, where different source articles contribute sentences to a summary. We conducted an exploratory study to determine how much variation humans would produce in a reordering task under different experimental conditions, in order to assess the issues for evaluating automated reordering.

While a good ordering is essential for summary comprehension (Barzilay et al., 2002), and recent work on sentence ordering (Bollegala et al., 2006) does show promise, it is important to note that determining an optimal sentence ordering for a given summary may not be feasible. The question for evaluation of ordering is whether there is a single best ordering that humans will converge on, or that would lead to maximum reading comprehension, or that would maximize another extrinsic summary evaluation measure. On texts of approximately the same length as summaries we look at here, Karamanis et al. (2005) found that experts produce different sentence orderings for expressing database facts about archaeology. We find that summaries of newswire have a relatively larger set of coherent orderings.

We conducted an experiment where human subjects were asked to reorder multi-document summaries in order to maximize their coherence. The summaries used in this experiment were originally produced by a different set of human summarizers as part of a multi-document summarization task that was conducted by NIST in 2004. We present quantitative results that show that there is a large amount of variability among the reorderings considered coherent. On this basis, we suggest that evaluation of sentence ordering should use multiple references.

For each such summary in the experiment, we create three initial sentence orderings: (a) original order (b) random order, and (c) the output of an automated ordering algorithm. We show that:

- The initial orderings presented to the human subjects have a statistically significant impact on the reorderings that they create.
- The set of individual human reorderings ex-

hibits a significant amount of variability.

The next section provides some background for the sentence ordering task and presents the automated sentence ordering algorithm used in our experiments. Section 3 describes the experimental design. Sections 4 and 5 present quantitative analyses of the results of the experiment. Section 6 discusses related work. We discuss our results in Section 7 and conclude in Section 8.

2 Sentence Ordering Algorithms

A number of approaches have been applied to sentence ordering for multi-document summarization (Radev and McKeown, 1999). The first techniques exploited chronological information in the documents (McKeown et al., 1999; Lin and Hovy, 2002). Barzilay et al. (2002) were the first to discuss the impact of sentence ordering in the context of multi-document summarization in the news genre. They used an augmented chronological ordering algorithm that first identified and clustered related sentences, then imposed an ordering as directed by the chronology. Okazaki et al. (2004) further improved the chronological ordering algorithm by first arranging sentences in simple chronological order, then performing local reorderings.

More recent work includes probabilistic approaches that try to model the structure of text (Lapata, 2003) and algorithms that use large corpora to learn an ordering and then apply it to the summary under consideration (Bollegala et al., 2005).

Conroy et al. (2006) treat sentence ordering as a Traveling Salesperson Problem (TSP), similar to Althaus et al. (2004). Starting from a designated first sentence, they reorder the other sentences so that the sum of the *distances* between adjacent sentences is minimized. The distance (c_{jk}) between any pair of sentences j and k is computed by first obtaining a similarity score (b_{jk}) for the pair, and then normalizing this score:

$$c_{jk} = 1 - \frac{b_{jk}}{\sqrt{b_{jj}}\sqrt{b_{kk}}}, \ (c_{jj} = 0) \quad (1)$$

Because a typical multi-document extractive summary usually contains a small number of sentences, a near-optimal solution to this TSP can be found either by exhaustive search or by random sampling. In this paper, we use this TSP ordering algorithm to construct one of the three experimental conditions.

3 Experimental Design

We designed an experiment to test two hypotheses: (1) that the initial orderings presented to the human subjects have a statistically significant impact on the reorderings that they create, and (2) that the set of individual human reorderings exhibits a significant amount of variability.

For our experiment, we randomly chose nine 100-word human-written summaries[†] out of 200 human written summaries produced by NIST; they were used as references to evaluate extractive multi-document summaries in 2004 (Harman, 2004). We later retrieved the quality judgments performed by NIST assessors on seven of the summaries; the remaining two were used as a reference model for assessors and had no quality judgments. The seven summaries for which we had judgments were all given high ratings of 1 or 2 (out of 5) on seven questions such as, *Does the summary build from sentence to sentence to a coherent body of information about the topic?*

The nine summaries were evenly divided into three different groups: S_{1-3}, S_{4-6} and S_{7-9}. For each summary, we used three orderings:

- **O**: the original ordering of sentences in the summary, as written by the author of the summary.
- **R**: a random ordering of the sentences
- **T**: an ordering created by applying the TSP ordering algorithm described in the previous section.

We constrained the random and the TSP orderings so that the first sentence of the human summary appeared first.

Eighteen human subjects were divided into three groups (I, II, and III), 6 subjects per group. We presented each subject with each of the nine summaries, in either its original ordering (condition C_O), random ordering (condition C_R), or TSP ordering (condition C_T), as described in the Latin square design of Figure 1. For example, the six subjects in group II were presented with summaries $1-3$ in random order, $4-6$ in original order, and $7-9$ in TSP order. Thus the experiment produced 18 reorderings for each of the nine summaries, six per initial order.

[†]D30024-C (Document set D30024, NIST author ID C), D31022-F, D31008-E, D30048-C, D30037-A, D30001-A, D30051-D, D30015-E, D31001-C

	S_{1-3}	S_{4-6}	S_{7-9}
C_O	I	II	III
C_R	II	III	I
C_T	III	I	II

Figure 1: Latin Square Design

The human subjects chosen for the experiment were all native English speakers. Subjects accessed the task on a website, including the instructions, which explained that they would be reading a document on the screen and could reorder the sentences in that document so as to make the document more coherent. In order to prevent the introduction of any bias, the order of presentation of summaries was randomized for every subject. The instructions clearly specified the possibility that summaries might need little or no reordering. It would be difficult to measure whether the instructions led subjects to believe that all summaries could be improved by reordering. We do not have objective criteria to identify a control set of summaries that cannot be improved by reordering; in fact, this is a subjective judgement that is likely to vary between individuals. Because the three experimental conditions had the same instructions, we believe the significant differences in *amount* of reordering across conditions is a real effect rather than an artifact.

4 Variability across Experimental Conditions

To measure the variability across the experimental conditions, we developed two methods that assign a global score to each set of reorderings by comparing them to a particular reference point.

4.1 Method 1: Confusion Matrices and κ

In NLP evaluation, *confusion matrices* have typically been used in annotation tasks (Bruce and Wiebe (1998), Tomuro (2001)) where the matrix represents the comparison of two judges, and the κ inter-annotator agreement metric value (Cohen, 1960) gives a measure of the amount of agreement between the two judges, after factoring out chance. However, κ has been used to quantify the observed distribution in confusion matrices of other types in a range of other fields and applications (e.g., assessing map accuracy (Hardin, 1999), or optical recognition (Ross et al., 2002)). Here we use it to quantify variability within sets of reorderings for a summary.

Given a representation of each summary as a set of sequentially indexed sentences (e.g., 1, 2, 3, 4,

	1	2	3	4	5
1	5	0	0	1	0
2	1	3	1	0	1
3	0	2	2	1	1
4	0	0	2	2	2
5	0	1	1	2	2

Figure 2: Confusion matrix for a set of reorderings (summary 1, condition=C_O, reference=O; κ=0.33)

5), and of each reordering as a corresponding sequence of positional indices, we can create confusion matrices as in Figure 2. The rows represent the sequential positions of the summary sentences in one of the three initial orders that subjects were presented with, the columns represent the sentence indices, and each cell value m_{ij} indicates how often sentence j occurred in position i. Figure 2 shows the confusion matrix obtained by comparing the 6 reorderings for summary 1, obtained under the C_O experimental condition, to the original order (O) for that summary. The first column of the figure indicates that among the reorderings under consideration, five have sentence 1 in the first position, and one has sentence 1 in the second position. If all reorderings reproduced the original order O, the five cells of the matrix on the main diagonal would all have the value 6, and all other cells would have the value 0. The column headings of the corresponding confusion matrix for the random order (R) correspond to the sequence R, and similarly for (T).

In the general case (any agreement matrix), κ measures whether the distribution of values within a matrix differs from the distribution that would be predicted by chance; the ratios of column and row marginals to the matrix total provide estimates of the expected values within each cell. Given a confusion matrix where the cells on the matrix diagonal are denoted as n_{ii}, the row marginals as n_{i+}, the column marginals as n_{+i} and the matrix total as n_{++}, the formula for κ is:

$$\kappa = \frac{\sum_i P_{ii} - \sum_i P_{i+}P_{+i}}{1 - \sum_i P_{i+}P_{+i}} \tag{2}$$

where $P_{ii} = \frac{n_{ii}}{n_{++}}$ (the proportion of cases where a sentence ended up in its original slot), $P_{+i} = \frac{n_{+i}}{n_{++}}$, and $P_{i+} = \frac{n_{i+}}{n_{++}}$. If all cells on the diagonal are 6, κ is equal to 1. The question of interest to us is how closely a given matrix approximates this degree of agreement with the initial order.

For each summary 1-9 and for each condition,

we construct three confusion matrices: one with each initial order O, R, and T as the *target* of comparison. We denote the corresponding κ values as κ_O, κ_R, and κ_T. In principle, κ values range from 1 to values approaching -1, with 1 indicating perfect agreement, 0 indicating no difference from chance, and negative values indicating disagreements greater than expected by chance. Here, because all row and column marginals necessarily sum to 6, κ ranges from 1 to 0, with 1 indicating that the set of reorderings all reproduce the initial ordering, and 0 indicating that the set of reorderings conforms to chance.

4.2 Method 2: Means Vectors and Three Correlation Metrics

Our second method for measuring the amount of variability in a set of reorderings is based on the observation that each reordering is the same length as the initial ordering, and that each sentence index must occur exactly once per reordering. Each set of reorderings can be represented by a *means vector*, where each element of the vector is the mean sentence index for all reorderings in that set. We use three correlation metrics to give different measures of how well a means vector correlates with the initial orderings O, R and T.

The mean of the indices in each sentence position will more nearly approximate the original sentence index in that position when there are fewer instances of substituting a different sentence, and when substitutions involve sentences that were originally closer to the given slot. Figure 3 gives a hypothetical example in which each of the 6 subjects used the same ordering shifted by one: half the subjects shifted the summary by starting with the last sentence, then continuing from sentence 1 through 5 in sequence; the other half shifted the summary by starting with sentence 2 and continuing in sequence, with sentence 1 in the last position. Comparison of the means vector to the original order (O) indicates that this set of reorderings is quite similar to the original for the second through fifth positions and different in the first and last positions.

There are many distributions of sentences within a set of reorderings that can lead to the same means vector, thus we lose the power to identify some of the differences between individual reorderings within an experimental condition. However, the question we want to assess is whether the pattern given by a set of reorderings taken as a whole correlates well with the initial presentation order. We

O	1	2	3	4	5	6
S_1	2	3	4	5	6	1
S_2	6	1	2	3	4	5
S_4	6	1	2	3	4	5
S_3	2	3	4	5	6	1
S_5	2	3	4	5	6	1
S_6	6	1	2	3	4	5
Mean	4	2	3	4	5	3

Figure 3: A hypothetical example illustrating Means Vectors

compute means vectors for each condition for each summary, giving 27 such vectors. We compare each means vector representing a set of reorderings to each initial ordering O, R and T using three correlation coefficients: Pearson's r, Spearman's ρ, and Kendall's τ (Lapata, 2006).

The three correlation coefficients test the closeness of two series of numbers, or two variables x and y, in different ways. Pearson's r is a parametric test of whether there is a perfect linear relation between the two variables. Spearman's ρ and Kendall's τ are non-parametric tests. Spearman's ρ is computed by replacing the variable values by their rank and computing the correlation. Kendall's τ is based on counting the number of pairs x_i, x_{i+1} and y_i, y_{i+1} where the deltas of both pairs have the same sign. In sum, the three metrics test whether x and y are in a linear relation, a rank-preserving relation, or an order-preserving relation. Since we are comparing a set of reorderings to an initial order, rather than two sequences, it is unclear to us what grounds there would be for preferring one correlation over another. Given the exploratory nature of this method, we chose to compare results across metrics in order to determine empirically whether they support the same conclusions.

4.3 Results

The two scoring methods yield 12 global scores‡ per summary per experimental condition, or twenty seven observations per score. We computed ANOVAs (analysis of variance) for each of the twelve scores in turn, with the score as the dependent variable and with summary number and condition as factors. Condition had a significant effect for all three κ metrics, and for r_O, ρ_O, τ_O and τ_T. This indicates that the mean score for the nine summaries differs, depending on the condition, for these seven

‡4 metrics (κ, r, ρ, τ) and three initial orders (O, R and T) as targets of comparison

Metric	p-value	HSD	D_1	δ_1	D_2	δ_2
κ_O	0.004027	0.1370	$C_O > C_R$	0.2768	$C_O > C_T$	0.2143
κ_R	0.0001682	0.0858	$C_R > C_O$	0.2279	$C_R > C_T$	0.1929
κ_T	0.002455	0.1356	$C_T > C_O$	0.2848	$C_T > C_R$	0.2325
r_O	0.00004985	0.1556	$C_O > C_R$	0.4646	$C_T > C_R$	0.3643
r_R	0.7604	-	-	-	-	-
r_T	0.1135	-	-	-	-	-
ρ_O	0.0003774	0.2006	$C_O > C_R$	0.5103	$C_T > C_R$	0.3983
ρ_R	0.931	-	-	-	-	-
ρ_T	0.09643	-	-	-	-	-
τ_O	0.0004306	0.2129	$C_O > C_R$	0.5338	$C_T > C_R$	0.4209
τ_R	0.8394	-	-	-	-	-
τ_T	0.03532	0.2482	$C_O > C_R$	0.3685	$C_T > C_R$	0.2957

Table 1: Analysis of variance (ANOVA) using Tukey's HSD for twelve global scores

of the twelve scores we computed. In all cases, summary was a non-significant factor, meaning that the means of the specified metric (e.g., κ_O) do not vary depending on the summary.

Table 1 presents the p-values for the analysis of variance of each metric with condition as a factor. A significant p-value indicates that there is a significant effect of condition on the mean, but does not indicate whether the means for each condition were significantly different from all others. We use Tukey's Honest Significant Difference (HSD) method to examine the significant differences in more detail. For each score, Table 1 shows Tukey's HSD (the delta at which two means become significantly different), the pairs of conditions whose difference in means was greater than the HSD, and the actual deltas. For example, row 1 of the table indicates that the mean κ_0 is higher in condition O (C_O) than in condition R (C_R) by 0.2768, which is approximately twice the HSD of 0.1370. In all cases where condition was significant, two out of the three possible differences were statistically significant.

For each κ row, the initial order that is used as the *target* is also the order defining the condition whose mean κ scores are significantly greater than both other conditions; thus for κ_O (comparison to the original order O), the C_O condition (where subjects reordered O) is the one that has statistically significant differences from the other two. In other words, no matter what the target is, analysis of variance of the mean κ scores shows that the reorderings created under condition C_O have a non-chance similarity to the O ordering that is significantly greater than the other two reordering conditions; the reorderings under condition C_R have a non-chance similarity to the R ordering that is significantly greater than the other two reordering conditions; the reorderings under condition C_T have a non-chance similarity to the T ordering that is significantly greater than the other two orderings. The sizes of the δs are roughly the same. There are no other significant differences.

The κ scores provide one type of evidence showing that taken as a set, the initial order that a set of subjects are presented with has a statistically significant effect on the reorderings that they produce; the reorderings they produce will always be significantly closer to the initial order they are presented with, with chance similarity factored out, than to any of the other two initial orders.

For the three correlation coefficients that compare the means vectors to one of the three possible targets, the experimental condition has a significant effect on the means of the coefficient only for the cases where the target is the original order (O). In other words, there is no significant difference, depending on experimental condition, in the mean r, ρ, or τ scores when the sets of reorderings are compared with the random (R) or TSP (T) order, with one exception. There is also a significant difference in the means of τ when the sets of reorderings are compared with the TSP ordering. However, the effect is less significant than when compared with the O ordering, and the HSD is greater.

The results for r scores indicate that sets of reorderings created under conditions C_O and C_T have significantly higher mean correlations with the original order (O) than those under the C_R condition. The other correlation analyses have parallel results: both the C_O and C_T conditions have mean correlations with the O ordering (and with the T ordering, for τ) that are significantly higher than the C_R condition. These results suggest that not only is there a significant effect of the initial order on the range of reorderings produced, but also that under the C_R condition (subjects see a random order), the orderings produced are far more variable (less correlated with anything) than under the C_O and C_T conditions. r seems more sensitive than ρ or τ in that the HSDs are smaller.

5 Variability among Individual Subjects

The second analysis we performed was to measure the amount of variability among individual subjects. For this analysis, we use a variant of a method used by Karamanis et al. (2005) (based on (Lapata, 2003)). They first computed the average distance between each pair of expert pairs among 4 experts (6 pairs). Experts were then compared based on their average τ value, $\overline{\tau}$. When the $\overline{\tau}$ for a pair of experts is high, the experts are quite similar on all reorderings. For three of the experts, the $\overline{\tau}$ scores for all pairwise combinations were found to be rather high, and not significantly different, while the fourth expert was different from the other three.

Where they had 16 observations for which they computed $\overline{\tau}$ scores (each expert performed 16 orderings of the same items), we have more observations overall, but far fewer on which to make a comparison among pairs of subjects. Within a given condition, we have 6 subjects (15 pairs) but only 3 summaries, which is not enough to justify comparing the mean τ scores. Thus, we measure the similarity of two subjects' orderings using Kendall's τ.

5.1 Results

For 18 subjects, there are $C(18, 2) = 153$ unique pairwise comparisons among subjects. We computed Kendall's τ for every pair of subjects and then applied analysis of variance to the τ scores. With τ score as the dependent variable, and summary number, pair id and condition as factors, all factors were highly significant ($p \simeq 0$).

From the fact that summary number is a significant factor in predicting mean τ scores, we can conclude that the 9 summaries differ from each other in terms of the variability among individuals. As in the earlier ANOVA presented in Table 1, we use Tukey's HSD to determine the magnitude of the difference in means that is necessary for statistical significance, and use this to identify which summaries have significant differences in the amount of similarity among subjects' reorderings.

Applying Tukey's method to summary number as a factor yields the differences shown in Table 2.

S_+	S_-
8, 9, 6, 5, 3, 1, 2, 4	> 7
8, 9, 6	$> 4, 2$
8, 9	$> 1, 3, 5$

Table 2: Tukey analysis of summary number as a factor on Kendall's τ scores between individual subjects' reorderings

Among the 36 pairs of comparisons, twenty were significantly different. Here we present only the significant comparisons, not the size of the HSD nor the deltas for each comparison. The column on the left (S_+) shows the summary numbers where the mean τ values for pairs of individuals were significantly greater than for the summary numbers in the right column (S_-). Each row summarizes $|S_+| \times |S_-|$ comparisons. With summary 7, there were lower τ values than for all other summaries, meaning individuals' orderings were least alike. There were two other sets of comparisons with significant differences: summaries 8, 9 and 6 had significantly higher τ values than 4 and 2, and summaries 8 and 9 had significantly higher τ values than 1, 3 and 5. No other comparisons among summaries had significantly distinct mean τ values.

If we were to apply Tukey's HSD to the pair id factor, which was also highly significant as a predictor of τ values, it becomes difficult to summarize the significant differences. There are $C(153, 2) = 11,628$ pairwise comparisons of pairs of subjects; of these, $4,225$ were found to be statistically significant, using Tukey's method, and an analogous table to Table 2 would have 210 lines. This demonstrates that, overall, there is a large amount of variability among the individuals' reorderings.

6 Related Work on Evaluating Sentence Ordering

Karamanis and Mellish (2005) also measure the amount of variability between human subjects. However, there are several dimensions of contrast between our experiment and theirs: Their experiment operates in a very distinct domain (archaeology) and genre (descriptions of museum artifacts) whereas we use domain-independent multi-document summaries derived from news articles. We use ordinary, English-speaking volunteers as compared to the domain and genre experts that they employ (archaeologists trained in museum labeling). In terms of the experimental design, we use a Latin square design with three experimental conditions whereas they have a single experimental condition. Another important difference is the nature of the ordering task itself—the task we chose was a simple text-to-text ordering task whereas their task was a modified fact-to-text ordering task, i.e., although their subjects saw sentences, it is not clear whether they were simply sentences corresponding to database facts and devoid of connectives, pronouns etc. We applied analysis of variance to all pairs of subjects' τ scores directly, rather than to the specialized scores that they compute, so we cannot directly compare results. However, the amount of variation we find seems far greater.

Barzilay et al. (2002) also conducted experiments that asked human subjects to create alternative orderings and showed that subjects rarely agreed on a single ordering for the given text. However, they did not conduct a detailed quantitative analysis of the amount of variability found in the set of human reorderings.

Okazaki et al. (2004) do ask the human judges to provide a corrected ordering for each ordering that they grade during evaluation. However, only *one* corrected ordering per summary is created. In addition, the number of humans subjects used for the evaluation task and the measures taken for circumventing bias, if any, are not reported. By contrast, our experiment uses a Latin Square with fully randomized presentation order to circumvent the introduction of any bias. Moreover, we create 18 corrected orderings for each summary and are, therefore, in a much better position to draw general conclusions about variability in sentence orderings for extractive news summaries.

Lapata (2003) required the human subjects to create multiple orderings so as to produce a coherent text but used all the human orderings solely for the purpose of comparing the proposed ordering technique and not for any form of variability analysis.

7 Discussion

Our most noteworthy finding is that for summaries of clusters of news articles, the degree of similarity of the reorderings to the original text is inversely related to the degree of randomness in the ordering that humans see. This gives us new insight into the sentence ordering task for humans. Our results suggest that humans are better at creating coherence from coherence than from incoherence. Even under the experimental condition with the lowest disorder (C_O), there is a significant amount of variation. While there is no single *best ordering*, there are better and worse orderings, and TSP generally seems better than a random set of orderings. This is clearly apparent from Table 1— if we look at the cases where we use the original order O as the target of comparison (first, fourth, seventh and tenth rows), column five shows that in 3 out of 4 cases, the C_T condition (where subjects were presented with the TSP ordered sentences) has significantly higher scores than the C_R condition (where they were presented with randomly ordered sentences). We conclude from this that evaluation of sentence ordering should use multiple references.

To evaluate against multiple references, we suggest that a variation of the metrics we present here can be used in which test orderings are each compared to a *set* of target orderings comprised of the multiple references for a given text, in contrast to our method of comparing a set to a single target ordering. In confusion matrices for each text, the columns would represent the sentence indices of the multiple references, the rows would represent the sequential positions of the algorithm output for that text, and the cell values m_{ij} would represent how often the ith sentence of the output ordering occurred in the jth position across the multiple references.

In using multiple references, we also need further research on how to assess the relative quality of each reference order, and how to assess whether differences in quality among the references affect the evaluation. We believe that the relative coherence of summaries depends on many factors besides sentence order. A raw comparison of the κ_O values for summary 8[‡‡], for example, gives unusual results: the C_R condition reorderings most closely reproduce the original summary, followed by the C_T condition. We had the impression on reading this summary that there is a relative lack of use of devices linking the sentences to one another, such as discourse connectives, lexical cohesion, or anaphora. This raises the question of whether such devices are less necessary to create readability in short texts. While the seven summaries for which we found quality ratings were of roughly equal quality (summary 8 had the highest possible quality ratings), the DUC quality assessments have been shown to differ between assessors (Passonneau et al., 2005).

In the DUC summarization evaluations, performance of systems is assessed by averaging over

[‡‡]Document Set: D30015, NIST Author ID: E

large numbers of conditions, e.g., different document sets with different characteristics. We believe our lack of knowledge about the range of factors affecting the ordering task, and the way they interact, can be partly compensated for by evaluating ordering algorithms over a wide range of inputs.

8 Conclusions and Future Work

We conducted a reordering experiment that aims to gauge the difficulty of the sentence ordering task in the context of short, domain-independent multi-document summaries. Our results indicate that the sets of reorderings produced by human subjects depend, in a statistically significant manner, on the initial orders that the subjects are shown. In addition, we also show the existence of significant variability among subjects' reorderings. Both facts support our claim that there are *multiple* coherent orderings for a given summary. We believe that this has a significant impact on the evaluation of automatic ordering algorithms—all such algorithms should be evaluated against multiple reference orderings.

Our experiment has quantified the range of variability in human generated orderings under three conditions. In our view, a second, extrinsic assessment of the quality of the various reorderings would be necessary in order to determine whether there are grounds for ranking different orderings of the same summary. An example of an extrinsic assessment would be reading comprehension under time constraints. In future work, we would like to extend our investigations to include extrinsic assessment.

9 Acknowledgments

We are indebted to Mirella Lapata for sharing resources useful for this work. This work has been supported under the GALE program of the Defense Advaned Research Projects Agency, Contract Nos. HR0011-06-2-001 and HR0011-06-C-0023. Any opinions, findings, conclusions or recommendations expressed in this paper are those of the authors and do not necessarily reflect the views of DARPA.

References

E. Althaus, N. Karamanis and A. Koller. 2004. Computing locally coherent discourses. In *Proceedings of ACL*.

R. Barzilay, N. Elhadad, and K. McKeown. 2002. Inferring strategies for sentence ordering in multidocument news summarization. *JAIR*, 17:35–55.

D. Bollegala, N. Okazaki, and M. Ishizuka. 2005. A machine learning approach to sentence ordering for multi-document summarization and its evaluation. In *Proceedings of IJCNLP*.

D. Bollegala, N. Okazaki, and M. Ishizuka. 2006. A bottom-up approach to sentence ordering for multi-document summarization. In *Proceedings of COLING/ACL*.

R. Bruce and J. Wiebe. 1998. Word-sense distinguishability and inter-coder agreement. In *Proceedings of COLING/ACL*.

J. Cohen. 1960. A coefficient of agreement for nominal scales. *Educational and Psychological Measurement*, 20:37–46.

J. M. Conroy, J. D. Schlesinger, D. P. O'Leary, and J. Goldstein. 2006. Back to basics: Classy 2006. In *Proceedings of DUC'06*.

P. Hardin. 1999. Comparing main diagonal entries in normalized confusion matrices: A bootstrapping approach. In *IEEE International GRS Symposium*.

D. Harman. 2004. *Proceedings of DUC'04*. Boston, MA.

N. Karamanis and C. Mellish. 2005. Using a corpus of sentence orderings defined by many experts to evalute metrics of coherence for text structuring. In *Proceedings of ENLG*.

M. Lapata. 2003. Probabilistic text structuring: Experiments with sentence ordering. In *Proceedings of ACL*.

M. Lapata. 2006. Automatic evaluation of information ordering: Kendall's tau. *Computational Linguistics*, 32(4):471–484.

C-Y. Lin and E. Hovy. 2002. Automated multi-document summarization in neats. In *Proceedings of HLT*.

K. McKeown, J. Klavans, V. Hatzivassiloglou, R. Barzilay, and E. Eskin. 1999. Towards multidocument summarization by reformulation: Progress and prospects. In *Proceedings of AAAI/IAAI*.

N. Okazaki, Y. Matsuo, and M. Ishizuka. 2004. Improving chronological sentence ordering by precedence relation. In *Proceedings of COLING*.

R. Passonneau, A. Nenkova, K. McKeown, and S. Sigelman. 2005. Applying the pyramid method in DUC 2005. In *Proceedings of DUC'05*.

D. R. Radev and K. McKeown. 1999. Generating natural language summaries from multiple on-line sources. *Computational Linguistics*, 24:469–500.

T. D. Ross, L. A. Westerkamp; R. L. Dilsavor, J. C. Mossing, and E. G. Zelnio. 2002. Performance measures for summarizing confusion matrices: The AFRL COMPASE approach. In *SPIE International Society for Optical Engineering Proceedings Series*.

N. Tomuro. 2001. Systematic polysemy and inter-annotator disagreement: Empirical examinations. In *Proceedings of the First International Workshop on Generative Approaches to Lexicon*.

Visualising Discourse Structure in Interactive Documents

Clara Mancini **Christian Pietsch** **Donia Scott**

Centre for Research in Computing
The Open University
Walton Hall, Milton Keynes, MK7 6AA, UK
{c.mancini,c.pietsch,d.scott}@open.ac.uk

Abstract

In this paper we introduce a method for generating interactive documents which exploits the visual features of hypertext to represent discourse structure. We explore the consistent and principled use of graphics and animation to support navigation and comprehension of non-linear text, where textual discourse markers do not always work effectively.

1 Introduction

There is a long and well-established literature within theoretical, computational and psycho-linguistics on textual devices that function to signal the coherence structure of a discourse to the reader. This work has addressed the traditional conceptualisation of text: a two-dimensional array on a physical page, traversed in a set pattern (e.g., left to right, top to bottom in the Western tradition). As texts are increasingly being read on a computer screen, the act of reading is progressively becoming one of hypertext navigation. However, hypertext presents a strikingly different conceptualisation of text, and brings with it new challenges for conveying discourse structure.

Hypertext is distinctive in that it is interactive and non-linear, with several reading paths available through the document. It is organised around *nodes* and *links*; the reader moves from node to node by mouse-clicking on links. A node can be the equivalent of a traditional text page or can contain just a few sentences; links can be words or graphical elements. Since nodes typically contain more than one link, the author can only partially control the order in which the reader will access them.

With hypertext, then, a new conceptualisation of text has emerged as a three-dimensional array on a computer screen, which can be traversed in any number of ways. One of the challenges this poses for text research is that coherence markers of the traditional notion of text often do not work for this new medium. We are exploring new possibilities for signalling coherence in non-linear documents, exploiting the graphical features of a visually rich medium yet to be systematically exploited as a dimension of signification. This work is set in the context of the textual presentation of medical records from a repository of data-encoded medical histories.

2 Structure representation in non-linear text

As we discuss elsewhere (Mancini et al., 2007), discourse markers such as adverbials, pronouns and connectives cannot reliably be used to signal the discourse relation between hypertext nodes, since nodes can be accessible in more than one way, via paths that reflect different relevancies. This restriction is less likely to apply to graphical features, because they are visual and work in space. Owing to its technical characteristics, hypertext is a spatial medium (Carter, 2000) as well as a temporal one (Luesebrink, 1998), in which spatial structures have a temporal dimension and realisation: both space and time can be exploited in hypertext to express discourse coherence through space-temporal configurations in a three-dimensional space.

At present, most hypertexts (especially on the Web) make no use of graphical features to signal discourse relations between nodes, and nodes often consist of long text pages with a few links targeting other pages, from where the source page can no longer be seen. We take a different approach whereby the text is made more readable in two ways: by making hypertext nodes much smaller and by using graphical features to signal the coherence relations between nodes. We use the screen as a visual field across which the text can dynamically distribute, as links are clicked and new nodes appear, composing meaningful patterns. The presentation and distribution of the nodes are intended to signify the rhetorical role that their content plays within the discourse. To achieve this, coherence relations are used as document structuring principles during discourse construction to define hypertext links. These are then dynamically rendered during navigation through the consistent and concurrent use of the medium's spatial and temporal graphic features connoting the nodes. We refer to this paradigm as *cinehypertext*.

Having established a parallel between textual and visual processing, research informed by Gestalt theory has proposed relevant principles of document design (Campbell, 1995; Riley and Parker, 1998). Additionally, a number of representational rules for visually expressing discourse relations between hypertext nodes can be derived from the semiology of graphics, according to which graphic features can be employed to express conceptual relationships of *similarity*, *difference*, *order* and *proportion*, exploiting the properties of the visual image (Koch, 2001). Following these principles and rules, we have designed and begun testing a series of prototype visual patterns expressing coherence relations in non-linear discourse (Mancini et al., 2007).

3 Graphics devices to visualise interactive text structure

Our empirical work so far shows that graphics can indeed be used to express abstract relational concepts (Power et al., 2003; Mancini, 2005). But can graphics usefully support the expression of discourse structure in hypertext navigation? Can visual discourse markers support comprehension, substituting or complementing textual discourse markers in non-linear documents? If so, how do these textual and graphical features interact: can they express the same semantic meaning by following the same principles or do they, due to their different semiotic characteristics, function in different ways to the same end?

Our starting point is two NLG systems that generate, as linear text, summaries of a cancer patient's medical history (respectively generated to be read by clinicians and medical researchers, or by patients) from a repository of data-encoded medical reports (Hallett et al., 2006; Williams et al., 2007). We are extending these systems to generate interactive text on the one hand, and its animated graphical presentation, on the other. Since textual and graphical discourse markers will interact with each other,

> You had a consultation with your doctor on September 20th 1993.
>
> On September 27th you did a self examination and you found that you had a lump in your right breast. A self examination is an examination of the breasts by running your hand over each breast and up under your arms and checking for changes to their size, shape or feel.
>
> On October 4th you did another self examination and you found that you had a lump in your right breast.
>
> On October 11th you had a radical mastectomy to treat cancer in your right breast. A radical mastectomy is an operation to remove the breast, along with the lymph glands under the arm and the muscles of the chest wall. Cancer is a tumour that tends to spread, both locally and to other parts of the body.

Figure 1: Example section of a linear report generated for a patient.

our interactive documents may not present some of the textual features that occur in the corresponding linear form. We aim to provide a principled account of this interaction, and start by studying the effect of using visual markers on an interactive version of the linear reports already produced by our generators. Figure 1 shows an example section of a linear textual report.

At present, we transform a linear medical report into an interactive one by dividing the text into related chunks within text nodes whose graphics and animation features signal the relations holding between the chunks. In our example, the relations holding between the nodes are SEQUENCE, ELABORATION, MOTIVATION and RESULT. We generate graphical presentations of these discourse relations, using motion trajectory, distribution, colour value and dimensions of text windows. Red arrows and bold fonts in the windows signal active links, whereas followed links are signalled by dark grey arrows and bold fonts.

Specifically, the SEQUENCE of events described in the report is expressed by the vertical alignment of text windows appearing one under the other and having the same width and background colour (Figure 2).

Causal relations, like RESULT and MOTIVATION, holding between events are expressed by the horizontal alignment of text windows having the same height, where the one representing the result slides out, moving from left to right, from behind the one representing the cause, having a darker background (Figure 3)

The expression of MOTIVATION is similar to that of RESULT, with the difference that this time the window representing the motivation moves from

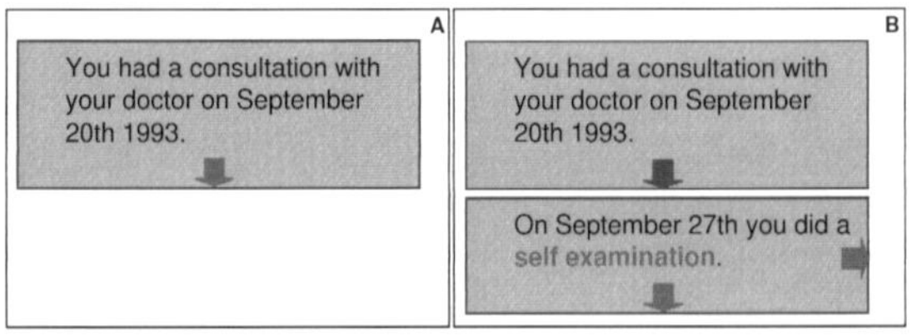

Figure 2: Representation of SEQUENCE: the red arrow link in the first node (A) is activated and the second node appears underneath it (B).

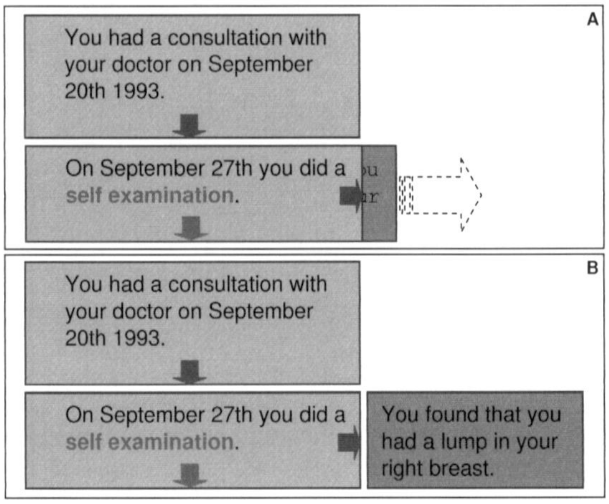

Figure 3: Representation of RESULT: the result-node slides out from behind the cause-node (A) placing itself next to it on the right hand side (B).

right to left and has a lighter background (Figure 4).

Finally, the definitions for which an explanation is available constitute links whose activation triggers an ELABORATION node, which appears slightly overlapped along a virtual third dimension. While the background of the other nodes is grey, the background of elaborative nodes is a lighter tone of red (Figure 5).

We have been evaluating the significance of these and other visual patterns, while exploring new designs to express discourse relations in interactive documents of different formats. We are also implementing a prototype system that employs a selection of patterns to carry out more empirical studies. The architecture of the prototype is described below.

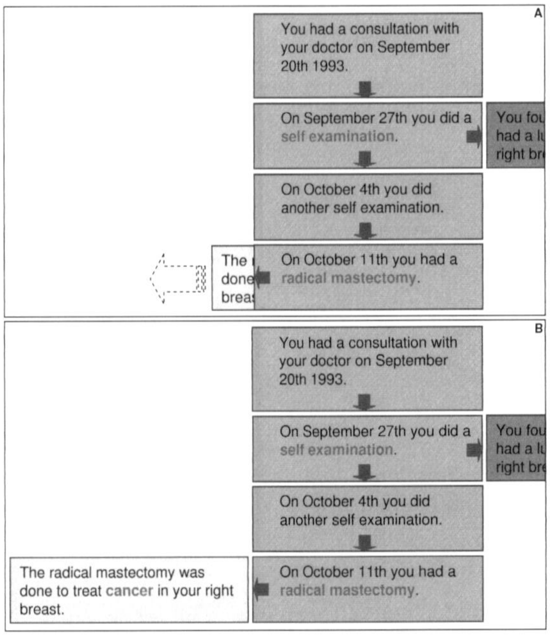

Figure 4: Representation of MOTIVATION: the motivation-node slides out from behind the consequence-node (A) placing itself to its left (B).

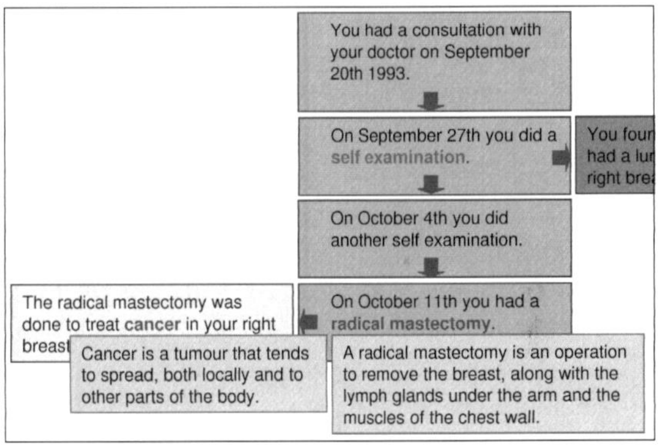

Figure 5: Representation of ELABORATION: the elaboration-node appears overlapped to the node containing the definition that is being elaborated on.

4 System architecture

Few existing text generators which produce HTML output actually use the properties of non-linear text fully. Sometimes HTML is used as a simple text formatting language. Where hyperlinks are provided, the rhetorical, semantic or pragmatic relation of the link target to the anchor is rarely made explicit. Our approach is a radical departure from this practise.

We propose an additional layer of abstraction embodied in a well-defined data format we call XCH (XML for CineHypertext), and describe a prototype architecture that extends previous approaches by providing a principled way of hyperlinking and animating content, thus encouraging the user to interact with the information dynamically presented. In fact

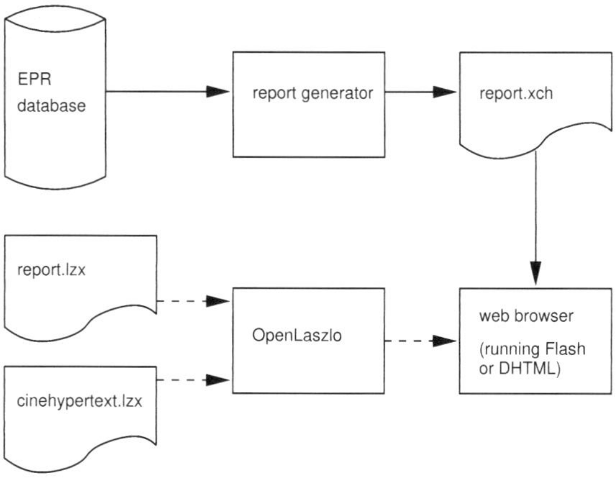

Figure 6: Prototype architecture. Solid arrows signify online data flow, dashed arrows signify data flow which occurred earlier.

we are crossing the border from document generation to application generation because the user interacts with a Rich Internet Application (RIA) which is very much data-driven.

Our XCH format is an instance of XML defined by two XML schema files. One is domain-independent and captures the range of semantic/pragmatic relations that can be encoded between chunks of information. The other is domain-specific and defines the document structure of (in the current prototype) a medical report.

Often, XML is processed using XSLT. Indeed a simple XSLT style sheet can be used to convert XCH to linear text. However, to transform XCH into the interactive and animated Web application we are aiming for, we prefer to use a Web toolkit. We chose OpenLaszlo which since version 4 is no longer restricted to one particular run-time platform for content delivery (Flash) but can also compile source code into AJAX-like DHTML code which is natively supported by most current browsers. OpenLaszlo also makes it very easy to animate any of its visual components (widgets). Its XML-based programming language (LZX) is as declarative as XSLT but adds object-orientation and supports creating reusable class libraries.

Figure 6 shows an overview of the current system architecture. Its upper half depicts an existing NLG system modified to produce XCH output. Its lower half outlines the new presentation module which takes XCH as input. Here, report.lxz is the domain-specific part of the presentation module implementation, and cinehypertext.lzx is the domain-independent, library part. We expect that our emerging cinehypertext library and format will prove useful in other domains and systems.

5 Conclusion

This work aims to identify ways of presenting hypertext discourse which employ graphics to signal discourse structure in a systematic and principled way, by making articulate use of the space-temporal dimensions of the electronic medium. The work is part of a larger effort in natural language generation, aimed at producing different renditions of the same semantic content for different purposes and for different media. One of the novel aspects of our work is that we are generating 'paraphrases' that vary not just along the traditional dimensions (discourse, syntax, lexicalisation) but also in terms of graphical presentation (e.g., as textual reports in different styles – including linear vs. non-linear – or as slides for a presentation).

References

K. S. Campbell. 1995. *Coherence, continuity, and cohesion. Theoretical foundations for document design*. Erlbaum, Hillsdale, NJ.

L. M. Carter. 2000. Arguments in hypertext. A rhetorical approach. In *Proceedings 11th ACM Conference on Hypertext and Hypermedia*, pages 87–91, New York. ACM.

C. Hallett, R. Power, and D. Scott. 2006. Summarisation and visualisation of e-health data repositories. In *UK E-Science All-Hands Meeting*, Nottingham, UK.

W. G. Koch. 2001. Jaques Bertin's theory of graphics and its development and influence on multimedia cartography. *Information Design Journal*, 10:37–43.

M. C. Luesebrink. 1998. The moment in hypertext. In *Proceedings 9th ACM conference on hypertext and hypermedia*, pages 106–112, New York. ACM.

C. Mancini, D. Scott, and S. Buckingham Shum. 2007. Visualising discourse coherence in non-linear documents. *Traitement Automatique des Langues, Special Issue on Computational Approaches to Document and Discourse*, 47(1). To appear.

C. Mancini. 2005. *Cinematic hypertext. Investigating a new paradigm*. IOS, Amsterdam.

R. Power, D. Scott, and N. Bouayad-Agha. 2003. Document structure. *Computational Linguistics*, 29:211–260.

K. Riley and F. Parker. 1998. Parallels between visual and textual processing. *IEEE Transactions on Professional Communication*, 41:175–185.

S. Williams, P. Piwek, and R. Power. 2007. Generating monologue and dialogue to present personalised medical information to patients. In *European Workshop on Natural Language Generation*, Prague. Submitted.

Abstract verbs

Richard Power
Department of Computing
Open University
Milton Keynes MK7 6AA, UK
r.power@open.ac.uk

Abstract

Existing generation systems use verbs almost exclusively to describe actions/events or to ascribe properties. In doing so, they achieve a direct concrete style of the kind often recommended in style manuals. However in many genres, including academic writing, it is common to find verbs expressing abstract relationships, with events etc. pushed down into nominalisations. This paper illustrates two important classes of abstract verb, one expressing discourse relations, the other expressing participant roles, and discusses some theoretical and practical reasons for studying such verbs and including them in generation systems.

1 Introduction

Many writing manuals enjoin us to freshen up our verbs. A bad writing style, they tell us, is characterised by overuse of abstract verbs like 'involve' and 'characterise' (oh dear), whereas good prose is enlivened by concrete verbs denoting actions and events. In his book *Style: Towards Clarity and Grace* (Williams, 1990) illustrates the two styles by comparing the following sentences:

> (A) Because we knew nothing about local conditions, we could not determine how effectively the committee had allocated funds to areas that most needed assistance.
>
> (B) Our lack of knowledge about local conditions precluded determination of committee action effectiveness in fund allocation to those areas in greatest need of assistance.

Sentence (A), most of us would agree, is clearly expressed, while its paraphrase (B) is turgid. The reason, according to Williams, is that the first sentence expresses actions through verbs (determine, allocate), while the second pushes them down into nominalisations.

Computational Linguists, like most academics, are often unable to resist the lure of the abstract verb. But how about our programs? Let us look at some output samples from Natural Language Generation (NLG) systems, as surveyed by Pavia (1998).

> Behrens's principal activities were architecture and industrial design. He made electrical appliances and prototype flasks. He built the high tension plant and the turbine factory for AEG in 1908-1910. He built a housing for the workers of AEG in Henningsdorf.
> *Komet, (Bateman and Teich, 1995)*

> To schedule the appointment:
> 1. Choose the start time of the appointment.
> 2. Enter the description of the appointment.
> 3. Click on the Insert button.
> *DRAFTER-2 (Power and Scott, 1998)*

> This jewel is a necklace and is in the Art Deco style. It was made in 1920. It is made from moonstone and silver rock-crystal. In colour, it is coral. It differs from the previous item, in that whereas that was made by Arthur and Georgie Gaskin, this was made by H.G.Murphy.
> *ILEX, (Oberlander et al., 1998)*

These typical products of current NLG present a paradox. On the one hand, they conform to the advice given by Joseph Williams and other style gurus. The verbs are concrete and usually denote actions (build, click, make). Noun phrases denote people and things rather than nominalised events or propositions. On the other hand, the texts are not really well-written; their short mechanical sentences suggest naivety and limited expressive resources. Concrete writing is not always good writing; turning this on its head, we might question whether the style manuals are really justified in dismissing an abstract style as necessarily bad. Perhaps we would do better to understand why abstract writing is common in some genres and whether it serves a purpose other than bamboozling the reader.

As Halliday among others has pointed out (Halliday and Martin, 1993), an abstract style is common in genres (like scientific writing) where **argument predominates over description**. In argument, it is often necessary to make comments upon propositions; therefore, we find many sentences in which the subject of the verb denotes a proposition (or a complex of propositions), either through a sentential complement, or a nominalisation, or an anaphoric reference to a proposition mentioned earlier. Because sentences of this kind are often needed in argumentative writing, they have taken on the significance of a hallmark through which academics can certify their distinctive professional expertise — the literary counterpart of the doctor's stethoscope or the lawyer's wig. As a result, academics (and bureaucrats, etc.) may feel **obliged** to write in this way, even when the subject-matter is not argumentative, and could be expressed through straightforward narration or description.

If this analysis is right, we should not dismiss abstract writing as bad writing, either when writing papers or when designing NLG systems. We should aim for mastery of both styles, so that the system can choose whichever is most appropriate in any given case.

2 Discourse verbs

The concept of an abstract verb is initially perplexing: when events or propositions are pushed down into nominalisations or sentential complements, what is left for the main verb to do? One obvious answer is that verbs can take over the task of signalling relations among propositions: in other words, they can express discourse relations.

Take for example sentence (B) from the last section, 'Our lack of knowledge about local conditions precluded determination of committee action effectiveness...'. The main verb here is 'precluded', and its meaning corresponds to the relation NON-VOLITIONAL CAUSE from Rhetorical Structure Theory (RST) (Mann and Thompson, 1987), with the extra twist that the nucleus is negated: in general, 'X precluded Y' means (roughly) 'Because X happened, Y could not happen'.

How common are verbs expressing discourse relations? This is a complex question that would require investigation of corpora from varied genres, but merely by consulting theasuruses or works like the *Cambridge English Lexicon* (Hindmarsh, 1980) we can confirm that there are many such verbs, especially for causal and inferential relations. Here for example are some causal verbs roughly grouped:

CAUSING: bring about, cause, induce, lead to, make
RESULTING: derive from, result from, stem from
INITIATING: launch, originate, set in motion, start
PROVOKING: arouse, elicit, evoke, provoke, trigger
HELPING: contribute to, facilitate, help, stimulate

Most of these can be used as alternatives to discourse connectives like 'because' and 'as a result', except that their meanings are usually more precise. For instance, 'Losing his job triggered John's depression' could be paraphrased roughly by 'John was depressed because he lost his job', but the discourse verb carries the extra implication that the depression acquired a momentum beyond the original cause.

Considering the obvious prevalence of such discourse verbs, the NLG literature is curiously silent. Almost everybody follows the standard line that rhetorical relations are realised by discourse connectives. In work based on RST, discourse relations are assumed to hold between clauses, as in the manual for marking up the RST Discourse Treebank (Carlson and Marcu, 2001), where discourse verbs are not mentioned at all. The only references we can find in NLG are from Laurence Danlos, who was the first to point out that verbs like 'cause' and 'precede' can signal the relations expressed by discourse connectives like 'because' and 'next', and to label such verbs *discourse verbs* (Danlos, 2006). Among other things, Danlos observes that the subject of a discourse verb is often an anaphoric reference to an event (or proposition) mentioned in a previous sentence, or sometimes to the agent of this event:

> Ted left. This preceded Sue's arrival.
>
> Ted didn't stop joking. This (He) caused hilarity among his friends.

We have seen examples of verbs for CAUSE and SEQUENCE; how about the other RST relations? Danlos does not pursue this issue because she is interested mainly in issues of lexical representation in the framework of Segmented Discourse Representation Theory. To show that verbs can be used across the whole spectrum of discourse relations, rather than one or two exceptional cases, the table below lists the original RST relations from Mann and Thompson (1987) with examples (where possible) using discourse verbs.

ANTITHESIS: Taking part in sport beats watching it on television
BACKGROUND: [No example]
CONCESSION: John's occasional mistakes do not mean he is not a good referee
ENABLEMENT: Filling in the enclosed form enables you to apply for membership
EVIDENCE: My learning the system in five minutes shows that it is easy to use
JUSTIFY: [No example]
CIRCUMSTANCE: The writing of his first novel coincided with his stay in Rome
SOLUTIONHOOD: Adding a scroll bar solves the problem of text not fitting on the screen
VOLITIONAL CAUSE: The dark clouds forming overhead motivated him to bring an umbrella
VOLITIONAL RESULT: Our boat journey was motivated by the serious flooding
NON-VOLITIONAL CAUSE: The abundant harvest brought about a surplus of corn
NON-VOLITIONAL RESULT: The bomb exploding in the shopping centre resulted in 30 people being hurt

PURPOSE: His trip to Selfridges served to buy a present for his sister
CONDITION: Claiming benefit requires that the mother is less than 18 years old
OTHERWISE: Late submission of papers will preclude their consideration
EVALUATION: Our offices being open 7 days a week adds up to a better service
RESTATEMENT: Omitting needless words means keeping your writing concise
SUMMARY: [No example]
SEQUENCE: Ted's departure preceded Sue's arrival
CONTRAST: John's liking for beetroot constrasts with Mary's disgust
JOINT: [No example]

3 Theta verbs

We have noted one kind of abstract verb, the category that Danlos calls 'discourse verbs'. Are there others? A plausible further candidate can be found in verbs like 'performed' and 'underwent' which express *thematic roles* — that is, relations between eventualities and their participants. When an event is described directly, these thematic roles are expressed implicitly by syntactic relations like subject and object:

The police interrogated the suspect

However, to highlight a thematic role we can also express it by a verb:

The police performed an interrogation
The suspect underwent an interrogation

As a label for this group I suggest *theta verbs*. Here is a list of examples for some common thematic roles; note that some circumstantial roles are equivalent to discourse relations so that we get some overlap with discourse verbs.

Participant roles

AGENT The doctor examined Mary ⇒ The doctor performed an examination (of Mary)
PATIENT The doctor examined Mary ⇒ Mary underwent an examination (by the doctor)
EXPERIENCER Mary feared her boss ⇒ Mary experienced a fear of her boss
BENEFICIARY John paid Mary compensation ⇒ Mary benefitted from (John's) payment of compensation
INSTRUMENT Mary opened the drawer with a hairpin ⇒ A hairpin was employed (by Mary) to open the drawer

Circumstantial roles

CAUSE John fell over by treading on a banana skin ⇒ Treading on a banana skin caused John's fall
PURPOSE John sacked Mary to reduce his costs ⇒ Reducing his costs motivated John's dismissal of Mary
MANNER John dismissed Mary quickly and insensitively ⇒ Speed and insensitivity characterised John's dismissal of Mary
PLACE The committee met in the city hall ⇒ The city hall housed the meeting of the committee
TIME The minister arrived in the afternoon ⇒ The afternoon saw the arrival of the minister

Some roles can be expressed by several verbs, with different shades of meaning (e.g., for AGENT we also have achieve, accomplish, commit, engineer, and so forth). There is also at least one verb that can express *any* thematic role, thus achieving a vagueness that may assist the non-commital writer (but not the reader):

AGENT: The dismissal involved an American employer
PATIENT: The dismissal involved an elderly secretary
EXPERIENCER: The fear of dismissal involved the staff
BENEFICIARY: The compensation payment involved the secretary
INSTRUMENT: Opening the drawer involved a hairpin
CAUSE: John's fall involved treading on a banana skin
PURPOSE: The dismissal involved reducing John's costs
MANNER: The dismissal of the secretary involved unseemly haste
PLACE: The committee meeting involved the city hall
TIME: The minister's arrival involved a Monday afternoon

4 Implications

One reason for studying abstract verbs is simply to enhance the quality and variety of generated texts. This would require (a) an expansion of grammars to cover formulations with abstract verbs, and (b) some kind of empirical investigation into when the use of an abstract verb is appropriate. However, discourse verbs (in particular) are also theoretically interesting because they challenge existing assumptions about rhetorical relations and their realization in discourse:

1. **Argument role**: In RST, argument roles are labelled *nucleus* and *satellite*; what happens to these roles when the relationship is expressed by a discourse verb? Using a verb introduces distinctions like given-new, and notions like agency, which are not relevant for discourse connectives.
2. **Syntactic features**: A discourse relation expressed by a verb can draw on the distinctions expressed by syntactic features like tense, aspect, voice, modality, and negation, most of which are irrelevant for discourse connectives. For instance, if the relation is EVIDENCE, the issue of when the evidential relationship was first noticed is made explicit by the tense of the verb.
3. **Span structure**: Discourse verbs provide additional evidence against RST's theory of span structure, as described by Knott et al. (2001).
4. **Repertoire of relations**: The classification of rhetorical relations might look very different

when based on evidence that includes discourse verbs as well as connectives.

Points 3 and 4 require some elaboration, which is given below.

4.1 Span structure

RST makes two central claims about span structure (Knott et al., 2001): first, that atomic spans are clauses; and second, that rhetorical relationships between spans (or their meanings) are expressed by combining adjacent spans through a schema application. The prototypical case is illustrated by the following text from the CLEF domain (Hallett et al., 2007) which realizes an EVIDENCE relation:

> The patient looks anaemic, so a packed red cell transfusion is probably needed.

The atomic spans are adjacent clauses, linked by a discourse connective ('so') expressing the rhetorical relation between them. Now consider the same message expressed using a discourse verb:

> The patient looks anaemic. This suggests the need for a packed red cell transfusion.

It is striking how an apparently minor change throws the RST analysis into confusion. First, the nucleus of the EVIDENCE relation is now expressed by a noun phrase; this means for example that it could not be marked up as a rhetorical argument in the RST Discourse Treebank (Carlson and Marcu, 2001). Second, this noun phrase is not linked directly to the span describing the anaemia, but rather to a pronoun ('this') coreferring anaphorically with this span. One could argue for some kind of presentational relation between the first sentence and the second (e.g., ELABORATION), but on such an analysis the rhetorical structure assigned to the text no longer addresses its main point.

4.2 Repertoire of relations

If we try to classify discourse relations with reference to discourse verbs rather than connectives, the most obvious change is that the verbs are more specific. We have illustrated this point already in listing causal verbs, which subclassify causal relations along several dimensions identified by Talmy (1988) (e.g., change/stasis, generation/enablement, weak/strong control, temporary/enduring effect). Consider for instance the following more specific alternatives to 'John was drowsy because he took antihistamines':

Taking antihistamines made John drowsy
Taking antihistamines kept John drowsy
Taking antihistamines enabled John to be drowsy
Taking antihistamines helped make John drowsy
Taking antihistamines triggered John's drowsiness

Such examples suggest that discourse verbs are far more effective than connectives in putting discourse relations under the microscope, at least for the groups of relations concerned with causality and inference.

References

J. A. Bateman and E. Teich. 1995. Selective information presentation in an integrated publication system: an application of genre-driven text generation. *Information Processing and Management*, 31(5):753–767.

Lynn Carlson and Daniel Marcu. 2001. Discourse tagging manual. Technical report, ISI Tech Report ISI-TR-545.

Laurence Danlos. 2006. Discourse verbs. In *Comparative study of connectives and discourse markers in the framework of a dynamic discourse semantics*, Toulouse, France.

Catalina Hallett, Donia Scott, and Richard Power. 2007. Composing queries through conceptual authoring. *Computational Linguistics*, page (forthcoming).

Michael Halliday and James Martin. 1993. *Writing Science: Literary and Discursive Power*. The Falmer Press, London, UK.

R. Hindmarsh. 1980. *Cambridge English Lexicon*. CUP, Cambridge, UK.

Alistair Knott, Jon Oberlander, Michael O'Donnell, and Chris Mellish. 2001. Beyond elaboration: The interaction of relations and focus in coherent text. In *Text representation: linguistic and psycholinguistic aspect*, pages 181–196, Amsterdam: Benjamins.

W. Mann and S. Thompson. 1987. Rhetorical structure theory: a theory of text organization. In L. Polyani, editor, *The structure of discourse*, Norwood, NJ. Ablex.

J. Oberlander, M. O'Donnell, A. Knott, and C. Mellish. 1998. Conversation in the museum: experiments in dynamic hypermedia with the intelligent labelling explorer. *New Review of Hypermedia and Multimedia*, 4:11–32.

Daniel S. Pavia. 1998. A survey of applied natural language generation systems. Technical report, ITRI Technical Report, University of Brighton, UK.

R. Power and D. Scott. 1998. Multilingual authoring using feedback texts. In *Proceedings of the 17th International Conference on Computational Linguistics and 36th Annual Meeting of the Association for Computational Linguistics*, pages 1053–1059, Montreal, Canada.

Leonard Talmy. 1988. Force dynamics in language and cognition. *Cognitive Science*, 12:49–100.

Joseph M. Williams. 1990. *Style: Towards clarity and grace*. University of Chicago Press, Chicago, USA.

An Architecture for Data-to-Text Systems

Ehud Reiter
University of Aberdeen
Aberdeen, UK
ereiter@csd.abdn.ac.uk

Abstract

I present an architecture for data-to-text systems, that is NLG systems which produce texts from non-linguistic input data; this essentially extends the architecture of Reiter and Dale (2000) to systems whose input is raw data instead of AI knowledge bases. This architecture is being used in the BABYTALK project, and is based on experiences in several projects at Aberdeen; it also seems to be compatible with many data-to-text systems developed elsewhere. It consists of four stages which are organised in a pipeline: Signal Analysis, Data Interpretation, Document Planning, and Microplanning and Realisation.

1 Introduction

Data-to-text systems are Natural Language Generation (NLG) systems which generate texts from non-linguistic input data, such as sensor data and event logs. Such systems need to perform data analysis as well as linguistic processing. In this paper I present a 4-stage pipeline architecture which I believe is suitable for many data-to-text systems. It is being used in a new project at Aberdeen, BABYTALK, and is partially based on our experiences with other data-to-text systems developed at Aberdeen.

Very briefly, the four stages are

1. *Signal Analysis:* Analysing numerical and other input data, looking for patterns and trends.
2. *Data Interpretation:* Identifying more complex (and domain-specific) messages from the patterns and trends detected in Signal Analysis; also identifying causal and other relations between messages.
3. *Document Planning:* Deciding which of the above messages should be mentioned in the generated text, and creating a document and rhetorical structure around these messages.
4. *Microplanning and Realisation:* Creating an actual text which communicates the document plan.

In the rest of this paper, I describe the above stages. I then explain why I think this architecture is an appropriate one for data-to-text systems; look at how well it fits existing data-to-text systems; discuss intermediate representations between the stages; and briefly describe software resources which we are (slowly) developing to support the architecture.

2 Background

2.1 Data-to-text

Data-to-text systems generate texts from non-linguistic input data, which is typically numerical. For example, SUMTIME (Reiter et al., 2005) and FOG (Goldberg et al., 1994) generate textual weather forecasts from numerical weather prediction data; ANA (Kukich, 1983) generates textual stock market reports from numerical stock market data; and VITRA (Herzog and Wazinski, 1994) and DESCRIBER (Roy, 2002) generate natural descriptions of visual scenes. Some work has also been done on generating texts from lists of events; for example PLANDOC (McKeown et al., 1994) generates summaries based on trace files from a simulator, and Hallett and Scott (2005) describe a system which generates summaries of events in a medical record.

Perhaps the biggest difference between data-to-text systems and NLG systems whose input is a knowledge base is that data-to-text systems must analyse and interpret their input data, as well as decide how to linguistically communicate it. While there is of course a substantial literature on data analysis, this primarily focuses on hypothesis testing and data mining; there are differences between this kind of data analysis and data analysis for the purposes of generating a textual summary (Sripada et al., 2003).

2.2 NLG Architectures

Perhaps the best-known architecture for general NLG systems is the three-stage pipeline model (Reiter and Dale, 2000), which divides NLG into document planning, microplanning, and realisation stages. This architecture focused on NLG systems whose input was a knowledge base. The architecture proposed here essentially extends the Reiter and Dale architecture by adding two new stages, Signal Analysis and Data Interpretation, which are placed before document planning in the pipeline; this extension allows the inputs to the system to be data instead of (or in addition to) knowledge.

The RAGS (Mellish et al., 2006) project conducted a survey of NLG systems, and concluded that they were architecturally quite diverse in terms of how they were modularised; it proposed a fairly abstract NLG architecture which described different representations which might be used in an NLG system, but did not commit to specific stages or modules.

The only proposal for an architecture which is specifically for data-to-text systems (which I am aware of) is Yu et al. (2004). The architecture given in that paper is quite detailed, and based on one system; the architecture presented here, in contrast, is higher-level and applies to many systems.

3 The Architecture

In this section I outline my proposed architecture, which is summarised in Figures 1 and 2. Note that some data-to-text systems only have some of the stages; Figure 2 explains when a stage is needed in a system.

I also explain how this architecture is being used in BABYTALK (Portet et al., 2007). BABYTALK is a new project at Aberdeen whose goal is to generate summaries of medical data about babies in a neonatal intensive care unit. BABYTALK systems have two types of inputs: (1) numerical sensor data about the baby, recording information such as heart rate, blood pressure and temperature; and (2) records of

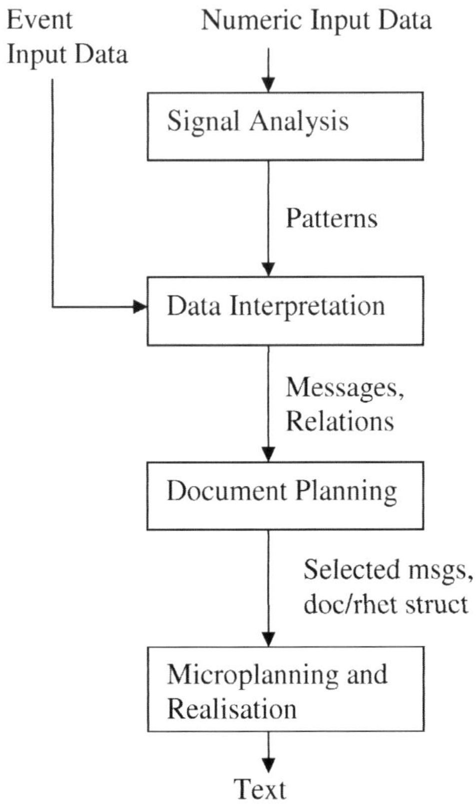

Figure 1: The Architecture

medical actions and observations, such as medication administered to the baby and blood test results. Different BABYTALK systems generate different kinds of texts from this input data; here I will focus on the BABYTALK BT45 system, which generates summaries of about 45 minutes worth of medical data which are intended to help doctors and nurses make appropriate treatment decisions (Law et al., 2005).

Figures 3 and 4 show examples of numeric and event inputs to BT45; Figure 5 shows the text that a doctor wrote to describe this data. This is an extract from a corpus text, not a generated text; it illustrates the type of text BT45 is trying to generate.

BABYTALK is a multi-person project, involving people with diverse backgrounds, ranging from signal analysis to computational linguistics. From this perspective, the architecture needs to not only be intellectually sensible, it also needs to modularise the system in a way which allows people to develop modules in their area of expertise without needing to become experts in all of the research areas involved in BABYTALK.

Stage	*input*	*output*	*needed if...*
Signal Analysis	numeric data	discrete patterns in data	there is numeric input data
Data Interpretation	basic patterns and events	higher-level messages, relations between messages	text communicates more than basic patterns
Document Planning	messages, relations	messages to be mentioned, document and rhetorical struct	only some messages are mentioned in text
Microplanning and Realisation	messages, structure	text	users want fluent texts

Figure 2: Stages in the Architecture

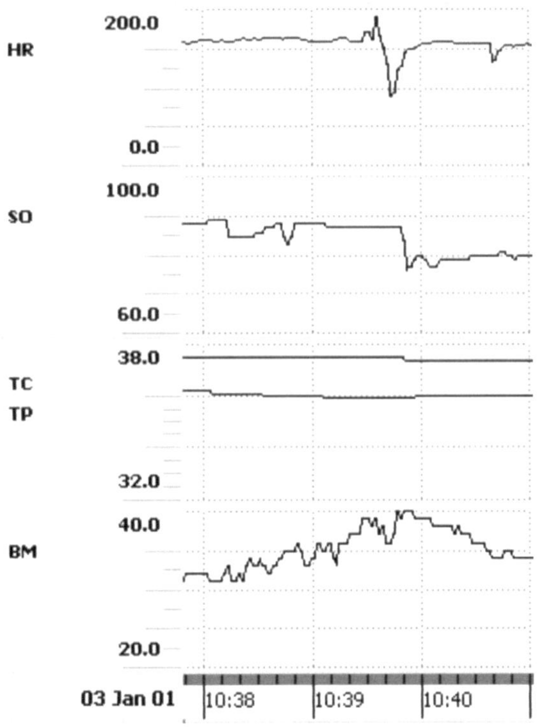

Figure 3: Example of BT45 numeric input data

time	*action*	parameters
10.38	FiO2 changed	new-value = 35%
10.39	morphine given	amt=50ug, route=IV
10.41	incubator opened	agent = doctor
10.51	baby intubated	agent = doctor

Figure 4: Example of BT45 event input data

3.1 Signal Analysis

The first stage in the architecture is to try to detect basic patterns in the numerical input data. Patterns are often organised into a taxonomy or ontology, although this is not required by the architecture. From a high-level perspective, the goal of signal analysis is to replace numerical data by a set of discrete patterns; this allows the remainder of the system to reason symbolically instead of numerically.

Signal analysis must also distinguish 'real' data from noise. For example, RR (Pianesi et al., 2007), which summarises the behaviour of participants in a meeting, must analyse audio signals and determine when a participant is talking (and hence contributing to the meeting), and when he or she is making non-communicative noises, such as coughing.

Input data which is already structured as discrete events, such as log files or records of medical actions, can bypass signal analysis. If all input data is of this form (as in PLANDOC (McKeown et al., 1994), for example), then the data-to-text system does not need to perform any signal analysis.

In my experience, signal analysis in data-to-text systems can usually be done with existing signal analysis algorithms. There is a substantial literature on signal analysis and pattern detection, including specialist journals such as *Pattern Recognition*. Quite sophisticated algorithms can be used in data-to-text systems; for example TREND (Boyd, 1998) used wavelet analysis. The basic challenge for the system developer is to understand the algorithms, the domain, and the way humans talk about the domain well enough to identify which algorithms are appropriate for a particular system.

In preparation for re-intubation, a bolus of 50ug of morphine is given at 1039 when the FiO2 = 35%. There is a momentary bradycardia and then the mean BP increases to 40. The sats go down to 79 and take 2 mins to come back up. The toe/core temperature gap increases to 1.6 degrees.

Figure 5: Extract from BT45 corpus text

BT45's signal analysis module uses three algorithms to detect patterns:

- Short-term changes in channels, such as spikes and steps, are detected using a simplified version of the algorithm proposed by Yu et al. (2007).
- Longer-term changes in the data, such as sensor values increasing or decreasing over time, are detected using linear segmentation (Keogh et al., 2001).
- *artefacts*, that is data which is corrupted or otherwise should be ignored (for example, because a sensor has fallen off the baby) are detected as described by Portet et al. (2007).

To take a concrete example, one pattern type in BT45 is SPIKE; this indicates that the values in a sensor channel have temporarily increased or decreased, but then reverted to their previous value. The SPIKE class has several parameters, including channel, direction, time, and extremeValue. One particular spike which is detected in the Figure 3 data has parameters channel=HR (Heart Rate), direction=Down, time=1039, extremeValue=90.

3.2 Data Interpretation

The second stage of the architecture analyses the patterns detected by signal analysis, and also any events which are directly specified in the input data, and infers more complex (and domain-specific) *messages* about the data set from these patterns and events. It may also infer relationships (such as causality) between patterns, events, and messages. From a high-level perspective, the goal of data interpretation is to map basic patterns and events into the messages and relationships that humans use when discussing this domain.

In some applications, such as marine weather forecasts (Reiter et al., 2005), humans only refer to basic patterns when discussing the domain, and do not refer to relationships. Systems in such domains do not need to perform data interpretation. But in other domains, humans also communicate about higher-level events or patterns. For example, SCUBATEXT (Sripada and Gao, 2007), which generates safety-oriented summaries of scuba dives from depth profiles and other dive computer data, looks for patterns that suggest potentially dangerous activities in a dive. For instance, one risky activity is a 'sawtooth' dive where the diver descends, ascends, and then descends again. SCUBATEXT creates sawtooth messages wherever it sees an increasing trend in depth, followed by a decreasing trend in depth, followed by another increasing trend; this is an example of data interpretation.

BT45 performs three basic activities in data interpretation:

- *Create messages:* This is similar to SCUBATEXT. For example, a BRADYCARDIA (heart rate is temporarily too low) message is created from downward spikes in heart rate which go below 100.
- *Decide how important events are:* BT45 assigns an importance to every message; this is needed by the document planner. For example, the importance of a BRADYCARDIA depends primarily on how long it lasts for (5 seconds is unimportant, 5 minutes is very important), and secondarily on how low heart rate goes.
- *Detect relationships between events:* BT45 looks for three kinds of relationships between messages: causality (for example, blood oxygen increases *because* the nurse increased oxygen levels in the ventilator); part of a procedure (for example, giving morphine is *part of* a re-intubation procedure); and other (for example, an increase in blood oxygen is *associated with* a decrease in blood CO2).

Currently, data interpretation in BT45 is primarily done by production rules written in JESS[1], which are based on knowledge-acquisition activities conducted with experienced doctors. We may in the future use KBTA (Shahar, 1997) for some of this reasoning.

To take a concrete example in BT45, the SPIKE event mentioned at the end of the Signal Analysis section is interpreted in Data Interpretation as a BRADYCARDIA. It has moderate importance (15 on a scale of 0 to 100), and has an *associated with* link to a drop in blood oxygen saturation (SO) which happens at about the same time.

3.3 Document Planning

The third stage of the architecture decides which events to mention in the text, and also on the text's rhetorical and document (e.g., paragraph break) structure. This is the same as the Document Planning stage in the architecture of Reiter and Dale

[1] `http://herzberg.ca.sandia.gov/jess/`

(2000). From a high-level perspective, signal analysis and data interpretation can produce a large number of messages, patterns, and events (often hundreds or thousands), but texts usually are limited to only describing a small number of messages (the actual number depends on the genre, but often is between 5 and 25 events). The Document Planner must decide which messages are actually communicated in the text; this decision is based on the domain and genre. It must also try to communicate how the messages mentioned in the text relate to each other; this can partially be done using rhetorical and document structure.

In some data-to-text applications, such as pollen forecasts (Turner et al., 2006), all the input data is communicated to the user, so document planning is a trivial task. But this is unusual, usually some selection is needed. Indeed, Law et al. (2005), who found that doctors made better decisions from textual summaries than from graphical displays, speculate that this happened precisely because the texts only communicated the most relevant information.

Document planning is perhaps the least-understood aspect of data-text systems, and indeed of NLG in general; in fact Evans et al. (2002) argue that document planning should not be considered part of NLG. Of course document planning still needs to be done in data-to-text systems regardless of whether it is regarded as an 'NLG' task.

Yu et al. (2007) treat document planning in data-to-text systems as the task of finding 'interesting patterns', and use two mechanisms to do this: rules acquired from domain experts, and novelty (how often a pattern has been seen before). They use simple schemas to specify document structure.

Hallett and Scott (2005), who summarise medical events, use a different approach. The input to their document planner is a graph of events and relations between events. Their system works by partitioning this graph into inter-connected clusters of events; dropping small clusters (unless they contain information which domain knowledge says must be reported); and then mapping clusters onto a specific *report spine* for the target type of report, which specifies which events are central for this type of report. Non-spinal events are linked to spinal events using rhetorical relations which are based on event relations; they may be dropped if they are too far away from a spinal event in the graph.

Document planning in BT45 is currently done in a similar fashion to Hallett and Scott, except that many decisions take into account the importance of messages (calculated by Data Interpretation). BT45's document planner decides on paragraph boundaries, but not sentence boundaries (sentence boundaries are chosen by the microplanner/realiser, as part of aggregation).

For example, the BRADYCARDIA message mentioned in the last section is included in a cluster of messages which happen at about the same time (these essentially are the messages mentioned in the text of Figure 5). This cluster is overall the second-most important message cluster, so it is included in the text; and the BRADYCARDIA message is moderately important, so it is included in the text describing the cluster. The cluster is realised at the document level as a single paragraph (this decision is based on its size). A simple SEQUENCE rhetorical relation is used to relate the BRADYCARDIA message to other messages, because it only has generic *associated with* links to other messages in its cluster.

3.4 Microplanning and Realisation

The fourth stage of the architecture generates actual texts based on the content and structure chosen by Document Planning. It corresponds to the two stages of Microplanning and Realisation in Reiter and Dale (2000). From a high-level perspective, microplanning and realisation must decide how to actually express in language the concepts and structure selected by earlier stages.

It is possible to perform microplanning and realisation using simple templates. Whether this is acceptable depends on what is appropriate for users. For example, IGRAPH (Ferres et al., 2006) uses templates to generate (spoken) descriptions of graphs for visually-impaired users. IGRAPH's texts look clumsy and repetitive on paper, and probably would not be acceptable as textual summaries for people who can read. But visually impaired users listening to a speech synthesiser have different requirements, and in some cases may prefer simple repetitive texts.

Microplanning and realisation in data-to-text are fairly similar to microplanning and realisation in other NLG systems, so I will not describe them in detail here. There are a few differences in emphasis, though.

One difference is that most (although not all) data-to-text systems produce simple language from a syntactic perspective, because their users prefer this. Syntactic realisation in such systems is relatively straightforward.

Another difference is that data-to-text systems must deal with differences in how readers interpret words that communicate data. For example, Reiter et al. (2005) found considerable differences in how different readers and writers of weather forecasts interpreted time phrases such as *by late evening* and *later*; and Roy (2002) found inconsistencies in the way that different people mapped colour terms such as *pink* into numerical RGB colour specifications. There is no clear solution to this problem, it is a major open research issue.

Finally, data-to-text system may need to communicate uncertainty about about the reliability of the input data or the system's analysis. Again this is an open research issue. There is a substantial literature in linguistics and psychology on communicating uncertainty, but I am not aware of attempts to incorporate these findings into data-to-text systems.

The current version of BT45 lexicalises the BRADYCARDIA message mentioned above as *There is a bradycardia to 90*; ie, it uses a there-is sentence and mentions the extreme value but not the duration. The corpus text shown in Figure 5, in contrast, uses the phrase *There is a momentary bradycardia*. '*momentary*' is a qualitative description of the duration of the bradycardia; determining when it can be used is not easy, in part because different people use it in different ways.

4 Justification for Architecture

The architecture presented here divides the data-to-text generation process into 4 stages. Obviously we could form an architecture with more stages by splitting the stages presented here into smaller stages (for example, split Microplanning and Realisation into two separate stages); we could also form an architecture with fewer stages by combining stages (for example, combine Signal Analysis and Data Interpretation into one stage). The stages of the architecture described here are based on the following criteria.

Types of processing performed and knowledge required. Signal analysis uses numerical pattern-recognition algorithms and is to some degree domain independent; data interpretation uses symbolic reasoning and relies on domain knowledge; document planning uses symbolic reasoning and relies on domain communication knowledge (Kittredge et al., 1991); and microplanning and realisation are based on linguistic reasoning and are partially domain-independent. This consideration is especially important in projects such as BABYTALK which involve developers from diverse backgrounds (as mentioned above).

Intermediate representations. Modules need clear API's which will remain fairly stable even if a module is re-implemented using different techniques. One of the primary reasons for combining Microplanning and Realisation into one stage is that it is difficult to define a generic API between a Microplanner and a Realiser, because the inputs expected by a Realiser depend on the syntactic formalism it is based on.

Perhaps the hardest decision to justify is the separation of Data Interpretation and Document Planning, as these both involve domain-dependent symbolic AI reasoning, and they tend to either both be present or both be absent in individual systems. My main reason for separating these is that they emerge from two very different research communities; Data Interpretation has been studies by researchers in knowledge-based (expert) systems, while Document Planning has been studied by researchers in the NLG community.

5 Applicability

Perhaps not surprisingly, the architecture described here fits many data-to-text systems developed at Aberdeen by the author and his colleagues, including SUMTIME (Reiter et al., 2005) (generates marine weather forecasts for offshore oil rigs); pollen forecast generator (Turner et al., 2006); SUMTIME-TURBINE (Yu et al., 2007) (generates summaries of sensor data from a gas turbine); and SCUBATEXT (Sripada and Gao, 2007) (generates safety-oriented summaries of scuba dives). It also seems to fit many data-to-text systems developed elsewhere.

For example, ANA (Kukich, 1983), which generates stock market summaries, is described as having 4 modules in a pipeline: fact generator, message generator, discourse organiser, and text generator. These correspond to the signal analysis, data interpretation, document planning, and microplanning/realisation modules described here.

Another example is PLANDOC (McKeown et al., 1994), which generates summaries of what happened in a simulation. It is described as having 5 modules: Message Generator, Ontologiser, Content Planner, Lexicaliser, and Surface Generator. The Message Generator is essentially an interface to the simulation package; the Ontologiser performs data interpretation; the Content Planner does document planning; and the Lexicaliser and Surface Generator perform microplanning and realisation (respectively). As mentioned above, PLANDOC does not need to perform signal analysis, because its input is already in the form of discrete events.

However, the architecture described here does not fit all data-to-text systems. For example DESCRIBER (Roy, 2002) takes a more integrated approach based on machine learning.

6 Representations

The above description of the architecture is of course very high-level. To make it more concrete, we need to specify intermediate representations (APIs) between the modules. As Mellish et al. (2006) point out, it is difficult to do this for NLG as a whole, because the field is very diverse. However, we believe this problem is more tractable (although still hard) in the more limited area of data-to-text.

In particular, we use the following intermediate representations in BT45, and believe these could be used in other systems as well:

- output of *Signal Analysis* is a set of patterns. Patterns are represented as objects in a Protégé[2] ontology, which includes types such as SPIKE and INCREASING TREND. Objects have parameters (feature values), such as the channel they occurred in and the time they occurred at.
- output of *Data Interpretation* is a set of messages which are again represented as objects in a Protégé ontology; all messages have an importance parameter. *Data Interpretation* also produces a set of relations between messages; these are represented as (RelationType, Message1, Message2) triples.
- output of *Document Planning* is a document plan. This is represented as a tree. Nodes in the tree can specify messages; they can also be annotated with document structure level (e.g., paragraph). Parent-child links can be annotated with rhetorical relations (which are finer-grained than the domain relations produced by Data Interpretation; e.g., VOLITIONAL-CAUSE instead of CAUSES). In RAGS (Mellish et al., 2006) terminology, a document plan is a tree which represents both document and rhetorical structure, and whose nodes can specify conceptual structures (ie, messages).
- output of *Microplanning and Realisation* is a text, which may include HTML mark-ups.

7 Software

An architecture should also be supported by software resources which help developers create systems based on the architecture. We are trying to create such resources for building data-to-text systems. In particular

- *Signal Analysis:* The TSNET (Hunter, 2006) system, which has been developed at Aberdeen over a number of years, includes many signal analysis algorithms for time series data. We are adapting TSNET so that it can be used to perform Signal Analysis in BABYTALK, and believe it could be used in other data-to-text systems as well.
- *Microplanning and Realisation:* We are developing a Java library called SIMPLENLG[3] to perform these tasks; again this is based on several previous projects. SIMPLENLG currently performs morphological processing, realisation of simple syntactic structures, and simple lexicalisation; we hope to add support for simple microplanning soon.

We hope over the next few years to expand the above, and in particular also provide software tools for Data Interpretation and Document Planning.

8 Conclusion

There is growing interest in data-to-text systems. Such systems are both practically useful (all fielded NLG systems that I am aware of are data-to-text systems) and scientifically interesting (in part because they help us study how language relates to the non-linguistic world). I have tried in this paper to outline the kinds of processing that data-to-text systems must perform, and show how this processing can fit into an architecture which is an extension of (not a replacement of) existing NLG architectures.

Acknowledgements

Many thanks to the reviewers and to my colleagues at Aberdeen for their comments on this paper. All opinions expressed here are of course mine alone. BABYTALK is supported by grant EP/D049520/1 from the UK Engineering and Physical Sciences Research Council (EPSRC).

[2] http://protege.stanford.edu

[3] http://www.csd.abdn.ac.uk/~ereiter/simplenlg/

References

Sarah Boyd. 1998. TREND: a system for generating intelligent descriptions of time-series data. In *Proceedings of the IEEE International Conference on Intelligent Processing Systems (ICIPS-1998)*.

Roger Evans, Paul Piwek, and Lynne Cahill. 2002. What is NLG? In *Proceedings of the Second International Conference on Natural Language Generation*, pages 144–151.

Leo Ferres, Avi Parush, Shelley Roberts, and Gitte Lindgaard. 2006. Helping people with visual impairments gain access to graphical information through natural language: The iGraph system. In *Proceedings of the 10th International Conference on Computers Helping People with Special Needs*.

Eli Goldberg, Norbert Driedger, and Richard Kittredge. 1994. Using natural-language processing to produce weather forecasts. *IEEE Expert*, 9(2):45–53.

Catalina Hallett and Donia Scott. 2005. Structural variation in generated health reports. In *Third International Workshop on Paraphrasing (IWP2005)*.

Gerd Herzog and Peter Wazinski. 1994. VIsual TRAnslator: Linking perceptions and natural language descriptions. *Artificial Intelligence Review*, 8(2-3):175–187.

Jim Hunter. 2006. TSNet a distributed architecture for time series analysis. In *Proceedings of IDAMAP 2006*, pages 85–92.

Eamonn Keogh, Selina Chu, David Hart, and Michael Pazzani. 2001. An online algorithm for segmenting time series. In *Proceedings of IEEE International Conference on Data Mining*, pages 289–296.

Richard Kittredge, Tanya Korelsky, and Owen Rambow. 1991. On the need for domain communication language. *Computational Intelligence*, 7(4):305–314.

Karen Kukich. 1983. Design and implementation of a knowledge-based report generator. In *Proceedings of ACL-1983*, pages 145–150.

Anna Law, Yvonne Freer, Jim Hunter, Robert Logie, Neil McIntosh, and John Quinn. 2005. Generating textual summaries of graphical time series data to support medical decision making in the neonatal intensive care unit. *Journal of Clinical Monitoring and Computing*, 19:183–194.

Kathleen McKeown, Karen Kukich, and James Shaw. 1994. Practical issues in automatic document generation. In *Proceedings of ANLP-1994*, pages 7–14.

Chris Mellish, Donia Scott, Lynn Cahill, Daniel Paiva, Roger Evans, and Mike Reape. 2006. A reference architecture for natural language generation systems. *Natural Language Engineering*, 12:1–34.

Fabio Pianesi, Massimo Zancanaro, Elena Not, Chiara Leonardi, Vera Falcon, and Bruno Lepri. 2007. Multimodal support to group dynamics. *Personal and Ubiquitous Computing*, 11. In press.

François Portet, Ehud Reiter, Jim Hunter, and Somayajulu Sripada. 2007. Automatic generation of textual summaries from neonatal intensive care data. In *Proceedings of AIME 2007*. Forthcoming.

Ehud Reiter and Robert Dale. 2000. *Building Natural Language Generation Systems*. Cambridge University Press.

Ehud Reiter, Somayajulu Sripada, Jim Hunter, and Jin Yu. 2005. Choosing words in computer-generated weather forecasts. *Artificial Intelligence*, 167:137–169.

Deb Roy. 2002. Learning visually grounded words and syntax for a scene description task. *Computer Speech and Language*, 16:353–385.

Yuval Shahar. 1997. A framework for knowledge-based temporal abstraction. *Artificial Intelligence*, 90:79–133.

Somayajulu Sripada and Feng Gao. 2007. Summarizing dive computer data. In *Proceedings of the Workshop on Multimodal Output Generation (MOG-2007)*, pages 149–157.

Somayajulu Sripada, Ehud Reiter, Jim Hunter, and Jin Yu. 2003. Generating English summaries of time series data using the Gricean maxims. In *Proceedings of KDD-2003*, pages 187–196.

Ross Turner, Somayajulu Sripada, Ehud Reiter, and Ian Davy. 2006. Generating spatio-temporal descriptions in pollen forecasts. In *Proceedings of EACL-2006 Poster Session*, pages 163–166.

Jin Yu, Ehud Reiter, Jim Hunter, and Somayajulu Sripada. 2004. A new architecture for summarising time series data. In *Proceedings of INLG-04 Poster Session*, pages 47–50.

Jin Yu, Ehud Reiter, Jim Hunter, and Chris Mellish. 2007. Choosing the content of textual summaries of large time-series data sets. *Natural Language Engineering*, 13:25–49.

An Experiment on "Free Generation" from Single RDF triples

Xiantang Sun
Department of Computing Science, University of Aberdeen
Aberdeen, UK, Ab24 3UE
xsun@csd.abdn.ac.uk

Chris Mellish
Department of Computing Science, University of Aberdeen
Aberdeen, UK, Ab24 3UE
cmellish@csd.abdn.ac.uk

Abstract

This paper introduces our domain independent approach to "free generation" from single RDF triples without using any domain dependent knowledge. Our approach is developed based on our argument that RDF representations carry rich linguistic information, which can be used to achieve readable domain independent generation. In order to examine to what extent our argument is realistic, we carry out an evaluation experiment, which is the first evaluation of this kind of domain independent generation in the field.

Introduction

In the Semantic Web, both instance data and ontological data[1] are represented as graphs based on the Resource Description Framework (RDF) (W3C 2004). In order to facilitate non-technician users to access the knowledge and information coded in RDF, we are eventually aiming at developing a domain independent approach to presenting RDF graphs in natural language, which can greatly reduce the cost of applying NLG techniques to various RDF domains (e.g., medical RDF data and chemical RDF data). In this paper we introduce our domain independent approach to generating phrases or sentences from single RDF triples[2] without using any domain knowledge but only generic linguistic knowledge sources. This contrasts with almost all existing work generating natural language from ontologies, which assumes the existence of domain-dependent lexicons. This work is a key part of our final system because generation from single RDF triples, which are the atomic units of RDF graphs, is the foundation and also the first step for any further generation from larger RDF graphs. In order to examine to what extent the linguistic structures can be used to achieve domain independent generation from single RDF triples, we have built a generation system, *Triple-Text (TT),* and here we compare TT's generation with human experts' generation in an evaluation experiment.

[1] Ontological languages are developed based on the RDF syntax, so ontological data are still RDF graphs.

[2] Generation from RDF triples in our case means only presenting the information in the triples, rather than explaining the information.

1 Linguistic structures in ontologies

Let's start with an example of a triple, which consists of a subject, a predicate (also known as a property) and an object. The triple *(LongridgeMerlot HasMaker Longridge)*, may be realised as, *LongridgeMerlot has a property 'HasMaker' with a value 'Longridge',* if this triple is viewed as a pure logical representation. But there could be a much better way of realising it, if the implicit linguistic information embedded in the triple could be correctly recognised and exploited:

Longridge Merlot has a maker, Longridge.

More interestingly, we find that the generation process in fact does not require understanding the real semantics of the terms, *'Longridge', 'Merlot', 'has', 'maker'* and *'Longridge'*. That is, the words embedded in the names of these terms could form most of the final sentence and they have been already placed in a sensible way by their creators. This implies that what is required to make the final sentence is to just to fill in "missing" words, e.g., determiners. Obviously, the name of the property in the triple plays the most crucial role in the generation.

As our earlier work (Mellish and Sun 2005) (Sun and Mellish 2006) shows, RDF representations indeed contain rich linguistic information. In our corpus of 882 OWL files which include 37260 class names and 1218 property names, only 14% of class names consist totally of meaningless strings and 97% of the properties' names fully or partially consist of natural words. Our further analysis has shown that the properties may be classified into 6 categories based on their "patterns". 37.2% of the properties start with '*has*', 12.3% start with '*is*', 11.3% end with a preposition, 18.0% are single words, 12.5% have two words, and 8.3% have more than two words. In each category, we further define some specific patterns[3], for instance those shown in figure 1. In total, we define 23 patterns in the six categories.

Patterns of 'has'	Examples
'has'+...+noun	*hasColor, hasName*
'has'+...+preposition	*hasExposureTo, hasShapeAnalagousTo*
'has'+...+adj	*hasTimeClose, hasTimeOpen*

Figure 1: examples of the patterns for '*has*'

2 Generating single sentences from RDF triples

Based on the patterns found from the corpus, we developed a system (TT) to generate single sentences from single RDF triples without any domain dependent knowledge. The key idea here is to construct VPs from the properties of input triples and treat the subjects and objects of the triples as domain dependent terms, which are simply seen as proper nouns e.g., *(John Surname Murphy)* "*John has a surname Murphy.*" So the main part of the system is about constructing proper VPs from properties. In the process of constructing VPs, every property is tokenised into a sequence of units, e.g., *hasEmail* is separated into *has* and *email*. Then, the property is classified into one of our 6 categories, and in this case *hasEmail* belongs to the *'has'* category. In each category, we have a set of rules to construct VPs from input properties. A rule's LHS is a pattern and the RHS is a corresponding linguistic form (VP) for the pattern. For example, we have a rule like,

LHS: 'has' + [unit] + [noun]*
RHS: 'has' + det[4] + 'units' + 'noun'*

which can construct a VP, *has an email,* for the property, *hasEmail.* Assuming that TT is given a triple, *(Peter, hasEmail, X@Y.com)*, then the generated single sentence is, *Peter has an email, X@Y.com,* where the subject and the object are treated as proper nouns without any analysis. In the case of input that our rules cannot cover, TT outputs a kind of "RDF flavoured" text, e.g., TT generates, *abg has a property k34 with value 377,* from the triple *(abg k34 377).*

3 Evaluation

In order to examine to what extent our domain independent generation is realistic in terms of syntax, comprehensibility and overall quality, we carried out an experiment to compare TT's generation with human experts' generation and pure "RDF flavoured" generation (the "RDF generator"), as our baseline (as in the example shown at the end of section 2).

3.1 Experiment design

We applied a "Two-Panel" methodology to compare the three kinds of generation, which is similar to the methodology applied in KNIGHT[5] (Lester and Porter 1997). The Two-Panel evaluation methodology can be used to empirically evaluate NLG generation by comparing computer generation with human generation. We take *Computer Blindness* as a central principle through the experiment in order to guarantee the integrity of the evaluation results. This means that our judges do not know that any texts are generated by computer..

[3] We use QTAG (Mason 2003) to recognise the parts-of-speech (POS) of the units extracted from the property names. For example, QTAG can recognise '*has*' and '*colour*' (from '*hasColour*') as a verb and a noun. We achieved 99.2% accuracy of POS recognition on our corpus using QTAG with the assistance of some manually-added rules.

[4] We simply add an indefinite determiner if the '*noun*' is not in its plural form.

[5] In KNIGHT only the system's generation and human generation are compared.

There are four steps in our methodology:

- randomly selecting 90 triples with different properties and then generating from them with TT and the "RDF generator" (we took the 90 triples from ontologies collected in an knowledge engineer's ongoing project);
- arranging two panels consisting of RDF experts and PhD students whose areas are irrelevant to computing. NB the RDF experts in the first panel did not know the domains that the 90 triples were from, in order to make their generation "domain independent" like TT;
- asking panel 1 to manually generate 90 short sentences from the triples;
- evaluating all generations by panel 2.

3.2 Experiment

The source RDF data for the experiment were collected from 7 domains in order to test TT's performance in general. The input data were not known to us until we started the experiment. 90 different single RDF triples were randomly collected from the data and input to TT and the "RDF generator". We avoided having 2 sentences with the same property. Now we had 90 sentences from TT and another 90 sentences from the "RDF generator". We invited 3 RDF experts (2 PhD students and a Post-Doc) for panel 1, 6 law PhD students for panel 2. Each of the experts in panel 1 was asked to present 30 different triples from the 90 triples in natural language. Panel 2 judged the generation in terms of syntax, comprehensibility, and overall quality. Panel 2 was given mixtures of the generations from TT, the "RDF generator" and the experts, but they were not shown the source triples and did not know that there were computers involved in the experiment. Each judge was given *90* short sentences and asked to judge them in terms of syntax, comprehensibility, and overall quality by choosing between possible options.

- Syntax: we asked *"does the sentence have any grammar mistakes?"* and gave five options, *A) all wrong B) basically wrong C) some mistakes but understandable D) minor mistakes E) no mistakes*
- Comprehensibility: we asked "do you understand what the sentence says?" and gave options, from *not at all, a little bit, some of it, understand most of it,* and *understand it all*
- Overall quality: we asked "*Do you like the way the sentence is written?"* and gave options from *not at all, a little bit, generally ok, good* and *excellent.*

When we distributed these sentences to the judges, we followed the four principles that applied in KNIGHT's evaluation. They are

- System-Human division: Each judge in panel 2 received 90 different sentences from TT, the "RDF generator" and experts in random order (30 of each).
- Domain Division: Each judge in panel 1 and panel 2 received sentences that were approximately evenly divided among the domains which the 90 RDF triples were from.
- Single-generation restriction: No judge in panel 2 received more than one sentence from the same RDF triple.
- Multijudge Stipulation: Each sentence is judged exactly twice in order to obtain relatively unbiased judgements.

3.3 Experiment results

After the experiment, for each triple we had 3 sentences (generated from TT, the "RDF generator" and panel 1) judged by panel 2. Then, we had three samples of quantitative data of the judges' opinions of each dimension by mapping options A-E onto 1-5 (a sample of TT, a sample of the "RDF generator" and a sample of the experts' text). The two-tailed Standard T-test is a good way to detect differences between these samples if the differences exist (as in KNIGHT). We compared TT with the experts, TT with the program and the program with the experts. Here are the results for the means[6] and the differences and their significance[7] (tables 1, 2, 3 and 4).

---

[6] ± in table1 stands for the standard error.

[7] The t-tests used in our case are unpaired, two-tailed. The results are reported for a 0.05 level of confidence. Significance does not depend on whether we apply a multiple test correction.

Generator	Syntax	Comprehensibility	Overall
RDF gen.	2.44±0.09	2.01±0.09	1.81±0.08
TT	3.14±0.12	2.76±0.12	2.29±0.11
Experts	3.3±0.12	2.88±0.12	2.4±0.11

Table1: Means

RDF gen. VS TT	Syntax	Comprehensibility	Overall
Difference	0.70	0.75	0.48
Significance	3.72E-06	1.89E-06	1.89E-06
Significant?	Yes	Yes	Yes

Table2: Differences and significance

RDF gen. VS Expert	Syntax	Comprehensibility	Overall
Difference	0.86	0.87	0.59
Significance	2.42E-08	1.16E-08	6.26E-06
Significant?	Yes	Yes	Yes

Table3: Differences and significance

TT VS Expert	Syntax	Comprehensibility	Overall
Difference	0.16	0.12	0.11
Significance	0.35	0.47	0.46
Significant?	No	No	No

Table4: Differences and significance

As shown in table 1, experts score the highest and the "RDF generator" scores the lowest in every dimension. TT's performance is worse than but close to the experts', however neither of them scores very high. Indeed, both of them score less than 2.5 in overall quality. The reason for the low scores is probably that the data for the test contained many domain dependent terms, which the readers did not understand or felt were "odd", e.g., *area125*. In syntax and comprehensibility, both experts and TT achieve an "average" level. However, it seems that the readers do not like the "RDF flavoured" text. We talked with the readers about the texts after the experiment and found out that the "odd" domain dependent terms lowered readers' scores, though the readers understood most of the texts. According to table 2 and table 3, both experts and TT differ significantly from the "RDF generator". According to table 4, we could not find a significant difference between the experts and TT. This does not indicate that TT is as good as the experts because a bigger sample may show a significant difference. As an example of where TT is not as good as the humans, one of our experts writes "*The industry of the North is manufacturing sector.*" from (*North industryOfArea manufacturing_sector*), which is more "natural" than TT's generation, "*North is the industry of area manufacturing sector.*" So we may only say that TT's performance is to some extent close to the experts. On the other hand, the fact that we were with this sample able to show a significant difference between the other pairs gives us some confidence in the adequacy of TT's output.

Conclusion

Our corpus analysis and the evaluation experiment show that there is an opportunity to achieve adequate quality domain independent generation from RDF data. Our future work will focus on generating from larger RDF graphs.

Acknowledgements

Our thanks go to EPSRC, who funds our research project through grant GR/S62932/01.

References

J. C. Lester, and B. W. Porter. (1997) Developing and empirically evaluating robust explanation generators: The Knight Experiments. *Computational Linguistics* 23(1):65–101.

O. Mason, (2003). *Qtag 3.1*. Department of English, School of Humanities, University of Birmingham,http://web.bham.ac.uk/O.Mason/software/tagger/

C. Mellish and X. Sun. (2006). The Semantic Web as a Linguistic Resource. *Knowledge Based Systems* 19, pp 298-303.

W3C, (1999). "Resource Description Framework (RDF) Model and Syntax Specification.", http://www.w3.org/TR/PR-rdf-syntax/.

X Sun and C. Mellish. (2006). Domain Independent Sentence Generation from RDF Representations for the Semantic Web. Combined Workshop on Language-Enabled Educational Technology (ECAI'06), Italy.

The Narrator: NLG for digital storytelling

Mariët Theune
Human Media Interaction
University of Twente
Enschede, The Netherlands
m.theune@utwente.nl

Nanda Slabbers
Human Media Interaction
University of Twente
Enschede, The Netherlands
nandaslabbers@hotmail.com

Feikje Hielkema*
Department of Computing Science
University of Aberdeen
Scotland, UK
fhielkem@csd.abdn.ac.uk

Abstract

We present the Narrator, an NLG component used for the generation of narratives in a digital storytelling system. We describe how the Narrator works and show some examples of generated stories.

1 Introduction

The automatic generation of narratives is still a largely unexplored field in NLG. Some exceptions are STORYBOOK (Callaway, 2000), a narrative prose generation system that can generate many different retellings of the same story (Little Red Riding Hood) and the architecture for a "narratologically enhanced NLG system" proposed by Lönneker (2005). An NLG system that is actually used in a digital storytelling application is PRINCE (Hervás et al., 2006).

Here we present the Narrator: the NLG component of the Virtual Storyteller, a multi-agent system that automatically creates fairy tales based on the actions of autonomous character agents in a simulated story world, where they can perform goal-oriented actions and experience emotions (Theune et al., 2004). The emerging story is captured in a formal representation and fed to the Narrator, which expresses it in natural language (in our case, Dutch). In the rest of this paper, we give a brief overview of the subsequent tasks the Narrator carries out to generate a fluent, well-formed narrative. We focus on the generation of referring expressions; a more detailed description of the entire generation process can be found in Theune et al. (2007). For more information concerning various design decisions see Theune et al. (2006).

* Feikje Hielkema carried out this work while she was at the University of Groningen, The Netherlands.

2 Document planning

The input for the Narrator is a Fabula (Swartjes and Theune, 2006): a story representation in the form of a causal network linking the following plot elements: actions, events, perceptions, goals, goal outcomes, and characters' "internal elements" such as emotions and beliefs. Possible links between these elements are motivation, enablement, mental and physical cause relations. Also, each plot element is associated with a time stamp (in terms of time steps in the story world). The (simplified) example Fabula in Figure 1 represents a very short story about a dwarf who is hungry and believes there is an apple in the house, leading to the goal to eat the apple. To achieve this, the dwarf carries out a simple plan: taking the apple and then eating it, which leads to the perception and the belief that the apple has been eaten, signifying a positive goal outcome.

As a first step in turning a Fabula into a Document Plan, all information that is not relevant for narration must be pruned away. An example is the standard perception-belief-positive outcome chain that follows a successful action: for the narrative, it is sufficient to mention only that the action was carried out. Currently, this process is not yet implemented in the Narrator; however, we assume that in the example Fabula, the nodes following the 'Eat Apple' action will be pruned away. The next step is to convert the pruned Fabula to a binary tree, replacing the causal links with appropriate rhetorical relations between plot elements. The basic rhetorical relations used in the Narrator are Cause, Contrast, Temporal and Additive, with more specific subclasses such as Purpose and Elaboration. When mapping the links in the Fabula to rhetorical relations, consecutive steps of a plan are connected using a Temporal

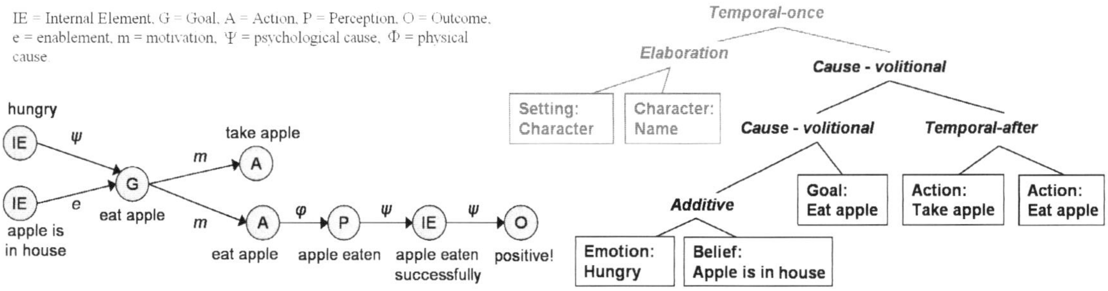

Figure 1: Fabula (left) and corresponding Document Plan (right).

relation. Motivation and psychological cause relations are mapped to Volitional Cause relations, and enablement and physical cause relations are mapped to Non-volitional Cause relations. Additive is the most general relation. It is used if two plot elements cause another plot element together, and more in general to connect two plot elements that do not have a more specific relation holding between them. We are currently investigating the automatic derivation of Contrast relations. The final step is to extend the Document Plan with a setting and background information about characters and objects. The example Document Plan in Figure 1 shows these extensions in grey: a Setting element introducing the protagonist, and an element specifying the name of the protagonist, connected via an Elaboration relation. They are in a Temporal-once (*Once upon a time...*) relation to the rest of the plot; this relation was added specifically for the fairy tale domain.

3 Sentence planning, lexicalisation and syntactic aggregation

Next, the leaves of the Document Plan are mapped to Dependency Trees. For each type of plot element a template is available telling exactly how its arguments should appear in the corresponding Dependency Tree. For example, actions are expressed using a straightforward active voice construction, with an optional PP argument to express instruments, e.g., *The knight opened the gate (with a key).*[1] For internal states, there are templates for standard sentences such as *The princess was scared* but also for storytelling-style constructions such as *Oh, how happy she was!* and *She had never been so happy!*, to be used for emotions with a high intensity. After the Dependency Trees are selected, their nodes are mapped to Dutch words (except the nodes referring to entities, which are lexicalised as part of referring expression generation). The lexical choice algorithm uses a discourse history, to achieve some variation in wording by taking into account which words have been used recently. The words added to the Dependency Trees are still uninflected, as morphology is taken care of during Surface Realization.

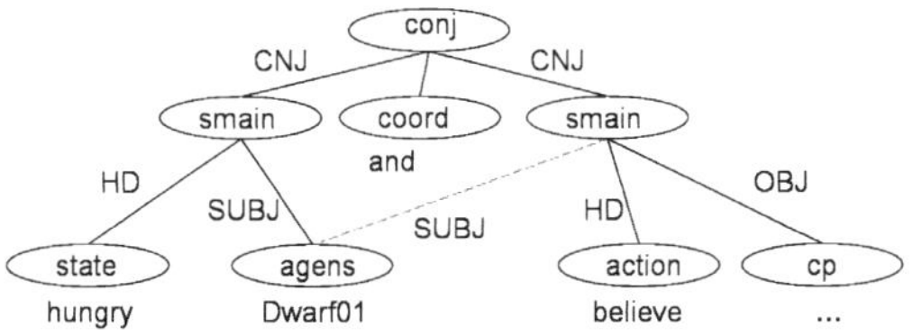

Figure 2: Aggregated Dependency Tree.

The Narrator uses a syntactic aggregation algorithm that combines pairs of Dependency Trees and adds an appropriate cue phrase to signal their rhetorical relation. The properties of this cue phrase determine which syntactic construction is used to combine the Dependency Trees. If the resulting tree contains repeated elements, these can be ellipted. Figure 2 shows an example where the subject of the second clause is deleted (Conjunction Reduction). A corresponding surface string could be *The dwarf was hungry and believed there was an apple in the house*, expressing the Additive relation in the Document Plan of Figure 1. To keep the aggregated sentences from getting too complex, at most three simple Dependency Trees can be combined. In cases where this restriction prohibits aggregation, rhetorical relations are expressed using adverbs such as *then*, *however* etc. For a more detailed description of the aggregation process, see Theune et al. (2006).

4 The generation of referring expressions

To determine whether a pronoun or a noun should be used to refer to a certain entity, we use a variant of the algorithms of McCoy and Strube (1999) and Henschel et al. (2000). Based on an analysis of

[1] For reading ease, Narrator output is translated to English.

human-written fairy tales we determined that pronouns are dispreferred (1) at the beginning of a paragraph, (2) if the antecedent has not been mentioned for two sentences, (3) if a pronoun has been used four times and the referring expression is the first one in the sentence. Also, pronouns cannot be used when the referring expression should express additional information (e.g., about a character's emotional state) in the form of an adjective or a relative clause. If the above conditions do not hold, a pronoun is used if there is either strong parallelism or a causal relationship with the previous clause or sentence (Chambers and Smyth, 1998; Kehler, 2002); otherwise the decision is based on the salience of the referent (Lappin and Leass, 1994).

If a noun phrase is to be generated, the referent's name (if available) is used in 25% of the cases, either on its own or in a construction such as *princess Amalia* if the noun describes a function, such as princess, king or knight. If a description is to be generated, first a noun has to be selected. Some concepts have both a preferred lexicon entry (the most common word for that concept) and one or more additional entries that are used occasionally for variation. After having selected the noun, different types of adjectives can be added. Distinguishing adjectives, necessary to create an unambiguous referring expression, are selected only for subsequent references using a modified version of the algorithm of Krahmer and Theune (2002). When introducing a new entity all its properties are mentioned, because they can be used as distinguishing properties later in the story. Non-distinguishing adjectives include adjectives describing a character's internal state, and 'decorational' adjectives used to spice up the descriptions of entities that have no specific properties except their type (e.g., *a heavy gate*). Finally, an indefinite article is added when the entity has not been mentioned before, and a definite article otherwise.

Simple inference rules are used to generate bridging descriptions. If the referent (e.g., a gate) is related to a discourse-old entity (e.g., a castle), the algorithm checks if there is a rule saying "all castles have gates". If there are no other salient entities for which the same rule holds (i.e., that they always have gates), then a bridging description like *the gate* can be used instead of *the gate of the castle*.

5 Surface form generation

When referring expression generation is finished, the Surface Realiser linearises the now fully lexicalised Dependency Trees. It traverses them depth-first, ordering the children of each node by grammar rules such as SMAIN → SU + HD + OBJ, which states that if a parent node has syntactic category 'SMAIN' (sentence) and three children with dependency labels 'SU' (subject), 'OBJ' (direct object) and 'HD' (main verb), then those children should be ordered in the above way. This particular rule would for instance be applied to produce the sentence *The prince loved Amalia*. Any nouns, adjectives and verbs are inflected at the moment they are linearised. Punctuation is added once linearisation is complete. This concludes our description of the Narrator; for more details see (Theune et al., 2007).

6 Examples

Our simple example story about the hungry dwarf is narrated as follows:

Once upon a time there was a dwarf called Plop. He was hungry and believed there was an apple in a house.[2] *Therefore he wanted to eat the apple. After Plop had taken the apple, he ate it.*

This story is well-formed and coherent, but also quite simple. The next story better illustrates the Narrator's potential, including examples of Document Plan extension, aggregation, pronominalization, and the use of 'decorational' adjectives (*a high tree*). It was generated from a hand-made Document Plan (shown in Figure 3), which contains Contrast relations and paragraph boundaries that cannot currently be generated automatically by the Document Planner. So the story illustrates the output quality that could be achieved by the Narrator once these remaining Document Planning problems are resolved:

Once upon a time there was a beautiful princess called Amalia. A knight from a far away country was in love with her, but she was in love with a young prince. The knight was jealous, so he wanted to abduct her.

After the knight had climbed a high tree, he jumped into the princess' bedroom. She was so scared that she screamed loudly, but nobody heard her.

The knight grabbed the princess and then he placed her on his horse. After that he took her to an old and narrow bridge. On the other side she saw the prince she was in love with. Oh, how relieved princess Amalia was!

[2]Assuming that the house belongs to Plop, the bridging description *the house* would be more appropriate here. However, in this case the Narrator lacked knowledge about the owner of the house, so a general indefinite description was produced.

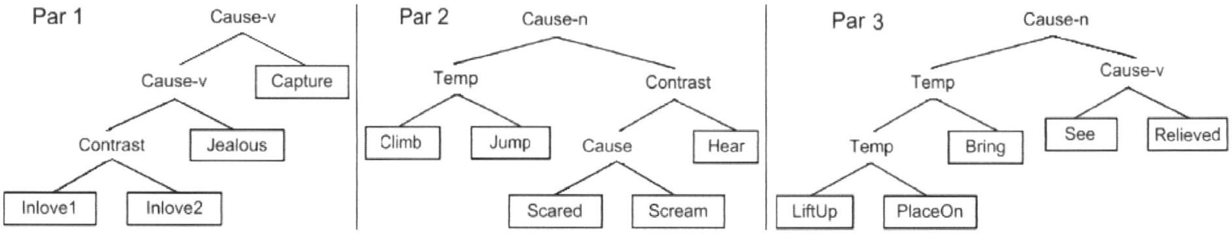

Figure 3: Initial Document Plan for the second example story.

7 Concluding remarks

The Narrator has been implemented (in Java), but so far has only been tested with hand-made input structures, because parts of the Document Planner and of the Virtual Storyteller's plot generation component are still under construction. So far, the only evaluations have been informal comparisons with earlier versions. The Narrator does not employ the kind of narratological knowledge proposed by Lönneker (2005), and unlike STORYBOOK it cannot handle narrative aspects such as multiple viewpoints or character dialogue. However, it can generate well-formed and fluent stories containing some typical narrative constructions. Currently being investigated are the automatic placement of paragraph boundaries, detection of contrast relations and lexicalisation of emotions, taking their intensity into account. In addition, as pointed out by one of our reviewers, it would be beneficial to add a form of semantic aggregation to the system, grouping related plot elements together during document planning.

Our main long-term challenge is to generate texts that are not only grammatical and coherent, but that can also really affect the reader by employing narrative techniques such as the use of subjective perspectives to heighten identification, and foreshadowing to increase suspense. Ablation tests in the style of Callaway (2000) could then be used to evaluate the effect of such techniques.

References

C. Callaway. 2000. *Narrative Prose Generation*. Ph.D. thesis, North Carolina State University, Raleigh, NC.

G.C. Chambers and R. Smyth. 1998. Structural parallelism and discourse coherence: A test of Centering Theory. *Journal of Memory and Language*, 39:593–608.

R. Henschel, H. Cheng, and M. Poesio. 2000. Pronominalization revisited. In *Proceedings of COLING*, pages 306–312.

R. Hervás, F. Pereira, P. Gervás, and A. Cardoso. 2006. Cross-domain analogy in automated text generation. In *Proceedings of the Third joint workshop on Computational Creativity, ECAI'06*.

A. Kehler. 2002. *Coherence, Reference, and the Theory of Grammar*. CSLI Publications.

E. Krahmer and M. Theune. 2002. Efficient context-sensitive generation of referring expressions. In K. van Deemter and R. Kibble, editors, *Information Sharing: Reference and Presupposition in Language Generation and Interpretation*, pages 223–264. CSLI Publications.

S. Lappin and H. Leass. 1994. An algorithm for pronominal anaphora resolution. *Computational Linguistics*, 20(4):535–561.

B. Lönneker. 2005. Narratological knowledge for natural language generation. In *Proceedings of the 10th European Workshop on Natural Language Generation (ENLG-05)*, pages 91–100.

K.E. McCoy and M. Strube. 1999. Generating anaphoric expressions: Pronoun or definite description? In *Proceedings of the ACL Workshop on The Relation of Discourse/Dialogue Structure and Reference*, pages 63–71.

I. Swartjes and M. Theune. 2006. A Fabula model for emergent narrative. In *Technologies for Interactive Digital Storytelling and Entertainment (TIDSE)*, LNCS 4326, pages 95–100.

M. Theune, S. Rensen, R. op den Akker, D. Heylen, and A. Nijholt. 2004. Emotional characters for automatic plot creation. In *Technologies for Interactive Digital Storytelling and Entertainment (TIDSE)*, LNCS 3105, pages 95–100.

M. Theune, F. Hielkema, and P. Hendriks. 2006. Performing aggregation and ellipsis using discourse structures. *Research on Language and Computation*, 4(4):353–375.

M. Theune, N. Slabbers, and F. Hielkema. 2007. The automatic generation of narratives. In *Proceedings of CLIN-17*. to appear.

Capturing Acceptable Variation in Distinguishing Descriptions

Jette Viethen and Robert Dale
Centre for Language Technology
Macquarie University, Sydney, Australia
{jviethen|rdale}@ics.mq.edu.au

Abstract

Almost all existing referring expression generation algorithms aim to find one best referring expression for a given intended referent. However, human-produced data demonstrates that, for any given entity, many perfectly acceptable referring expressions exist. At the same time, it is not the case that all logically possible descriptions are acceptable; so, if we remove the requirement to produce only one best solution, how do we avoid generating undesirable descriptions? Our aim in this paper is to sketch a framework that allows us to capture constraints on referring expression generation, so that the set of logically possible descriptions can be reduced to just those that are acceptable.

1 Introduction

The literature contains many algorithms for the generation of referring expressions: see, for example, (Dale, 1989; Dale and Haddock, 1991; Gardent, 2002; Varges and van Deemter, 2005; Gatt, 2006). These algorithms generally attempt to produce a single 'best' referring expression for a given intended referent. What counts as 'best' is generally defined in terms of minimality and the redundancy of information: the best referring expression is the shortest possible distinguishing description, usually defined in terms of the number of properties expressed. At the same time, some researchers (for example, (Dale and Reiter, 1995; Krahmer et al., 2003)) have noted that human-produced referring expressions are often not minimal in this sense, and so variations on these algorithms weaken this requirement, while still tending to embody a 'shorter is better' criterion.

This focus on minimality has the consequence that it allows us to ignore the abundant evidence that any intended referent can be successfully and appropriately referred to by a large number of referring expressions, many of which involve some redundancy; see, for example, the data described in (Viethen and Dale, 2006). Once we remove the requirement of minimality, and admit that there are many possible acceptable solutions to the problem of how to refer to an intended referent, we are faced with a new problem: for any given entity, there are many logically possible distinguishing descriptions, and we need some way to navigate this space of possibilities, so that we can at least separate the acceptable from the less acceptable. This paper attempts to establish a framework for thinking about this problem.

In Section 2, we begin by first discussing the question of domain-specificity; our argument here is that we are at too early a stage to come up with a definition of 'acceptable reference' that is universally applicable, and so we must begin by acknowledging what we call *the hierarchy of referential domains*. We also introduce the domain that we use as the focus of discussion in this paper. Then, in Section 3, we discuss the idea of a *space of descriptions*, distinguishing the two notions of *logically possible description* and *acceptable description* and presenting some statistics that demonstrate the scale of the problem we face. In Section 4, we enumerate a collection of constraints on acceptable reference that we have identified as being applicable in the domains under consideration here. Finally, in Section 5, we draw some conclusions and consider how the ideas presented in this paper might be taken further.

2 Domain Specificity

2.1 On the Generality of Solutions

Early algorithms for referring expression generation (for example, (Dale, 1989)) attempted to provide domain-independent characterisations of what makes a good referring expression. Subsequent work, and specifically that in the spirit of the Incremental Algorithm (IA; (Dale and Reiter, 1995)) acknowledged that there were domain-specific aspects to the problem; in the case of the IA, this involved using a general, domain-independent algorithm in conjunction with domain-specific preference orderings over the available properties to be used in descriptions. With the question of domain-specificity conveniently delegated to the subtask of determining appropriate preference orderings, research in this area typically then goes on to explore only a single chosen domain.[1]

Our suspicion is that domain-specific characteristics have a much greater impact on the problem of referring expression generation than this simple view suggests. Dale et al. (2002) suggested that additional higher-level domain-specific *reference strategies* were required to provide more guidance over the process of referring expression generation. Here, we note that a monotonic combination of the costs or rankings of potential attributes, as suggested by Krahmer et al. (2003), is based on the assumption that adding another property to an already distinguishing referring expression will never make the expression better; but this is by no means always the case. In many instances the incorporation of another property — such as a visually very salient one — can increase the usefulness of a referring expression for the hearer, but this very much depends upon the domain. Research into how to effectively rank referring expressions for entities in a specific domain therefore first requires an exploration into the characteristics of the properties that occur in that domain and the dependencies between these properties. In short, we do not believe there is a short-cut around the problem of domain-specificity.

This does not mean that we are reduced to providing algorithms that are devoid of any generality. Rather, as we argue below, we may be able to determine a structure over the space of domains that makes it possible to provide solutions that apply at varying degrees of domain-specificity.

2.2 Grid-Based Domains

Our recent work on referring expression generation (Viethen and Dale, to appear) is based on a domain which has arguably very specific characteristics compared to many other application domains in NLG. It consists of 16 filing cabinet drawers which form a four-by-four grid. Four drawers each have one of four colours (yellow, orange, pink and blue); the colours are distributed randomly over the grid, as shown in Figure 1.

[1] Interestingly, as far as we are aware, no significant studies have been carried out to determine how such preference orderings might actually be identified in any given domain.

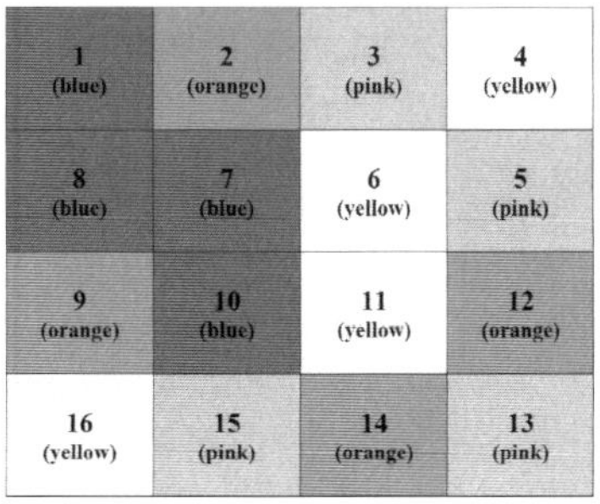

Figure 1: The filing cabinets

In exploring the generation and evaluation of referring expressions in this domain, we determined that specific characteristics of the domain have a considerable influence on the performance of different algorithms. In (Viethen and Dale, 2006) we discuss how the very good performance of the IA, and the contrasting unexpectedly bad results for the Relational Algorithm (Dale and Haddock, 1991), are mainly due to the peculiarities of the drawer domain. In particular, the domain's regular grid-like layout and the uniformity of the possible referents with regard to their types and properties put the Relational Algorithm, at least as originally specified, at a great disadvantage.

This does not mean, however, that more specifically-tailored solutions for reference in this domain are then so tied to the description of filing cabinets that they cannot be used for anything else. Rather, we take the view that our specific domain of enquiry is an instance of a more general class of domains, which we refer to as the *grid-based domains*. This class of domains shares a set of common characteristics:

Type homogeneity: All potential referents are of the same type; related objects of other types might be used to describe the referent, but these objects are not considered distractors.

Positional precision: Every entity has an exact position in the grid, allowing a unique description using only positional information.

Connectedness: Every entity is connected to each of its neighbours in the grid by a spatial relation, such as above or left-of.

Also, in domains like this, the properties of the entities fall into two categories: they are either *positional* (for example, row or column, and corner-hood or other special positional information such as on-an-edge or in-the-middle) or *intrinsic* (for example, colour, size, or shape).

Many domains share these properties: for example, blocks or buildings on a street map with a grid layout, as can be found in many inner cities of Australia or the United States; cubicle layouts in open-plan offices; cells in spreadsheets or tables of many different kinds; the boards of many games such as checkers; windows in large building blocks; and cars in car parks, perhaps as imagined from an aerial view. We might consider these all to be *regular* grid-based domains; we can then also identify somewhat less regular grid-based domains, such as map references, books in bookshelves, bricks in a wall, or pictures on display.

Our proposal here is that, while we carry out our experimentation in one particular grid-based domain, we can still identify strategies for reference that work across all grid-based domains; consequently, we can provide solutions that, while they are clearly not domain-independent, are of more value than strategies tied to a single very specific domain.

2.3 A Hierarchy of Referential Domains

The basic idea underlying the above proposal is that we can impose some structure over the space of possible *referential domains* (domains in which we want to refer to things) that allows us to determine different degrees of domain-specificity. It is too early to determine what such a hierarchy of domains would look like, but there are some reasonable suggestions we might make. For example, it is plausible that, at the top level, we can partition the space of all referential domains into those that are physical or concrete, on the one hand, and those that are abstract (such as the domains of beliefs, or mathematical objects) on the other hand, with different strategies for reference appropriate in each.

Similarly, we can hypothesise some domain structure from the bottom-up. Above, we identified a subset of domains that we referred to as grid-based; we might consider the set of grid-based domains to be a subtype of the set of 'physical layout' domains, such as a collection of objects on a table or plants in a garden. Such domains clearly share some of the characteristics of grid-based domains that will be relevant for reference, but at the same time embody significant differences that will render some specifically grid-based reference strategies inappropriate.

These are only suggestions; our view is that detailed consideration of quite different domains is required before we can properly establish the relationships between these domains. The main point we are arguing for here is that some degree of domain specificity cannot be ignored. To put the point more strongly: we argue that further progress on the development of algorithms for referring expression generation will only result if we move away from a focus on domain-independent aspects of the problem.

2.4 Reference in Grid-Based Domains

The special characteristics of grid-based domains noted above have an impact on the kinds of referring expressions that we might generate.

First, as already noted, the property of *positional precision* means that for every entity in a grid-based domain, there exists a unique description which only uses the row and column properties of that object, such as *the drawer in the bottom row, third column* for d14 in Figure 1.

The property of *type homogeneity* means that the entities in the domain often share a set of grid-independent properties. In the case of the drawer domain, this set only consists of colour; in the car park domain, this would include properties such as make and model, colour, or modifications such as spoilers. This characteristic adds to the uniformity of descriptions across objects, and therefore allows for reference strategies to be quite generally applicable in the domain.

The *positional precision* and *connectedness* characteristics mean that it is possible to infer the exact grid location of one entity from that of another whose location is specified. For example, if we know that one object is in row 2 and column 4, then we know that the object to the right of it is in row 2 and column 3. As we will see in Section 4, this has an influence on the usefulness of grid-dependent properties of objects that are spatially related to the referent.

Another consequence of *connectedness* is that the normal transitivity of spatial relations such as above, below, and left-of does not play a role in these domains. Of course, it is logically true that if object2 is below object1 and object3 is below object2, then object3 is also below object1. However, this relation between object1 and object3 would never be used in a referring expression describing either of these two entities. In the drawer domain, a hearer would always understand *the drawer below the orange drawer in the top row* to be d7, the drawer *directly* below d2, not d10 or d15.

Our point here is that the nature of the domain has an impact on how the properties available in that domain might be used to refer to entities. Most importantly, these domain characteristics impact on the applicability of 'general purpose' algorithms, as we saw in (Viethen and Dale, 2006) with regard to the poor performance of the relational algorithm of Dale and Haddock (1991) in a new domain.

3 The Space of Descriptions

3.1 The Possible and the Acceptable

In any domain where entities are described via a finite set of properties and relations, there are a finite number of possible descriptions of a given entity. We might think of these as the set of *logically possible referring expressions*. This set will of course be combinatorial in the number of properties and related entities. Even if we limit the set to those which are *distinguishing* descriptions,we are still faced with a large set of descriptions to choose from.

Existing algorithms effectively provide ways to search this space, generally oriented towards finding shorter solutions before longer ones are considered. These strategies favour referring expressions which avoid or minimise redundancy and stop as soon as one referring expression is found, but as we know, human descriptions are often redundant and there is usually more than one acceptable solution; these algorithms therefore will fail to find many descriptions which are in fact quite acceptable from the point of view of readers or listeners. This is in effect taking an engineering perspective: find one good solution that can do the job, then stop exploring other possibilities. A more interesting approach to the problem might be from the speaker's and the listener's perspectives: identify all the acceptable referring expressions for an object and then rank them by usefulness to the parties involved.

These observations then raise some questions. In particular, are all logically possible distinguishing descriptions also *acceptable* to the speaker or listener? And if not, how do we rule out those which are not acceptable descriptions? It seems likely that many of these descriptions—especially the very long, multiply redundant ones—will not be particularly useful.

Below, we provide some basic statistics that demonstrate the size of the space of possible descriptions that are available in even a simple domain like the one focussed on here. Then, in Section 4, we propose some plausible constraints on this space of possible descriptions.

3.2 The Size of the Space

In our present work, we use an algorithm which is based on the graph-based framework for referring expression generation described in Krahmer et al. (2003) to generate all logically possible distinguishing descriptions for a target referent. We concentrate on referring expressions containing simple attributive properties and binary relations between pairs of entities. More complex expressions involving plurals, and Boolean combinations of properties or quantifiers (see among others (Gatt, 2006), Varges and van Deemter (2005) and van Deemter and Krahmer (2007 to appear)) are not included in our current investigation; but even without these, the number of possible descriptions we have to consider is very large.

The attributive properties we encode for the drawer domain are colour, row and column for all drawers, and position with the value corner for the four corner drawers. Of the relational properties, only above and left-of are explicitly encoded, so as to avoid circularity. It is left to the realisation level to determine whether to realise the edge (a above b) as *A which is above B* or *B which is below A*, depending on whether A or B is the entity being described.[2]

We use a parameter maxNodes to delimit the set of descriptions produced by our algorithm; this determines how many entities can maximally be included in each referring expression. We currently investigate referring expressions involving no more than two entities. Three reasons justify this seemingly low cut off: firstly, as each entity in our domain has 3–4 attributive properties, it seems unnecessary to consider descriptions containing long chains of relations such as *the blue drawer above the blue drawer left of the drawer in the third row below the yellow drawer*; secondly, our set of 140 human-produced descriptions for

[2]For representational issues in the drawer domain and the graph-based framework, see (Viethen and Dale, 2006) and (Krahmer et al., 2003) respectively.

this domain contains only four relational descriptions with more than one relation; and finally and most practically, allowing more than two entities in a description extends the set of descriptions to be considered from hundreds to thousands.

If we allow maximally one related entity to be included alongside the intended referent, it turns out that we have an average of about 212 possible distinguishing descriptions per drawer. For example, for drawer d1 in Figure 1, the number of candidate descriptions consists of the following sets, where 'DD' means 'distinguishing description':

- $|\{\text{DDs of d1}\}| = 8$
- $|\{\text{DDs of d1}\} \times \{\text{DDs of d2 or d8}\}| = 8 \times (4{+}2) = 48$
- $|\{\text{DDs of d1}\} \times \{\text{non-DDs of d2 or d8}\}| = 8 \times (4{+}6) = 80$
- $|\{\text{non-DDs of d1}\} \times \{\text{DDs of d2 or d8}\}| = 8 \times (4{+}2) = 48$
- $|\{\{\text{non-DDs of d1}\} \times \{\text{non-DDs of d2 or d8}\}$, where the resulting description is distinguishing$\}| < 8 \times (4{+}6) = 80$. In fact, for this drawer the number is 44.

This results in a total of 228 candidate descriptions for drawer d1 using at most one relational property.

Taking into account that, depending on a drawer's position in the grid, there are between 4 and 12 distinct possible combinations of two neighbours in a relational description; that each candidate description only needs to describe one of the contained drawers distinctly to distinguish the intended referent; and that there are a large number of non-distinguishing descriptions that become distinguishing when combined with a non-distinguishing description for one or more other drawers, it becomes clear that the number of candidate descriptions involving three drawers lies in the thousands. In fact, there are between 5136 and 8834 relational descriptions with up to two relatees for each drawer, or about 6764 on average.

4 Constraints on Acceptability

Of course, no sensible algorithm would generate the set of all possible descriptions and then attempt to select from amongst these. However, as we noted above, generate-and-test search strategies like those present in existing algorithms will fail to discover many acceptable descriptions. We would like, therefore, to see if we can identify ways of constraining this space of possible descriptions to a more manageable set; any constraints so determined might then form the basis of a revised generate-and-test search strategy that does not focus on minimality, but rather on acceptability, and is able to find all acceptable solutions, not just one.

On the basis of an examination of the kinds of referring expressions produced by our graph-based algorithm for this domain, we first define in Section 4.1 two 'whitelist' rules that allow us to identify a number of referring expressions that are considered acceptable under all circumstances. We then go on in Section 4.2 to describe a collection of 'blacklist' constraints which exclude certain types of referring expressions as unacceptable. Finally, in Section 4.4 we provide three examples of rules that can be used for ranking the remaining referring expressions in this domain and, we believe, other grid-based domains.

4.1 Whitelist rules

Minimality: In any domain, if the description is a minimal distinguishing description, it is considered acceptable, where a *minimal* referring expression is definedas a *shortest possible* one.[3]

Non-relationality: In domains with only a small number of available attributive properties for each entity, as is the case in the drawer domain, we will consider all non-relational distinguishing referring expressions as acceptable, regardless of any redundancy they contain. In other domains, descriptions using long lists of attributive properties may become too long and cumbersome, and may lead to false implicatures.

4.2 Blacklist constraints

After applying these two white-list rules, we can direct our focus towards the remaining descriptions, which will either be non-minimal (i.e., overspecified), relational, or both. We make two general observations regarding constraints on the acceptability of these types of referring expressions.

Firstly, the two categories of properties in grid-based domains discussed in Section 2.2 have an impact on the acceptability of overspecification in referring expressions. We observe that it seems to be the case that informationally redundant *intrinsic* properties are more useful—or even desirable— than redundant *positional* properties.

[3]See (Dale, 1989). For present purposes, we will assume that all descriptions are 'accessible', in that they can be determined by the listener to be true of the intended referent.

For example, while the mention of the relatee and its colour in *the pink drawer in the far right that's below the yellow drawer* is unnecessary, this description is clearly more acceptable than *the pink drawer in the far right that's below the drawer in the top row*, where instead of colour, the row property is included for the relatee.

Secondly, we observe that, in our human-produced data, relations are only used under two circumstances:

(a) The attributive properties of the relatee are more visually salient than those of the target. So, the target gets described mainly in terms of its relation to a more salient entity, as for example in *the book left of the huge black lexicon in the bottom shelf.*

(b) The combination of properties of target and relatee, including the relation holding between them, is more or as visually salient as the target alone. An example of this, taken from our human-produced data set, is *the yellow drawer that's above another yellow drawer* for drawer d6.

Note also, as discussed in Section 3.1, that we have already ruled out those descriptions which are not distinguishing descriptions. We then propose the following constraints to further reduce the space of acceptable referring expressions.

C1: No relatees without attributes: A referring expression should at least contain one attributive property for each relatee to the referent. In most domains the minimum requirement is that the type of each entity is included. This is a commonly observed phenomenon, of course, and is often catered for in algorithms by means of a special case 'necessary-inclusion' rule. Note, however, that for highly connected domains where all the referents are of the same type (as in our drawer domain), this constraint also excludes descriptions containing only type as the attributive property used for a relatee. Consequently, Examples (1) and (2) are excluded by this constraint, while Example (3) is not:

(1) the blue drawer in the first column below another drawer

(2) the thick book in the third shelf from the top, left of another book

(3) the bush under the tree

This constraint reduces the average number of descriptions per drawer from about 212 to 200.

C2: No relatee without salient properties: Either the relatee itself or the combination of the relatee and the intended referent need to be as readily locatable as the referent described in only attributive terms. If this is not the case, the mention of the relatee renders the expression more informative than required and adds the potential for confusion. While the visual salience of an entity or specific properties is difficult to determine for most domains, in the drawer domain it is straightforward that the two properties that can contribute to the visual salience of an entity are its colour and its being in the corner position. We therefore exclude descriptions containing relatees without either of these two properties, such as:

(4) the yellow drawer in the second row, third column that's left of the drawer in the second row, fourth column

(5) the pink drawer left of the drawer in the bottom row, third column.

This constraint reduces the average number of descriptions per drawer by another 65 to about 135.

C3: No grid properties for less salient relatees: In regular grid-based domains, it appears there is no good reason to include row and column properties for relatees. This information can either be inferred from the intended referent, or forces the listener to perform the opposite inference to find the location of the intended referent. This constraint excludes descriptions such as the following:

(6) the big red book next to the little booklet, which is the fourth book from the left in the second shelf from the bottom

(7) the blue drawer in the second row left of the yellow drawer in the third column

The only cases where grid information for a relatee might be useful are (i) situations where the relatee is more easily locatable than the intended referent (as in Example 8), and (ii) situations where the relatee only has the bit of grid property it shares with the intended referent and no other grid information is contained in the referring expression (as in Example 9).[4]

[4]Note that, in the second case, the PP attachment ambiguity means that we can see *in the leftmost column* to be either

(8) the blue book below the fat brown dictionary in the third shelf from the top

(9) the blue drawer above the orange drawer in the leftmost column

4.3 Status of the Constraints

In the previous section, we offered three domain-specific constraints on acceptable reference that substantially reduce the number of logically possible descriptions that we might want to consider. The constraints are based on our observations on the data; while the real status of the constraints requires more rigorous experimental testing, we would suggest that they do seem intuitively plausible when expressed as general rules, and they also succeed in ruling out specific referring expressions that are plausibly dispreferred.

To back up our intuition, we conducted a small evaluation exercise where seven native English speakers were asked to directly compare pairs of randomly chosen descriptions. One description in every pair was from the set of left over acceptable descriptions for one drawer; the other one was taken from the set of descriptions for the same drawer that were excluded by the constraints. Each participant could choose to compare between 5 and 20 pairs for 4 drawers each, which resulted in 361 comparisons.

Overall, the participants preferred the description from the set deemed acceptable in 69% of the cases. The descriptions considered acceptable by C1 and C3 were chosen in 64% of the cases, while the hypothesis of C2 was supported in 78% of the cases. Interestingly, there were two participants who overall slightly preferred the descriptions excluded by the constraints.

While these numbers are mildly encouraging in the characterisation of the constraints presented here, we do not claim that it is ultimately the correct one. Our main point here is that we need to identify such constraints for any given domain or class of domains.

4.4 Rules for Ranking

After applying the black-list constraints, we are still left with a fairly large number of possible descriptions. We are less confident of ruling subsets of these out as unacceptable, but it does seem to us that some are more acceptable than others.

a property of the intended referent or of the relatee. This constraint results in an average of about 66 descriptions per drawer.

We suggest, therefore, that we may also require a number of general ranking rules along the following lines.

R1: Not too many positional properties: In small grid domains, it seems desirable to either exclude all positional properties, or to use at most one bit of grid information. The smaller a domain, the less need there is to direct the hearer's focus towards the intended referent by the use of more and more precise position information.

Most relational descriptions in our human-produced set for the drawer domain are of the type ⟨colour–relation–colour⟩:

(10) the yellow drawer that's above another yellow drawer

(11) the blue drawer above the pink drawer

However, there are three examples of relational descriptions containing one bit of grid information in our human-produced data, and other examples with more position information than this cannot be excluded on the grounds of not being contained in a data set of only 140 items.

If we choose to limit relational descriptions in the drawer domain to at most one bit of grid information, the average number of descriptions after applying the blacklist constraints decreases by 35 to about 31.

As this is a fairly large reduction, we included this rule in our evaluation exercise and found that only 54% of the comparisons turned out in its favour. However, without the vote of the two participants who overall preferred the excluded descriptions, the hypothesis of R1 was supported in 70% of the cases.

R2: Always use location: The opposite effect emerges in larger domains: the bigger the search space, the more helpful positional information is in directing the hearer's focus into the relevant area of the domain. This is especially true for uniform domains, where most entities have the same type and other attributive properties of similar salience. For example, in a large bookshelf containing only randomly-ordered small paperbacks in many different colours, a referring expression only containing *intrinsic* properties such as colour, size, or title is unlikely to be very helpful.

R3: No relational descriptions: In very small domains, it can be best to exclude all relational descriptions, given that each object can be described uniquely using only attributive properties. In a 3×3 grid, descriptions such as *the small blue object left of the red object in the top right corner* or even *the blue object left of the red object* will always be significantly more cumbersome than non-relational descriptions.

5 Conclusions and Future Work

In this paper, we have taken the view that the process of referring expression generation fundamentally involves domain-specific principles. This position does not need to result in chaos, with every domain having its own hand-crafted rules for reference; rather, we propose that referential domains are ordered in a subsumption hierarchy, which allows us to group domains according to common characteristics. These characteristics can help us define what counts as an acceptable referring expression for domains of a given type. To illustrate our claim, we explore the use of constraints in grid-based domains, using our drawer domain as a specific example, and show how this allows us to reduce the very large set of logically possible descriptions to a more manageable set of acceptable descriptions.

Evidence from human-produced referring expressions shows that for any given object a variety of acceptable descriptions exist. This runs contrary to the prevailing assumption that the aim of a referring expression generation system should be to find only one best description for a target referent. We have provided an approach to determining acceptability that denies this assumption, and is more in line with real human behaviour.

There are some clear steps forward from the position taken in this paper.

- First, we need to develop algorithms that can use the kinds of constraints we have discussed, so that we don't have to generate all the bad referring expressions to find the good ones.
- There are a range of psycholinguistic experiments that could be carried out both to validate the constraints and rules we have identified, and to test algorithms based on these constraints.
- More generally, the notion of a hierarchy of referential domains requires further exploration.

In conclusion, it is clear that humans can produce many acceptable referring expressions for a given intended referent. We have argued that a focus on minimality and single 'best' solutions has allowed the field to avoid the fact that the range of acceptable descriptions can only be characterised by reference to characteristics of the domain in question.

References

Dale, R. and Haddock, N. 1991. Generating referring expressions involving relations. In *Proceedings of the 5th Conference of the European Chapter of the ACL*, 161–166, Berlin, Germany.

Dale, R. and Reiter, E. 1995. Computational interpretations of the Gricean maxims in the generation of referring expressions. *Cognitive Science*, 19(2):233–263.

Dale, R., Geldof, S., and Prost, J. 2002. Generating more natural route descriptions. In *Proceedings of the Australasian Natural Language Processing Workshop*, Canberra, Australia.

Dale, R. 1989. Generating recipes: An overview of EPICURE. In *Proceedings of the 2nd European Workshop on Natural Language Generation*, Edinburgh, UK.

Gardent, C. 2002. Generating minimal definite descriptions. In *Proceedings of the 40th Annual Meeting of the Association for Computational Linguistics*, Philadelphia, PA, USA.

Gatt, A. 2006. Generating collective spatial references. In *Proceedings of the 28th Annual Meeting of the Cognitive Science Society*, Vancouver, Canada.

Krahmer, E., van Erk, S., and Verleg, A. 2003. Graph-based generation of referring expressions. *Computational Linguistics*, 29(1):53–72.

van Deemter, K. and Krahmer, E. 2007, to appear. Graphs and Booleans: On the generation of referring expressions. In Bunt, H. and Muskens, R. (Eds.), *Computing Meaning*, vol. 3, 17–53. Kluwer, Dordrecht, The Netherlands.

Varges, S. and van Deemter, K. 2005. Generating referring expressions containing quantifiers. In *Proceedings of the 6th International Worskhop on Computational Semantics*, Tilburg, The Netherlands.

Viethen, J. and Dale, R. 2006. Algorithms for generating referring expressions: Do they do what people do? In *Proceedings of the 4th International Conference on Natural Language Generation*, 63–70, Sydney, Australia.

Viethen, J. and Dale, R. to appear. Evaluation in natural language generation: Lessons from referring expression generation. *Traitement Automatique des Langues*, 47(3).

Papers Presented as Posters

Determining tutorial remediation strategies from a corpus of human-human tutoring dialogues

Charles B. Callaway and **Johanna D. Moore**
Human Communication Research Centre
University of Edinburgh
2 Buccleuch Place
Edinburgh, EH8 9LW, United Kingdom
{ccallawa, jmoore}@inf.ed.ac.uk

Abstract

We present an empirical approach to adaptively selecting a tutoring system's remediation strategy based on an annotated corpus of human-human tutorial dialogues. We are interested in the remediation selection problem, that of generating the best remediation strategy given a diagnosis for an incorrect answer and the current problem solving context. By comparing the use of individual remediation strategies to their success in varying contexts, we can empirically extract and implement tutoring rules for the content planner of an intelligent tutoring system. We describe a methodology for analyzing a tutoring corpus and using the resulting data to inform a content planning model.

1 Introduction

The goal of an Intelligent Tutoring System (ITS) is not simply to confer knowledge to a student or explain how to solve problems, but to give students help and feedback as they solve problems. Dialogue-based ITS's principally contribute to student learning by providing targeted remedial feedback when the student gives an incorrect answer. The success of a remediation depends both on the content of a remediation and on selecting the right strategy at the right time – for instance, a remediation strategy without content ("No") may be best. Additionally, unlike explanation generation, an ITS shouldn't tell the student everything it knows since the goal is to get the student to do the problem solving, not have the tutor do it for them.

There are many competing theories about what leads students to learn. For instance, VanLehn et al. (2003) propose that students learn when they experience an impasse, such as getting stuck, are correct but uncertain, or make a known type of error. Posner et al. (1982) believe that cognitive dissonance occurs when a student is forced to confront an inconsistency between a strongly held but inaccurate expectation and an actual outcome. Wolf et al. (2005) credit students with generating "accountable talk" when they use valid examples or reasoning strategies from within the domain of interest to back up their claims, and when they make appropriate connections between elements of the domain. Meanwhile Thomas and Rohwer (1993) explain learning gains by the extent to which students apply cognitive effort when processing the new material.

Just as important as the error diagnosis itself then is understanding how to present that diagnosis to the learner, which requires knowing what options are available for varying remedial feedback. Each type of error the student makes can be remediated using many styles varying along social, motivational, content and contextual dimensions even though the diagnosis from the domain reasoner is the same.

One way to discover which of these multiple potential remediation strategies would perform best after an incorrect answer in a given context is to systematically analyze a corpus of tutoring dialogues for (1) remediation strategies, (2) the student's performance after the remediation, and (3) any contextual factors that may have influenced which strategy was selected by the human tutor. Indeed annotation of tutoring dialogue corpora is becoming more common (Cabrera et al., 2007).

But even corpus analysis is difficult due to factors such as data sparsity: (1) there is a large range of potential contextual factors leading to low counts of many phenomena for each specific context, (2) individual remediation strategies don't occur in all domains making it harder to share annotation schemes,

(3) remediation strategies that do occur across domains may have different success rates for different domains, and (4) few dialogues can be collected since a large amount of time is needed to organize and conduct corpora collection between scarce human experts and students. For instance, in the corpus described below, 25 hours of dialogue were required to obtain 198 instances of remedial feedback (i.e., 8 per hour of collected dialogue).

To provide an empirical basis for selecting remediation strategies, we have explored the use of remedial feedback in our tutoring system in the domain of symbolic differentiation (Callaway et al., 2006). By annotating remediation dialogue acts, adjacent dialogue acts related to remediation, along with features such as problem type, we hope to find evidence of patterns in existing human-human dialogues that can be correlated with measures of problem-solving success. To measure the degree of success, we defined a performance metric to compare remediation strategies with their local outcomes, rewarding remediations that led to the student overcoming an impasse and penalizing cases where the tutor's remediations were ineffective or the tutor was forced to "bottom out" by supplying the correct answer.

We then statistically analyzed the resulting data in order to provide advice to an intelligent tutoring system on which strategy to use in a given context. We hope to be able to empirically answer four questions: (1) what is the variation of success of individual remediation strategies, (2) do multiple remediations have better results than single remediations, and (3) which remediation strategies are correlated with particular types of problems (such as polynomials or trigonometric functions). The resulting information can be directly used to help decide which remediation strategy is best to use when the student answers incorrectly in a particular context.

We begin by examining related work in dialogue generation and tutoring, then introducing our tutoring domain of symbolic differentiation and the corpus we analyzed, describing the annotation scheme and evaluation methodology, presenting and analyzing the resulting empirical data, and discussing its implications for NLG.

2 Related Work

Adding generated natural language dialogue to a tutorial system is a complex task whether using templates or deep generation since interactivity allows for a wide range of local variation in context. Many existing tutorial dialogue systems rely on pre-authored curriculum scripts (Person et al., 2000) or finite-state machines (Rosé et al., 2001) without detailed knowledge representations. These systems are easier to design for curriculum providers, but offer limited flexibility because the writer has to predict all possible student responses. Representations of domain knowledge and reasoning, along with a record of past student problem solving behavior and misconceptions, is vital for adaptively interacting with students via natural language.

Newer generations of tutoring systems have concentrated more on the tutor's utterances than on being able to understand free natural language input. CIRCSIM is a tutor in the cardiac physiology domain (Michael et al., 2003) that parses student input via finite state machines, arrives at a diagnosis, and then selects and realizes a response for the student, notably with the systematic use of discourse markers. This project also used annotation as a means of identifying key domain phenomena, but without relating it to a success measure (Kim et al., 2006).

The BEETLE1 system (Moore et al., 2004) describes a tutor for teaching basic electricity concepts and components in circuits. The focus of this work was to explore how affective factors should effect the response given. The DIAG-NLP2 system (Eugenio et al., 2005) in the domain of appliance repair takes menu-based input for determining students' actions in a schematic environment and employs high-level abstract revision operations when creating tutorial feedback to make the tutor's responses sound more natural. A formal evaluation showed that a version with revision significantly improved learning gain over a version without it.

In addition to CIRCSIM, annotation has been used in the generation community to attempt to discover relationships or prove effectiveness. Litman and Forbes-Riley (2006) annotated a large array of factors that might potentially affect learning and used χ-square tests over sequences of dialogue moves to discover which of those factors had the greatest influence on learning gain. The GNOME project (Poesio, 2004) created annotation schemes of noun phrases and their co-referring pronouns in order to be able to utilize them for evaluating pronominalization algorithms.

3 Background

We are attempting to semi-automatically formulate remediation strategies using a corpus of human-

Tutor: Differentiate sin(2x)
Student: cos(x)
Tutor: Again we have to use the chain rule.
Tutor: So the answer you gave isn't right.
Student: cos(2x) (x)
Student: sorry
Student: it is cos(2x) (2)
Tutor: Yes, well done.
Tutor: And well done for spotting your mistake.

Figure 1: Extract of a tutoring dialogue

human tutoring sessions in the symbolic differentiation domain. At an abstract level each tutoring session consists of a short subdialogue where a preparatory exchange occurs, followed by a series of math problems proposed by the tutor and solved by the student whenever possible, until a preset time limit is reached. A segment of a typical tutoring dialogue is shown in Figure 1.

Each individual math problem consists of a problem proposal followed by attempts by the student to determine the next correct substep (or the final solution). When a student answers incorrectly, the tutor may immediately respond with remedial feedback to help the student learn from that mistake or wait for the student to ask for help before providing the remediation. Tutors then advance to a subsequent problem either when the student has produced a correct answer, the student is unable to solve the problem and the tutor is forced to produce the answer (a "bottom out"), or the tutor tries a simpler, but related, differentiation problem.

Symbolic Differentiation Domain: The subject area for our human-human corpus data is the differentiation of polynomials and other functions, which involves significant use of the Chain Rule:

$$\frac{d}{dx}\left[f(g(x))\right] = \frac{d}{dg}\left[f(g(x))\right] \cdot \frac{d}{dx}\left[g(x)\right]$$

Its application involves several steps that can be formalized in a task model describing the step-by-step task of building a derivative in terms of simpler, partially ordered sub-tasks, helps to identify which parts of the task a student is currently attempting to solve, and can aid a tutoring system in deciding how to address student actions and provide corrective feedback on the current problem.

The high-level task description for solving derivatives of a given function $y = f(g(x))$ consists of (1) rewriting y to a form $\overline{y}$ which the student already knows how to solve; (2) identifying the component elements of $\overline{y}$ as two nested functions $f(g(x))$; (3) identify the "inner" ($z = g(x)$) and "outer" ($w = f(z)$) layers of $\overline{y}$; (4) differentiate each of the layers, $\frac{dz}{dx}$ and $\frac{dw}{dz}$; (5) combine the results appropriately $\frac{dy}{dx} = \frac{dw}{dz} \cdot \frac{dz}{dx}$; and (6) use algebra to convert the result to a canonical form.

In these dialogues, tutors proposed problems drawn from six fundamental types: polynomials ($3x^4 - 2x$), trigonometric functions ($sin(5x^2)$), square roots ($\sqrt{4x + 6x^5}$), logarithms ($log(7x)$), inverses ($1/sin(4x)$) and combinations ($\sqrt{sin(3x^2)}$).

Corpus: The human-human corpus of tutored differential calculus for this study was conducted at the University of Edinburgh as part of an effort to associate subjective situational factors with learning in the domain (Porayska-Pomsta et al., 2007) and implement the newly discovered principles in an intelligent tutoring system (Callaway et al., 2006)

The data consists of 33 transcripts of tutoring sessions conducted via a chat interface and lasting about 40 minutes each. During each session, the tutor gave the student a sequence of problems to solve until they ran out of time, regardless of the number of problems completed. Five experienced mathematics instructors (as tutors) and 28 first-year mathematics or science undergraduate students who were learning differentiation in a calculus course at the University of Edinburgh were paid to participate.

The data collection environment separated students from tutors physically. They could, however, communicate via a chat interface where the two interlocutors could send each other their typed utterances. Complex mathematical expressions could be entered using a special editor, and text and formulas could be intermixed. The tutor could observe the student's actions in real-time on a second screen. Students and tutors were trained to use the interfaces prior to the data collection session. The resulting corpus consists of 33 dialogues (5 students returned twice) and contains 1650 utterances, 5447 words and 559 formulas.

Domain Reasoning: A domain reasoner supports a model that describes correct actions and relationships within that domain. To support a tutoring system, a domain reasoner must be capable of determining whether a student's answer is correct or not, and if not, what is the most likely explanation for the error. This is usually accomplished by model-tracing using both correct and buggy rules (Brown and Burton, 1978). For symbolic differentiation,

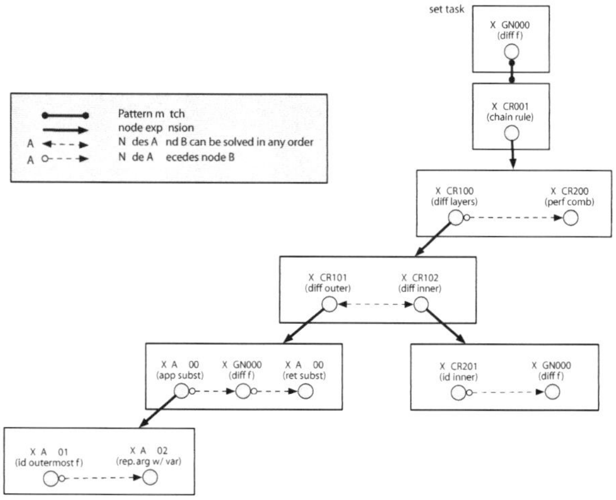

Figure 2: A graphical depiction of the task model

this translates to correct and buggy rules not only for differentiation itself, but also the algebraic rewriting techniques necessary for problem solving.

In tutoring systems based on chat-style text interfaces, the tutor's dialogue acts are the sole means for the system to exhibit adaptivity. Of the possible range of tutor utterances, remediations and proactive hints are most likely to introduce adaptive behavior that will lead to increased student problem solving performance.

Remediations and hints are based directly on the task model itself, where the domain reasoner plays an important role in ensuring that both student and computer tutor are in step when solving problems. A domain reasoner for symbolic differentiation for instance should minimally be capable of judging the correctness of both intermediate steps and final solutions, using buggy rules to be able to interpret the most likely reason for student errors, knowing how far the student has progressed through the current problem, and producing diagnoses that allow the tutoring system to provide feedback to the student.

Given a student solving the differentiation problem x^{-3} by answering $-3 * x^{-2}$ instead of the correct $-3 * x^{-4}$, our domain reasoner would produce:

```
[bg-pl111, type(buggy), rule(power_rule),
 tmc(basic,null), expr(x^(-3)),
 student_answer(-3*x^(-2)),
 wrong_part(exponent, -2),
 corrected_part(exponent, -4)]
```

A non-adaptive template system would match this with a single tutorial utterance which would be the same in every context. However here we are trying to use the dialogue context and problem solving history to vary tutor feedback where the diagnosis serves as the starting point but not the final determinant of remediation content.

4 Annotation Scheme

As mentioned earlier, we are interested in using the corpus to identify which remediations are most likely to lead to improved student performance in a given context. We have ignored clarification dialogues and in-depth follow-ups to mistakes, as they are not easily classifiable and dialogue interpretation components would have a difficult time distinguishing their intent. We have instead concentrated on (1) student answers, (2) tutor responses to those answers, and (3) utterances involved in cognitive impasses, such as help requests. Given a corpus annotated for remediation, we can then use empirical techniques to determine the success or failure of particular remediation strategies in given contexts and adjust the tutorial content planner's high level generation rules accordingly.

The following annotation scheme describes the types of utterances (out of a larger annotated set) that we assume have a strong bearing on remediation and adaptivity of tutorial utterances in general:

Giving and Repairing Answers: Once the tutor has proposed a problem or presented feedback from a previous substep, the student is expected to either provide the next substep or the final solution, or else declare to the tutor that he can't advance by requesting help. Answers are either correct or wrong (we coded partially correct answers as wrong), while step type indicates whether the answer is considered an intermediate step or final solution in terms of the domain model.

We coded correct answers differently depending on whether they occured within normal problem solving or during remediation. In the latter case, answers are instead termed repairs, and rather than being marked for correctness (since repairs are correct by definition), they were instead annotated according to whether the answer was given without an intervening tutor turn (*immediately*) or if there was a discussion of the error before the repair (*delayed*). Figure 3 shows examples of answers in lines 4, 6, 12 and 19 and repairs in lines 8 and 17.

Local Remediation Strategies: If instead the student's answer is incorrect, the tutor must first make the student aware of the mistake and then decide how best to get the student to understand and then fix it. In procedural problem solving domains like

```
Student-01:  Hi.                            No-Annotation
Tutor---02:  Welcome back.                  No-Annotation
Tutor---03:  Try sqrt(3x^2)                 Propose-Problem/Sqrt
Student-04:  (3x^2)^(1/2)                   Give-Answer/Correct/Substep
Tutor---05:  good                           Accept-Answer/Move-On
Student-06:  then (3x^2)^(-1/2)             Give-Answer/Wrong/None
Tutor---07:  you're missing the factor      Remediation/Hint-Error-Location-General
Student-08:  1/2 (3x^2)^(-1/2)              Repair-Answer/Immediate/Substep
Tutor---09:  right                          Accept-Answer/Move-On
Student-10:  then i'm not sure              Help-Request
Tutor---11:  use the chain rule here        Hint-Not-Remediation/Hint-Relevant-Rule-Name
Student-12:  1/2 (6x)^(-1/2) 3x^2           Give-Answer/Wrong/None
Tutor---13:  no, not quite.                 Remediation/Rejection-Only
Tutor---14:  (3x^2)^(-1/2) was right        Remediation/Bottom-Out-Substep
Student-15:  oh, the other way around?      No-Annotation
Tutor---16:  yep                            No-Annotation
Student-17:  1/2 (3x^2)^(-1/2) (6x)         Repair-Answer/Delayed/Substep
Tutor---18:  right                          Accept-Answer/Move-On
Student-19:  (6x)/[2*sqrt(3x^2)]            Give-Answer/Correct/Solution
Tutor---20:  Great!                         Accept-Answer/Positive
```

Figure 3: Condensed dialogue demonstrating typical dialogue moves and their annotation

differentiation, these options are limited to techniques like rejections, hints, and bottoming out. Remediations can occur *singly* (line 7 of Figure 3) or in *multiples* (lines 13–14).

Rejections: The tutor indicates the answer/repair is incorrect without elaborating why. Rejections can appear alone, forcing the student to discover the underlying cause, or in combination with a hint in the same utterance that provides more detail.

```
Tutor:  No.       Remediation, Reject-Only
Tutor:  No, but good try!
                  Remediation, Reject-Positive
Tutor:  That's not what I meant.
                  Remediation, Implied-Rejection
Tutor:  Very close!
                  Remediation, Almost-Complete
```

Hints: The tutor indicates how the student should proceed after the error (Zhou et al., 1999). Most hints in our differentiation domain concern the location of the error.

```
Tutor:  Check the numerator
        Remediation, Hint-Error-Location-General
Tutor:  Are you sure about the 4?
        Remediation, Hint-Error-Location-Specific
Tutor:  Use the power rule.
        Remediation, Hint-Relevant-Rule-Name
Tutor:  The power rule is n*x^(n-1)
        Remediation, Hint-Relevant-Rule-Form
Tutor:  Think of sin^3x as (sin x)^3
        Remediation, Hint-Rewrite
```

Bottoming Out: The tutor supplies the answer.

```
Tutor:  The chain rule gives you (3x^3-3)
             Remediation, Bottom-Out-Substep
Tutor:  No, the answer is 3(x^3-1)
             Remediation, Bottom-Out-Complete
```

Requesting Help If the student is blocked on a problem and prefers not to make an incorrect guess or provide an uncertain answer (hedging), he will often immediately ask for help. The student may also give no answer, and after a short time the tutor typically then supplies a hint to keep the tutoring session on track. Line 10 of Figure 3 shows a typical help request in our domain.

```
Tutor:     Let's try (x^3-3x)^2
                   Propose-Problem
Student:   Where do I start?
                   Help-Request
```

Using this scheme, two annotators coded three of the larger corpus dialogues, obtaining a Kappa of 0.88 considering only top level tags, and 0.78 when the additional lower-level dependent features described below were also taken into account. A single annotator then coded the remaining dialogues.

5 Data Analysis

When students provide incorrect answers, the natural reaction for a tutor is to remediate. There are then a small number of responses that students make to that remediation: (1) immediately repairing the error, (2) repairing with some delay after additional information has been given or requested, (3) explicitly making a request for help, (4) responding with another incorrect answer, and (5) not responding, forcing the tutor to provide further remediation or else directly supply the correct substep or solution.

The success of a remediation can thus be deduced from the subsequent outcome, where we might assume that an immediate repair indicates that an

Remediation Strategy	Immed. Repair	Delayed Repair	Help Request	Wrong Answer	Bottom Out Substep	Bottom Out Complete	Count Totals	Scores
Reject-Only	1 / 6	0 / 3	2 / 1	3 / 7	3 / 1	2 / 2	11 / 20	-21 / +4
Reject-Positive	0 / 2	1 / 2	0 / 1	0 / 3	0 / 0	1 / 0	2 / 8	-2 / +5
Implied-Rejection	2 / 3	0 / 5	1 / 1	3 / 2	0 / 2	1 / 0	7 / 13	-3 / +11
Almost-Complete	3 / 5	0 / 0	0 / 0	3 / 3	0 / 2	2 / 2	8 / 12	-2 / 0
H-E-Loc-General	5 / 8	5 / 3	0 / 1	4 / 9	0 / 6	0 / 3	14 / 30	+22 / -11
H-E-Loc-Specific	13 / 7	3 / 3	0 / 1	2 / 5	0 / 0	2 / 0	20 / 16	+46 / +23
Hint-Rule-Name	0 / 2	1 / 0	0 / 0	3 / 2	0 / 0	0 / 0	4 / 4	-4 / +4
Hint-Rule-Form	2 / 1	0 / 0	1 / 1	0 / 4	0 / 0	1 / 4	5 / 10	+3 / -25
Hint-Rewrite	1 / 2	3 / 4	1 / 0	1 / 2	0 / 0	0 / 0	6 / 8	+7 / +12
Totals	27 / 36	13 / 20	5 / 6	19 / 38	3 / 11	10 / 11	77 / 121	+46 / +23

Table 1: Frequencies of 198 single/multiple remediation dialogue acts by strategy and outcome

"optimal" remediation was selected, while bottoming out indicates a poor remediation was selected. We are thus measuring performance (Aleven et al., 2002) rather than learning gain, where the former is a finer-grained metric. To do this we created an ad-hoc scoring metric that reflects this assumption: for positive outcomes, 4 points for an immediate repair and 2 points for a delayed repair; for negative outcomes, subtracting 1 point for a help request, 2 for a wrong answer, 3 for bottoming out of a substep and 4 points for bottoming out of the entire problem.

The 33 dialogues in the corpus contained 198 total remediations, 77 of which were *single* (occurring alone) and 121 in combination. Table 1 presents the number of each remediation type (rows) as described in Section 4 grouped by outcome (columns) for single/multiple remediations in the entire corpus. The final column lists the score for that remediation type using the scoring metric described above. A positive score thus indicates that that remediation type (when used without other remediations) on average led to the student successfully solving a substep or the entire problem, while a negative score indicates that that remediation type was in general not successful. A score near zero indicates that the outcome averaged out. Pearson's correlation shows remediation as a whole was slightly correlated with successful remediations (those followed by repairs) at $R = 0.13$, and the strongest remediation type was `hint-location-specific` ($R = 0.23$).

The frequency data also indicate which remediations are most often used by tutors. For instance, both `hint-error-location-general` and `hint-error-location-specific` score well, but the former is just as likely as not to involve a discussion with the tutor before the student arrives at the correct answer. (This is not to say that having discussions is a bad thing, we merely score delayed repairs less highly than immediate repairs, but both positively. Also, very specific hints give away more information and so may result in lower longer-term learning.) Negative conclusions can also be drawn, for example that direct rejections ("No.") are very rarely used as a sole remedial utterance.

The right half of each column in Table 1 contains frequencies for multiple remediations, where a student's incorrect answer is followed by two or more adjacent remediation strategies before an outcome is registered. Here, `hint-error-location-specific` continues to correlate strongly with positive outcomes, while `hint-error-location-general` has switched from a positive to a negative correlation.

We were also interested in seeing how problem type (e.g., polynomial) and remediation type correlates with outcome. Table 2 presents frequencies and scores for each remediation type, where for instance `hint-error-location-general` is shown to fare better on polynomials (+11) than square roots (-4) while `hint-error-location-specific` resulted in successful outcomes regardless of problem type. We conclude that the type of differentiation problem can thus have a sizeable impact on the types of remediations a tutor should select in this domain and that this factor should be considered when writing content planning rules.

The data shows that not only are certain tutor remediation strategies better than others overall, but these strategies are also correlated with problem solving performance when the type of differentiation problem is taken into account. Single re-

Remediation Strategy	Poly-nomial	Square Root	Trigono-metric	Logari-thmic	Combin-ation	Inverses	Count Totals
Reject-Only	7 – +2	6 – +5	7 – -11	3 – -1	1 – -1	7 – -11	31
Reject-Positive	4 – -5	1 – +4	2 – -4	1 – +2	1 – +4	1 – +2	10
Implied-Rejection	12 – +9	0 – 0	4 – +3	1 – +2	0 – 0	3 – -2	20
Almost-Complete	9 – -4	3 – -2	3 – -2	2 – +8	2 – +2	1 – -4	20
H-E-Loc-General	16 – +11	5 – -4	10 – -5	4 – +8	2 – +6	7 – -5	44
H-E-Loc-Specific	12 – +7	6 – +16	5 – +10	1 – +4	0 – 0	12 – +32	36
Hint-Rule-Name	3 – +6	1 – +2	2 – -4	1 – -2	0 – 0	1 – -2	8
Hint-Rule-Form	2 – -4	2 – -8	5 – -16	2 – +8	2 – +3	2 – -5	15
Hint-Rewrite	3 – +6	1 – -2	3 – +4	1 – +4	0 – 0	6 – +7	14
Totals	68 – +28	25 – +11	41 – -25	16 – +33	8 – +14	40 – +12	198

Table 2: Combined frequencies and scores for remediations split by problem type

mediations are also more highly correlated with performance than are multiple remediations. This may be because a low aptitude student will perform poorly regardless of whether one or more remediations are administered, but the tutor may feel the need to give more than one remediation type to such a student. Similarly, more specific hints (like `hint-error-location-specific` and `hint-rule-form`) may be given immediately, and the next step in the tutor's remediation sequence after a highly specific hint is to bottom out, resulting in a lower score. Both multiple remediations and highly specific hints may also be given depending on how difficult a step the tutor thinks the student is facing (rather than the overall problem difficulty).

Even more variation is seen when problem type is taken into account. With the differences apparent in Table 2, it becomes possible to write the remediation rules of a tutoring component directly from such data. For instance, we could extract a rule that says if the student is working on a logarithmic function, then select randomly among `almost-complete`, `hint-error-location-general+` and `hint-rule-form`, and otherwise default to selecting `hint-error-location-specific`. This method also points to baseline strategies to use in evaluating an implemented tutoring system against a more sophisticated strategy.

6 Tutorial Generation Component

We have implemented a text generation component (named BUG) in the symbolic differentiation domain that produces turns for the computer in its role as tutor. BUG generates a variety of verbalizations for system feedback within the current context and automatically pronominalizes, aggregates dialogue segments, and inserts discourse markers appropriately. The remediation content planner is included as part of a dialogue manager (Callaway et al., 2006) based on TRINDIKIT which manages the dialogue context and generates all dialogue acts for verbalization within a single turn. As the tactical generator, BUG accepts dialogue moves (sequences of dialogue acts interrelated by rhetorical relations) and information about the dialogue context.

To illustrate, if the dialogue manager decides it would be best to correct a student's wrong answer with a `hint-error-location-specific` remediation type, it gathers details from the diagnosis and constructs a dialogue move such as:

```
[[id1,[concession,id2,id3]],
 [id2,[assert,correct,diff_outer]],
 [id3,[join,id4,id5]],
 [id4,[assert,location,factor,missing]],
 [id5,[assert,location,factor,correct_value,2]]]
```

producing the tutorial utterance "You differentiated the outer layer correctly. However, you missed the factor: it should be 2." where the first clause corresponds to `id2`, the second to `id4`, and the third to `id5`. BUG first converts the dialogue move to deep linguistic representations based on a version of the STORYBOOK system (Callaway and Lester, 2002) modified for use in dialogue systems, and which includes modules for pronominalization, clause aggregation and discourse marker insertion. In this example, it pronominalizes a repeated use of "factor" as "it", revises `id4` and `id5` as indicated by the `join` relation, and inserts the discourse marker "However" into the resulting sentence to connect it to `id2` as indicated by the dialogue move above.

7 Conclusions

We have described natural language generation in the setting of intelligent tutoring systems, focusing on empirically acquiring tutorial (content) planning rules directly from a corpus of human-human tutoring dialogues. We developed an annotation scheme and local performance metric for tutorial remediations within that corpus, and constructed a framework for analyzing the resulting data. The analysis supports an initial baseline and set of parameters that will be extremely useful when the tutorial feedback generator selects remediation rules when we formally evaluate our computer tutor.

References

V. Aleven, O. Popescu, and K. Koedinger. 2002. More on pilot-testing a tutorial dialog system that supports self-explanation: Good feedback on explanations helps, how we can generate more of it? In *ITS 2002 Workshop on Empirical Methods for Tutorial Dialogue Systems*.

John Seely Brown and Richard R. Burton. 1978. Diagnostic models for procedural bugs in basic mathematical skills. *Cognitive Science: A Multidisciplinary Journal*, 2(2):155–192.

Anita Ferreira Cabrera, Johanna D. Moore, and Chris Mellish. 2007. A study of feedback strategies in foreign language classrooms and tutorials with implications for intelligent computer-assisted language learning systems. *International Journal of AI in Education*. In Press.

Charles B. Callaway and James C. Lester. 2002. Narrative prose generation. *Artificial Intelligence*, 139(2):213–252, August.

Charles Callaway, Myroslava Dzikovska, Colin Matheson, Johanna Moore, and Claus Zinn. 2006. Using dialogue to learn math in the LeActiveMath project. In *Proceedings of the ECAI Workshop on Language-Enhanced Educational Technology*, pages 1–8, August.

B. Di Eugenio, D. Fossati, D. Yu, S. Haller, and M. Glass. 2005. Natural language generation for intelligent tutoring systems: A case study. In *Proc. of the 12th International Conference on Artificial Intelligence in Education*, pages 217–224, Amsterdam, The Netherlands, July.

Jung Hee Kim, Reva Freedman, Michael Glass, and Martha W. Evens. 2006. Annotation of tutorial dialogue goals for natural language generation. *Discourse Processes*, 42(1):37–74.

Diane Litman and Kate Forbes-Riley. 2006. Correlations betweeen dialogue acts and learning in spoken tutoring dialogues. *Natural Language Engineering*, 12(2):161–176.

Joel A. Michael, Allen A. Rovick, Yujian Zhou, Michael Glass, and Martha Evens. 2003. Learning from a computer tutor with natural language capabilities. *Interactive Learning Environments*, 11(3):233–262.

Johanna D. Moore, Kaŝka Porayska-Pomsta, Sebastian Varges, and Claus Zinn. 2004. Generating tutorial feedback with affect. In *Proceedings of the Seventeenth International Florida Artificial Intelligence Research Sociey Conference*, Miami Beach, FL, May.

N. Person, A. C. Graesser, D. Harter, and E. Mathews. 2000. Dialog move generation and conversation management in autotutor. In *Workshop Notes of the AAAI '00 Fall Symposium on Building Dialogue Systems for Tutorial Applications*.

Massimo Poesio. 2004. Discourse annotation and semantic annotation in the GNOME corpus. In *Proceedings of the ACL Workshop on Discourse Annotation*, Barcelona, Spain, July.

K. Porayska-Pomsta, M. Mavrikis, and H. Pain. 2007. Diagnosing and acting on student affect: the tutors' perspective. *User Modelling and User-Adapted Interaction, Special Issue on Affective Modelling and Adaptation*. Submitted.

G. J. Posner, K. A. Strike, P. W. Hewson, and W. A. Gertzog. 1982. Accommodation of a scientific conception: Towards a theory of conceptual change. *Science Education*, 66(2):211–227.

C. P. Rosé, P. Jordan, M. Ringenberg, S. Siler, K. VanLehn, and A. Weinstein. 2001. Interactive conceptual tutoring in Atlas-Andes. In *Proc. AI-ED 2001*.

J. W. Thomas and W. D. Rohwer. 1993. Proficient autonomous learning: Problems and prospects. In M. Rabinowitz, editor, *Cognitive Science Foundations of Instruction*, pages 1–32. Erlbaum.

K. VanLehn, S. Siler, C. Murray, T. Yamauchi, and W. Baggett. 2003. Why do only some events cause learning during human tutoring? *Cognition and Instruction*, 21(3):209–249.

M. K. Wolf, A. C. Crosson, and L. B. Resnick. 2005. Classroom talk for rigorous reading comprehension instruction. *Reading Psychology*, 26:27–53.

Yujian Zhou, Reva Freedman, Michael Glass, Joel Michael, Allen Rovick, and Martha Evens. 1999. Delivering hints in a dialogue-based ITS. In *Proceedings of the Sixteenth AAAI Conference*, pages 128–134, Orlando, FL.

Deep-reasoning-centred Dialogue

Debora Field
Department of Computer Science,
University of Liverpool, L69 3BX.

Allan Ramsay
Department of Computer Science,
University of Manchester, M60 1QD.

Abstract

This paper discusses an implemented dialogue system which generates the meanings of utterances by taking into account: the surface mood of the user's last utterance; the meanings of all the user's utterances from the current discourse; the system's expert knowledge; and the system's beliefs about the current situation arising from the discourse (including its beliefs about the user and her beliefs, and its beliefs about what is 'common knowledge'). The system formulates the content of its responses by employing an epistemic theorem prover to do deep reasoning. During the reasoning process, it remembers the proof tree it constructs, and from this derives the meaning of an explanatory response.

1 Introduction

We are building a system that offers users expert advice (on health, but the particular domain is unimportant) by means of multiple-turn natural language dialogue. The work presented in this paper concerns largely the generation of the *meanings* of utterances, meanings which contain all the information necessary for their realisation in grammatical surface form. (The surface realiser is as yet unfinished, but we do not envisage many problems in completing it, as will be discussed.) In answer to the old chestnut, "Generation from what?", the system generates the meanings of its utterances by analysing and manipulating a range of different sorts of information, including: the surface mood of the user's last utterance; the meanings of all the user's utterances from the current discourse; the system's expert knowledge about health; and the system's beliefs about the current situation arising from the discourse (including its beliefs about the user and her beliefs, and its beliefs about what is 'common knowledge'). To describe what the system is generating and how it does this therefore requires description of the entire process from analysis of the surface structure of a user's utterance, right through to the point at which an utterance meaning is finished and ready to be sent to the surface realiser. We will start with a brief outline of this process, which will be expanded upon in the body of the paper.

The anticipated user is a person wanting health advice, who engages the system in a turn-by-turn NL dialogue by typing in utterances in grammatical English, requesting responses from the system, and responding to them. The system understands users' utterances, in the sense that for each utterance it derives a meaning expressed in intensional logic. As the conversation proceeds, the system also maintains an understanding of the discourse as a whole, in that after each utterance it updates a growing model of the discourse, enabling it to remember everything that has been said during the discourse, who said what, which order the utterances were made in, which entities have been mentioned during the discourse (and during which turn), and how they were referred to.

The system has its own belief state—including its beliefs about what the user believes—which it continually updates, as it keeps track of the meanings of what has been said by whom during the dialogue, and as it refers to its bank of 'common' knowledge. The system also has a bank of expert knowledge on health, expressed as rules which describe causal relations between conditions, foods, activities, *etc.*, which enable it to reason about the consequences of particular choices and actions.

The system's epistemic theorem prover does deep reasoning over its understanding of and beliefs about what the user has said (expressed as logical forms), its expert knowledge, and its memory of the contents of the whole discourse, in order to formulate accurate and appropriate response meanings during dialogue with users. The system also enhances its responses by making them explanatory, which it does by using the edited contents of the proof tree that gets constructed during the first stages of calculating the system's response to an utterance.

Having formulated an utterance meaning that it believes will be accurate and appropriately explanatory, the system's belief state and discourse model are accordingly updated, and the system fleshes out the utterance meaning by deriving descriptions for all the nominal entities in the utterance meaning, so that the user will be able to dereference them, and so that natural-sounding discourse results. Then the system maps the fleshed-out utterance meaning into grammatical surface form. The system's surface realiser is unfinished, however, we are confident that the nature of the input to the realiser is what is needed for our system to produce grammatical surface text, and that we have a suitable architecture for realising it.

2 NL understanding

We can view our system as an utterance generator whose input is user utterances. On receiving a user's utterance, the system derives a logical representation of its meaning (Ramsay, 2001b; Ramsay, 1997):

(1) U: *I am allergic to eggs.*

Figure 1: Logical form of (1) after analysis: 30 ms

```
utt(claim,
 exists(B :: {aspect(now,simple,B)},
  state(B)
  & theta(B,pred,lambda(C,allergic(C)))
   & theta(B,topic(ref),ref(lambda(D,speaker(D)))!0)
    & lambda(E,to(B,E)) < lambda(F,egg(F))))
```

Fig. 1 shows the logical form of (1) after analysis. While the system understands that Fig. 1 is the meaning of the user's utterance, it also has the ability to reason about what follows from this, because it has its own banks of common sense knowledge and expert knowledge. The expert knowledge is expressed in the form of rules which describe causal relations between conditions, foods, activities, *etc.*, which enable the system to reason about and discuss the consequences of particular choices and actions. For example, it knows that if a person has an allergy to a substance, the allergy will be to some set of things that contain that substance, that it is dangerous for that person to eat things that belong to that set, and that something cannot be both safe and dangerous (Fig. 2). If the user follows (1) with:

(2) U: *Is it safe for me to eat pancakes?*

the system is able to use its knowledge about the consequences of having an allergy, and about the ingredients of pancakes, plus one or two other meaning postulates, to work out that it is not safe for the user to eat pancakes. What is more, the system uses the knowledge it discovers (while formulating its response) to construct an explanatory utterance which answers the user's question *and* gives justification for the answer (see section 7).

Note that the implication in the final rule of Fig. 2 is between two situation types (denoted by propositions). Reasoning about situation types seems to be essential for the correct analysis of terms like 'safe' and 'dangerous', and so we are forced to use a fine-grained intensional logic as our basic framework in

Figure 2: Some of the system's beliefs

```
bel(system,
forall(A,
 forall(O :: {allergy(O, A)},
  forall(H :: {have(H) & theta(H, object, O)},
   forall(S :: {theta(H, agent, S)},
    allergic(S, A)))))
&
forall(S :: {theta(S, pred, lambda(X, allergic(X)))},
 forall(T :: {theta(S, topic(ref), T)},
  forall(A :: {subset(lambda(X, to(S, X)), A)},
   allergic(T, A))))
&
forall(A,
 forall(S1 :: {allergic(A, S1)},
  dangerous(exists(EAT,
   eat(EAT)
   & theta(EAT, agent, A)
   & exists(X, theta(EAT, object, X)
    & exists(Y, contains(X, Y) & (S1:Y)))))))
&
forall(SOA1,
 forall(SOA2,
  not(safe(SOA1)
   & dangerous(SOA2)
   & (SOA1 => SOA2)))))
```

the same way that situation semantics is grounded in (Aczel, 1988)'s notion of non-well-founded sets. Our theorem prover (Ramsay, 2001a) allows us to perform inference over intensional rules of this kind.

3 Mood and extra-linguistic plans

Notice from Fig. 1 that the logical form of the meaning of (1) is nested inside the expression `utt(claim...)`. This arises from analysis of the surface mood of the utterance. We consider that linguistic actions are generally intended to help with underlying extra-linguistic plans, so we analyse the surface mood to determine the answer to the most basic goal-related question: What does the user want? Does she want to know whether something is true? Does she want to know the identity of something? Does she want the system to do something? We take it that: for a statement P there is some action A which the hearer ('H') could do if H knew that the propositional content P was true; for a query P there is something the speaker ('S') could do if S knew that P was true; and for an imperative P there is something that someone (probably S or H, but not necessarily) could do if H carried out the action described by P.

4 Discourse model

Having derived the meaning of a user's utterance, the system adds the meaning plus a record of who uttered it to the 'minutes' (after (Thomason, 1990; Lewis, 1979; Stalnaker, 1972)). Individual entities (including the events) that have been mentioned during the discourse are represented in a 'discourse model' as unique skolem constants, while n-place predicates describe the detail of what has been said about each entity (Ramsay and Seville, 2000). The skolems are anchored (Barwise and Perry, 1983) and note is taken of the order of centres (Grosz et al., 1995) so that NPs in later user utterances can be dereferenced successfully, and that in its own utterances, the system will know how to refer to entities in ways which enable the user to dereference them.

The discourse model enables the system to remember everything that has been said during the discourse, who said what, which order the utterances were made in, which entities have been mentioned during the discourse (and on which turn), and how they were referred to. This enables the system, during the formulation of a response to a user, to use information that she introduced into the conversation during turns preceding the most recent one, or to use information that she has introduced over a number of separate turns, as in this example ('C' is 'computer'):

(3) U: *I am allergic to eggs.*
C: *Please go on.*
U: *Is it safe for me eat pancakes?*
C: *No, it is not safe for you to eat pancakes.*
U: *What about Yorkshire pudding?*
C: *No, it is not safe for you to eat Yorkshire pudding either.*

5 System's private beliefs

The system has its own set of beliefs. These include 'common knowledge' beliefs (things the system believes everyone can be expected to know), beliefs about the system's current situation arising from the dialogue (including beliefs about what the user believes), and expert knowledge about health. Having understood the meaning of a user's utterance, and updated the minutes, the system adjusts its private beliefs about the current situation in light of what has just been said. (Note that the minutes do not contain what the user believes or what the system believes concerning what has been said, it is purely a record of what has been said, and by whom.)

In adjusting its private beliefs following a user utterance, the system makes a significant default assumption. We consider that, in a purely neutral context where neither party has any specific views on the reliability or cooperativeness of the other, it is rational for a speaker to produce utterances that she believes, and for the hearer to believe this is what the speaker is doing. This default assumption, that people are committed to what they say, arises as a consequence of our assumption that linguistic actions are generally intended to help with underlying extra-linguistic plans. Since I cannot be expected to help you unless I know something about your plan, there is no point in you telling me about things that will not help me identify your plan.

Under the assumption that people are committed to what they say, during its update step following a user's utterance, the system assumes that the user has been honest in the declaration of her extra-linguistic plan (Section 3), and if the user has made a statement, it also adds to its beliefs that it believes: (i) what the user has stated; (ii) the user believes what she has stated.

The assumption we make that people are committed to what they say ignores the fact that in normal human-to-human conversation, people often say things that they themselves do not believe (lying, bluffing, or using sarcasm, for example). Enabling a dialogue system to handle conversations in which users say things they do not believe is work we have in mind for the long-term future (after (Field and Ramsay, 2004)). It is not an ability we consider essential for the proper functioning of a dialogue system whose role is to advise users who willingly approach with a genuinely enquiring attitude, in contrast to users who are perhaps obliged to use a 'counselling system' (as part of a compliance programme, perhaps), and as a consequence may attempt to deceive or be uncooperative in other ways.

6 Response strategy

Surface mood gives a strong starting point for how the system will go about working out a suitable response to a user's utterance. If the utterance is a polar query, for example:

(4) U: *Is walking good for me?*

Figure 3: Logical form of (4) after analysis: 20 ms

```
utt(query,
 exists(B
 ::{aspect(now,simple,B)},
  state(B)
  & theta(B,pred,lambda(C,good(C)))
   & lambda(D,theta(B,topic(ref),D))
    < lambda(E,exists(F,walk(F) & theta(F,agent,E)))
    & for(B,ref(lambda(G,speaker(G)))!4)))
```

the system's analyses its mood as *query* (Fig. 3) and then the system's theorem prover reasons about the proposition `PROP` nested inside `utt(query,PROP)`. It first tries to prove `PROP` is true. If this fails, it tries to prove that `PROP` is false. If both proofs fail, the system has nothing concrete to report to the user.

If the user's utterance was a WH query:

(5) U: *Which foods contain eggs?*

the NL understander analyses its mood as *whquery* (Fig. 4), and then the theorem prover tries to find a proof that there is something that satisfies the given property, *i.e.*, tries to find a value of `B` which makes the embedded proposition true.

Figure 4: Logical form of (5) after analysis: 10 ms

```
utt(whquery,
 lambda(B,
  exists(C :: {aspect(now,simple,C)},
   contain(C)
   & lambda(D,theta(C,object,D)) < lambda(E,egg(E))
    & theta(C,agent,B))
  & food(B)))
```

If the user's utterance was a statement, the only implemented strategy the system currently has is to say something polite and banal to indicate that it is listening, as in:

(6) U: *I am overweight.*
C: *Please go on.*
U: *Is walking good for me?*

Since the system remembers everything that has been said during a conversation, if it is presented with a statement it is not sure what to do with, it is able to wait and see whether the user adds something to the discourse that makes her goal clearer.

There is a lot of work to be done to enable the system to respond more intelligently to statements, but nothing that cannot be done by approaching utterances as declarations of complex goals requiring recognition by the system, and by having plenty of meaning postulates (and an appropriate theorem prover) which enable the system to understand what follows from users' utterances. Immediate plans include treating discourse markers in user utterances as clues to the user's goal. Another is trying to judge whether the statement might be a comment on an earlier utterance from the current discourse, to analyse what kind of comment it is (dissatisfaction with, surprise at, anger at an earlier utterance, *etc.*), and to decide what would be an appropriate response.

We have not yet given much thought to how the system should respond to utterances in the imperative mood, since it is an unlikely occurrence in the context of a dialogue between a human non-expert and a disembodied machine expert that has no ability to do anything but communicate through text, apart from instances where the user explicitly instructs the system to communicate things to her (*Tell me ...*, *Explain why...*, *List...*, *etc.*), and perhaps instances where the user is insulting the system (*Get lost!*, *Go and learn English!*, *etc.*).

7 Generating explanatory responses

Let us assume the system has reached a point at which it has formulated the meaning of an accurate and relevant response to the user's utterance. We want the system to give a reply to the user which not only satisfies her communicative goal, but which satisfies it in a way that is as helpful as possible to her. With respect to WH queries to which there are several, or even very many possible answers, the issue of the relevance or helpfulness of different ways of responding has been discussed at length (see (Groenendijk and Stokhof, 1997)). If a user asks:

(7) U: *Which foods should a person with acne avoid?*

there may be hundreds or even thousands of foods which enable the proof of *A person with acne should avoid eating [what]* to be completed. We consider (following (Ginzburg, 1996)) that a descriptive or 'explanatory' answer is more useful or appropriate to the user than a list of instances, in cases where there is more than a handful of instances. By 'explanatory answer', we mean that, where possible, responses by the system should inform the user about causal relations between entities, so that she will be able to re-use her new information in other situations by making new inferences of her own. For example, rather than making the following accurate but minimal responses:

(8) U: *I have acne.*
C: *OK.*
U: *Is eating chocolate good for my skin?*
C: *No.*
U: *What about bacon?*
C: *No.*
U: *What about ... No ... What about ...*

the system should produce an explanatory response which aims to educate the user:

(9) U: *I have acne.*
C: *OK.*
U: *Is eating chocolate good for my skin?*
C: *No, because chocolate is a fatty food, and fatty foods aggravate acne.*

Now the user can infer for herself that bacon, chips, mayonnaise and cream cakes are bad for acne, whereas carrots, cod and honey are not (if she knows which foods are fatty foods and which are not).

A side-effect of the fundamental design of our system—to use a theorem prover for property theory to do deep reasoning with logical forms derived from NL utterances, in conjunction with its own expert knowledge—is that during the process of formulating a response to a user, the system discovers a lot of information which it knows could be of great potential benefit to the user. If the system is privy to all this information, why waste it by keeping it secret? Why not pass it on to the user? This is far from suggesting that the system dump all its expert knowledge on the user at once, regardless of the user's desires and needs. It is viewing the user's own utterances as insights into the gaps in the user's knowledge that the user is keen to have filled, and then attempting to fill those particular gaps as precisely as possible, neither being more informative than necessary, nor less.

Technically speaking, the explanatory information contained in the 'because...' clause in (9) is drawn from the proof tree that was constructed by the theorem prover while working out its response to the user's question (after (Fiedler, 1998)).[1] The structure of all proof trees is as follows:

```
(10) g1 +[g11 +[g111 +[]
              ],
         g12 +[g121 +[],
               g122 +[g1221 +[]]
              ]
        ]
```

where `G +[LIST...]` means `[LIST...] are the subproofs of GOAL.`

Fig. 5 is the proof tree that the system constructs while it is formulating its response to utterance (11):

(11) U: *I am overweight. Is walking good for me?*

One change has been made to make this proof tree easier to read. In the tree from the implementation, the skolem function `#813(lambda(B, exists(C, walk(C) & theta(C, agent, B))))` appears many times, and means roughly *There is a set of walking events C whose agent is some individual B.* This expression has been simplified to skolem `#813`.

Figure 5: Proof tree for response to (11): 20 ms

```
answer::[bel - computer]
 + [for(#813,S)::[bel - computer]
 + [lambda(B,exists(C,walk(C) & theta(C,agent,B)))
  < lambda(D,exercise(D))::[bel - computer] + [],
  overweight(S)::[bel - computer] + []],
 lambda(E,theta(#813,topic(ref),E))
 < lambda(B,exists(C,walk(C) & theta(C,agent,B)))
  ::[bel - computer]
 + [lambda(B,exists(C,walk(C) & theta(C,agent,B)))
  < lambda(F,exercise(F))::[bel - computer] + [],
  overweight(S)::[bel - computer] + []],
 theta(#813,pred,lambda(G,good(G)))::[bel - computer]
 + [lambda(B,exists(C,walk(C) & theta(C,agent,B)))
  < lambda(H,exercise(H))::[bel - computer] + [],
  overweight(S)::[bel - computer] + []],
 state(#813)::[bel - computer]
 + [lambda(B,exists(C,walk(C) & theta(C,agent,B)))
  < lambda(I,exercise(I))::[bel - computer] + [],
  overweight(S)::[bel - computer] + []],
 aspect(now,simple,#813)::[bel - computer]
 + [lambda(B,exists(C,walk(C) & theta(C,agent,B)))
  < lambda(J,exercise(J))::[bel - computer] + [],
  overweight(S)::[bel - computer] + []]]
```

In the construction `P::[bel-computer]` (from Fig. 5), `[bel-computer]` is the 'epistemic context' of `P`. `P::[bel-computer]` means *The system believes P* (see Section 7.1). You will notice that the epistemic context of *every* proposition in Fig. 5 is `[bel-computer]`. The system has, however, used beliefs with different epistemic contexts to construct this tree. For example, since the user has just told the system she is overweight, the fact that she is overweight is in the common ground (is assumed to be mutually believed by system and user) before the system starts to formulate its response and derive the proof tree. We do not see common-ground contexts in the proof tree, because the system's goal was to prove that it *privately* believed something, and when reasoning with common-ground propositions, the system knew that `P::[bel-commonground([user,computer])]` subsumes `P::[bel-computer]`. Fig. 6 is a paraphrase of Fig. 5 from which the epistemic context `[bel - computer]` has been removed.

Figure 6: Paraphrase of (5)

```
answer::[bel-c]
 + [(#813 is something which is 'for' S)
   + [(the set of walking events is a
       subset of type 'exercise')
      + [],
      (S is overweight) + []],
   (the set of topics of #813 is a
    subset of the set of walking events)
   + [(the set of walking events is a
       subset of type 'exercise')
      + [],
      (S is overweight) + []],
   (The predicate of #813 is type 'good')
   + [(the set of walking events is a
       subset of type 'exercise')
      + [],
      (S is overweight) + []],
   (#813 is a state)
   + [(the set of walking events is a
       subset of type 'exercise')
      + [],
      (S is overweight) + []],
   (The tense and aspect of #813 are
    'present' and 'simple')
   + [(the set of walking events is a
       subset of type 'exercise')
      + [],
      (S is overweight) + []]]
```

7.1 Explanatory responses: difficulties

In line with (Grice, 1975), we consider that a guiding principle when it comes to formulating natural responses to users' utterances is to not be overly informative, which means the user's knowledge must be taken into account (Cawsey, 1990; Paris, 1991). If a user has said the following:

(12) U: *I have acne. Is eating chocolate good for my skin?*

we think that most people would consider the following explanatory response to be odd, even though

[1]This is achieved by using an abbreviated copy of the proof stack in a 'label' (after (Gabbay, 1996)). The label carries non-logical, arbitrary information about the progress of a proof, and is used for a variety of purposes in addition to keeping a note of the proof trail. Labels are threaded through the clause, so that information can be passed from one subgoal to the next.

all of its parts are necessary in constructing the system's proof of the answer "No":

(13) C: *No, because you have acne, and eating fatty foods aggravates acne, and chocolate is a fatty food.*

The system knows (from (12)) that the user knows she has acne, so it is odd-sounding for the system to say *because you have acne* to the user, even though this proposition forms a requisite part of the system's own proof that chocolate is bad for the user's skin. In order to prevent the system being more informative than required, we eliminate from the explanatory bit of the response the parts of the proof tree that the system believes the user already knows.

Technically speaking, this is achievable on account of a significant design feature of the theorem prover, namely that it is an epistemic one (see (Field and Ramsay, 2006)). We take the view that the best way to reason about what someone else believes is to see which conclusions you would draw if your view of the world matched theirs, and to express this, we use the notion of the 'epistemic context' in which a proposition is available. We write `P::C` to say that the proposition `P` is available in the context `C` (after (Wallen, 1987)), and we let belief statements introduce contexts. Each proposition in the proof tree from which explanatory answers are derived has its own epistemic context. This information, along with the contents of the discourse model, and axioms defining the properties of knowledge and belief, enable the system to establish which parts of the proof tree it thinks are things that are already known by the user, and which parts are not already known.

A harder problem than avoiding being too informative in an explanatory response is the problem of spotting the occasions when it is not appropriate at all to give an explanatory response. Consider:

(14) U: *I am allergic to eggs. Is it dangerous for me to eat pancakes?*
C: *Yes, because if you are allergic to a substance, it is dangerous to eat foods containing that substance, and pancakes contain egg.*

We would argue that most Western readers would judge from (14) that the user probably already knows that the consequences of having an allergy to a substance are that it is dangerous to eat foods containing that substance. So it seems overly informative and even patronising for the system to explain these consequences to the user. We would also argue that, although she has not declared it explicitly, the thing the user wants to achieve in making this utterance is to find out whether pancakes contain egg, and that an accurate and minimal "Yes" would be the ideal system response. The system's problem is, it is difficult to spot when it is appropriate to assume that a user understands a relationship that she has not explicitly declared. Making decisions like this would require judgements about the inferences a particular user is likely to be able to make (Horacek, 1997; Zukerman and McConachy, 1993)—just one of the many refinements in the queue.

8 From meaning to message skeleton

In technical terms, the content of the system's proof tree is the bulk of the meaning that becomes the input to the surface generator. Formulae in proof trees are an alternative representation of the logical forms that the system has been reasoning with: the logical forms have been skolemised and anchored to make them more suitable as input for NL generation.

Let us return to user query (11), and let us assume that the system wants to use the full proof tree (Fig. 5) in an explanatory response to the user. To express Fig. 5 to the user in a natural-sounding way, the system makes an utterance with the structure *A because B*, where *A* constitutes a response that would stand alone in being accurate and appropriate, and *B* constitutes additional explanatory information. The part of the proof tree that provides the content for *A* is the list of the 'principal subgoals', which in (10) are `[g11,g12]`. The part of the proof tree that provides the content for part *B* of the response *A because B* is a list of the 'secondary subgoals', items that are nested inside the top-level subgoals, which in (10) are `[g111, g121, g122, g1221]`. Parts *A* and *B* are then somewhat crudely glued together with a `because`, to make what we are calling a 'message skeleton', which is the skolemised and anchored meaning (of the system's utterance) that will soon become the input to the surface realiser (illustrative figure coming shortly).

9 Fleshed-out message skeletons

Before the message skeleton is sent to the surface realiser, work is done to decide how to refer to nominal entities in such a way as is natural-sounding, and will enable the user to dereference them. This involves determining whether entities have been mentioned in the discourse thus far, or are in the common ground for some other reason, and if so, how they are described. An entity which is not yet in the common ground needs slightly different treatment—the system examines what it knows about that entity, and uses that information to look in a 'reverse dictionary' (in which entries are meanings, and definitions are words) for a suitable word or phrase to describe it. Additionally, after (Dale, 1988; Reiter, 1990), if an entity has not been mentioned before, it is marked for the realiser as *indefinite*. If it has been mentioned before, and can be realised by a pronoun without being misleading (*e.g.*, due to gender confusion), it is marked as *pronoun*. Otherwise, entities are marked as *definite* and minimal distinguishing descriptions obtained for them.

Fig. 7 (actual output) shows the fleshed-out message skeleton for the system's response to (11). `BECAUSE` has been added to the message, as discussed, to separate the explanatory part from the remainder in a way that reflects surface order. `YES` has been added because the system *has* constructed a proof of the proposition the user is querying, and so some surface affirmative is required. Of course, `YES` does not appear in all system utterances, since sometimes the system wants to say `NO`, sometimes it is answering a WH query, and sometimes it is making a statement. Notice the item `PRON(S,lambda(N,user(N)))`. This instructs the realiser that `S` is the user, and to realise `S` with a pronominal form. `PRON(S,lambda(N,user(N)))` was added to the bare message skeleton during the fleshing-out process. The realiser knows that the pronoun to use to refer to the user while talking to her is *you*.

It is probably unwise to show what the surface realiser outputs, given Fig. 9 as input, because it is unfinished, and its output is odd and incomplete. However, for the sake of evaluation, here it is, the time taken to produce it (from being asked the question by the user) being 590 ms:

(15) C: *[Yes, ????, because, you, be, overweight]*

This messy output should and will soon be:

(16) C: *Yes, walking is good for you, because you are overweight, and walking is a type of exercise.*

How natural this response is, and whether it should contain more information or less information, is under on-going scrutiny, as is the exploitation of the proof trees in general.

10 Conclusion

We consider the surface realiser to be the main weakness in the current implementation, but believe this should not present too many difficulties, since we already have one of the most important ingredients of a surface realiser: comprehensive input that contains all the information necessary for the generation of natural-sounding discourse turns. Also helping us is that we have resources available to us in the architecture of the system, namely, those that are used in the analysis of surface form during NL understanding. A reverse dictionary is also already in place, which is being used to flesh out message skeletons with appropriate referring and indefinite expressions for skolem constants. We intend to exploit previous work on bag generation to help finish off the realiser.

Concerning evaluation, we have included timings in the figure captions, and one timing of 590 ms for the system's complete response to (11). Its response to (2) takes 451 ms. These timings are slightly lower than they will be when the realiser is finished.

We are at pains to point out that the system is not a health expert, and the expert rules it uses are not rules that actual doctors and nutritionists use—they are rules that we have made up, and they certainly are not fine-grained or precise enough for the health domain. It is our priority to get the basic architecture and functioning complete before the system would be suitable for developing into an actual health advisor. Having said that, we are shortly about to incorporate a nutrition ontology into the system, to enable it to answer detailed questions about which foods contain which substances, and which foods should be avoided or promoted under various conditions. We are interested to see how difficult it would be for us to exploit an ontology of expert knowledge for our dialogue purposes.

The proof trees that the system's theorem prover constructs provide us with much food for thought, and could be used in ways not discussed in the paper. One use would be to generate dialogue clarification questions (after (Cawsey, 1991)). Instead of using the full proof tree, the system could cherry pick from the proof tree, and query the user on her knowledge of the different parts of the proof, with the aim of finding where the user's reasoning had gone wrong, and correcting it.

With regard to answering questions to which there is more than a handful of answers, we acknowledge that there are many occasions when using the content of a proof tree as the substance of the system's answer, with a few odd words crudely inserted, will not be satisfactory. For example, if a user said:

(17) U: *I have heart disease. What lifestyle advice can you give me?*

the natural response would be a piece of prose in which several different kinds of lifestyle change were discussed. To do this, the system would require the ability to write an appropriate summarised text on the basis of its expert knowledge. This would require the additional knowledge of how to construct an argument, as well as more in-depth knowledge of discourse structure (unless stock answers to anticipated questions had been prepared manually in advance for such occasions), work we consider feasible, given collaboration with argumentation experts, and considerable further development.

We acknowledge that our work is just one of many in a tradition of dialogue system implementations, (TRAINS (Allen et al., 1996), TRINDIKIT (Larsson and Traum, 2000), and GoDiS (Larsson et al., 2000), to mention a few).

11 Acknowledgements

Our thanks go to Floriana Grasso for her valuable input. This work was funded under EU-grant

Figure 7: Fleshed-out message skeleton in response to (11)

```
[YES,
 aspect(now,simple,#813(lambda(B,exists(C,walk(C) & theta(C,agent,B))),S)),
 state(#813(lambda(D,exists(E,walk(E) & theta(E,agent,D))),S)),
 theta(#813(lambda(F,exists(G,walk(G) & theta(G,agent,F))),S),pred,lambda(H,good(H))),
 lambda(I,theta(#813(lambda(J,exists(K,walk(K) & theta(K,agent,J))),S),topic(ref),I))
 < lambda(J,exists(K,walk(K) & theta(K,agent,J))),
 for(#813(lambda(L,exists(M,walk(M) & theta(M,agent,L))), S), S),
 PRON(S,lambda(N,user(N))),
 lambda(H,good(H)),
 BECAUSE,
 overweight(S),
 lambda(O,exists(P,walk(P) & theta(P,agent,O)))
 < lambda(Q,exercise(Q))]
```

FP6/IST No. 507019 (*PIPS*: Personalised Information Platform for Health and Life Services).

References

P Aczel. 1988. *Non-Well-Founded-Sets*. Stanford: CSLI Publications.

J. F. Allen, B. W. Miller, E. K. Ringger, and T. Sikorski. 1996. A robust system for natural spoken dialogue. In *Proc. ACL'96*.

J. Barwise and J. Perry. 1983. *Situations and Attitudes*. Cambridge, MA: Bradford Books.

A. J. Cawsey. 1990. Generating explanatory discourse. In Mellish, C., Dale, R. and Zock, M. (eds) *Current Research in Natural Language Generation*, Academic Press, pp. 75-101.

A. J. Cawsey. 1991. Generating interactive explanations. In *Proc. 9th National Conference on Artificial Intelligence (AAAI-91)*, pp. 86–91.

P. R. Cohen, J. Morgan, and M. E. Pollack. 1990. Editors. *Intentions in communication*. Cambridge, Massachusetts: MIT.

R. Dale. 1988. *Generating Referring Expressions in a Domain of Objects and Processes*. PhD Thesis, Centre for Cognitive Science, University of Edinburgh.

A. Fiedler. 1998. Macroplanning with a cognitive architecture for the adaptive explanation of proofs. In *Proc. 9th International Workshop on Natural Language Generation (INLG-98)*.

D. Field and A. Ramsay. 2004. Sarcasm, deception, and stating the obvious: Planning dialogue without speech acts. *Artificial Intelligence Review* 22(2): 149–171.

D. Field and A. Ramsay. 2006. Planning ramifications: When ramifications are the norm, not the problem. In *Proc. 11th International Workshop on Non-Monotonic Reasoning (NMR'06)*, 30 May–1 June 2006, Lake District, England, pp. 343-351.

D. M. Gabbay. 1996. *Labelled deductive systems*. Oxford University Press: Oxford.

J. Ginzburg. 1996. The semantics of interrogatives. In S. Lappin (ed) *Handbook of contemporary semantic theory*, Oxford: Blackwell.

H. P. Grice. 1975. Logic and conversation. In P. Cole and J. Morgan (eds) *Syntax and semantics, Vol. 3: Speech acts*, pp. 41–58. New York: Academic Press.

J. Groenendijk and M. Stokhof. 1997. Questions. In J. van Benthem and A. ter Meulen (eds) *Handbook of Logic and Language*, Amsterdam/Cambridge, MA: Elsevier/MIT Press, pp. 1055-1124.

B. J. Grosz, A. Joshi, and S. Weinstein. 1995. Centering: a framework for modeling the local coherence of discourse. *Computational Linguistics* 21(2): 175–204.

H. Horacek. 1997. A model for adapting explanations to the user's likely inferences. *User Modeling and User-Adapted Interaction* 7(1):1–55.

S. Larsson and D. Traum. 2000. Information state and dialogue management in the TRINDI Dialogue Move Engine Toolkit. In *Natural Language Engineering Special Issue on Best Practice in Spoken Language Dialogue Systems Engineering*, CUP, UK pp. 323-340.

S. Larsson, P. Ljunglf, R. Cooper, E. Engdahl, and S. Ericsson. 2000. GoDiS - an accommodating dialogue system. In *Proc. ANLP/NAACL-2000 Workshop on Conversational Systems*, pp. 7-10.

D. Lewis. 1979. Scorekeeping in a language game. *Journal of Philosophical Logic* 8: 339–59. Reprinted in D. Lewis *Philosophical papers Volume I*, 1983, New York and Oxford: Oxford University Press, pp. 233–249.

C. Paris. 1991. The role of the user's domain knowledge in generation. *Computational Intelligence* 7:71–93.

A. Ramsay and H. Seville. 2000. Models and discourse models. *Journal of Language and Computation 1(2).*

A. M. Ramsay. 1997. Dynamic and underspecified semantics without dynamic and underspecified logic. In H. C. Bunt and L. Kievit and R. Muskens and M. Verlinden (eds) *Computing Meaning* 1: 208–220, Dordrecht: Kluwer Academic Publishers (SLAP 73).

A. M. Ramsay. 2001a. Theorem proving for untyped constructive λ-calculus: implementation and application. In the *Logic Journal of the Interest Group in Pure and Applied Logics*, Vol. 9(1): 83–100.

A. M. Ramsay. 2001b. Weak lexical semantics and multiple views. In H. C. Bunt and R. Muskens and E. G. C. Thijsse (eds) *Computing Meaning* Vol. 2: 97–112, Dordrecht: Kluwer Academic Publishers (SLAP 77).

E. Reiter. 1990. Generating descriptions that exploit a user's domain knowledge. In R. Dale, C. Mellish, and M. Zock (eds) *Current Research in Natural Language Generation*. London: Academic Press, pp. 257-285.

R. Stalnaker. 1972. Pragmatics. In D. Davidson and G. Harman. Editors. *Semantics of natural language (Synthese Library, Vol. 40)*, pp. 380–97. Dordrecht, Holland: D. Reidel.

R. H. Thomason. 1990. Accommodation, meaning, and implicature: Interdisciplinary foundations for pragmatics. In (Cohen et al., 1990), pp. 325–63.

L. Wallen. 1987. Matrix proofs for modal logics. *Proc. 10th IJCAI*, pp. 917–23.

I. Zukerman and R. McConachy. 1993. Generating concise discourse that addresses a user's inferences. In *Proc. IJCAI*, Chambery, France, Morgan Kaufmann, pp. 1202–1207.

Extending the Entity-grid Coherence Model to Semantically Related Entities

Katja Filippova and **Michael Strube**
EML Research gGmbH
Schloss-Wolfsbrunnenweg 33
69118 Heidelberg, Germany
http://www.eml-research.de/nlp/

Abstract

This paper reports on work in progress on extending the entity-based approach on measuring coherence (Barzilay & Lapata, 2005; Lapata & Barzilay, 2005) from coreference to semantic relatedness. We use a corpus of manually annotated German newspaper text (TüBa-D/Z) and aim at improving the performance by grouping related entities with the WikiRelate! API (Strube & Ponzetto, 2006).

1 Introduction

Evaluation is a well-known problem for Natural Language Generation (NLG). Human labor required to evaluate the output of a NLG system is expensive since every text should be read by several human judges and evaluated according to several parameters. Automatic summarization is an application using a NLG component which is hard to evaluate. The Document Understanding Conference[1], which every year issues a summarization task, distinguishes five aspects of linguistic quality of a summary: grammaticality, non-redundancy, referential clarity, focus and coherence. The parameter for which most participants get very low scores is coherence. This may reflect the difficulty which (mostly) extractive methods face during the ordering phase. Even if selected sentences are relevant and related, being in a wrong order they will make the summary hard to understand. The same is true for any other text-to-text generation system with a multisentential output.

In this paper we consider a way of automatic coherence assessment (Barzilay & Lapata, 2005) which is beneficial for such NLG systems. This method is based on how patterns of entity distribution differ for coherent and incoherent texts. It utilizes information of three kinds: coreference, salience and syntax. As a suggestion for future work, Barzilay & Lapata hypothesize that integrating semantic knowledge for entity grouping (as opposed to coreference) should improve the results. So, the purpose of the current study is threefold:

- to check how the method performs on a language other than English;
- to estimate the contribution of the three knowledge sources on mannualy annotated data;
- to see whether semantic clustering of entities outperfoms the coreference baseline.

2 The Entity-based Approach

Barzilay & Lapata (2005) describe a method for coherence assessment which grounds on the premises that (1) for a text to be globally coherent it has to be locally coherent as well; and (2) the patterns of how entities appear throughout the text differ for coherent and incoherent data.

To test their method, they consider a collection of coherent texts[2] and for each of them generate a number of incoherent variants by putting the sentences in a random order. Then, for each rendering, they create an *entity-grid* where each column represents an entity and each row represents a sentence from the text. A cell in a grid tells which syntactic function a given entity has in a given sentence. The set of possible functions is reduced to four: subject (**s**), object (**o**), other (**x**), or nothing (**-**) if the entity is not mentioned in a sentence. Two example grids

[1] http://duc.nist.gov

[2] They experiment with a corpus of newspaper articles and a corpus of accident reports, all in English.

	e_1	e_2	e_3	e_4	e_5	e_6
s_1	**S**	**O**	**X**	**-**	**-**	**-**
s_2	**O**	**S**	**-**	**O**	**-**	**-**
s_3	**S**	**-**	**-**	**-**	**-**	**-**
s_4	**-**	**-**	**-**	**-**	**-**	**S**

Table 1: Coherent text grid

	e_1	e_2	e_3	e_4	e_5	e_6
s_4	**-**	**-**	**-**	**-**	**-**	**S**
s_1	**S**	**O**	**X**	**-**	**-**	**-**
s_3	**S**	**-**	**-**	**-**	**-**	**-**
s_2	**O**	**S**	**-**	**O**	**-**	**-**

Table 2: Incoherent text grid

– for a coherent text and for its shuffled version – are presented in Tables 1 and 2 respectively.

To compare two texts which differ only in their sentence order, each of them is represented by a feature vector. A feature stands for a possible transition between syntactic functions of an entity (e.g. **-o**, **sx**, **sso**). Unigram, bigram and trigram transitions are distinguished. The value of a transition feature is its probability calculated from the grid. For binary transitions there are, thus, 4×4 possible features. If there are no full parses available so that one cannot distinguish between syntactic realizations and fills a cell with **x** or **-** only, the number of binary transitions is reduced to $2 \times 2 = 4$. These simplified (i.e. without syntactic information) feature vectors for the grids in Tables 1 and 2 are given in Table 3.

	xx	**x-**	**-x**	**--**
g_1	0.17	0.28	0.17	0.39
g_2	0.11	0.22	0.33	0.33

Table 3: Feature vectors for grids in Tables 1 & 2

The coherence assessment is then formulated as a ranking learning problem. SVM^{light} (Joachims, 2002) is used for this task. Pairwise rankings (a coherent text vs. an incoherent rendering) are supplied to the learner as the relative quality of incoherent renderings is not known. For each document 20 pairs are generated in total.

Barzilay & Lapata (2005) obtain impressive results – about 90% of *ranking accuracy* which is the ratio of how often a coherent order is ranked higher than its incoherent variant[3]:

$$RA = \frac{correct\_pairs}{all\_pairs}$$

Barzilay & Lapata (2005) demonstrate that richer syntactic representation, as well as coreference resolution instead of string identity for entities identification, improve the performance. Another finding is that it is effective to distinguish between *salient* entities (those mentioned more than once: e_1, e_2 in Tables 1 & 2) and the rest. Given that they preprocess the data automatically by employing a state-of-the-art parser and a noun phrase coreference resolution system, manual annotation is expected to refine the model.

3 Reimplementation

We reimplemented the algorithm of Barzilay & Lapata (2005) and tested it on a German corpus of newpaper articles TüBa-D/Z (Telljohann et al., 2003). This corpus provides manual syntactic[4], morphological and NP coreference annotation (Hinrichs et al., 2004). We used the same SVM^{light} package for learning of a ranking function. Like Barzilay & Lapata, we took 100 articles for training, testing and development sets each. The results we report below are all computed from the development set. As results might differ considerably depending on how incoherent random orders are, for every article we continued to use the set of random orders generated during the first try. This allowed us to make objective judgements about the impact of a certain parameter on the performance. We also selected a subset of articles from the TüBa-D/Z in order to make the average article length equal to the average length of the articles Barzilay & Lapata used (i.e. 10.5 sentences).

3.1 Settings

Similar to Barzilay & Lapata, we experimented with the following settings:

COREF: coreference vs. word identity for entity identification;

SYNT: syntax-rich vs. simplified representation;

SAL: distinguishing between salient entities (mentioned exactly once) and the rest vs. without this distinction.

[3]Note, that random baseline ensures RA of 50%.

[4]Yannick Versley kindly helped us to to convert the syntactic annotation (Versley, 2005).

	+COREF	-COREF
+SYNT+SAL	72%	62%
+SYNT-SAL	69%	53%
-SYNT+SAL	75%	66%
-SYNT-SAL	71%	59%

Table 4: Ranking accuracy for different settings

The results for each of the settings are presented in Table 4. Although obtained from human-annotated data, they are strikingly lower than the results Barzilay & Lapata report for English. We concluded the following:

1. Coreference information definitely improves the performance. Using word match for entity clustering works only if combined with salience, otherwise the method is hardly better than the baseline.
2. The fact that quite some correct decisions could be made with all parameters set negative (-SYNT-SAL-COREF) brought us to the idea that there is a difference in the amount of entities mentioned in the first, the last and a middle sentences of a text. Having calculated the average number of entities[5] in these three types of sentences, we concluded that indeed the amount decreases as the text continues. In a coherent text the first sentence generally introduces more entities than any further sentence mentions. The last sentence is shorter and, on average, contains less entities than other ones.
3. Surprisingly, for our data syntactic information turned out to have a negative impact on the results, although it may be that a larger training set is needed to benefit from it.
4. The RA of 59% for -SYNT-SAL-COREF demonstrates that the method can be of use even if applied to data without any information but sentence boundaries.

3.2 Extended Rankings

Apart from the settings described above, we also experimented with the training data representation by extending the pairwise ranking to longer rankings. According to Lapata's (2006) psycholinguistic experiment, Kendall's τ correlates reliably with human judgements regarding ordering tasks. It varies between -1 and 1 and is calculated as $1 - 4\frac{t}{N(N-1)}$, where t is the number of interchanges of adjacent elements required to bring the total of N elements in the right order. Assuming that the lower the τ, the less coherent a text is, we supplied the learner with rankings of 3 sentences instead of pairwise rankings as well as with rankings of all 21 renderings. Unfortunately, this modification did not improve the results but caused a slight drop in performance: for the best setting (-SYNT+SAL+COREF) the RA was 73%.

3.3 Beyond Entities

For entity clustering we used the WikiRelate! API (Strube & Ponzetto, 2006) to compute relatedness between entities. We preferred it to the GermaNet API (Gurevych, 2005) because the latter works better for computing semantic similarity whereas the former is more suitable for computing semantic relatedness. Apart from that, given that our data is a collection of newspaper articles containing named entities (persons, locations, organizations) which can be related as well, Wikipedia is a better choice as it covers named entities as well as common nouns (the version from 09/25/2006 has 471,065 entries). Future work should make use of both semantic resources. From the 6 possible measures implemented in WikiRelate!, we selected the Wu&Palmer measure as Strube & Ponzetto (2006) report that it demonstrated the highest correlation with humans.

The experiments with semantic relatedness had two goals:

- to see whether it can improve the best results achieved with coreference sets,
- to check whether semantic relatedness alone can be reliably used for entity clustering in case there is no coreference resolution system available.

Since syntactic information affects the results negatively while distinguishing between salient entites and the rest has a positive impact on them, we did not further experiment with all possible settings combinations and used -SYNT+SAL.

To group similar entities together, our algorithm proceeds as follows: when a new entity e_i is encountered, it is measured whether it is related to already found entities E. If there is an entity $e_j \in E$ such that $SemRel(e_i, e_j) > t$, where t is a threshold, then its history is further assigned to this entity. We experimented with different values for t:

[5] Both new and already mentioned entities count.

the smaller the value, the denser the grid but the less related words within one entity group are.

t	-SYNT+SAL+COREF	-SYNT+SAL-COREF
w/o	75%	66%
0.1	71%	66%
0.2	72%	66%
0.3	72%	68%
0.4	73%	68%
0.5	73%	69%

Table 5: Ranking accuracy with different relatedness thresholds

The results demonstrate a significant improvement over the word-identity model although semantic relatedness is not as good as coreference, the difference between them still being about 5%. Semantic clustering of entities on top of coreference grouping does not bring an improvement, at least when done incrementally. A better approach might be to require any two entities from one cluster to have the minimum relatedness of t rather than adding an entity to a cluster when it is related to at least one element from the cluster.

4 Conclusions and Future Work

We presented our work on extending the entity-based coherence assessment from coreference to semantic relatedness and its application to German. In spite of the fact that we used human-annotated data, our results are considerably worse than the results for English. This may be caused by differences between the corpora. We analysed the impact of different settings and problem formulations (pairwise vs. multi-element rankings) and reported the best parameters for German.

Our initial experiments with entity clustering using semantic relatedness gave us some evidence that this is a promising direction to pursue. In particular, we would like to depart from the manually annotated data and explore cheaper approaches which require neither a deep parser, nor a coreference resolution system and work fully automatically. The RA of 69% obtained without syntactic and coreference information motivates this direction of research. Such an approach would provide a low-cost coherence evaluation strategy for NLG applications with a multisentential output.

Future work should compare (or combine) the information from Wikipedia with information from GermaNet and determine constraints on entity grouping. We experimented with incremental clustering although it may be that "shrinking" of a complete grid with a constraint on the size of a cluster would be more effective. We would also like to test the extended model on the data sets used by Barzilay & Lapata (2005).

Acknowledgements: This work has been funded by the Klaus Tschira Foundation, Heidelberg, Germany. The first author has been supported by a KTF grant (09.009.2004).

References

Barzilay, Regina & Mirella Lapata (2005). Modelling local coherence: An entity-based approach. In *Proceedings of the 43rd Annual Meeting of the Association for Computational Linguistics,* Ann Arbor, Michigan, 25–30 June 2005, pp. 141–148.

Gurevych, Iryna (2005). Using the structure of a conceptual network in computing semantic relatedness. In *Proceedings of the 2nd International Joint Conference on Natural Language Processing,* Jeju Island, South Korea, 11-13 October, 2005, pp. 767–778.

Hinrichs, Erhard, Sandra Kübler, Karin Naumann, Heike Telljohann & Julia Trushkina (2004). Recent developments in linguistic annotations of the TüBa-D/Z treebank. In *Proceedings of the 3rd Workshop on Treebanks and Linguistic Theories,* Tübingen, Germany, 10–11 December 2004.

Joachims, Thorsten (2002). Optimizing search engines using clickthrough data. In *Proceedings of the 8th International Conference on Knowledge Discovery and Data Mining,* Edmonton, Canada, 23–26 July 2002, pp. 133–142.

Lapata, Mirella (2006). Automatic evaluation of information ordering: Kendall's tau. *Computational Linguistics*, 32(4):471–484.

Lapata, Mirella & Regina Barzilay (2005). Automatic evaluation of text coherence: Models and representations. In *Proceedings of the 19th International Joint Conference on Artificial Intelligence,* Edinburgh, Schotland, 30 July–5 August, 2005, pp. 1085–1090.

Strube, Michael & Simone Paolo Ponzetto (2006). WikiRelate! Computing semantic relatedness using Wikipedia. In *Proceedings of the 21st National Conference on Artificial Intelligence,* Boston, Mass., 16–20 July 2006, pp. 1219–1224.

Telljohann, Heike, Erhard Hinrichs & Sandra Kübler (2003). *Stylebook for the Tübingen treebank of written German (TüBa-D/Z).* Technical Report: Seminar für Sprachwissenschaft, Universität Tübingen.

Versley, Yannick (2005). Parser evaluation across text types. In *Proceedings of the 4th Workshop on Treebanks and Linguistic Theories,* Barcelona, Spain, 9-10 December 2005.

Generating Multilingual Descriptions from Linguistically Annotated OWL Ontologies: the NaturalOWL System

Dimitrios Galanis and **Ion Androutsopoulos**
Department of Informatics
Athens University of Economics and Business
Patission 76, GR-104 34 Athens, Greece

Abstract

We introduce NaturalOWL, an open-source multilingual natural language generator that produces descriptions of instances and classes, starting from a linguistically annotated ontology. The generator is heavily based on ideas from ILEX and M-PIRO, but it is in many ways simpler and it provides full support for OWL DL ontologies with RDF linguistic annotations. NaturalOWL is written in Java, and it is supported by M-PIRO's authoring tool, as well as an alternative plug-in for the Protégé ontology editor.

1 Introduction

In recent years, considerable effort has been devoted to the Semantic Web (Antoniou and van Harmelen, 2004), which can be thought of as an attempt to establish mechanisms that will allow computer applications to reason more easily about the semantics of the Web's resources (documents, services, etc.). Domain ontologies play a central role in this endeavour: in effect, they establish domain-dependent semantic vocabularies (classes of entities; particular entities, called instances; properties of instances; axioms governing their use) that can be used to publish on the Web knowledge in shared machine-readable representations, and to annotate other resources (e.g., documents, videos) with machine-readable metadata describing aspects of their semantics.

In the case of natural language documents, some semantic annotations can be produced automatically via ontology-aware information extraction (Bontcheva and Cunningham, 2003); but information extraction can currently provide reliably only relatively simple types of semantic information, mostly by identifying and classifying named entities, and, less reliably, relations between them. When texts are generated automatically from formal knowledge bases, however, the generator can easily annotate the texts with much richer information, including full representations of their semantics, expressed in machine-readable markup. In fact, an entire strand of work in natural language generation (NLG) has focused on generating textual descriptions of an ontology's classes or instances. A well-known example of such work is ILEX (O'Donnell et al., 2001), which was demonstrated mostly with ontologies of museum exhibits. More recently, the M-PIRO project (Androutsopoulos et al., 2007) developed a multilingual extension of ILEX, which was tested in several domains, including museum exhibits and computing equipment. In this type of work, the ontology's role is no longer simply to provide a semantic vocabulary; the ontology acts as a repository of knowledge, and parts of the knowledge (e.g., information pertaining to particular instances or classes) can be rendered automatically in multiple natural languages or in a machine-readable form that carries the same semantic content. For example, M-PIRO's generator can deliver a description like the following to a human on-line shopper,

> A110: This is a laptop, manufactured by Toshiba. It has a Centrino Duo processor, 512 MB RAM, and an 80 GB hard disk. Its speed is 1.7 GHz and it costs 850 Euro.

and the following semantically equivalent formal representation to a software agent.[1] Alternatively, each individual sentence of the text could be marked up with a machine readable semantic representation.

```
<Laptop rdf:ID="A110">
 <manufacturedBy rdf:resource="#toshiba" />
 <hasProcessor rdf:resource="#centrinoDuo" />
 <hasMemory rdf:datatype="...#string">512 MB</memory>
 <hasDisk rdf:datatype="...#string">80 GB</disk>
 <speed rdf:datatype="...#string">1.7 GHz</speed>
 <cost rdf:datatype="...#string">850 Euro</cost>
</Laptop>
```

The standard formalism for publishing ontologies on the Semantic Web (SW) is currently OWL.[2] There are application domains (e.g., on-line shops) where one can envisage future SW sites that will maintain and publish their content entirely in the form of OWL ontologies. Then, NLG technology, embedded in server or browser plug-ins, could be used to render parts of the OWL ontologies in multiple natural

[1]For simplicity, we show scalar values as strings that include the units of measurements. More principled, language-independent representations of these values are also possible.

[2]Consult http://www.w3.org/TR/owl-features/.

languages or equivalent machine-readable representations on demand (Androutsopoulos et al., 2007). NLG can, thus, be seen as a key technology of the SW, which makes knowledge accessible to both humans and computers, a major target of the SW.

In this paper, we introduce NaturalOWL, a prototype open-source natural language generator intended to demonstrate what NLG can offer to the SW.[3]will be announced in the final version of this paper. NaturalOWL is heavily based on ideas from ILEX and M-PIRO, but unlike its predecessors it provides full support for OWL DL, the most principled version of OWL that corresponds to description logic (Baader et al., 2002); many NLG researchers will be familiar with this form of logic. Our previous attempts to support OWL in M-PIRO's generator ran into problems, because of incompatibilities between OWL and M-PIRO's ontological model (Androutsopoulos et al., 2005). Compared to ILEX and M-PIRO, NaturalOWL is also simpler; for example, it is entirely template-based, as opposed to the Systemic Grammars its predecessors employed.[4] Although future work may enhance some of NaturalOWL's components, the simplicity of the current system makes it easier to explain to SW researchers, who may not be familiar with NLG. It also simplifies the task of extending the system to support additional natural languages. NaturalOWL currently supports English and Greek.

It has been argued (Mellish and Sun, 2006) that in most OWL ontologies, classes and properties are given names that are either English words (e.g., `Laptop`, `cost`) or concatenations of English words (e.g., `manufacturedBy`, `hasMemory`). Based on this observation, Sun and Mellish (2006) generate texts from RDF descriptions, RDF being the description formalism on which OWL is based, without any domain-dependent linguistic resources. They use WordNet to tokenize the names of classes and properties, as well as to assign part-of-speech (POS) tags to tokens, and this allows them to guess that a class name like `Laptop` above is in fact a noun that can be used to refer to that class, or that `<manufacturedBy rdf:resource="#toshiba" />` should be expressed in English as "[This laptop] was manufactured by Toshiba". Hewlett *et al.* (2005) adopt very similar techniques. This approach, however, is problematic when texts have to be generated in multiple languages. Even in the monolingual case, there are significant problems: for example, a POS-tagger is often needed to distinguish between noun and verb uses of the same token, and morphological or even syntactic analysis is needed (especially in highly inflected languages) to extract tokens from class and property names and convert them into grammatical phrases; in effect, this re-introduces the need to interpret texts. Furthermore, our experience is that generating high-quality texts often requires linguistic information that is not present, not even indirectly, in OWL ontologies, nor can it be embedded conveniently in them (Androutsopoulos et al., 2005).

We, therefore, propose to annotate OWL ontologies with stand-off RDF markup that associates elements of the ontologies (e.g., classes, properties) with domain-dependent linguistic resources (e.g., lexicon entries, templates). We believe that this kind of linguistic annotation should be a standard part of ontology engineering for the SW; apart from allowing parts of the ontology to be presented to end-users in natural language, it facilitates presenting ontologies to domain experts for validation; and the annotations can also be useful when querying or extending ontologies via natural language (Katz et al., 2002; Bernstein and Kaufmann, 2006). NaturalOWL's RDF linguistic annotations will hopefully contribute towards a discussion in the NLG community on how to annotate OWL ontologies with linguistic information, and this may eventually produce standards that will allow alternative NLG components to render OWL ontologies in natural language, in the same way that alternative browsers can be used to view HTML pages.

Below we present briefly NaturalOWL's processing stages and its annotations of OWL ontologies. Following Wilcock (2003), the processing stages communicate in XML, but they are implemented in Java, instead of XSLT, and there is a clearer separation between processing code and linguistic resources.

2 Document planning

When instructed to produce a natural language description of an instance, NaturalOWL first selects from the ontology all the logical facts that are directly relevant to that instance; for example, when describing the laptop of the first page, it would select the fact that the instance is a `Laptop`, the fact that its manufacturer is Toshiba, etc.[5] NaturalOWL may be instructed to include facts that are further away in a graph representation of the ontology, up to a maximum (configurable) distance; setting the distance to two when describing a statue, for example, would also include in the selected facts information about the statue's sculptor (e.g., the country and year they were born in). This is very similar

[3]NaturalOWL and its Protégé plug-in can be downloaded from `http://www.aueb.gr/users/ion/publications.html`.

[4]Consult `http://www.ltg.ed.ac.uk/methodius/` for another offspring of M-PIRO's generator that uses CCG grammars.

[5]To save space, we restrict the discussion to descriptions of instances. NaturalOWL can also describe classes, but it conveys only information that is explicit in the ontology, unlike the work of Mellish and Sun (2005), where class descriptions also convey inferred facts. There are also separate stand-off annotations that specify how interesting each type of fact is per user type, and other user modelling information, much as in ILEX and M-PIRO. The ordering annotations could also be made sensitive to user type and target language.

to ILEX's content selection, but without employing rhetorical relations.

The selected facts of distance one are then ordered by consulting ordering annotations (see `owlnl:order` below), which specify a partial order of properties (e.g., that the manufacturer should be mentioned first, followed by the processor, memory and disk in any order, and then the price); is-a facts are always mentioned first. Second distance facts are always placed right after the corresponding directly relevant facts, producing texts like "This is a statue. It was sculpted by Nikolaou, who was born in Athens in 1968. This statue is made of marble and it...". In the application domains we have considered, this ordering scheme was adequate, although in other domains more elaborate text planning approaches may be needed; consult, for example, Bontcheva and Wilks (2004) for an application of text schemata to NLG from ontologies.

3 Microplanning, surface realisation

For each property, one or more micro-plans need to be specified per language. NaturalOWL's micro-plans are templates, each consisting of a sequence of slots. Each slot can be filled by an expression referring to the owner of the property (the laptop, in the case of `manufacturedBy`), the value (filler) of the property (Toshiba), or a string. The following RDF annotations refer to the `manufacturedBy` property.[6] After setting the property's order, they define an English micro-plan, according to which `<manufacturedBy rdf:resource="#toshiba" />` should be rendered in English as a phrase starting with (first slot) a nominative expression referring to the owner (the laptop). The `owlnl:retype` element of the first slot allows the system to select automatically among using the owner's name in natural language (if it has one), a noun phrase (e.g., "this laptop"), or a pronoun to refer to the owner, depending on context. The second slot will be filled by the string "was manufactured", which is marked up as being a past passive verb form; this additional markup is needed when aggregating phrases to form longer sentences. The third and fourth slots will be filled by the string "by" and an accusative automatically selected referring expression corresponding to the filler, respectively. The micro-plan may generate, for example, a phrase like "It was manufactured by Toshiba".[7]

[6]The linguistic annotations are kept in separate files from the OWL ontology, but they refer to its elements via their unique identifiers; we abbreviate the identifiers to save space.

[7]Although OWL properties (and other elements of OWL ontologies) can be associated with strings in multiple languages via `rdfs:label` tags, this mechanism is inadequate for template micro-plans; for example, it provides no principled way to indicate positions where referring expressions should be placed, or to annotate sub-strings with syntactic categories.

```
<owlnl:property rdf:about="...#manufacturedBy">
  <owlnl:order>1</owlnl:order>
  <owlnl:EnglishMicroplans ...>
    <owlnl:microplan ...>
      <owlnl:aggrAllowed>true</owlnl:aggrAllowed>
      <owlnl:slots ...>
        <owlnl:owner>
          <owlnl:case>nominative</owlnl:case>
          <owlnl:retype>re_auto</owlnl:retype>
        </owlnl:owner>
        <owlnl:verb>
          <owlnl:voice>passive</owlnl:voice>
          <owlnl:tense>past</owlnl:tense>
          <owlnl:val>was manufactured</owlnl:val>
        </owlnl:verb>
        <owlnl:text>
          <owlnl:val>by</owlnl:Val>
        </owlnl:text>
        <owlnl:filler>
          <owlnl:case>accusative</owlnl:case>
          <owlnl:retype>re_auto</owlnl:retype>
        </owlnl:filler>
      </owlnl:slots>
    </owlnl:microplan>
  </owlnl:EnglishMicroplans>
  <owlnl:GreekMicroplans ...>
  ...
</owlnl:Property>
```

NaturalOWL currently employs a very simple algorithm for generating referring expressions: once the instance being described has been introduced by mentioning its class (e.g., "This is a statue."), it uses pronouns to refer to that instance (e.g., "It was sculpted by Nikolaou."), until the focus moves to another instance ("Nikolaou was born in Athens. He was born in 1968."). Then, when the focus returns to the original instance, a demonstrative is used ("This statue is made of..."). As in M-PIRO, some properties may contain canned strings, and there are special annotations to flag canned strings that change the focus. Again, more elaborate referring expression generation algorithms can be added.

To be able to generate expressions like "this is a statue" or "this laptop", NaturalOWL requires OWL classes to be associated with noun phrases (more precisely n-bars). This is illustrated in the RDF statements below, where the class `Laptop` is associated with a noun phrase entry `laptop-NP` of NaturalOWL's domain-dependent multilingual lexicon, also expressed in RDF. The lexicon entry lists the various forms of the noun phrase, provides information on gender etc. The nominative singular form in Greek would be "φορητός υπολογιστής" (portable computer). We have considered associating classes with WordNet (or EuroWordNet) synsets, but the domain ontologies we have experimented with contain highly technical concepts, which are not covered by WordNet. Nevertheless, we plan to consider emerging standards for linguistic annotations (Ide and Romary, 2004), especially regarding the lexicon.

The phrases of the micro-plans are then aggregated in longer sentences, using roughly M-PIRO's aggregation rules (Melengoglou, 2002). This produces the final text, and, hence, there is no separate surface realization phase, apart from adding presentation markup, markup for speech synthesizers etc.

```
<owlnl:owlClass rdf:about="...#Laptop">
  <owlnl:hasNP rdf:resource="#laptop-NP"/>
</owlnl:owlClass>

<owlnl:NP rdf:ID="laptop-NP">
  <owlnl:LanguagesNP ...>
    <owlnl:EnglishNP>
      <owlnl:gender>nonpersonal</owlnl:gender>
      <owlnl:singular ...>laptop</owlnl:singular>
      <owlnl:plural ...>laptops</owlnl:plural>
    </owlnl:EnglishNP>
    <owlnl:GreekNP>
      <owlnl:gender>masculine</owlnl:gender>
      <owlnl:singularForms>
        <owlnl:nominative ...>...</owlnl:nominative>
        <owlnl:genitive ...>...</owlnl:genitive>
        <owlnl:accusative ...>...</owlnl:accusative>
      </owlnl:singularForms>
      ...
</owlnl:NP>
```

4 Source authoring

NaturalOWL is supported by M-PIRO's authoring tool (Androutsopoulos et al., 2007), which has been extended by NCSR "Demokritos" to be compatible with OWL DL. The tool helps "authors" port NaturalOWL to new application domains, including the tasks of ontology construction, defining micro-plans, creating the domain-dependent lexicon, etc. NaturalOWL is also accompanied by a plug-in for Protégé, an ontology editor most SW researchers are familiar with.[8] The plug-in provides the same functionality as M-PIRO's authoring tool. Consult also Bontcheva (2004) for related work on authoring tools.

5 Conclusions and further work

We introduced NaturalOWL, an open-source natural language generator for OWL DL ontologies that currently supports English and Greek. The system is intended to demonstrate the benefits of adopting NLG techniques in the Semantic Web, and to contribute towards a discussion in the NLG community on relevant annotation standards. NaturalOWL was partly developed and is being extended in project Xenios, where it is used by mobile robots acting as museum guides, an application that requires, among others, extensions to generate spatial expressions.[9]

References

I. Androutsopoulos, S. Kallonis, and V. Karkaletsis. 2005. Exploiting OWL ontologies in the multilingual generation of object descriptions. In *10th European Workshop on NLG*, pages 150–155, Aberdeen, UK.

I. Androutsopoulos, J. Oberlander, and V. Karkaletsis. 2007. Source authoring for multilingual generation of personalised object descriptions. *Natural Language Engineering*. In press, available on-line.

G. Antoniou and F. van Harmelen. 2004. *A Semantic Web Primer*. MIT Press.

F. Baader, D. Calvanese, D.L. McGuinness, D. Nardi, and P.F. Patel-Schneider, editors. 2002. *The Description Logic handbook: theory, implementation and application*. Cambridge University Press.

A. Bernstein and E. Kaufmann. 2006. GINO – a guided input natural language ontology editor. In *5th Int. Semantic Web Conference*, pages 144–157, Athens, GA.

K. Bontcheva and H. Cunningham. 2003. The Semantic Web: a new opportunity & challenge for Human Language Technology. In *Workshop on Human Language Technology for the Semantic Web and Web Services, 2nd Int. Semantic Web Conf.*, Sanibel Island, FL.

K. Bontcheva and Y. Wilks. 2004. Automatic report generation from ontologies: the MIAKT approach. In *9th Int. Conf. on Applications of Natural Language to Information Systems*, pages 324–335, Manchester, UK.

K. Bontcheva. 2004. Open-source tools for creation, maintenance, and storage of lexical resources for language generation from ontologies. In *4th Conf. on Language Resources & Evaluation*, Lisbon, Portugal.

D. Hewlett, A. Kalyanpur, V. Kolovski, and C. Halaschek-Wiener. 2005. Effective NL paraphrasing of ontologies on the Semantic Web. In *Workshop on End-User Semantic Web Interaction, 4th Int. Semantic Web conference*, Galway, Ireland.

N. Ide and L. Romary. 2004. International standard for a linguistic annotation framework. *Natural Language Engineering*, 10(3/4):211–225.

B. Katz, J. Lin, and D. Quan. 2002. Natural language annotations for the Semantic Web. In *International Conference on Ontologies, Databases, and Application of Semantics*, University of California, Irvine.

A. Melengoglou. 2002. Multilingual aggregation in the M-PIRO system. Master's thesis, School of Informatics, University of Edinburgh, UK.

C. Mellish and X. Sun. 2005. Natural language directed inference in the presentation of ontologies. In *10th European Workshop on NLG*, Aberdeen, UK.

C. Mellish and X. Sun. 2006. The Semantic Web as a linguistic resource: opportunities for Natural Language Generation. *Knowledge Based Systems*, 19:298–303.

M. O'Donnell, C. Mellish, J. Oberlander, and A. Knott. 2001. ILEX: an architecture for a dynamic hypertext generation system. *Natural Language Engineering*, 7(3):225–250.

X. Sun and C. Mellish. 2006. Domain independent sentence generation from RDF representations for the Semantic Web. In *Combined Workshop on Language-Enabled Educational Technology and Development and Evaluation of Robust Spoken Dialogue Systems, European Conference on AI*, Riva del Garda, Italy.

G. Wilcock. 2003. Talking OWLs: towards an ontology verbalizer. In *Workshop on Human Language Technology for the Semantic Web, 2nd Int. Semantic Web Conf.*, pages 109–112, Sanibel Island, FL.

[8]See http://protege.stanford.edu/.

[9]Xenios is funded by the European Union and the Greek General Secretariat for Research and Technology; consult http://www.ics.forth.gr/xenios/ for further information.

Cryptic Crossword Clues: Generating Text with a Hidden Meaning

David Hardcastle
Open University, Milton Keynes, MK7 6AA
Birkbeck, University of London, London, WC1E 7HX
d.w.hardcastle@open.ac.uk
ahard04@dcs.bbk.ac.uk

Abstract

This paper discusses the generation of cryptic crossword clues: a task that involves generating texts that have both a **surface reading**, based on a natural language interpretation of the words, and a **hidden meaning** in which the strings that form the text can be interpreted as a puzzle. The process of clue generation realizes a representation of the hidden, puzzle meaning of the clue through the aggregation of chunks of text. As these chunks are combined, syntactic and semantic selectional constraints are explored, and through this language understanding task a meaningful surface reading is recovered. This hybrid language generation/language understanding process transforms a representation of the clue as a word puzzle into a representation of some meaningful assertion in the domain of the real world, mediated through the generated multi-layered text; a text which has two separate readings.

1 Introduction

This paper discusses a system called ENIGMA which generates cryptic crossword clues: fragments of text that also have a **hidden meaning**, quite different from the **surface reading**. This raises an interesting research question: how to generate text that has multiple layers of meaning based on different syntactic rules and different semantic interpretations. The input to the realizer is a production of a high-level cryptic clue grammar whose terminals are the strings that participate in the puzzle presented by the clue. These conceptualizations of possible crossword clues contain no implicit syntactic or semantic information, and so a mechanism is required to ensure that the resulting surface text is syntactically correct and semantically appropriate while the meaning of the text, derived directly from the input, is not disturbed during lexicalization. As with computational humour and poetry generation the process of generation is unusual in that the content is not specified in the input (Ritchie, 2001; Manurung, 2000), and this leads to tractability problems when considering the wide range of lexicalization options (see also Ritchie, 2005: 4) requiring a bespoke solution.

1.1 Cryptic Crossword Clues

The cryptic crossword clues generated by ENIGMA consist of two separate indications of the solution word, one of which is a definition, the other a puzzle based on its orthography. Consider, for example, the following simple clue for *noiseless*:

`Still wild lionesses (9)`

Here *noiseless* is represented both by the synonym *still* (the definition) and a wordplay puzzle (an anagram of *lionesses*) indicated by the convention keyword *wild*. All of the clues generated by the system conform to Ximenean conventions (Macnutt, 1966), a set of guidelines that impose restrictions on inflection and word order to ensure that clues are 'fair' and also encourage the use of homographs and convention vocabulary to make them cryptic in nature.

It is important to note here that there are two separate readings of this clue: a surface reading in which the clue is also a fragment of English text, and the puzzle reading required to solve the clue. In the surface reading the word *still* is an adverb qualifying the adjective *wild*, while in the puzzle reading it is an adjective that is a synonym for *noiseless*.

There are many different types of crossword clue wordplay, including anagrams, homophones, writing words backwards, appending words together, and more besides. ENIGMA generates clues using seven of the eight main types listed in (Macnutt, 1966) and can also generate complex clues with subsidiary puzzles. This coverage combined with the richness of lexical choice in cryptic crossword convention vocabulary means that it is not uncommon for ENIGMA to generate several hundred valid clues for a single input word.

1.2 Requirements for Generation

Given a particular solution word, such as *noiseless*, the first step for the system is to determine the different ways in which the letters of the solution could be presented as a puzzle. For example, the basis of the clue could be that *noiseless* is an anagram of *lionesses*, or that it can be formed by running *noise* and *less* together, or that it is composed of a river (*Oise*) followed by the letter *l* all placed inside the word *ness*. In its present form ENIGMA locates 154 such formulations for the input word *noiseless*. Each of these formulations can be represented as a clue tree under ENIGMA's domain grammar for cryptic crosswords in which the terminal elements are the strings used to compose the solution word. The sample clue tree in Figure 1 represents the fact that *noiseless* can be formed by running *noise* and *less* together, a puzzle type known as a Charade (Macnutt, 1966; Manley, 2001).

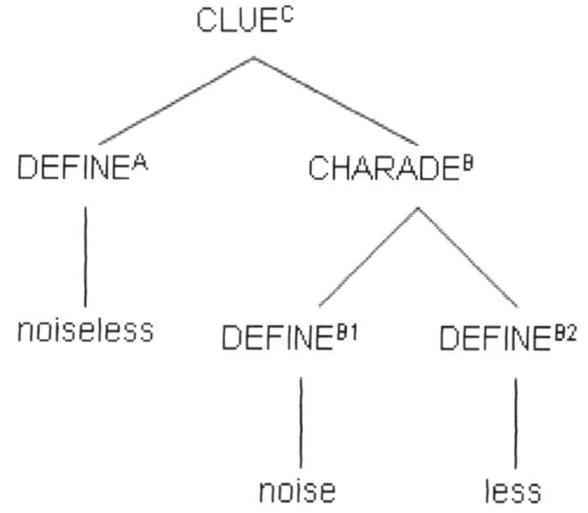

Figure 1. A clue tree that represents appending *noise* and *less* to form *noiseless*.

These clue trees contain no linguistic information - the terminals should be thought of as strings not as words. To lexicalize this data the system must construct a fragment of natural language that can be reinterpreted - through the resolution of homographs and a knowledge of special conventions - as a valid cryptic clue puzzle based on this non-linguistic structure. Along the way the syntax and semantics of the puzzle reading must not be disturbed or the clue will lose its hidden meaning. At the same time, the natural language syntactic and semantic information that is missing from the input data must be imposed on the clue so that a valid surface reading is achieved.

2 Chunk by Chunk Generation

A complete clue does not need to be a sentence, or even a clause, it can be any valid fragment of text, and ENIGMA takes advantage of this fact to simplify the generation algorithm. The clue tree shown in Figure 1 is realized through a process of composition. First the symbol labeled A is realized. Next B1 and B2 are realized individually and then combined to form B. Now, A and B can themselves be combined to form the clue. Each realization is a fragment of text, and I refer to each of these fragments as a *chunk*, although I note that they are rather different from chunks based on major heads (Abney, 1989), for the reasons set out below. To implement this process the system needs to be able to do two things: create chunks for each terminal in the clue tree, and merge chunks into successively larger ones until the root of the tree is reached. This recursive process enables ENIGMA to construct complex clues with subsidiary puzzles using the same implementation it uses for simple puzzles.

2.1 Word Order

When chunks are combined together they cannot interleave or nest. The reason for this is that each chunk represents a part of the hidden meaning of the clue, and word order is central to its interpretation. This is why ENIGMA uses a flat structure rather than a tree structure to build up the clue.

3 Implementation

Each chunk can attach to another chunk to its left, to its right, or via an intermediary word or phrase, such as a conjunction, something I call 'upward attachment'. The grammar that underpins these attachments is encoded as a set of three *extension points*[1] to each chunk: one specifying the relationships that can occur to the left, another those that can occur to the right, and the third specifying upward attachments. For example the chunk *wild lionesses* has, amongst many others, an extension point to the left indicating that it can attach as direct object to a verb, one to the right indicating that it can attach to a verb as subject and an upward attachment through which it can attach via a coordinating conjunction to another noun.

In addition to specifying the relationship and target type each extension point also specifies an *erasure*[2] for the chunk to which it belongs - this erasure indicates a word in the chunk that can stand in for the chunk as a whole when determining attachment. It is important to note that the erasure is not equivalent to the syntactic head and that different extension points on the same chunk may have different erasures. For example, in addition to looking for a verb to the left, the chunk *wild lionesses* also has an extension point looking for an adverb to the left, since an adverb could qualify the adjective *wild*. Therefore, the extension point looking for a verb erases *wild lionesses* to *lionesses*, so that a verb chunk looking for a noun to its right as direct object will accept it, whereas the extension point looking for an adverb erases this same chunk to *wild*, so that an adverb looking to its right for an adjective to qualify could also accept it. In this way the concept of erasure makes it possible for a wider variety of syntactic dependencies to be encoded in the same way on a single chunk, enabling polymorphic behaviour.

In some respects the extension points and associated erasures encoded onto each chunk act like the categories on functors in Combinatory Categorial Grammar (Clark et al, 2002), or edges on the agenda used in chart generation (Kay, 1996) as they specify the type and directionality of the arguments available and the type of the result. However, in addition to this syntactic information the grammar also provides the mechanism through which semantic selectional constraints are enforced. The erasures do not just specify a type (such as noun or adjective) but also a **member** of the chunk: *wild* or *lionesses* in this case. This enables the erasures to be used to determine which semantic checks are required to validate the attachment, adding to ENIGMA's implementation of chunks the semantic constraints that Abney notes as missing from his formulation (1989: 15). For example, if the chunk *wild lionesses* attaches to a chunk to its left that erases to a verb and is looking for a direct object then the extension point governing this attachment enforces syntactic correctness, but this is not enough. Since the clue tree only contains information about crossword conventions a separate semantic check is now required to ensure that it makes sense for the verb to take the noun *lionesses* as its direct object, and this semantic check will be performed using the relation and the erasures as arguments.

So, for example, when the chunk *still* is combined to the left of *wild lionesses* the system performs a semantic check to ensure that *still* can qualify *wild*. If the verb *calm* (an alternative homograph of a synonym for *noiseless*) is attached to the left then the system checks that *lionesses* can be the direct object of *calm*, and so on.

4 Sample output

Figure 2 depicts system output from ENIGMA representing the sample clue given in the introduction. Since so many clues are generated the system also generates a list of justifications which it uses to determine a score and rank the clues. The output shown in Figure 2 only includes information that relates to this paper; the full listing also contains information about the structure of the clue and the difficulty of the clue as a word puzzle. All of the explanatory text is generated using templates.

```
Clue for [noiseless]
Clue [Still wild lionesses (9)]
POS [still/AV0 wild/AJ0 lionesses/NN2]
Homograph pun: to solve the clue 'still'
must be read as Adjective but has surface
reading Adverb
Sense: dependency fit 'wild lionesses' of
type Adjective Modifier characterized as
'inferred'
```

[1] The term extension point is more commonly used to define the interfaces to plug-in components in extensible computer systems.

[2] In Object-Oriented Programming an erasure is a simplification or genericisation of a type through some interface, see for example (Bracha et al, 2001).

```
Attachment: 'wild lionesses' attached via
type Attributive Adjective Modifier
Sense: 'still wild' sense-checked for In-
tensifying Adverb attachment using the
lexicon
Attachment: 'still wild' attached via
type Adverbial Qualifier (of Adjective)
Thematic Fit: 'wild' and 'lionesses'
share common thematic content.
```

Figure 2. Sample output from ENIGMA.

5 Discussion

ENIGMA constructs clues using their hidden meaning as the starting point. Lexical choice is very unrestricted, while word order is quite tightly constrained. This leads to combinatorial explosion in lexical choice, but of the intractably large number of possible productions for each clue very few also function as viable fragments of natural language. ENIGMA's approach is to work through the structure of the hidden clue and determine constraints on the surface reading on the fly. The compositional process reins in the combinatorial explosion by pushing language constraints down to the most local level at which they can operate.

ENIGMA uses various generic language understanding resources built specifically for the application during the generation process to ensure that the syntactic relationships behind the clue's surface reading are semantically supported.

- A Collocational Semantic Lexicon mined from British National Corpus and augmented using WordNet determines if a proposed dependency relation between two words is semantically probable (Hardcastle 2007). This lexicon is used to impose selectional constraints on syntactic dependency relations, such as between a verb and its direct object.
- A Word Association Measure based on a distributional analysis of data in the British National Corpus is used to evaluate the thematic coherence of the clue (Hardcastle 2005).
- A Phrase Dictionary derived from the Moby Compound word list[3] is used to identify aggregations that result in the creation of multi-word units such as compound nouns or phrasal verbs.

[3] http://www.dcs.shef.ac.uk/research/ilash/Moby/.

The resulting clue texts are syntactically and semantically valid under the symbolic language grammar of the domain, and at the same time are plausible fragments of natural language. I plan to perform a mix of qualitative and quantitative evaluations on a set of generated clues, a reference set of clues published in newspapers and a set of control clues generated with no syntactic or semantic constraints, grouped into subsets that share the same solution word.

References

S. Abney. (1989). Parsing by Chunks. In *The MIT Parsing Volume,* edited by C. Tenny. The MIT Press.

G. Bracha, N. Cohen, C. Kemper, S. Mark, M. Odersky, S.-E. Panitz, D. Stoutamire, K. Thorup, and P. Wadler. (2001). *Adding generics to the Java programming language: Participant draft specification.* Technical Report, Sun Microsystems.

S. Clark, J. Hockenmaier, and M. Steedman. (2002). Building deep dependency structures with a wide-coverage CCG parser. In *Proceedings of the 40th Meeting of the ACL,* pages 327–334.

D. Hardcastle. (2007). *Building a Collocational Semantic Lexicon.* Technical Report BBKCS-07-02. Birkbeck, London.

D. Hardcastle. (2005). An examination of word association scoring using distributional analysis in the British National Corpus: what is an interesting score and what is a useful system? In *Proceedings of Corpus Linguistics*, Birmingham.

M. Kay. (1996). Chart Generation. In *Proceedings of the 34th Meeting of the ACL,* pages 200-204.

D. S. Macnutt. (1966). *On the Art of the Crossword.* Swallowtail Books.

D. Manley. (2001). *Chambers Crossword Manual.* Chambers.

H. Manurung, G. Ritchie and H. Thompson. (2000). *Towards a Computational Model of Poetry Generation.* In *Proceedings of AISB Symposium on Creative and Cultural Aspects and Applications of AI and Cognitive Science*, pages 79-86.

G. Ritchie. (2001). Current Directions in Computational Humour. In *Artifical Intelligence Review 16(2)*, pages 119-135.

G. Ritchie. (2005). Computational Mechanisms for Pun Generation. In *Proceedings of the 10th European Natural Language Generation Workshop*, pages 125-132.

Combining Multiple Information Layers for the Automatic Generation of Indicative Meeting Abstracts

Thomas Kleinbauer and **Stephanie Becker** and **Tilman Becker**
German Research Center for Artificial Intelligence (DFKI)
Stuhlsatzenhausweg 3, 66123 Saarbrücken, Germany
<firstname.lastname>@dfki.de

Abstract

We describe a new application for NLG technology: the generation of indicative, abstractive summaries of multi-party meetings. Based on the freely available AMI corpus of 100 hours of recorded meetings, we are developing a summarizer that uses the rich annotations in the AMI corpus.

1 Introduction

The automatic summarization of documents has been a research topic for half a century now. Most prominently, the automatic creation of document *extracts* has been studied extensively. However, when applying such approaches to natural dialogs, such as meetings, the resulting texts may differ vastly from hand-written summaries: instead of concise and coherent prose, the expected output consists of a concatenation of speaker contributions taken from the original dialog. Yet, these utterances were made from each speaker's own perspective and thus are likely to contain first-person wording, inept for a comprehensible summary. Additionally, speech disfluencies or–in automated settings–speech recognition errors might further decrease the readability of the text. Finally, the extracted utterances are reproduced out of context which can be problematic in numerous ways, including the acceptance of the service by the meeting participants.

In this paper, we present our ongoing research on the generation of meeting abstracts that aims at overcoming the outlined shortcomings. So far, we have concentrated on *indicative* summaries that allow the reader to quickly assess whether the underlying meeting is relevant for her current information need.

2 Related Work

Extractive summarization of documents has been studied extensively over the last decades (s. Mani and Maybury (1999) for an overview), but faces additional challenges when applied to natural language dialogs. Unlike carefully authored articles, spontaneous utterances are often ungrammatical and contain speech disfluencies (Liu et al., 2006). Moreover, free discussions are naturally less well structured, e. g., when speakers switch topics or digress. For an automated system, additional difficulties arise from the limitations of current ASR systems, introducing recognition errors into all subsequent processing steps. Zechner (2001) and Murray et al. (2005) show ways to cope with such issues.

Generative approaches, on the other hand, are based on an internal representation of summary contents verbalized through NLG techniques (e. g. Kan et al. (2001)). Such approaches have been applied to natural discourse domains before, for instance, Alexandersson (2003) generates summaries of machine–translated phone conversations. However, we are not aware of any prior work attempting to generate full abstracts of multi-party interaction.

3 Annotated AMI Meetings

In the AMI project[1], circa 100 hours of meetings have been recorded, annotated and stored in a freely available multimodal corpus (McCowan et al., 2005). The meetings are semi-staged, in the sense that they are based on the predefined scenario of a virtual company in which a project team works on the task of designing a new innovative remote control. The roles of the four project team members are played by

[1] http://www.amiproject.org

subjects which act as a project manager, a user interface designer, a production designer, and a marketing expert. However, the discussions of the meeting participants are free and not prescripted. Meetings typically last about 30-40 minutes.

In addition to multiple video and audio streams, a number of annotations are included in the corpus, such as speech transcription, syntactic chunks, named entities, dialog acts, addressing, argumentative structure, hot spots, decision points and topics.

The goal of the AMI project is to develop automatic recognition systems for all of these annotation layers. In section 4 we show which layers are already used by our summarizer, see figure 5 for an example from the current system. However, all of these annotations are potentially useful, very rich resources for further extensions of our system.

3.1 Propositional Content

Additionally, we have annotated a small subset of the AMI corpus with categories from a domain ontology to represent the propositional content of speaker utterances. The AMIMATTER ontology that we created for this purpose models the remote control design scenario in a formal ontology based on Dolce-Lite-Plus (Masolo et al., 2003). Embedded in a comprehensive theory of representing situations and descriptions, it provides a taxonomy of relevant terms, ordered by an `IS-A` relation that expresses subsumption, or specialization. For instance, it contains information such as (remote_control IS-A technical_device) which expresses that the category remote_control is a sub-category of the category technical_device. Hence, a reasoner can infer that all remote controls (which technically would be considered *instances* of the category remote_control) are technical devices.

The AMIMATTER ontology covers over 20 different subdomains, with a total of 53,319 categories. 52,072 of those are extracted from WordNet (Fellbaum, 1998), the remaining 1,247 cover scenario-specific concepts and the Dolce-Lite-Plus upper model. Three subdomains—physical objects, meeting-related categories and project-related categories—were used to annotate the discourse transcription. The current system relies only on the annotation of relevant categories, ignoring relations within or beyond the dialog act segment boundaries[2]. Fig. 1 shows an example of such an annotation: three instances from the physical object subdomain were created (shown as boxes) and linked to the respective words in the source utterance above.

4 Summary Content Representation

We currently concentrate on three of the above annotation layers, topic labels, dialog acts and propositional content. For the pre-existing topic annotation, the recordings were split into larger segments and labeled with one of 24 topics matching typical activities in the remote control design scenario, e. g., "discussion" or "presentation of prototype(s)". These segments are used by our system as the basic structuring unit for the summaries. In most cases, the label can be used to verbalize the general subject of the topic segment, with the exception of the "other" label which is used for unknown topics.

In a similar practice, all participants' utterances in the manual transcript of the meeting discourse were segmented and labeled with dialog acts such as "inform", "suggest", etc. according to a scheme consisting of 15 distinguished dialog acts. However, our system currently discards the labels themselves, but uses the segments as a common unit for the propositional content annotation outlined in section 3.1. We perform a frequency analysis of all annotated ontology instances and select the three items that occur most often. We found this a useful heuristic, although it sometimes produces unexpected results (s. fig. 5: the term "beep" stems from an ontology category of the same name that was used to annotate a discussion about audio signals in the corpus).

5 Text Generation

The actual generation of the abstracts is done in a three-step pipeline:

1. Analysis of meeting annotation layers
2. Sentence planning
3. Surface realization

In the first step, information drawn from the annotation layers (s. section 3) is transformed

[2]More precisely, annotators were asked to identify those terms in a speaker utterance that belong to one of the three subdomains, identify the appropriate AMIMATTER category and create an instance of it, and connect the instance with the original word.

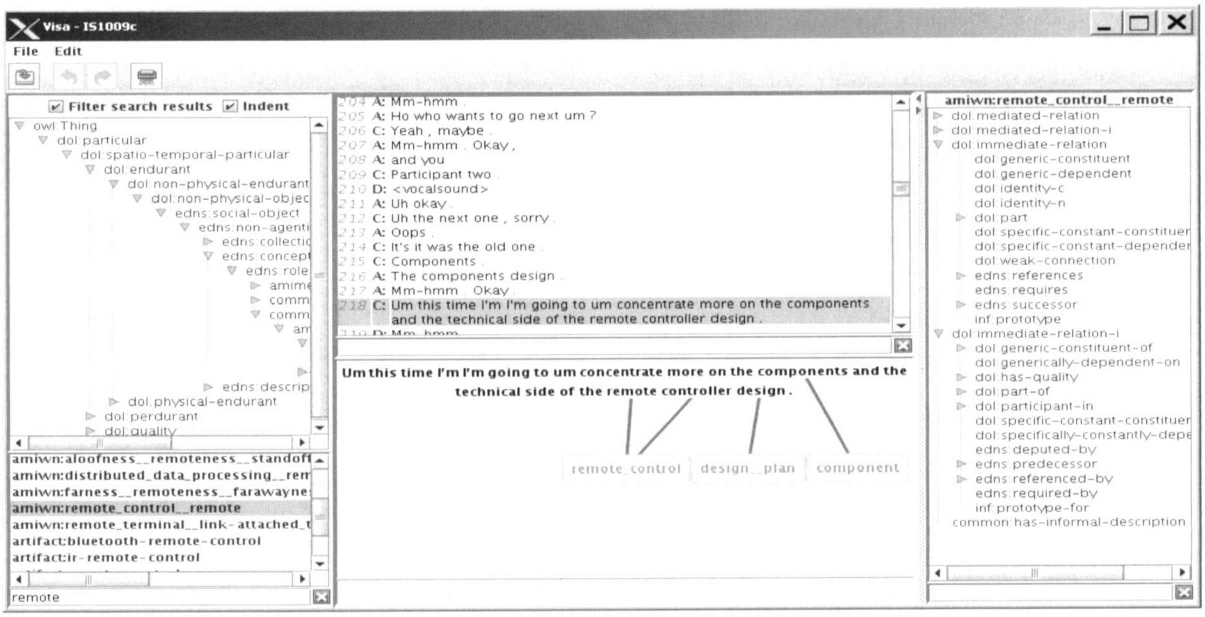

Figure 1: Example annotation of an utterance in meeting IS1009c in the AMI corpus. The outer sides display categories and relations of the AMIMATTER ontology in tree views, the center part contains the meeting transcript (top) and the annotation area (bottom).

into expressions in a propositional logic-like formalism (figure 2). These assertions are used

```
(topic "t0")
(about "t0" "opening")
(content "t0" "introduction")
(content "t0" "project manager")
(after "t0" "t1")  ...
```

Figure 2: The input for the sentence planner: topic t0 which is the opening of the meeting occurs before topic t1 and contains the content items "introduction" and "project manager".

as a knowledge base by the sentence planner PREPLAN, a hierarchical, goal-driven planner (André, 1995). In addition to the assertions, PREPLAN is provided with a library of plan operators, each of which encodes strategies how to reach a given goal. Figure 3 shows an example of such an operator which describes how to reach the goal "ShowSummary" as the result of solving three subgoals, one of which is an iteration over all topics. Here, the "with"-condition is matched against the knowledge base that was generated before.

```
strategy: (ShowSummary)
subgoals: (WriteXMLHeader)
          (for-each ?t with (topic ?t)
             (ShowTopic ?t))
          (WriteXMLFooter)
```

Figure 3: A complex plan operator in PREPLAN

PREPLAN successively finds matching plan-operators until all goals and subgoals are resolved. The outcome of this process is an XML-encoded description of instructions in a logical form which is passed to the surface realizer, NIPSGEN (Engel, 2006), a template-based generator. NIPSGEN converts the semantic input into typed feature structures which are then transformed into a natural language utterance. A derivation tree for the XTAG-grammar (XTAG Research Group, 2001) is created using transformation rules which are applied to the input structure (see figure 4 for a sample rule). The actual syntax tree is constructed using the derivation tree. The generation of the correct morphological inflections is achieved by percolating the morphological features through the XTAG tree and looking up the correct inflections for all lexical leaves in the XTAG lexicon for English. Traversing the lexical leaves from left to right produces the natural language ut-

```
$VP=VP(o:Introduction(has-topic:$T,
           has-agent:$A), not(lex:))
 -> $VP(lex:introduce, sub:NP(o:$A),
        obj:NP(o:$T))
```

Figure 4: A NipsGen rule: the semantic concept 'Introduction()' is lexicalized with the verb 'introduce'. The values of the features 'has-topic' and 'has-agent' are realized as NP's in object and subject position, respectively.

terance.

> *"The meeting was opened and the meeting group talked about the user interface, the remote control and the design. They debated the costs, the company and the project while discussing the project budget. The signal, the remote control and the beep were mentioned afterwards. They talked about meeting before closing the meeting."*

Figure 5: Example of a meeting summary.

6 Current and Future Work

We are currently developing the summarization system further by adding more annotation layers to the processing pipeline.

Work has also begun on the evaluation of meeting summaries. To this end, we will use a task based evaluation scheme where summaries are used by subjects to better understand previous meetings in order to join the team, replacing a previous member. The quality of summaries will degrade when we move from hand-annotated layers to automatically generated annotations. Extrinsic evaluations as described above will be a realistic measure for the level of degradation.

Given the richness of the data in the AMI corpus, we have also started work on multimedia summaries that will combine text with pictures from the video signals and links into the meetings[3]. We are experimenting with result-based summaries, presented in a newspaper style and timeline-based summaries, presented in a comic-strip style.

In general, summarization of multi-party meetings poses further challenges, like summaries from a personal perspective, and moving to related domains like instant messaging and IRC interactions.

[3]These links are timestamps that are used by a meeting player to show relevant segments.

References

Jan Alexandersson. 2003. *Hybrid Discourse Modelling and Summarization for a Speech-to-Speech Translation System*. Ph.D. thesis, Universität des Saarlandes, Germany.

Elisabeth André. 1995. *Ein planbasierter Ansatz zur Generierung multimedialer Präsentationen*. Infix, St. Augustin.

Ralf Engel. 2006. SPIN: A semantic parser for spoken dialog systems. In *Proceedings of the Fifth Slovenian And First International Language Technology Conference (IS-LTC 2006)*.

Christiane Fellbaum, editor. 1998. *WordNet–An Electronic Lexical Database*. MIT Press.

Min-Yen Kan, Kathleen R. McKeown, and Judith L. Klavans. 2001. Applying natural language generation to indicative summarization. In *Proceedings of 8th European Workshop on Natural Language Generation*, pages 92–100, Toulouse, France, July.

Y. Liu, E. Shriberg, A. Stolcke, D. Hillard, M. Ostendorf, and M. Harper. 2006. Enriching speech recognition with automatic detection of sentence boundaries and disfluencies. *IEEE Transactions on Audio, Speech and Language Processing*, 14(5):1526–1540.

Inderjeet Mani and Mark T. Maybury, editors. 1999. *Advances in automatic text summarization*. MIT Press.

C. Masolo, S. Borgo, A. Gangemi, N. Guarino, and A. Oltramari. 2003. Wonderweb deliverable D18 ontology library (final), December.

I. McCowan, J. Carletta, W. Kraaij, S. Ashby, S. Bourban, M. Flynn, M. Guillemot, T. Hain, J. Kadlec, V. Karaiskos, M. Kronenthal, G. Lathoud, M. Lincoln, A. Lisowska, W. Post, D. Reidsma, and P. Wellner. 2005. The Ami meeting corpus. In *Proceedings of the Measuring Behavior 2005 symposium on Annotating and Measuring Meeting Behavior*, Wageningen, NL, September.

G. Murray, S. Renals, and J. Carletta. 2005. Extractive summarization of meeting recordings. In *Proceedings of the 9th European Conference on Speech Communication and Technology*, Lisbon, Portugal, September.

XTAG Research Group. 2001. A lexicalized tree adjoining grammar for english. Technical Report IRCS-01-03, IRCS, University of Pennsylvania.

Klaus Zechner. 2001. *Automatic Summarization of Spoken Dialogues in Unrestricted Domains*. Ph.D. thesis, Carnegie Mellon University.

A Comparison of Hedged and Non-hedged NLG Texts

Saad Mahamood, Ehud Reiter, and Chris Mellish
Department of Computing Science
University of Aberdeen, Untied Kingdom
{smahamoo, ereiter, cmellish}@csd.abdn.ac.uk

Abstract

We assess the use of hedge phrases in "affective" NLG texts. A simple experiment suggests non-native speakers prefer texts that contain hedge phrases, but native speakers prefer texts that do not contain hedge phrases.

1 Introduction

In recent years there has been growing interest in "affective" Natural Language Generation (NLG). Affective NLG has been defined as: "NLG that relates to, arises from or deliberately influences emotions or other non-strictly rational aspects of the Hearer" (de Rosis, 2001).

One open issue in affective NLG is how texts that communicate emotionally sensitive information should be worded. In this paper we focus on the usage of 'hedge phrases' which communicate empathetic information, such as "unfortunately." An experiment in the domain of communicating exam results to students suggests that such emphathetic hedge phrases are appreciated by non-native English speakers, but disliked by native English speakers.

2 Motivation

Some NLG systems produce texts that communicate emotionally sensitive information. In particular, the BT-Parent system, which is part of the BabyTalk project (Portet et al., 2007; Reiter, 2007), produces texts that summarise the condition of a baby in a neonatal intensive care unit, for the baby's parents. Such texts must be worded in a way which minimises emotional distress, while of course still being truthful. The work here is an initial attempt to explore one aspect of how sensitive information should be communicated. Because of ethical considerations, we have conducted this initial experiment with a different group, students who are being told about exam results.

3 Hedge Phrases

Hedging can be described as a strategy by which speakers mitigate and soften the force of their utterances (Nikula, 1997). The term was first coined by Lakoff (1973), but the original definition has been widened in part due to the observation that certain verbs and syntactic constructions convey hedged performatives (Markkanen and Schröder, 1997a). Verbs such as *suppose*, *guess*, and *think* are examples of these hedged performatives. However these verbs have also been defined as hedges that affect the amount of commitment which a speaker may have to the truth-value of a particular sentence (Markkanen and Schröder, 1997a). Prince et al. (1982) in their analysis on hedging found that hedges can be be classified into two distinct groups with respect to their effect on the truth-value.The first are *approximators* which do modify the truth-condition of the proposition (e.g. I *suppose* the sky is blue). The second is *shields* which unlike *approximators* do not affect the truth-conditon of the proposition, but instead show the amount of commitment that the speaker/writer has to the proposition (e.g. I *think* his feet are blue) (Markkanen and Schröder, 1997a).

In the hedging literature distinctions are not always made between the strategies to be applied and the modifying devices used to achieve the hedging (Clemen, 1997). The five distinct strategies defined by Clemen (1997) are: *Politeness*, *Indirectness*, *Mitigation*, *Vagueness*, and *Understatement*. It can be argued that hedging is determined by a combination of factors, namely the type of context (discourse type), the colloquial situation, the speaker's/writer's intention and knowledge of the background dialogue/conversation (Clemen, 1997).

The aspects of hedging that were of interest to us was the usage of evaluative adverbs (Bonami and Godard, 2006) as a modifying device (such as *unfortunately*, *sadly*, etc.) combined with aspects of the *Indirectness* and *Mitigation* hedging strategies defined by Clemen (1997).

4 Empathy in NLG

Reiter et al. (2000) asked two doctors to rewrite a computer-generated smoking cessation letter, with one doctor asked to enhance the empathy of the letter and another doctor asked to enhance the readability of the letter, thus producing two differing letters. They then asked 20 smokers which version they preferred, and why. They found strong individual differences, with 8 smokers preferring one version and 9 smokers preferring the other (and 3 expressing no preference). In terms of qualitative comments, some of the participants finding the empathic version too "patronising", whilst others found it to be "encouraging".

Perhaps the most important lesson from this experiment is that there seem to be major individual differences in how diffent people react to "empathetic" texts. Hence it would be very helpful if we could create rules which predicted which texts people prefer, based on their characteristics.

5 System Implementation

We created a simple NLG system which generated short texts which summarised the exam results of a student; this used the simplenlg API (Reiter, 2007). The system can insert evaluative adverbs (words and phrases) into generated sentences. These adverbs were classified into two distinct groups: Negative hedges and Positive hedges. Negative hedges were adverbs that were used when a given proposition was negative in content. While the positive hedges were used when dealing with a positive content. The example below illustrates these two types of hedges:

(1) ***Unfortunately***, *you got CAS 9 in CS5038*

(2) ***Happily***, *the CAS result for CS5035 was 19*

The Common Assessment Scale (CAS) score is a scoring mechanism used by the University of Aberdeen. The scale comprises of 21 discrete points with 0 being the lowest and 20 being the highest score. For the NLG system, a student's score was used to determine whether a given proposition was positive or negative.

There were also two different types of hedges deployed; Front hedges and back hedges. Front hedges, as illustrated above, are hedges in which an adverb is injected in front of a given proposition, whereas back hedges are phrases that are inserted after a proposition:

(3) ***Sadly***, *you got CAS 9 in CS5035 and CS5037.* ***Hopefully, this won't effect your degree result by much***.

Our system randomly chooses which hedge phrase to use; however, it will never insert more than one front hedge or more than one back hedge into a sentence.

The system differs from the ADVISOR expert system (Elhadad, 1991) because of its focus on a specific collection of adverbial words that act as hedges rather than using adjectives for argumentative usage.

6 Experiment

6.1 Aims

This initial experiment compared the individual preference of participants when presented with hedged and non-hedged texts from our system. The texts gave results for mythical students, not for the experiment participants.

6.2 Participants

The trial for this experiment was organised as follows. A 1-page, double-sided questionnaire was distributed to a total of 37 Masters students (9 females and 28 males). A total of 5 questionnaires were rejected as incomplete. In the experiment 14 participants were native and fluent in English (Native speakers), whilst 18 participants were not native to the English language. The 18 non-native English speakers were asked if they were fluent in English: 7 said they were (Fluent speakers), and 11 said they were not (Non-fluent speakers).

6.3 Procedure

The questionnaire in the experiment showed to each participant an artificially generated exam test result for two differing scenarios. The first was in a positive context in which a hypothetical student has achieved a set of high results. The second in a negative context in which a set of low results was presented. For each scenario participants were shown two texts summarising the exam results: one without hedges (Text A) and one with hedges (Text B). The participants were asked to state which of the two texts they would prefer in the context of having their results delivered to them.

6.4 Evaluation Criteria

The questionnaire asked each participant for a set of personal details; Age, English fluency level, and gender. The main questionnaire then consisted of two sections as described in the previous section.

Here are two possible letters that could be sent to the student by the University:

Text A: "You can get a Master's Degree. You got CAS 18 in CS5037, CS5038, CS5052 and CS5549. Average CAS results were achieved in CS5540 and CS5541. You got CAS 9 in CS5548 and CS5942. You got CAS 19 in CS5035."

Text B: "You can get a Master's Degree. Fortunately, you got CAS 18 in CS5037, CS5038, CS5052 and CS5549. Thankfully, average CAS results were achieved in CS5540 and CS5541. Unfortunately, you got CAS 9 in CS5548 and CS5942. Happily, the CAS result for CS5035 was 19."

Which of these two letters do you think is best? :

Definitely A **Both the Same** **Definitely B**

☐ ☐ ☐ ☐ ☐ ☐ ☐

Why?:

Figure 1: A section of the questionnaire given to participants

Subjects were asked to state a preference which ran from -3 for Text A to + 3 for Text B. If both texts were considered by a participant to be the same then a score of 0 was given. The participants were asked to provide free text comments on why they made their particular choice of text.

6.5 Results

The overall results in this experiment were calculated by a mean average of the participants selection of hedging preference in sections 1 and 2 of the questionnaire. These results are presented in table 1. It is quite clear that on average most participants favoured texts without any form of hedging. However, if we break the results down by language fluency a different picture emerges.

A one-way ANOVA statistical analysis shows a significant effect by group ($p = 0.01$). Further analysis using Post-Hoc Tukey HSD shows a significant difference ($p = 0.013$) between native and fluent speaker groups. This significant difference is also present between native and non-fluent ($p = 0.002$) speaker groups. There was no significant difference ($p = 0.487$) between the fluent and non-fluent speaker groups. It can be concluded from this statistical analysis that there is a correlation between native/non-native status and the amount of preference for hedged and non-hedged texts.

In comparing the number of participants that preferred hedged text in sections 1 & 2 it seems that 16 people preferred the hedged text in section 1 compared to 8 people who preferred the opposite tendency in section 2. However, there was no statistical significant factor found which determined the preference of either hedged text when a univariate analysis of variance was conducted.

7 Discussion

From the results above we can see that there is a statistical correlation between the overall preference for these types of hedges and whether the participant is a native speaker. This correlation between being a native speaker and preference for hedging may be partially due to the differing cultural expectations in text of non-native speakers compared to those that have English as their primary language. This is consistent with research conducted by Crismore et al. (1993) which has shown that there is a difference in the amount of hedges used in written text between Finnish and American University students.

The scenario in which the hedges were inserted may play a role in defining the preference for hedging. One of the typical comments which was repeated by several native speakers was that the hedges were less favourable since they were inappropriate for the textual content type. In general the hedges were perceived to be adding opinion to text or were just "wishy-washy". The quote below is from a native speaker and is a good overall representative of the comments received:

> "[Text] B is over-personal, yet in this context it could be constructed as condescending as well. Although [Text] A is a bit more abrupt, it's more formal and suited to University letters."

Such sentiments were not as pervasive in the other speaker groups, which instead commented on how the hedged text was more "humanised" and comfortable. An example of this from a non-fluent speaker is shown below:

> "Good result, so 'wonderful' can make the student happy. Humanised."

It is possible that cultural expectations may play a big role in the wide disparity in perception between the native and non-native speaker groups. However, it is also possible that the preference for such hedges

Speaker Group	Total Mean	Section 1	Section 2
Native Speakers	-1.75	-1.42	-2.07
Fluent Speakers	0.27	0.09	0.45
Non-Fluent Speakers	1.14	2	0.28
All Groups	**-0.48**	**-0.14**	**-0.82**

Table 1: Overall average participant preferences for sections 1 & 2 by language fluency

just reflects the varying degrees of English understanding by the different groups. Such "hedges" may act as "emotional navigators" for those who aren't fluent with English language conventions. On the other hand it is quite possible that the preference for hedging is based upon personal preference rather than any singular principle.

8 Future Work

There are at least two areas that need further investigation. The first is to explore the impact that cultural background may have on a particular individual's preference for hedging. It would be interesting to see the types of hedges preferred by some cultures and the ones that aren't. It is possible that this line of research could in turn allow a NLG system to adapt its textual output depending on the cultural background of the recipient.

The second area would look into defining a model for hedging. Currently there is no model for the placement and frequency of hedges within NLG text. One approach for defining such a model would be to look into the statistical frequency of hedges within different corpora to see whether there are any particular defining grammatical or contextual features that are shared between hedges.

References

Olivier Bonami and Danièle Godard. 2006. Lexical semantics and pragmatics of evaluative adverbs.

Gudrun Clemen. 1997. In Markkanen and Schröder (Markkanen and Schröder, 1997b), chapter The Concept of Hedging: Orgins, Approaches and Definitions, pages 235–248.

Avon Crismore, Raija Markkanen, and Margaret S. Steffenson. 1993. Metadiscourse in persuasive writing: A study of texts written by american and finnish unversity students. *Written Communication*, 10(1):39–71, January.

Fiorella de Rosis. 2001. Towards adaptation of interaction to affective factors. *User Modelling and User-Adapted Interaction 11*.

M. Elhadad. 1991. Generating adjectives to express the speaker's argumentative intent. In *Proceedings of the 9th National Conference on Artificial Intelligence (AAAI 91)*, pages 98–104.

George Lakoff. 1973. Hedges: A study in the meaning criteria and the logic of fuzzy concepts. *Journal of Philosophical Logic 2*.

Raija Markkanen and Hartmut Schröder. 1997a. In Markkanen and Schröder (Markkanen and Schröder, 1997b), chapter Hedging: A Challenge for Pragmatics and Discourse Analysis, pages 3–18.

Raija Markkanen and Hartmut Schröder, editors. 1997b. *Hedging and Discourse: Approaches to the Analysis of a Pragmatic Phenomenon in Academic Texts*. Walter de Gruyter.

Tarja Nikula. 1997. In Markkanen and Schröder (Markkanen and Schröder, 1997b), chapter Interlanguage View of Hedging, pages 188–207.

François Portet, Ehud Reiter, Jim Hunter, and Somayajulu Sripada. 2007. Automatic generation of textual summaries from neonatal intensive care data. In *Proceedings of the 11th Conference on Artificial Intelligence in Medicine (AIME '07)*. LNCS, July.

Ellen F. Prince, Joel Frader, and Charles Bosk, 1982. *Linguistics and the Proffessions*, chapter On hedging in physician-physician discourse, pages 83–97. Ablex.

Ehud Reiter, Roma Robertson, and Liesel Osman. 2000. Knowledge acquisition for natural language generation. In *First International Conference on Natural Language Generation (INLG-2000)*, pages 217–224.

Ehud Reiter. 2007. An architecture for data-to-text systems. In *Proceedings of the 11th European Workshop on Natural Language Generation (ENLG'07)*, June.

Cueing the Virtual Storyteller: Analysis of cue phrase usage in fairy tales

Manon Penning and **Mariët Theune**
Human Media Interaction
University of Twente
Enschede, The Netherlands
m.p.j.penning@student.utwente.nl, m.theune@utwente.nl

Abstract

An existing taxonomy of Dutch cue phrases, designed for use in story generation, was validated by analysing cue phrase usage in a corpus of classical fairy tales. The analysis led to some adaptations of the original taxonomy.

1 Introduction

A taxonomy of Dutch cue phrases, used to signal rhetorical relations between text segments, has been developed for the generation of narratives in the Virtual Storyteller project (Theune et al., 2006; Theune et al., 2007).[1] The taxonomy includes only the most frequent cue phrases found in the Spoken Dutch Corpus.[2] Because the Spoken Dutch Corpus consists largely of spontaneous speech, the taxonomy might not be fully representative of cue phrase usage in the target domain of the Virtual Storyteller, which is fairy tales. In this paper we describe a corpus analysis we carried out to investigate this issue, and we discuss the modifications we made to the taxonomy based on the results. We also present a preliminary comparison of cue phrase usage in direct and indirect discourse in fairy tales.

2 The corpus

The Dutch "Stichting Beleven" has a large on line collection of Dutch translations of classical fairy tales and fables (Stichting Beleven, 2006). They tried to collect translations that are as true to the stories in the original tales as possible, while avoiding archaic language. Therefore, we considered this website to be a useful source for the purpose of this research. From the website we selected 8 fairy tales by Aesop, 25 by Andersen and 25 by the brothers Grimm. In the case of Aesop, this included all available stories by this author. In the cases of Andersen and Grimm, selections were made based on the popularity of the stories on the website. This resulted in a corpus of 97.000 words.

3 Procedure

The goal of our analysis was to find out whether the 36 cue phrases in the taxonomy of Theune et al. (2006) were in fact among those most frequently used in fairy tales. We also wanted to find any cue phrases that did appear in fairy tales but were not in the taxonomy. To identify potential cue phrases we first collected a list of all unique words occurring in the fairy tale corpus, and then determined for each word whether it could be used as a cue phrase by formulating one or more sentences in which the word occurred as a cue phrase. This resulted in a list of 85 potential cue phrases of which we wanted to determine the frequency in the corpus. A complicating factor here was that words that are used as cue phrases can sometimes also have a different function. Litman (1996) has labeled these two types of occurrences with 'discourse sense' (when actually used as a cue phrase) and 'sentential sense' (when used as some sort of filler, noun, verb or other non-cue phrase type of word). For example the Dutch word 'maar' (but) can be used to indicate contrast as in "Zij hadden mooie blanke gezichtjes, *maar* ze waren lelijk en zwart van hart." (They had beautiful white faces, but their hearts were ugly and black), but also as some sort of filler "Wacht *maar*, ik krijg je nog wel!" (Just wait, I'm gonna get you yet!).

Indicators whether a potential cue phrase is used in its sentential or discourse sense include part of speech, the presence of collocations and ortho-

[1] http://wwwhome.cs.utwente.nl/~theune/VS/index.html
[2] http://lands.let.kun.nl/cgn/ehome.htm

graphic markers, and the position of the cue phrase in the utterance (Hirschberg and Litman, 1994; Litman, 1996; Oates, 2000; Louwerse and Mitchell, 2003; Zufferey and Popescu-Belis, 2004). For the potential cue phrases in our corpus, we determined manually for each occurrence whether it was a case of discourse or sentential use.[3] In the case of discourse use, it was determined which relation from the taxonomy was signalled: causal, additive, contrastive or temporal (or more specific subtypes of those relations), or possibly another relation not included in the taxonomy. This was done largely based on intuition, but when in doubt we used a variant of the substitutability test of Knott and Dale (1994), allowing all substitutions that did not influence the meaning of the sentence. This was done independently by two annotators. We did not measure annotator agreement, but only compared the resulting classifications, resolving any differences through discussion. A few uncertain cases remained, so this procedure did not result in exact counts, but it was sufficient to get a general idea of how often the various cue phrases were used.[4]

4 Results and adaptation of the taxonomy

Table 1 gives an overview of the frequencies of the cue phrases in our corpus. The cue phrases from the original taxonomy are given in italics. As can be seen in Table 1, there are a lot of cue phrases that only occur rarely and a few cue phrases that occur quite often. Temporal relations seem to be signalled much less often than additive, cause and contrast relations. Some of the words that had been identified as potential cue phrases did not occur as actual cue phrases in the corpus at all (#cue = 0). This category also included a few of the cue phrases from the original taxonomy. The table also shows that some of the newly identified cue phrases seem to be good alternatives for less used ones that already were in the taxonomy. For example, the word 'toen' (then) is a temporal marker that was not in the original taxonomy but occurs very frequently in fairy tales.

The analysis did not give rise to adaptations of the structure of the taxonomy, because most of the cue phrases found in the corpus could be easily fitted into the existing relation (sub)categories. One exception was the cue phrase 'anders' (otherwise) which signalled an 'Otherwise' relation not in the taxonomy. However, we decided not to add it to the taxonomy because our generation system currently cannot produce this type of relation (Theune et al., 2007). We also added a new category for negative additives ('evenmin' and 'noch', meaning something like 'neither'), but we did not add these to the taxonomy because their counts were very low and 'noch' in particular is a bit archaic.

All in all, we kept the structure of the original taxonomy as it was, but we did make some changes in the cue phrases included in the taxonomy. For a start, the cue phrases that did not occur in the corpus at all were removed ('ooit', 'uiteindelijk', 'vervolgens' and 'waardoor'). Secondly, some of the cue phrases that did not occur very often and did not seem to differ in meaning from other, more frequent alternatives were removed: 'en...ook', 'zowel...als' (additive), 'en' (causal) and 'doordat' (involuntary cause-last).[5] Also, we replaced the less frequent cue phrase 'plotseling' (suddenly) by the more frequent synonym 'opeens'. Based on the high counts of 'eerst' (first) and 'toen' (then), it was decided to add those to the taxonomy. The cue phrases that we kept in, or added to, the new version of the taxonomy are shown in bold face in Table 1.

5 Direct vs. indirect discourse

It has been noted that cue phrase usage differs between monologues and dialogues (Louwerse and Mitchell, 2003). Since in addition to just descriptive, indirect discourse, fairy tales tend to have pieces of direct speech in them (e.g., "What big ears you have, grandma"), we carried out an additional small-scale investigation to find out if there were any differences between those two text types in our corpus. For this study we selected 20 fairy tales that contained at least 5 lines of direct discourse and split them into collections of direct and indirect discourse (8.493 and 24.967 words respectively).

The cue phrase frequencies in these collections are summarised in Table 2. Because we had about three times as much data for indirect discourse, for a fair comparison we used relative counts here (number of occurrences every 10.000 words) instead of

[3]Implementing precise rules to automatically distinguish between these cases would have been more time consuming. Also, the use of different character encodings in the corpus hindered automatic processing.

[4]Only for the potential cue word 'en' another procedure was used: since it occurred over 4000 times in our corpus, checking each instance by hand was infeasible. Therefore, in this case we extrapolated from a number of random samples.

[5]We regard the (equally frequent) cause-first version of 'doordat' as the preferred alternative, because mentioning the cause first makes the generated stories easier to read.

Relation	Primitive			#cue = 0	0 < #cue ≤ 10	10 < #cue ≤ 50	50 < #cue ≤ 100	#cue > 100
Cause	voluntary		cause-first	hierdoor, vandaar	zodoende	***daarom***, ***dus***, ***omdat***, dan ook		
			cause-last		tenslotte	immers		***want***
			purpose		ervoor	opdat, zodat		***om***
	involuntary		cause-first	*waardoor*	***daardoor***, ***doordat***, dus	***zodat***		
			cause-last		*doordat*			
						en, ***omdat***		
Additive	moreover				***bovendien***, daarbij, ook nog	zelfs		
					alsmede, daarbij, verder, evenals, *zowel . . . als*	*en. . . ook*		***en***, ***ook***
	negative				evenmin, noch			
Contrast	unrealized cause			evengoed	daarentegen, evenwel, ***hoewel***, niettegenstaande dat, ofschoon, ondanks, ook al, weliswaar			***toch***
					alleen	***echter***		***maar***
Temporal	after		gap	*ooit*	***later***			
			sequence	*vervolgens*	***nadat***, sinds, sindsdien, straks, vanaf, waarop	***daarna***, na		**toen**
	before		gap	*ooit*	eerder, laatst, ***vroeger***			
			sequence		daarvoor, eer, ***voordat***, tevoren, totdat	**eerst**		
	finally			*uiteindelijk*	op het laatst	***eindelijk***, ***tenslotte***		
	suddenly				ineens, *plotseling*	**opeens**		
	during			gedurende, tussendoor	daarbij, in de tussentijd, ondertussen, intussen, onderwijl, zolang	***terwijl***		
	once					***eens***		
	when		as soon as			***zodra***		
							wanneer	**toen**, ***als***
Other						anders		

Table 1: Counts of cue phrases (#cue) organised by the relations they signal (based on (Theune et al., 2006)). Cue phrases from the original taxonomy are shown in italics; cue phrases included in the adapted taxonomy are shown in bold face.

Indirect discourse	Direct discourse #cue = 0	0 < #cue ≤ 5	5 < #cue ≤ 20	#cue > 20
#cue = 0	alleen, daarvoor, eer, in de tussentijd, ineens, laatst, niettegenstaande dat, noch, ondertussen, straks, tevoren, totdat, uiteindelijk, vanaf, vroeger, waarop, zodoende	daarentegen, eerder, ervoor, ofschoon, onderwijl, zowel. . . als		
0 < #cue ≤ 5	alsmede, bovendien, daarbij, daardoor, evenals, evenmin, evenwel, in de tussentijd, intussen, later, ondanks, opeens, op het laatst, plotseling, sinds, sindsdien, verder, weliswaar, zodra, zolang	anders, doordat, dus, echter, eerst, en. . . ook, hoewel, immers, na, nadat, opdat, tenslotte, voordat	wanneer	
5 < #cue ≤ 20	ondanks	daarna, daarom, eindelijk, eens, omdat, terwijl, zelfs	als, zodat	toch
#cue > 20		toen	om, want	en, maar, ook

Table 2: Cross-table for counts of cue phrases (#cue) in direct and indirect discourse (per 10.000 words).

absolute numbers. Since the total number of cue phrases was much smaller than in the full corpus, the ranges used in Table 2 were adapted accordingly. The cue phrases with #cue < 0 in Table 1 were left out since they would only meaninglessly clutter up the table. Still, quite a number of cue phrases that did appear in the total collection of fairy tales, did not occur in the selection of 20 fairy tales used here.

Table 2 shows that the most frequent cue phrases from the overall collection, also occur most often in both direct and indirect discourse. An exception is 'omdat' (because), which occurs more often in indirect than direct discourse. This is consistent with research by Degand and Pander Maat (2003) showing that the alternative 'want' is preferred when the speaker is somehow personally involved with the action being described (which is more typically the case in direct speech). Furthermore, in indirect discourse more cue phrases are used than in direct discourse. Responsible for this difference are mostly the less common causal cue phrases and temporal cue phrases. This can be explained intuitively by the difference in nature between direct and indirect discourse. When characters in a story engage in conversation, they are likely to discuss simple, current events without using elaborate language. But in narrating a story, a number of events is summed up mentioning actions, consequences, causes and temporal span. All in all, our findings are in line with earlier research, but the small number of data does not allow us to draw substantial conclusions.

6 Concluding remarks

We carried out an analysis of cue phrase usage in fairy tales in order to validate a cue phrase taxonomy for story generation in Dutch. This led to some modifications of the taxonomy such as leaving out the least frequent phrases and replacing others by more frequent alternatives. Limiting the taxonomy in this way to a small number of the most common cue phrases could make the generated stories easier to read (Williams and Reiter, 2005), but on the other hand it could also make them more boring (Knott and Dale, 1994). However, the adapted taxonomy seems to contain a sufficient number of alternatives for each cue phrase to limit the latter risk, as we hope to show during future evaluations.

Although differences in cue phrase usage between different text types are to be expected, the limited extent to which modifications to the taxonomy were necessary shows that the difference between cue phrase usage in the Spoken Dutch Corpus and cue phrase usage in classical fairy tales is quite small. This indicates that the taxonomy is usable for a broader scale of texts than just fairy tale-like stories. However, when comparing direct and indirect discourse in fairy tales, some differences surface that might indicate a need for different taxonomies for both kinds of discourse. A larger scale study is needed to further investigate this.

References

L. Degand and H. Pander Maat. 2003. A contrastive study of Dutch and French causal connectives on the speaker involvement scale. In A. Verhagen and J. van de Weijer, editors, *Usage based approaches to Dutch*, pages 175–199. LOT, Utrecht.

J Hirschberg and D. Litman. 1994. Empirical studies on the disambiguation of cue phrases. *Computational Linguistics*, 19(3):501–530.

A. Knott and R. Dale. 1994. Using linguistic phenomena to motivate a set of coherence relations. *Discourse Processes*, 18(1):35–62.

D. J. Litman. 1996. Cue phrase classification using machine learning. *Journal of Artificial Intelligence Research*, 5:53–94.

M. M. Louwerse and H. H. Mitchell. 2003. Toward a taxonomy of a set of discourse markers in dialog: A theoretical and computational linguistic account. *Discourse Processes*, 35(3):199–239.

S.L. Oates. 2000. Multiple discourse marker occurrence: Creating hierarchies for coherence relations. In *Proceedings of the ANLP-NAACL 2000 Workshop on Student Research*.

Stichting Beleven. 2006. Wereld volksverhalen almanak. Retrieved on 18-09-2006, from: http://www.beleven.org/verhalen/.

M. Theune, F. Hielkema, and P. Hendriks. 2006. Performing aggregation and ellipsis using discourse structures. *Research on Language and Computation*, 4(4):353–375.

M. Theune, N. Slabbers, and F. Hielkema. 2007. The Narrator: NLG for digital storytelling. These proceedings.

S. Williams and E. Reiter. 2005. Generating readable texts for readers with low basic skills. In *Proceedings of ENLG-05*, pages 140–147.

S. Zufferey and A. Popescu-Belis. 2004. Towards automatic identification of discourse markers in dialogs: the case of like. In *Proceedings of SIGdial 2004*, pages 63–71.

Atlas.txt: Linking Geo-referenced Data to Text for NLG

Kavita E. Thomas and Somayajulu Sripada
Department of Computing Science
University of Aberdeen
Aberdeen, UK
{tkavita,ssripada}@csd.abdn.ac.uk

Abstract

Geo-referenced data which are often communicated via maps are inaccessible to the visually impaired population. We summarise existing approaches to improving accessibility of geo-referenced data and present the Atlas.txt project which aims to produce textual summaries of such data which can be read out via a screenreader. We outline issues involved in generating descriptions of geo-referenced data and present initial work on content determination based on knowledge acquisition from both parallel corpus analysis and input from visually impaired people. In our corpus analysis we build an ontology containing abstract representations of expert-written sentences which we associate with macros containing sequences of data analysis methods. This helps us to identify which data analysis methods need to be applied to generate text from data.

1 Introduction

Currently there is a plethora of geo-referenced statistical data such as census data publicly accessible on the World Wide Web. Much of this data is provided by governmental organisations like National Statistics which provides the UK census 2001 data online[1]. Such organisations are legally required to make this data accessible to user groups with visual impairments. However the majority of this data is currently displayed in the form of chloropleth maps which shade regions according to the mean value of a given variable in that region, as is typically exemplified in Figure 1[2] and is described by the expert authored text:

"Of Scotland's Census Day population of 5,062,011, close to 2 million people live in large urban areas".

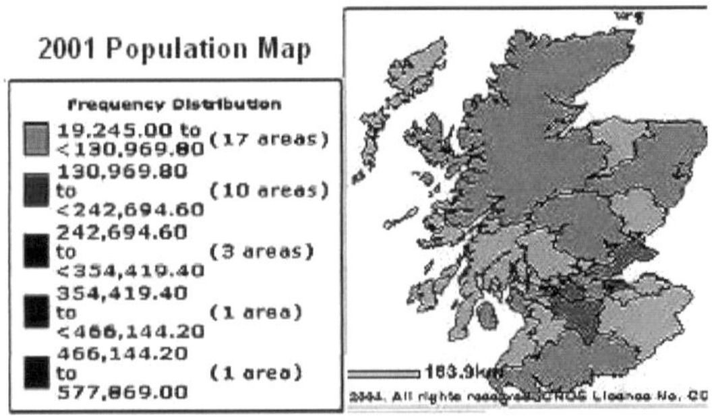

Figure 1: A map showing geo-referenced data

Such maps of geo-referenced data aid sighted users to quickly comprehend spatial patterns and trends, e.g., that the Scottish population is largely concentrated among the urban areas in Figure 1. However, visually impaired users have to listen to each of the individual frequency values corresponding to the census area units before comprehending the spatial distribution of population. The Atlas.txt project aims to improve access to such geo-referenced data using NLG technology by determining the salient features which best explain the data and communicating this relevant information as text summaries like the one above, which can then be read out via a screen-reader. The project initially addresses predominantly census data, but aims to develop techniques that can be applied on other geo-referenced data such as land-use data.

2 Related Work

Systems which generate descriptions of numerical data are not uncommon, e.g., the FOG system (Goldberg et al, 1994), TREND (Boyd, 1997) and MULTI-METEO (Coch, 1998) all generate textual summaries of numerical weather data. (Ferres et al, 2006) generates textual descriptions of informa-

[1] At http://www.statistics.gov.uk/census2001/census2001.asp .

[2] Scotland's Census Results Online, www.scrol.gov.uk.

tion in graphs and enables user querying. SumTime (Sripada et al, 2003) summarises time-series data. While there is no prior work on generating textual descriptions of geo-referenced data, there have been studies on describing spatial data in the context of route directions ((Geldof, 2003); (Marciniak and Strube, 2004)), scene descriptions (Novak, 1986), geometric descriptions (Mitkov, 1990) and spatial descriptions (Ebert et al, 1996). RoadSafe[3], which generates weather forecast texts for road maintenance based on spatio-temporal weather prediction data, also explores similar issues. However, in the Atlas.txt project our main focus is on describing geo-spatial data to visually impaired users.

Other projects address the issue of accessibility with other user interaction paradigms in mind, for example haptic interfaces and non-speech sonic interfaces. Of these, the most closely related are sonification (non-speech audio) approaches to data communication. (Stockman, 2004) discusses issues involved with sonification of spreadsheet data. Of particular interest is the iSonic (Zhao, 2005) data exploration tool which uses sonification techniques to aid interactive exploration of geo-referenced data displayed as chloropleth maps. Such approaches can be seen as complementary to our approach.

3 Knowledge Acquisition

In order to elicit end-user requirements and coordinate evaluation subjects, we interviewed a visually impaired volunteer at the Grampian Society for the Blind[4] (GSB) who is responsible for helping blind users with computer accessibility. He demonstrated how he and other blind users he knows currently explore data; if the data is in tabular form, they use spreadsheet applications which compute descriptive statistics such as the mean and range of a column (row) and use these statistics to gradually build a mental picture of the distribution of the data. Analysing geo-referenced data additionally needs to be associated with corresponding geographical areas. Textual descriptions, he felt, would certainly help visually impaired users to quickly gain an overview of the underlying data provided they present the same information a sighted person extracts from a visual representation of the data.

3.1 Parallel Corpus

In order to model the process of mapping geo-referenced data to its textual description we need to understand how humans perform this activity. There is a huge amount of geo-referenced data online, and we start by considering a few such expert (i.e., statistician) written texts and their corresponding data, which can be found online via organisations like National Statistics. Using such parallel data and text corpora for knowledge acquisition (KA) is a fairly common approach (Sripada et al, 2003). An example from Lambeth Council's website of the sort of texts we are looking at follows below, and the corresponding data appears in Table 1. Such pairings of sentences and tables containing the data communicated in the sentences form our growing corpus. The corpus collection is in an initial stage, and we currently have about 300 such pairs of sentences and data tables gleaned from a handful of online documents.

(1) *Example 1:* People from Non-white ethnic groups constituted 30.3 % of Lambeth's population in 1991, compared with 6.1% of the country as a whole.

(2) *Example 2:* Black African residents have increased in Lambeth by 5.1%. This is also reflected London wide and nationally.

We distinguish content depending on whether it classifies strictly spatial data (e.g., the first sentence in Ex. 2), compares areas (e.g., the second sentence in Ex. 2 and the last phrase in Ex. 1), or compares spatial data across different times. Another way we can distinguish message content has to do with whether messages describe factual information or communicate inferences. Following (Law et al, 2005), we distinguish between *descriptive* messages which are based on data analysis and factual features of the data, and *interpretative* messages which involve expert knowledge about the domain, which can include everything from inferences on the data to the communication of specific domain knowledge. The interpretative features which arise generally involve inferences drawn by the experts about the data, e.g., explanations, cause-effect, etc. Although performing these sorts of inferences is currently beyond the project's scope, our initial studies show a predominance of descriptive messages like those in Ex. 1 and 2, which seems to indicate that addressing these sorts of messages will enable us to address a decent proportion of the sorts of messages we want to communicate. Another point to bear in mind is that the documents we're webscraping are designed for sighted users, which means that one cannot assume that the modalities of text and data

[3]See www.csd.abdn.ac.uk/research/roadsafe.

[4]See www.grampianblind.co.uk

	White		Black Caribbean		Black African		Black Other		Indian		Pakistani		Bangladeshi		Chinese	
	1991	2001	1991	2001	1991	2001	1991	2001	1991	2001	1991	2001	1991	2001	1991	2001
Lambeth	69.7	62.4	12.6	12.1	6.5	11.6	2.7	4.9	2.1	2	0.8	1	0.7	0.8	1.3	1.3
Inner London	74.4	65.7	7.1	6.9	4.4	8.3	2	3.3	3	3.1	1.2	1.6	2.8	4.6	1.1	1.4
Greater London	79.8	71.2	4.4	4.8	2.4	5.3	1.2	2.3	5.2	6.1	1.3	2	1.3	2.1	0.8	1.1

Table 1: The Corresponding Data for Examples 1 and 2

contain the same information. However, although the two modes often contain complementary information, informal analysis indicates that official reporting of geo-referenced data often contains both maps and text to communicate important information, making webscraping fairly viable for corpus collection.

3.2 Corpus Analysis

We index data tables like the one shown in Table 1 to the corresponding texts which describe them in a database, thereby linking information in different modalities and forming a parallel corpus. Essentially the core of KA from corpus analysis lies in the mapping from a (manually interpreted) abstract representation (AR) of an expert textual description or *message* (Reiter and Dale, 2000) to an AR of the data, as is shown in Figure 3. Note that the textual analysis takes place on the sentential level currently; we leave higher-level discourse structure for future work. Abstract representations of data (ADR) contain the results of applying data analysis methods (which can range from simple descriptive statistics to spatial data mining methods) on the raw data found in tables in the documents.

AR of textual descriptions proceeds in several steps. We started building up an ontology of spatial relations by labelling texts at the sentential level according to the messages communicated; these message labels abstract over texts and indicate the primary spatial relation communicated, e.g., $category : location - density$, which for example labels the text: "The Black Caribbean community is concentrated in the wards around Brixton". Here $category$ is a higher level class in the ontology corresponding to messages communicating information to do with a category of data, in this case the Black Caribbean population, and $location - density$ indicates the particular feature ($location$) and property of this feature ($density$) under discussion. Message labels indicate information content. We indicate sentential rhetorical/discourse content via a set of around ten message predicates adopted from McKeown's message predicates (McKeown, 1985) and RST (Mann and Thompson, 1988). These message predicates communicate contrast, causality, etc. Message predicates and message labels constitute the highest level of abstraction at the sentential level in our ATR.

At a lower level we create ARs for the messages which can be seen as an intermediary level of abstraction between message labels and predicates and the texts themselves and correlate roughly to cue-phrases. We find all cue-phrases which indicate spatial relations in the corpora, e.g., "constituted", "concentrated", to get a range of the sorts of contexts these cues can appear in and then abstract over the cues, forming mostly synonymous classes of cues which can be associated with the same message labels and predicates. The text above has as its message content, the frame $concentrated[Group, Location]$.

3.2.1 Initial Methodology and Findings

We map from ATRs to ADRs by (manually) associating simple sequences of data analysis methods (which we term *macros*) with ATRs, so the previous text's ATR is associated with the method spatial segmentation. The text "A higher number of Black African people live in the north of the borough than in the south" would be associated with first spatial segmentation (Haining, 2003), and then, given that the distribution is not uniform, summation of the population values for the category in geographic regions with different frequencies.

The macros serve as an initial indication of which data analysis methods we should apply to the data and in which order so that we can generate the kinds of texts produced by the experts. We expect that the findings from data analysis will mostly lie at the sentential level, e.g., descriptive statistical information, or information from spatial segmentation. The idea is that these mappings between data and text can be used as a backbone for describing new data sets which share similar findings from spatial data analysis.

From an initial analysis of 70 texts, we found that spatial segmentation was the most common method invoked, occurring 17% of the time, followed by comparisons of values, which occurred 14% of the time. We found that 13% of the texts involved a sequence of data analysis methods, e.g., segmenta-

Figure 2: The Text to Data Mapping Process

tion followed by breakdown analysis, and another 13% invoked multiple (non-sequential) data analysis methods like reporting the minimum and maximum values. This leaves the majority (74%) as simply invoking a single data analysis method. Ignoring whether methods are invoked sequentially or in multiples, we found that the largest number of methods invoked involve simply giving significant values, ranking values, summing them or comparing them. However the extent to which these findings (as opposed to others arising from the same data) are significant needs to be resolved so that given a data set, we can determine which findings are "interesting".

4 Future Work

This paper describes work in progress on the Atlas.txt project, which just started in January 2007. As such, our goal here is to introduce the project and initial KA work in the hopes that we will receive useful feedback about our initial methodology which will then guide future work. In this paper we have presented initial ideas about mapping geospatial data to text via the data analysis macros necessary for communicating the corresponding texts with the goal of driving generation of similar sentences for unseen data. We still need to account for discourse level structuring of these messages. We have implemented our ATR in the SimpleNLG framework and toolkit[5], enabling us to generate text from ATRs. However much work still needs to be done toward implementing the data to ADR and ADR to ATR stages.

An immediate area of future work involves analysing more corpora in order to expand our set of data analysis macros. We also need to specifically investigate the extent to which the data analysis macros we associate with ATRs actually do produce the information communicated in the texts. Additionally we need a better understanding of the informational requirements of visually-impaired end-users, and the extent to which results from a survey we are currently running including "think aloud" descriptions of census data from sighted users needs to be adapted for the visually-impaired.

[5] See www.csd.abdn.ac.uk/ẽreiter/simplenlg/.

References

S. Boyd. 1997. Detecting and Describing Patterns in Time-varying Data Using Wavelets. In *Advances in Intelligent Data Analysis: Reasoning About Data, Lecture Notes in Computer Science*, 1280.

J. Coch. 1998. Multimeteo: Multilingual Production of Weather Forecasts. *ELRA Newsletter*, 3:2.

C. Ebert, D. Glatz, M. Jansche, R. Meyer-Klabunde, R. Porzel. 1996. From Conceptualization to Formulation in Generating Spatial Descriptions. In *Proceedings fo the 5th European Conference on Cognitive Modelling*, 96-39.

L. Ferres, A. Parush, S. Roberts, G. Lindgaard. (2006). 2006. Helping People with Visual Impairments Gain Access to Graphical Information Through Natural Language: The iGraph System. In *Proceedings of ICCHP 2006, Lecture Notes in Computer Science*, 4061.

S. Geldof. 2003. Corpus Analysis for NLG. In *Proceedings of the 9th EWNLG*.

E. Goldberg, N. Driedger, R. L. Kittredge. 1994. Using Natural-Language Processing to Produce Weather Forecasts. *IEEE Expert*, 9:2.

R. Haining. 2003. Spatial Data Analysis: Theory and Practice. *Cambridge University Press*.

A. S. Law, Y. Freer, J. R. Hunter, R. H. Logie, N. McIntosh, J. Quinn. 2005. A Comparison of Graphical and Textual Presentations of Time Series Data to Support Medical Decision Making in the Neonatal Intensive Care Unit. *Journal of Clinical Monitoring and Computing*, 19:183–194.

T. Marciniak, M. Strube. 2004. Classification-based Generation Using TAG. In *Proceedings of Natural Language Generation: 3rd International Conference, Lecture Notes in Artificial Intelligence*, 3123.

W. Mann, S. Thompson. 1988. Rhetorical Structure Theory: Towards a Functional Theory of Text Organization. In *Text:3*.

R. Mitkov. 1990. A Text-Generation System for Explaining Concepts in Geometry. In *Proceedings of the 13th Conference on Computational Linguistics*.

H. J. Novak. 1986. Generating a Coherent Text Describing a Traffic Scene. In *Proceedings of the 11th Conference on Computational Linguistics*.

E. Reiter and R. Dale. 2000. Building Natural Language Generation Systems. Cambridge University Press.

S. Sripada, E. Reiter, J. Hunter, J. Yu. 2003. Exploiting a Parallel TEXT-DATA Corpus. In *Proceedings of Corpus Linguistics*.

S. Somayajulu, E. Reiter, I. Davy. 2003. SumTime-Mousam: Configurable Marine Weather Forecast Generator. In *Expert Update* 6(3):4-10.

T. Stockman. 2004. The Design and Evaluation of Auditory Access to Spreadsheets. In *Proceedigns of the 10th International Conference on Auditory Display*.

H. Zhao, C. Plaisant, B. Shneiderman. 2005. I Hear the Pattern - Interactive Sonification of Geographical Data Patterns. In *Proceedings of ACM SIGCHI Extended Abstracts on Human Factors in Computing Systems*.

Generating monologue and dialogue to present personalised medical information to patients

Sandra Williams, Paul Piwek and Richard Power
Department of Computing Science
The Open University
Walton Hall, Milton Keynes, MK7 6AA, U.K.
{s.h.williams, p.piwek, r.power}@open.ac.uk

Abstract

Medical information is notoriously difficult to convey to patients because the content is complex, emotionally sensitive, and hard to explain without recourse to technical terms. We describe a pilot system for communicating the contents of electronic health records (EHRs) to patients. It generates two alternative presentations, which we have compared in a preliminary evaluation study: the first takes the form of a monologue, which elaborates the information taken from the patient's EHR by adding explanations of some concepts and procedures; the second takes the form of a scripted dialogue, in which the content is recast as a series of questions, answers and statements assigned to two characters in the dialogue, a senior and a junior nurse. Our discourse planning method designs these presentations in tandem, first producing a monologue plan which is then elaborated into a dialogue plan.

1 Introduction

Increasingly, health service providers are storing patient medical histories in machine-usable form – i.e., in databases of Electronic Health Records (EHRs) – and are obliged by legislation to make this information accessible to patients. We explore here an application in which material from EHRs is selected and organised for presentation to patients either as a monologue or as a script for a dialogue. Emphatically these are not intended to replace face-to-face consultation with a specialist. Rather, the aim is to help patients use consultations to better effect.

We have constructed a natural language generation (NLG) system that generates monologue or dialogue scripts which are spoken by synthetic voices. If a patient were to listen to a review of her recent record (but not, of course, containing any new diagnoses of which she was previously unaware) it could potentially help her in her next consultation in a number of ways:

- by reminding her of her own case history;
- by giving her practical examples of the meaning and usage of medical terms relating to her case;
- by demonstrating how to ask practical medical questions relating to her case (dialogues only).

We generate dialogue because it opens up new ways of making rhetorical and argumentative information explicit (Piwek et al., 2005). Also, as Craig et al. (2000) and Cox et al. (1999) found, it would help the patient recall the current state of her treatment, it would encourage her to ask questions during the subsequent consultation by reminding her of the exact meaning of technical terms, and would give her more confidence in expressing herself both in technical language and informal language. It could also save doctors' time by providing an additional source of explanation for patients.

The CLEF system (Hallett and Scott, 2005) summarises EHRs of breast cancer patients for *clinical staff*. We have implemented a pilot system for *patients* that selects and describes events from the same EHR repository. At present the wording of utterances is somewhat stilted, since our initial focus is on designing a discourse planner for both monologue and dialogue. Below is an extract from a monologue generated by the current system.

> On November 27th you had an examination. The doctor found that you had lymphadenopathy in your right axillary lymphnodes. Lymphadenopathy is swelling of the lymph nodes which the doctor can feel when you are examined. The commonest cause of lymphadenopathy is infection. Lympadenopathy can also be caused by a build up of cancer cells within the lymph nodes. Axillary lymphnodes are rounded masses of tissue under the arm containing white blood cells.

A dialogue script generated from the same data follows. The characters are two nurses, one junior and one senior, where the junior is an eager but not very knowledgeable character while the senior is an experienced, trustworthy instructor whose words carry weight. The junior reads from a report which contains some terms that she does not understand; the senior nurse explains them.

Junior Nurse: On November 27th she had an examination.

Senior Nurse: What did the examination find?

Junior Nurse: The doctor found that she had lymphadenopathy. What is lymphadenopathy?

Senior Nurse: Lymphadenopathy is swelling of the lymph nodes which the doctor can feel when you are examined. The commonest cause of lymphadenopathy is infection. Lympadenopathy can also be caused by a build up of cancer cells within the lymph nodes.

Junior Nurse: The lymphadenopathy was in her right axillary lymphnodes. What are axillary lymphnodes?

Senior Nurse: Axillary lymphnodes are rounded masses of tissue under the arm containing white blood cells.

We have piloted the system with colleagues to find out whether monologue and dialogue would be successful at conveying information in the EHR. Many useful ideas for improving the system emerged, as can be seen in Section 4.

2 Generating monologues and dialogues

2.1 Input

The system's input comes from a relational database representing medical histories of simulated breast cancer patients. The patient simulator was developed by Rogers et al. (2006) for the CLEF project. Database entries describe medical interventions, investigations, problems, drugs and patients. Primary keys provide relational links between database tables in the usual manner; additionally, a *Relations* table specifies explicit rhetorical relations – e.g., the evidential relation *HAS_FINDING* which indicates that an investigation provided evidence for diagnosis of a medical problem. Twenty types of relation are present in the *Relations* table, although our current prototype only describes a subset of them.

2.2 Discourse planning

Document planning has two or four stages depending on whether monologue or dialogue output is required. First, we select content and arrange it into a discourse structure. Second, we add explanation relations. At this stage, the discourse structure is complete for monologue generation and the final task is to recast it into a series of sentence templates. Discourse planning for dialogue output has two further stages: the third adds questions and answers, and the last allocates portions of the discourse structure to each conversational partner and recasts them into a series of utterance templates from which dialogue turns are to be generated. These stages are described in more detail below.

Content selection (stage 1a) queries the database for records on a particular simulated patient. These are scanned for recent medical investigations and interventions that are linked to medical problems via explicit evidential and motivational relations present in the *Relations* table. Selection of EHR data is the same for dialogue and monologue.

Initial discourse structures for medical episodes are built from the selected content (stage 1b). Fig. 1 (A) shows a *medical episode* where *Investigation* and *Problem* concepts are linked to each other by a *HAS_FINDING* relation and to a *Locus* concept by *HAS_TARGET* and *HAS_LOCUS* relations. The nodes in the diagram represent instances of concepts, while the arcs represent relations. Instances generally represent records found in database tables; here they are records from the *Investigation*, *Problem* and *Locus* tables; the nodes contain all the fields that were present in the record, e.g. Fig. 1 (A) shows the "Name" fields "examination", "lymphadenopathy" and "axillary lymphnodes". The arcs in the diagram represents relations present in the *Relations* table mentioned above. *Medical episodes* like the one in Fig. 1 (A) are ordered sequentially according to the date fields of the retrieved data.

Explanations are added (stage 2) as shown in Fig. 1 (B). The program consults a table of term definitions and introduces *EXPLANATION* relations linking instances of concepts to glosses that explain these concepts. At present, we do not have an automatic procedure for deciding which concepts require explanations; concepts like "examination" are left unexplained because they seem intuitively well-known, while less familiar concepts like "axilla" are explained. A search in the BNC confirmed that raw BNC frequencies correspond well with our intuitions: e.g., "examination" has high frequency, whereas "axilla" has low frequency. Our technical term definition glossary currently has 73 entries comprising canned phrases and sentences from trusted sites such as Cancer Research UK patient information pages (www.cancerresearchuk.org). Where appropriate these have been simplified slightly and their tenses have been changed.

Questions and Answers are added (stage 3) through the relations *RAISES_Q* (i.e., a concept raises a question) and *HAS_ANS* (i.e., a given question has an answer), as shown in Fig. 1 (C). Two question types are illustrated: firstly "What is it?" questions, which are subgraphs spanning *EXPLANATION* relations; and secondly a "What was found?" question asking about a specific argument in a specific relation (in this case about the finding of the *HAS_FINDING* relation, i.e., the *Problem*

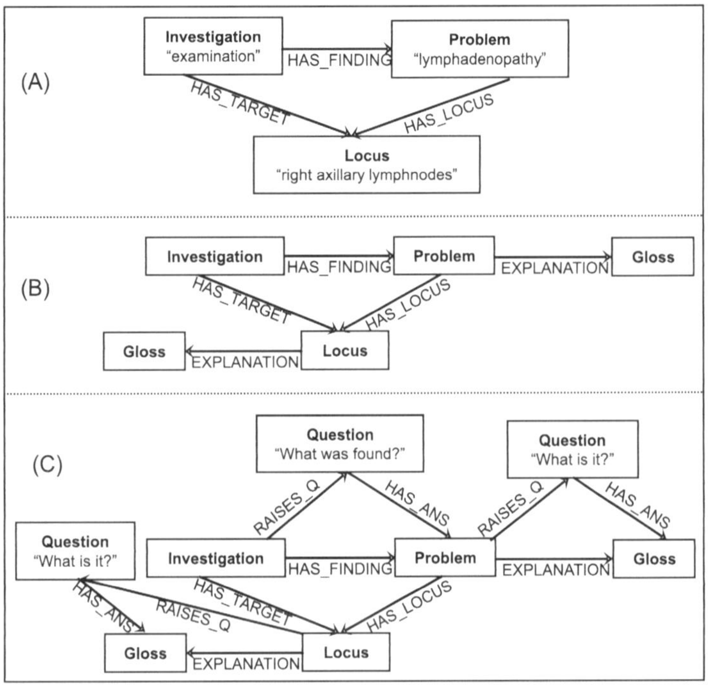

Figure 1: Stages in discourse planning.

that the evidence suggested). Note that questions ask about both concepts and relations.

Assignment to dialogue turns (stage 4) is achieved by mapping parts of the discourse structure to utterance specifications (i.e. questions, answers and statements) and by using dialogue templates to assign these to the dialogue partners. Below is a list of utterance specifications generated from Fig. 1 (C). The resulting dialogue script is given in section 1 where, for example, "On November 27th she had an examination" realises the utterance specification *inform(Investigation)*.

Speaker	**Specification**
Junior	inform(Investigation)
Senior	question(HAS_FINDING)
Junior	answer(Problem)
Junior	question(Problem.Name)
Senior	answer(Gloss)
Junior	inform(HAS_LOCUS)
Junior	question(Locus.Name)
Senior	answer(Gloss)

Note that a single turn can contain several moves and that both characters ask questions, thus avoiding 'conversational ping-pong' (Davis, 1998) — i.e., exchanges where turns degenerate into nothing more than a sequence of alternating questions and answers.

2.3 Microplanning, realisation and output

These are achieved through simple string processing with reference to a discourse history which maintains a list of entities mentioned so far, prohibits questions and explanations being generated more than once, and allows determiners such as "another" to be generated when an action is performed repeatedly. The output is formatted as web pages with embedded Active X commands to control text-to-speech. Examples of the system's output were given in section 1.

3 Pilot evaluation

As a preliminary test of our system, we piloted the effectiveness of communicating medical information through scripted dialogue and monologue by conducting a small evaluation with eleven colleagues from The Open University, divided randomly into two groups, Group A (five people) and Group B (six people).

Materials: We generated a monologue and dialogue from the same simulated patient's EHR. Loquendo text-to-speech voice Kate read the monologue, while in the dialogue Simon read the junior nurse and Kate the senior. Section 1 illustrates fragments of the materials that were actually used in the pilot. A practice monologue was also produced by hand, with both voices reading alternate paragraphs from a cancer patient web site.

Method: Both groups listened to the practice monologue and answered questions about the voices and a practice multiple-choice comprehension question. Group A then listened to the monologue and answered multiple-choice questions. Afterwards, this group listened to the dialogue, stated their preferences, and were asked for comments. Group B listened to the dialogue first, answered questions, listened to the monologue, stated their preferences, and added comments.

Results: Participants' comments were very informative. People particularly did not like pronunciations of technical terms and thought that the synthetic voices spoke too fast; these are problems that can be addressed by configuring the text-to-speech system. Furthermore, the general impression was that too much information was given too quickly, although one person commented that the dialogue was better because information was presented in shorter "chunks".

Both groups performed well on comprehension (their mean scores out of 10 were 8.6 for Group A and 7.5 for Group B), and an independent samples t-test showed no significant difference between them. A few people told us that they already knew some of the medical concepts queried by the comprehension questions; however, performance on questions for which the answers could not have been known in advance was also slightly (but not significantly) higher in Group A (monologue).

A Pearson chi-square test showed no difference between groups' monologue/dialogue preferences. Despite that, none of the participants were neutral about the choice — i.e., none selected the option "I have no preference".

Discussion: The most important outcome is that the system ought to communicate information at a slower rate and present it in smaller chunks. This could be achieved by adding conversational padding that would enable the density of new information to be finely tuned. Piwek and van Deemter (forthcoming) have proposed a possible solution to this problem.

4 Conclusion

Patients accessing their EHRs have very different needs from doctors: configuring a suitable presentation is not merely a question of replacing technical language. Doctors have to treat many patients every day, under severe time pressure; what they want is a condensed version of the facts relating to each individual case. Patients have plenty of time to view a single presentation of intense personal interest, and so are likely to prefer a gentler information flow with informal touches (i.e., dialogue rather than monologue) and some easily assimilated instruction. We have not tried to eliminate technical terms altogether, but to give patients some mastery of technical concepts that are highly relevant to their case. This is an original communication genre with subtle aims: the patient learns by viewing a conversation in which she is not addressed directly.

Technically, the planning of the patient communications is achieved through a process in which an initial plan, similar to that for generating condensed reports for doctors (Hallett and Scott, 2005), is progressively *overlaid* with further rhetorical and semantic content — first, by adding explanations, secondly by recasting assertions as conversational response pairs, and thirdly by grouping moves into turns. Our pilot evaluation suggests that the resulting dialogues are still too dense: they lack the reassurance that comes from a lighter, more discursive style, and some repetition of information that is *already familiar* — the equivalent of small talk. There are obvious more superficial ways in which our demonstrator could be improved (e.g., using more pronouns instead of ponderous repetition of nouns like 'lymphadenopathy'), but the crucial challenge lies in pushing our approach to discourse planning much further, so that the content from the EHR is folded into a plan that meets the special needs of this new genre.

References

Cox, R., McKendree, J., Tobin, R., Lee, J. and Mayes, T. (1999) Vicarious learning from dialogue and discourse: a controlled comparison. *Instructional Science* 27: 431-458.

Craig, S D., Gholson, B., Ventura, M., Graesser, A (2000) Overhearing Dialogues and Monologues in Virtual Tutoring Sessions: Effects on Questioning and Vicarious Learning. *International Journal of Artificial Intelligence in Education*, 11, 242-25.

Davis, R. (1998) *Writing Dialogue for Scripts*, A & C Black Ltd., London, ISBN 0-7136-4802-3.

Hallett, C., and Scott, D. (2005). Structural variation in generated health reports. *Proceedings of the 3rd International Workshop on Paraphrasing.*

Piwek, P., Power, R., Scott, D., and van Deemter, K. (2005) Generating Multimedia Presentations: From Plain Text to Screen Play. In O. Stock and M. Zancanaro, eds., *Multimodal Intelligent Information Presentation*. Springer.

Piwek, P., van Deemter, K. (forthcoming). Generating under Global Constraints: the Case of Scripted Dialogue. *Research on Language and Computation*. Kluwer.

Rogers, J., Puleston, C., Rector, A. (2006) The CLEF Chronicle: Patient Histories derived from Electronic Health Records. *Proc. of the 22nd International Conference on Data Engineering Workshops*, IEEE.

Author Index